EXPLORING COMMUNICATION THEORY

EXPLORING COMMUNICATION THEORY

Making Sense of Us

KORY FLOYD

University of Arizona

PAUL SCHRODT

Texas Christian University

LARRY A. ERBERT

University of Colorado Denver

ANGELA TRETHEWEY

California State University, Chico

Exploring Communication Theory: Making Sense of Us
© 2016 by Kory Floyd, Paul Schrodt, Larry A. Erbert, and Angela Trethewey

ISBN: 1519631677
ISBN 13: 9781519631671
Library of Congress Control Number: 2015920201
CreateSpace Independent Publishing Platform
North Charleston, South Carolina

CONTENTS

1

MAKING SENSE OF COMMUNICATION

INQUIRING MINDS WANT TO KNOW

M OMENTS AFTER BEING announced as the recipient of the 2015 Grammy Award for album of the year, singer-songwriter Beck nearly had his acceptance speech interrupted by Kanye West. Six years earlier, West had infamously stormed the stage at the MTV Video Music Awards, interrupting Taylor Swift's acceptance speech for best music video of the year to argue that Beyoncé should have won instead. As he approached Beck at the Grammy Awards, many in the audience thought he was spoofing his earlier interruption of Taylor Swift. In a backstage interview later that night, however, West expressed his dissatisfaction with the Grammy selection committee for not recognizing true artistry.

Whether you watched the Grammy Awards or heard later about Kanye West's antics, you likely noticed his bizarre behavior. Like most people do when they're confused, you search for a reason, an explanation for why West expresses himself the way he does.

You search, that is, for a communication theory.

We know the feeling. Each of us—Kory, Paul, Larry, and Angela—wants to understand why people communicate the way they do. That's what led us to take communication courses, as you

— 1 —

are doing now, and eventually to teach and study the many ways in which people interact. One lesson we've learned is that communication is often more complex than it appears. You may easily be able to come up with reasons why Kanye West behaves as he does, but does your explanation take the right factors into consideration? Does it ignore causes that are relevant, or take account of factors that don't really matter?

Those are the types of questions that communication scholars deal with every day. Most communication behaviors can be explained in more than one way, and it is the job of communication scholars—such as the ones we'll introduce you to in this book—to examine which explanations are the most useful.

Before we start looking at communication theories, let's take some time to talk about communication itself. In this chapter, we'll discuss the characteristics that communication behaviors share. Then we'll explore the communication discipline by looking at our past, our present, and our future. We believe having that background will be useful as you begin your study of communication theories.

How We Think About Communication

Although you communicate virtually every day of your life, you probably don't think very often about what communication is, exactly. If you asked 20 friends to define the term, you might find little agreement on what *communication* means, despite the fact that they all know how to do it. The situation isn't much different among communication scholars, who have also generated many dozens, if not hundreds, of definitions for what we study.

It's not essential that we all agree on precisely what communication is—and is not—before we can explore the value of theories. Discussions about the definition of communication can be valuable and we believe they should be encouraged. At the same time, however, it's useful to begin our journey into the world of communication theory with some shared ideas in mind. Therefore, instead of impos-ing one necessarily limited definition of what communication is, we have chosen to describe some of the most important characteristics of communication. Our list certainly won't be exhaustive, but it will introduce you to some of the features of communication that matter most.

1. *Communication is a process.* Communication is something we *do.* As a **process,** communication unfolds over time, and what happens at one point can affect what occurs later. If a friend violates your trust by sharing information you expected her to keep secret, that communication act might prevent you from confiding in her the next time you have something to share.

2. *Communication is symbolic.* We can never get into other peo-ple's brains to know exactly what they're thinking, so we rely on **symbols,** which are representations of ideas, to under-stand each other. Words are symbols. The word *tree* isn't actu-ally a tree; it just represents the idea of one. Gestures, facial expressions, and many other communicative behaviors are also symbols because they signify ideas.

3. *Communication focuses on meaning.* Because communication is symbolic, an important task is to figure out what **meaning,** or message, each symbol conveys. When you say "I love you," what does that *mean?* What message are you sending through your posture, or through your silence? You've probably had the experience of being misunderstood and telling another person "That isn't what I meant." If so, then you understand how challenging the process of meaning-making can be.

4. *Communication is ever-present.* Finally, communication is with us constantly. Your behaviors can send messages to other people whether you intend those messages or not. Have you ever tried hard to stay awake during class? In spite of your

efforts to look interested, your slouching posture and droopy eyelids were likely communicating your fatigue to others. Likewise, you are continually receiving messages from the people around you, whether those messages are intentional or unintentional.

Now that we understand some of the fundamental features of communication, let's look at how communication came to be a focus of academic study.

▲ ▲ ▲

Let's Discuss

1. How do you see the process of communication unfold in your own life?
2. What does it mean to call communication "ever-present"? Is it possible not to communicate at all?

▲ ▲ ▲

WHERE THE COMMUNICATION DISCIPLINE CAME FROM

The study of communication has a long, rich history. Each of us has our own personal story to tell, filled with the important people and life events that have made us who we are today. Similarly, every field of study has its own biography or "story" that helps others understand how that field came into being.

The communication process is fundamental to everything we do as human beings. As a result, the question of *how we communicate with each other* has been a topic of fascination for centuries. Scholars and laypersons alike have been motivated to understand what communication is, how it works, why it works better in some instances than others, and how it can best be taught. In fact, many of the communication principles we teach today can be found in the writings and teachings of such classical philosophers as Plato and Aristotle. Thus, by briefly reviewing the historical roots of the communication discipline, we can gain insight into where we are today as a field of study and catch a glimpse into our future.

In this section, we will briefly review three classical patterns of thought about communication that emerged in ancient Greece: the Sophistic tradition, the Platonic tradition, and the Aristotelian tradition.[1] We will then discuss how each of those traditions continues to inform the study of communication, as scholars in both the humanities and the social sciences further our understanding of how our everyday lives are created and sustained out of our continuing and constant interaction.[2]

COMMUNICATION AND THE CLASSICS

The formal study of communication began with the rise of democracy in Greece during the fifth century B.C.[3] It came about largely in response to the conceptual and practical concerns of the Greek people. Philosophers in ancient Greece were debating such timeless questions as *What is real?*, *What is truth?*, and *What is knowledge?* The practical concerns of the Greeks, however, were focused more on certain political events and economic self-interest. For instance, the citizens of Syracuse had overthrown their tyrannical governor and established democratic rule. As a result, the courts were flooded with lawsuits for the return of confiscated property. Because Greek culture valued the spoken word and citizens were required to argue their own cases in court, a tremendous need arose for someone to teach plaintiffs and defendants how to effectively argue their cases. Thus, the birth of communication theory was a practical response to a social dilemma, and the person credited by most classical theorists and historians with inventing communication theory was **Corax** of Syracuse.

The Sophistic tradition. In ancient Greece, the term **rhetoric** was used to refer to the study of communication, and those who taught communication were called **rhetoricians.** Corax was a specialist in forensic rhetoric who started his own business teaching Greek citizens how to effectively argue their cases in court.[4] In the *Art of Rhetoric*, Corax outlined a series of legal communication strategies and public speaking principles to help people win their lawsuits. His theories of legal and public communication were then introduced to Athens and the Greek mainland by his student **Tisias** in 428 B.C. Corax and Tisias defined rhetoric as "the craft of persuasion," and they developed a following of traveling teachers—known as the **Sophists**—who practiced and refined the theories taught by Corax.[5]

The Sophists believed that reality, truth, and knowledge were socially constructed through communication. In other words, they acknowledged that language could name things that had not yet been seen, and could conceal as well as reveal aspects of reality. Their beliefs and teaching practices, however, would come under the scrutiny of philosophers such as Plato, who argued that Sophists did little more than use clever arguments to deceive audiences. Critics believed that Corax and Tisias were simply teaching Greeks a set of persuasive "tricks" to make a weak case sound strong. As a result, the Sophists have been disparaged throughout much of Western history.

Despite those criticisms, the Sophists were the first among classical theorists to identify social needs and practical dilemmas that could be addressed using communication theory. Not only did they develop debating exercises to help individuals win their lawsuits, they also recognized the expectation of every Greek citizen to participate personally in government, as well as the importance of ceremonial gatherings in Greek culture. In response to those social needs, the Sophists developed schools of rhetoric and communication where they taught the use of persuasive and ornamental language to accomplish legal and political goals.

Many of the practical questions and social dilemmas that the Sophists attempted to address 2,500 years ago are still with us today. In February 2008, for instance, Roger Clemens testified before Congress that he had not used performance-enhancing drugs during his career as a major league baseball player. Despite his efforts to defend his professional and personal reputation, Congress concluded that his testimony was not believable or persuasive enough to settle the case and to avoid perjury charges. Ceremonial gatherings also remain an important context in which public speakers must carefully craft and deliver persuasive appeals to win over their audiences. In January 2011, President Barack Obama was faced with the daunting task of delivering a eulogy for the six victims of a gunman who attempted to murder Representative Gabrielle Gifford of Arizona, including Christina Taylor Green, a nine-year-old girl who was shot and killed while meeting her congresswoman at the local Safeway. In the days surrounding the victims' funerals, many legal and political correspondents debated the merits of President Obama's eulogy and the implications it had for gun-control laws in the United States.

Many of us have also had friends participate in student government. To get elected, they had to present their ideas publicly in a manner that persuaded other students to vote for them. As those examples reflect, practical questions—such as how best to defend a case before a jury of peers, how to present a set of ideas publicly in a competent manner, and how to deliver a persuasive speech effectively—all remain relevant today. Although they developed their schools of rhetoric to teach Greeks how to speak in public, the Sophists recognized that the most valuable communication theories were those that help people answer practical questions and achieve their personal goals. Consequently, the Sophistic tradition represents a pattern of thinking about communication that is still evident in some approaches to communication theory today.

The Platonic tradition. The second pattern of thought about communication to emerge in ancient Greece came from **Plato** (427–347 B.C.), who was a student of Socrates and a serious critic of life in Athens. Plato was convinced that Greek democracy had resulted in a public rejection of timeless ideals, such as truth and justice. In fact, he held the Sophists primarily responsible for misleading the Greek people about the true nature of reality and language. When Plato began his writing, rhetoric had become an important part of Greek academic life, so much so that it was considered the "queen of subjects" as "higher education meant taking lessons from the rhetor."[6] Schools of rhetoric were competing successfully with schools of philosophy, and many Greek citizens were more attracted to rhetorical teachings than to philosophical teachings. In response to the growing success of the Sophists, Plato established himself as the greatest critic of their approach to communication. He argued that rhetoric was not a science based on knowledge of right and wrong, but was instead a mere skill that depended on knowledge of human weakness and a manipulation of human language.

Plato started the *Academus,* a formal school where he argued for a theory of communication based on knowledge of a *true reality.* For Plato, reality consisted of timeless, changeless forms that exist beyond the evolving world of appearances and perceptions. He argued that through proper training, philosophers could attain knowledge of reality and could offer the truth—rather than mere opinions—to listeners. Plato believed that language was a necessary evil, an imperfect means of expressing inner thoughts and desires that could only distort true reality. Thus, he established his school, wrote *The Republic,* and used his writings to train the intellectual elite to critique and censor those who used language irresponsibly (such as the Sophists).

In essence, the Sophists and Plato represent opposite ends of a continuum regarding the nature of reality, truth, and language. The Sophists believed in a subjective reality that was socially constructed through language. In contrast, Plato believed in an objective reality that could only be revealed through critical inquiry by trained philosophers. Whereas the Sophists embraced ornamental language and taught ordinary citizens rhetorical strategies to help them win their cases, Plato trained future philosophers how to critique communication practices that distorted the true nature of reality. In the end, Plato argued that communication theory must be concerned not only with public speaking strategies and eloquence, but also with human communication in general. His writings outlined a philosophical theory of human communication that would later serve as a guide for the third pattern of thought to emerge from ancient Greece.

The Aristotelian tradition. No one from ancient Greece was more influential in the development of communication theory than **Aristotle** (384–322 B.C.). As one of Plato's former students, Aristotle tried to bridge the gap between the Sophists' attention to the practical questions driving the actual world of human affairs, and Plato's philosophical quest for truth and certainty. He believed theories of human behavior should be based on **empiricism,** or careful observation of the physical world, and meticulous reasoning according to the standards of logic. Aristotle established his own school in Athens in 335 B.C. called **the Lyceum**, and his *Rhetoric* is considered by many scholars to be the single most influential work in the history of Western thought about communication.[7]

In his efforts to balance the philosophical training of Plato with the pragmatic concerns of the Sophists, Aristotle reported the first systematic, empirical investigation of human communication. He defined *rhetoric* as "an ability, in each case, to see the available means of persuasion,"[8] and he argued that communication theory is a science concerned with understanding human thought and action through analysis of language behavior. Aristotle devoted quite a bit of time to teaching his students how to build successful arguments, how to arrive at truthful conclusions, and how to make the best use of different kinds of evidence. He identified various topics they address when engaged in legal, political, or ceremonial speaking. He also suggested that speakers could persuade audiences using three general sources of proof: **logos**, which is established through the wording and logic of the message; **pathos**, which is established through emotional appeals; and **ethos**, which is established through the personal character and integrity of the speaker. In fact, through his discussions of ethos, Aristotle became one of the first scholars to identify **source credibility**—which is the audience's perceptions of the speaker's competence, character, and goodwill—as an important component of public speaking. Consequently, those fortunate enough to study with Aristotle would have left his Lyceum with a better understanding of the rules for effective arguments, the role that human emotions play in persuasion, the importance of understanding and audience, the methods for improving style and delivery, and the value of rhetoric in discovering and communicating truth.

Considered together, the Sophistic, Platonic, and Aristotelian traditions that emerged from ancient Greece provide us with a brief glimpse of where the communication discipline came from. Some classical theorists were primarily interested in teaching (and selling) speaking strategies to help people achieve their personal and professional goals. Others were more interested in using rhetoric to pursue truth and justice; still others wanted to understand the pervasiveness of communication at all levels of human interaction. Across each of those schools of thought, however, the classical theorists recognized the "futility of prescribing practice without a theoretical framework as well as the emptiness of theory without reference to practice."[9] In fact, the recognition that communication practices should be guided by empirical theories, and that empirical theories should never be divorced from the social and practical concerns of the people using them, remains a primary concern of scholars today.

▲ ▲ ▲

Let's Discuss

1. In what ways do you use communication to be active in civic life?
2. Think of a speaker you find to be highly credible. What does that speaker say or do that give him or her credibility in your mind?

▲ ▲ ▲

Test Your Understanding

Many of the ideas represented in the three classical patterns of thought about communication are still evident today. Read each of the examples below and see if you can identify which example best represents the Sophistic, Platonic, and Aristotelian tradition:

In 1991, marketing consultants recognized the negative health connotations associated with the word "fried" and recommended that Colonel Sanders change the name of his company from Kentucky Fried Chicken to KFC. (**Answer: Sophistic tradition**)

After observing his elite skill as a professional golfer and his tremendous success on the PGA circuit, Gatorade and Gillette hired Tiger Woods to endorse their respective lines of product. In November 2009, however, Tiger was involved in a car accident that launched several investigations and ultimately revealed his marital infidelity. In the months following his car accident, both companies ended their endorsement deals with Tiger, citing reasons other than their concerns about Tiger's character. (**Answer: Aristotelian tradition**)

In the 2004 documentary, "Super Size Me," Morgan Spurlock attempts to reveal the effects of fast food by going on a 30-day diet in which he eats only McDonald's food. His film documents the drastic effects of eating only McDonald's food on his physical and psychological well-being, and he exposes the fast food industry's corporate influence and their attempts to encourage poor nutrition for its own profit. (**Answer: Platonic tradition**)

▲ ▲ ▲

From Ancient Greece to Contemporary Times

The study of human communication continued to evolve in the centuries following ancient Greece, and scholars built and extended the theoretical ideas and speaking principles outlined in the classics.[10] Historically, the study of rhetoric had focused on oral communication and public speaking, yet by the late 19th century, that focus had shifted to written communication. The study and teaching of rhetoric eventually became the province of departments of English,[11] and English teachers were stressing written arguments and the study of literature to the exclusion of oral communication. On the other hand, a separate group of teachers who emphasized **elocution**—the study of voice, articulation, and gesture—had become so focused on the details of speech delivery that their work started drawing criticism in the early 20th century. In response, dissatisfied English and elocution teachers joined forces and created many of the early departments of speech. Two traditions emerged during the early part of the 20th century that are still influential today: the humanistic tradition and the social scientific tradition.

The humanistic tradition. Despite the movement of some away from the focus on literature found in English departments in the early 1900s, the study of rhetoric was well established and a number of rhetorical scholars began to revitalize traditional studies of rhetorical theory. The humanistic approach to rhetorical theory began to take shape in the early 1920s as scholars used rhetorical criticism to analyze the methods used by a public speaker to influence an audience. Today, rhetoricians use the historical and critical methods of the humanities to examine how messages and other symbols influence public responses to political events and ethical dilemmas. For such scholars, the study of communication is a humanistic endeavor, one with a rich and long tradition that emerged from classical writings such as Aristotle's *Rhetoric* and Plato's *The Republic*. With a focus on human values and a desire to improve the human condition, communication scholars in the humanities examine how reason, ethics, and social justice inform our understanding of what it means to be human in cultural, social, and personal contexts. Students interested in the humanistic approach to communication typically take classes in classical, medieval, and modern rhetorical theory, rhetorical criticism, and public address, as well as courses in related fields of history or political science.

The social scientific tradition. Unlike the rhetoricians, others were interested in creating a new discipline of communication that would focus on interaction between people. As a result, they began searching for appropriate ways (or methods) to observe human communication. During that time, many disciplines were being influenced by the **scientific method**, a method of research in which a problem is identified, relevant data are gathered, and hypotheses are formed and empirically tested. By 1915, the National Association of Academic Teachers of Public Speaking (which today is called the National Communication Association) was recommending that communication scholars take courses in departments of physiology, psychology, and sociology to learn the methods of science.[12] Those scholars believed they could understand something only by reducing it to its most basic elements, manipulating those elements in controlled laboratory environments, and observing the results. In many ways, those social scientists subscribed to Aristotle's belief in using empirical observation and reasoning draw conclusions about our social world.

By the 1920s, communication researchers who were employing social scientific methods began publishing research reports on oral communication. One of the most influential bodies of research to emerge during that period examined audience psychology and attitude change. Early communication scientists explored audience reactions to public speeches and debates, as well as the effects of different kinds of message content on attitudes, opinions, and information retention. For instance, scholars used structured interviews to examine audience reactions to such events as the 1939 radio broadcast of H. G. Wells's *War of the Worlds*. After World War II, scholars in the late 1940s and early 1950s began investigating the effects of propaganda, which in turn prompted communication theorists to view human interaction as a *process* consisting of different kinds of *variables* (sender, message, channel, receiver, feedback, etc.). From the 1950s to the 1970s, many social psychologists and communication scholars conducted experiments in which they manipulated the credibility of a source, the content of a message, and/or the structure of a message to observe the effects on audience attitude. Other scholars used laboratory experiments to examine group dynamics and leadership, surveys to study audience reactions to various print and electronic media, and both forms of research to examine interpersonal relationships.

As a result, the late 1960s witnessed a growing tension between communication scholars in the humanities and those in the social sciences, as each community viewed the other as conducting different kinds of scholarship. By the 1970s and early 1980s, however, communication scholars started to seek an integration of the two traditions. Today, many departments of communication teach both humanistic and social scientific approaches. Let's look more closely at the contemporary discipline of communication in the next section.

The Communication Discipline Today

The history of the discipline is an important story reminding us all that the past matters. But the story of today's communication discipline may be even more compelling because communication is such an indispensable part of our daily lives. The contemporary communication field is made up of scholars and practitioners who seek to explore, invent, and understand communication in dynamic, complex, and ever-changing social and cultural landscapes. In this section we focus on three organizing frameworks for communication that reflect important contemporary principles and practices: communication contexts and interdisciplinary challenges; professional organizations and networks; and, diversity and growth of the discipline.

Communication Contexts and Interdisciplinary Challenges

Our review of the past recognized that the communication field includes rhetorical, humanistic, and social scientific traditions, each with the goal of understanding human interaction. But in what ways do scholars and practitioners in the discipline organize the study of human communication? How do we make sense of the overwhelming complexity of communication and meaning-making in our everyday lives? One way to answer those questions is to focus on a specific framework of experience.[13] We have already discussed the social scientific, rhetorical, and humanistic traditions as one framework for analysis, but scholars often distinguish *communication studies,* with a primary focus on different forms of human face-to-face interaction, from *media studies,* with a primary focus on the mediated forms of human interaction where technologies connect people in non face-to-face interactions, such as texting, radio broadcasts, newsprint, tweets, blogs, and Skype.[14] Although that distinction might be a good starting point for organizing communication theory and practice, it implies that technology does not influence and intersect directly in our human face-to-face encounters. On the contrary, one of us (L.E.) attended a conference recently where he was talking face-to-face with four other colleagues, only to notice that all four were texting other people at the same time! Perhaps the distinction between media and communication studies is not quite as useful as it may first appear.

Understanding communication in context. A common framework for understanding communication studies is the delineation of communication contexts. Put simply, a **context** can be thought of as a situation, environment, or particular type of experience.[15] For example, having your "first big fight" with a new romantic partner could be studied from the context of romantic relationships or from the context of conflict communication.[16] Similarly, you could study the promotion to a new leadership position in your marketing firm in either an organizational context or a leadership context. Thus, *context* provides a more focused orientation to your experiences in a given situation. One way to determine which contexts communication scholars find compelling is to look at the types of courses offered in departments of communication. A recent study of course offerings at 4-year colleges and universities found that the top ten courses offered in our discipline are:[17]

1. Interpersonal communication
2. Group communication
3. Organizational communication
4. Persuasion
5. Public speaking
6. Intercultural communication
7. Communication research methods
8. Communication theory
9. Argumentation and debate
10. Gender and communication

Of course, communication courses also cover a broad spectrum of other topics, including family communication, instructional communication, rhetoric and public address, health communication, conflict and negotiation, nonverbal communication, language and oral interpretation, and communication and aging. Is majoring in communication a good choice? Check out "Communication as a Unique Discipline?" to find out.

▲   ▲   ▲

Communication as a Unique Discipline?

Over the last 20 years or so communication scholars have asked about the relevance or importance of the discipline. What is unique about the communication discipline? Why do we need departments of communication studies? Is there any context in communication programs that can't be better addressed in other university departments? Consider these examples:

> You want to study intimacy in interpersonal relationships, so why not get a degree in psychology rather than communication studies? Is it possible that a degree in psychology will result in the same types of knowledge as a degree in communication? What if you want to study group dynamics? Wouldn't a degree in sociology make as much sense as a degree in communication? Imagine that you want to focus on intercultural communication so you can work overseas. Since anthropology has traditionally studied cultures, wouldn't a degree in anthropology better serve your interests?

Throughout this course, one important task is to consider the ways in which communication is separate and distinct from other disciplines. Work with your instructor and other students to consider why communication studies matter and what unique features our discipline possesses. As a hint, consider the role of symbols in defining and understanding communication. Also, ask your instructor or other communication instructors what practical implications they think the study of communication has for everyday interactions.

▲ ▲ ▲

Questions about communication also vary by *level of analysis*.[18] That way of framing questions asks us to consider differences between individual-level issues (self-talk), pair-level issues (friendships, romantic relationships), group-level issues (families, work teams), organizational-level issues (corporations, non-profit groups), and public-level issues (national elections, government protests). A *level of analysis* approach is useful for exploring potential differences in communication and human experience. For example, communication between two friends is vastly different than communication between two political parties. Likewise, communication with oneself may operate very differently than communication in an Alcoholics Anonymous group. Differences and similarities in communication levels may emerge based on the number of people involved, whether the people like or want to like each other, what goals the people are pursuing, and many other factors.

▲ ▲ ▲

Let's Discuss

1. The modern communication discipline addresses a wide variety of questions. Which questions about communication do you find most compelling?
2. Suppose you wanted to know more about how people can persuade others effectively. How would you approach that question from a humanistic perspective? How about a social scientific perspective?

▲ ▲ ▲

Crossing boundaries. A large part of what makes communication so interesting to learn about is that it intersects with so many other fields of study. It infiltrates our interior spaces (cognitive, biological, emotional) as well as our exterior spaces (social networks, work-life, public and cultural spheres). Understanding the influences on communication from the perspectives of other disciplines—such as psychology, anthropology, business, medicine, theater—allows us to recognize those places where we share ideas, theories, and practices. To call the communication field **interdisciplinary** means we recognize and value the contribution of other fields' philosophies, theories, practices, and knowledge as a way to enhance our understanding of communication.

Think about how you communicate with your friends, for instance. You make decisions about what messages to send, and how to send them, based on what meanings you want to convey. Your decisions may also be affected, however, by your state of mind (a psychological influence), your physical or mental health (a medical influence), your cultural traditions and practices (a sociological influence), and the availability of WiFi wherever you like to hang out (a technological influence). Knowledge from those other disciplines is therefore useful for understanding the many factors that affect the communication process.

PROFESSIONAL ORGANIZATIONS

The health of any discipline is reflected in the quality and strength of its professional organizations and networks of association. Three prominent professional organizations in the communication field are the *National Communication Association* (NCA: www.natcom.org), the *International Communication Association* (ICA: www.icahdq.org), and the *Association for Education in Journalism and Mass Communication* (AEJMC: www.aejmc.org). One of the benefits of professional organizations is that they provide a sense of coherence in mission and goals for the scholars they represent. For example, NCA's goals include:

Fostering research and teaching addressing the most pressing public problems at the dawn of the 21st century.

Advancing the communication disciplines role in reducing
prejudice and hateful acts based on racial, ethnic, religious,
and other human differences and increasing society's ability
to embrace opportunities of diversity was, and is, a critical
part of this effort.[19]

Notice how the goals of NCA focus on inclusiveness rather than division, and current problems rather than esoteric theories. ICA identifies four purposes in the accomplishment of its mission. They are:

(1) to provide an international forum to enable the development, conduct, and critical evaluation of communication
research; (2) to sustain a program of high quality scholarly
publication and knowledge exchange; (3) to facilitate inclusiveness and debate among scholars from diverse national
and cultural backgrounds and from multi-disciplinary perspectives on communication-related issues; and (4) to promote a wider public interest in, and visibility of, the theories,
methods, findings and applications generated by research in
communication and allied fields.[20]

As you might expect from an international organization, ICA focuses strongly on multiple disciplines, multiple national and cultural
backgrounds, and critical evaluation of research. Finally, AEJMC's
stated mission is:

To promote the highest possible standards for journalism
and mass communication education, to cultivate the widest
possible range of communication research, to encourage the
implementation of a multi-cultural society in the classroom
and curriculum, and to defend and maintain freedom of
communication in an effort to achieve better professional
practice and a better informed public.[21]

Although AEJMC emphasizes journalism and mass communication, specifically, all thsree organizations have a common interest in exploring communication phenomena and educating students and the public about communication theory, research, and application.

Professional organizations also promote *networking* among members. The importance of networking should not be underestimated. Communication networks allow for the development of new ideas, methods, and practices that are tested through debate, discussion, and dialogue. Close associates in a professional network can provide important feedback on principles and practices before we communicate them to wider audiences. Another important benefit of networking is that the interaction and dialogue can reflect changes and innovation in the discipline. What better way to explore a new idea than to test its assumptions and principles with other professionals in an environment designed to create new knowledge!

DISCIPLINARY DIVERSITY AND MULTICULTURALISM

Journalist and writer Thomas Friedman argued that we live, increasingly, in a *flat* world (and hot and crowded!) where our global connections to one another are more immediate, instantaneous, and complex than they have ever been before.[22] We might argue that we are encouraged, cajoled, and even forced to think globally. As you read earlier, communication scholars have embraced a spirit of multiculturalism and diversity that is important to where we are today as a discipline. Let's briefly explore two trends or growth areas in the discipline that influence how we study communication.

International perspectives. One of the most obvious and compelling areas of growth is in international communication studies.[23] Many scholars have argued that American and European theories and practices dominate the communication discipline. The fact that communication is a growing area of study around the globe is an encouraging sign, however. If one of our goals is to embrace diversity, then this trend is further evidence of a healthy discipline. Since many international scholars study in American universities, they are introduced and trained in particularly Western orientations (including theories and methods) to communication phenomena. A useful question is "Are American communication theories and practices a good reflection of the social and cultural experiences of international students?" At least one expert has argued that "the Asian communication scholar for the 21st century" will envision new theories and practices of communication that don't depend on Western paradigms, theories, and methods.[24] But we also want to encourage you to consider what insights and ideas international students have to offer us! At a minimum, international students and scholars can test the extent to which our theories and practices are unique to our social and cultural conditions or are more universal.

Diversity within the communication field. A second trend is the growth of majors in communication and the diversity of contexts studied. NCA examined the number of degrees earned by communication majors between 1970 and 2000. For undergraduate degrees alone, the number of majors increased roughly five-fold in that time period, from 10,802 in 1970 to 56,810 in 2000. The number of students earning master's degrees in the same period rose from 1,856 to 5,605. Although increases in student enrollments are one indicator of a healthy and vibrant discipline, communication scholars have also expanded areas of specialization to include strong emphases in emerging areas of study, such as communication about health, the environment, and national security. Let's take a closer look at some of these new trends in the next section, as they have some important implications for your work, life, and overall communication experiences.

LOOKING AHEAD: THE FUTURE OF COMMUNICATION STUDIES

Our rich and varied past will inform the future of our discipline, as it will inform your future personal and professional lives. The kinds of problems and opportunities you will likely face over the course of your lifetime will, increasingly, have much to do with communication. Your ability to understand your local and global context, effectively respond to, and perhaps even transform your identity, relationships, and communities will depend on your ability to apply communication theories and skills.

Although we cannot predict with absolute certainty how the future of communication studies will unfold, we have good reason to believe that communication scholars will continue to explore "big questions" to provide informed answers to some of society's most relevant and perplexing problems, including:

1. How is communication changing in a global, mediated world?
2. How can communication enhance our individual, relational, and community health?
3. How can communication reduce violence and enhance our security?

Many communication scholars are becoming more and more interested in applying communication theories to real-world problems. Applied communication research, sometimes referred to as *use-inspired* or *phronetic* scholarship, is motivated by the drive to provide individuals and communities with communication solutions to real world individual, relational, organizational, and even national problems.[25] Let's take a look at how the field of communication is currently addressing these applied questions.

How is Communication Changing in a Global, Mediated World?

Over the next several years, communication theories will likely focus on how communication practices in a variety of contexts—interpersonal relationships, organizational relationships, and even political landscapes—are being transformed as a result of new communication technologies. In the past, the communication discipline has distinguished face-to-face communication from mass mediated communication, and some communication programs and theories are still organized around that divide. The current generation of communication students and scholars, however, has grown up in a "wired" culture in which online interactions, information seeking, and self-expression in mediated forms are routine. Consequently, as we move into the future of communication studies, the lines between mediated and interpersonal, group, and political communication will become more and more blurred.[26]

Communication scholars in the future will explore the benefits and burdens of communication technologies. One challenge you might face right now, for instance, is figuring out how to match audience expectations across various types of communication media. The way you communicate in a text message to your friend may not be appropriate for an e-mail message to your professor. In a recent study, communication researchers Keri Stephens, Marian Houser, and Renee Cowan examined differences between college students' and their instructors' perceptions of e-mail messages.[27] Although students may feel comfortable using shorthand phrases, such as "C U l8r," "R U," or "LOL," instructors—even those who are members of the "millennial generation"—tend to view such casual messages negatively. Overly casual messages are likely to be viewed negatively by potential employers as well. The good news is that eliminating spelling errors and abbreviations and developing the ability to make clear requests and arguments are all strategies for improving your e-mail message's positive impact. Learning how to communicate effectively across always-changing media and audiences will help you to solve many of your own challenges, such as communicating with your instructors, finding a job, or making a romantic connection. Find out more about the effects of communication technology in "Taming the Wild Beast."

▲ ▲ ▲

Taming the Wild Beast: "Domesticating" Google

In the future, communication scholars are likely to explore how people use and appropriate new media technologies in all aspects of their everyday lives and how their use of new media shapes future technological developments. Domestication theory uses the metaphor of *taming wild animals* to explain how information communication technologies are introduced into our homes and "domesticated," such that they become a regular and routine feature of our public and private lives. As we domesticate technology, technology itself and our lives are shaped by our uses of it.

Consider Google. It was developed by Stanford University graduate students Larry Page and Sergey Brin as part of a digital library project. Their original search engine—which they called BackRub—used links to determine the relevance of individual webpages. Since its introduction, Google has grown exponentially and is now the most dominant search engine in the world. If we have a question, we often turn to Google to find the answer. You may have "googled" a topic, a person, or a place today. Indeed, through our collective use and appropriation of this particular technology, we have turned Google (a noun, a thing) into "googling" (a verb, a process). This communication technology impacts how we understand the value of information; at the same time, it discourages other types of information-seeking behavior. In response, other communication technologies, such as smart phones, are morphing to support our increasing demands for information seeking.

Consider this:

1. How do you use Google in your everyday life?
2. What benefits does Google offer you? What benefits does Google offer to society?

3. Some have criticized Google for potentially violating privacy (such as collecting children's Social Security numbers), censorship (such as complying with the Chinese government's request for Internet control), and "googlization" (Google's dominance and corporate privatization of digital information). What do you think are the potential problems with Google for you individually, and for society?

▲   ▲   ▲

Let's Discuss

1. To what extent do you think your own understanding of communication behavior is limited to the norms and social structures of the United States?
2. Has technology fundamentally changed how we communicate with each other? Or, has it simply given us more ways to communicate?

▲   ▲   ▲

HOW CAN COMMUNICATION ENHANCE OUR INDIVIDUAL, RELATIONAL, AND COMMUNITY HEALTH?

Communication studies continue to focus on how communication practices make us healthier. Health communication research is a growing area of our field. Scholars in that area explore how patients can improve their experiences, health outcomes, and satisfaction with their health care providers through more effective communication, how organizations can enhance the safety and well-being of their workers, communication strategies dating partners can use to reduce their risk of contracting sexually transmitted diseases, and ways public health officials can encourage healthier behaviors through persuasive health campaigns. A new but growing area of research examines the health and physiological impacts of communication behaviors.[28] For example, work at several universities—including one of our own programs of research (K.F.)—illustrates how emotionally supportive, affectionate communication in close relationships can reduce stress and improve a person's physical and mental health.[29] Other research documents the negative health effects of various conflict behaviors.[30] Studies such as those are promising because they identify ways we can communicate that will enhance and support our well-being.

How Can Communication Reduce Violence and Enhance Our Security?

Your lifetime will likely be characterized by increased globalization. That globalization brings with it wonderful opportunities, such as new economic markets and international collaborations. As the September 11 terror attacks made painfully clear, however, globalization also has the potential to bring national and regional conflicts over resources and ideologies into our daily lives. Communication researchers and practitioners have long been committed to providing theories and practices to manage conflict, communicate across cultures, and collaborate in diverse groups ethically and effectively. In the coming years, communication scholars will increasingly turn their attention to providing research and protocols to help government, military, non-government, and business leaders understand, navigate, intervene, and defuse ideological conflicts, particularly those that inspire violence.

A group of organizational, rhetorical, and new media scholars in the Consortium for Strategic Communication at Arizona State University is doing just that. Using humanistic concepts of narrative and ideology, the team collects and analyzes extremists' rhetoric from around the world to determine how violent extremists recruit and socialize new members, justify violence, and frame international conflicts.[31] In the future, this team hopes to develop an iPhone app that will help military and diplomatic personnel understand the narratives of an area. That is an important endeavor because, according to the U.S. Joint Forces Command, many of the "Internet-fueled" wars of the future will be carried out through narratives designed to influence public opinion.[32] Communication scholars and practitioners are poised to provide answers to the pressing question of how we can win the "battle of hearts and minds" as we move through the 21st century.

WHY LEARN ABOUT COMMUNICATION THEORIES?

When we started this chapter, we were perplexed about Kanye West's bizarre behavior. As you've seen, people have been intrigued and confused by human behavior for centuries. More than two thousand years ago, Corax of Syracuse wondered why some people were more persuasive in court than others, so he developed theories about persuasion and taught people public-speaking skills based on his ideas. In the early 1900s, researchers wondered what types of messages would influence people's attitudes, so they developed theories about attitude change and set up experiments to test their effects. As we begin the 21st century, communication scholars are wondering about all sorts of things, from the relational consequences of compulsive Internet use[33] to the effects of humor in political television[34] to the public's understanding of cancer clinical trials.[35] In each case, they test existing theories—or develop new ones—to help them understand human behavior better.

As the examples in this chapter illustrate, communication research has tremendous potential to help solve real-world problems—but addressing people's problems starts with understanding why people do what they do. That is the mission of communication theories. Let's say you want to design a website to discourage distressed teenagers from committing suicide, such as author Dan Savage did in 2010 when he created the It Gets Better Project (www.itgetsbetter.

org). How would you know what to say to dissuade people from taking their own lives? It would help to be familiar with theories that explain how communication influences behavior—as well as with theories about why people commit suicide. If you had that understanding to work with, you could craft messages that may actually save the lives of adolescents who found your webpage. Without those theories, however, you might end up creating messages that don't help at all, because they are irrelevant or unpersuasive.

Not every communication issue is a matter of life or death, but many everyday problems—from simple, mundane ones to complex, global ones—are, at their core, *communication problems*. Understanding how and why humans communicate as they do will give you tools to improve life for yourself, your family, your community, your country, and your world.

FOR FURTHER DISCUSSION

1. Go online and search the communication department website at your college or university for course listings. What contexts and areas of study are represented by the courses taught? Do you think the communication department strikes a balance among rhetorical, humanistic, and social scientific traditions? Does the department emphasize one more than the others? How can you tell?

2. If you were to create your own blog about communication, what are the topics, issues, and problems you would address? Whom would you want to read your blog? Why?

3. What "big questions" do you hope communication scholars will address in the future?

KEY TERMS

Aristotle
Context
Corax
Elocution
Empiricism
Ethos
Interdisciplinary
Logos
Lyceum
Meaning
Pathos
Plato
Process
Rhetoric
Rhetoricians
Scientific method
Sophists
Source credibility
Symbols
Tisias

2

CONCEPTUALIZING
COMMUNICATION THEORY

WHY DON'T HOLLYWOOD MARRIAGES LAST?

A S YOU WALK in the door after another day of school, one of your roommates says "Not again!" You ask, "What's going on?" and your roommate reads the following headline from her laptop: "Will Smith and Jada Pinkett Smith appear headed for divorce." You ask your roommate why she is so surprised by the news, and as she begins to defend one of her favorite actresses, you quickly point out that Hollywood marriages never last. To back up your argument, you remind your roommate of several Hollywood couples who divorced within weeks of getting married, such as Britney Spears and Jason Alexander (2 days), Carmen Electra and Dennis Rodman (9 days), Renee Zellweger and Kenny Chesney (4 months), and Bradley Cooper and Jennifer Esposito (4 months). Your roommate is a hopeless romantic, however. "Why don't Hollywood marriages ever last?" she wonders aloud.

How would you answer that question? To begin, you might consider whether there's something about being a movie star that would help you make sense of why Hollywood marriages struggle:

1. Perhaps Hollywood actors are lulled into thinking marriage is "easy" by the romantic films in which many of them have appeared.
2. Famous people are constantly monitored by tabloids, so maybe that creates a great deal of stress on their romantic relationships.
3. The demanding schedules of movie production companies may reduce the amount of quality time needed to connect and maintain a healthy relationship.
4. Perhaps movie stars have so many opportunities to cheat on their spouses that they wind up having affairs.

Those explanations may all be plausible, and you might be able to think of other factors that could explain why famous marriages struggle. On the other hand, maybe the answer to the question has more to do with marriage, in general, than with Hollywood.

1. Maybe people experience more marital strain nowadays because of financial pressures.
2. Many spouses might lack good conflict management skills, making it difficult to resolve their problems.
3. Because divorces aren't difficult to get—and they don't carry the social stigma that they used to—perhaps couples see them as an easy solution to their problems.

Those ideas could explain why Hollywood marriages never seem to last. It might also be that we've all been tricked into thinking that Hollywood marriages always fail just because we hear so much about them. All of your explanations make sense, but you don't just want a list of possibilities—you want to figure out which explanation is the *best* one.

In a very elementary way, you have just begun to create a communication theory.

This chapter explains what theories are and how they help us make sense of the world. We'll define the term *theory*, distinguish it from other terms commonly found in communication research, and describe four different parts of a theory. We will then discuss five philosophical assumptions that will help you understand the functions and goals of the communication theories you'll encounter in this book. By examining what theories consist of and what functions they serve, we believe you will develop a greater appreciation for using communication theory to address the social and practical problems we face in everyday life.

WHAT IS A COMMUNICATION THEORY?

In simplest terms, a **theory** is an organized set of statements that explains some phenomenon.[1] Theories are abstract, general ideas that are subject to rules of logic and organization. They help us make sense of our experiences by tying certain facts or observations to general principles and processes. In other words, theories provide us with interpretations and explanations of the world so that our experiences are easier to understand.[2]

Various fields of study use different theories to make sense of the world. To explain why Hollywood marriages rarely last, for instance, psychologists might use personality theories to clarify how narcissism makes it difficult for famous movie stars to focus on their spouses. Sociologists might use cultural theories to analyze how marriage has become less stable in Western society, particularly as people attain a higher socioeconomic status. Communication scholars might use conflict management theories to examine how Hollywood spouses resolve their differences, or dialectical theories to understand how they manage the competing tensions of their public and private lives. Although those explanations focus on different aspects of the question, they may each provide a piece of the answer.

Communication theories focus on how people send and receive messages to create shared meaning in cultural, societal, relational, and mediated contexts. Although communication theories share a basic goal of extending our knowledge and understanding of human communication, they accomplish that goal in varying ways. Some communication theories offer predictions and identify cause-and-effect relationships between various dimensions of the communication process. Other theories are used as sensitizing devices, or guides, to getting started in a research study, generating fruitful insights into people's meaning-making processes. Still other theories are based on critical examinations of institutional or ideological power for the purposes of uncovering voices that have been marginalized or silenced by dominant groups.[3] Later in this chapter, we will discuss three worldviews—what scholars call *paradigms*—that correspond with each type of theory. For now, we'll focus on how theories answer questions and extend our knowledge about the communication process.

One way to understand what theories are is to explore what they are not. Our next section compares and contrasts communication theories with three related but separate products: conceptual frameworks, models, and paradigms. We will then describe five philosophical assumptions that help us understand the similarities and differences among communication theories before concluding this chapter with a discussion of the functions and goals of communication theory.

WHAT IS NOT A COMMUNICATION THEORY?
A conceptual framework is not a communication theory. Our ability to communicate with each other depends, in large part, on using a shared language. The languages we use have vocabularies and rules for grammar that let us connect words and nonverbal gestures into meaningful statements. Our vocabularies operate like dictionaries, helping us identify meaning in the language we use. Similarly, communication theories include a vocabulary of defined terms, or a

conceptual framework, that helps us use the theory to understand some form of human interaction. If we wanted to develop a communication theory about troubled Hollywood marriages, for instance, we may need to define such key terms as *marriage, infidelity, celebrity, divorce,* and *tabloids.* By itself, that set of concepts isn't a theory. Rather, it provides a basic foundation for understanding the general ideas and principles in the theory. We cannot have a communication theory without a conceptual framework, but the framework by itself is not enough to comprise a communication theory.[4]

A model is not a communication theory. How would you describe the process of communicating with another person? Communication scholars have answered that question by offering a variety of models. A **model** is a formal description of a process. It is an abstract representation of how something works, or a simplified picture of complex relationships between phenomena. Communication models depict communication processes by graphing, plotting, or diagramming the essential elements of those processes and fitting them into an organized structure.[5] Early attempts to define the essence of communication led to a variety of general models. In the early 1950s, for example, Shannon and Weaver developed an influential communication model based on a mathematical theory of information transmission.[6] Schramm offered a communication model that included classic concepts such as source, encoder, and decoder, as well as more the novel concept of "fields of experience."[7] In the 1960s, Berlo developed the Sender Message Channel Receiver (or SMCR) model to depict what he believed were the four most essential elements to human communication.[8] In later years, scholars have developed more elaborate and specific models of communication, such as Barnlund's interpersonal communication model.[9]

As you can see from each of those examples, models are tools that help us to connect the essential elements of a communication process together. They are not theories, however. Models merely describe a process—theories, on the other hand, *explain* them.[10]

Nonetheless, models remain useful tools for communication scholars. For instance, communication professor Brian Spitzberg recently developed a model of computer-mediated communication (CMC) competence that identifies certain skills, media factors, message factors, and contextual cues that influence perceptions of media use in personal relationships.[11] Other scholars have used models to help organize lines of research on a topic for which no theories exist. For example, one of us (P.S.) recently described a divorce disclosure model (DDM) along with communication professors Tamara Afifi and Tara McManus. The DDM describes parents' motivations for disclosing negative information about their divorce to their adolescent children, the factors that influence those disclosures, and their effects on well-being.[12] Whether they depict a specific communication event or a general communication process, models are useful for identifying the essential elements within the process and describing how those elements relate to each other.

▲ ▲ ▲

Test Your Understanding
Suppose two movie stars are discussing whether they should divorce after six months of marriage. How could we describe that process? What would our communication model look like? What key elements, or important factors, would we want to include in our model? How many of our key elements would be related to the individual personalities of the partners? To the social and cultural environment? Or more important, to the *communication patterns* between the two partners? And how would we represent those elements using pictures, diagrams, or other symbols in a manner that communicates clearly what is happening in this type of interaction? Work with your instructor and other students to create verbal-graphic models that help describe some of the factors that influence the decision of some Hollywood couples to divorce so quickly.

▲ ▲ ▲

A paradigm is not a communication theory. Communication theories don't just magically appear. Rather, they are human creations that require the ability to interpret and make sense of our experiences. They are often created and altered over time by scholars who work together to validate and extend their ideas. Various **schools of thought** represent scholars who share certain assumptions and procedures for organizing their ideas about human communication. For example, the Sophists, Plato's *Academus,* and Aristotle's *Lyceum* each represented classical schools of thought that held different assumptions about the nature of reality, truth, and language. Members of such *schools*—groups of scholars—interact on a regular basis and jointly create ideas and practices. They may create new theories, new methods of research, or other bodies of knowledge. Scholars in each school of thought share a **paradigm**, which is a set of general assumptions, ideas, and procedures for viewing and studying a phenomenon such as human interaction.[13] Whereas a school of thought is a group of people who share ideas about the communication process, a paradigm is the set of ideas that they share.

It is helpful to think about communication theories in terms of the paradigms they represent. To understand the practical value of theories, it is important to identify the assumptions shared by the theorists who developed them. Different paradigms and schools of thought produce different kinds of theories, but the schools and paradigms are not theories themselves. Rather, paradigms are broader sets of assumptions that support the general ideas and principles contained within a communication theory.

The field of communication includes at least three general schools of thought, each with its own paradigm: the *post-positivist, interpretive,* and *critical* paradigms. Later in this chapter, we will compare and contrast those paradigms in detail. Before we explore the three major paradigms in our field, however, let's briefly discuss the four different parts of a communication theory.

▲ ▲ ▲

Let's Discuss

1. How do you form your own theories about communication behavior in everyday life?
2. If you were to develop a theory about why marriages succeed or fail, which concepts would be included in your conceptual framework?

▲ ▲ ▲

PARTS OF A COMMUNICATION THEORY

A useful way to study communication theories is to think about their common organizational structure. Every theory consists of identifiable parts. First, each theory has an **intellectual tradition**, or a general way of thinking about some aspect of the communication process that has been shared by a community of scholars.[14] Every communication theory has its own history or biography that tells the story of who developed the theory, under what circumstances, and for what purposes. Thus, our understanding of a specific communication theory depends, in part, on when and how we look at it. Some theories may not make sense unless we understand their historical context. A theory of failed Hollywood marriages, for instance, might begin with the story of Rudolph Valentino, a famous Italian actor who married American actress Jean Acker in 1919. After only six hours, Acker regretted her decision to marry and locked Valentino out of their honeymoon suite. In their divorce proceedings, Acker claimed that they never consummated their union.[15]

The second part of every communication theory is a set of assumptions about focus and scope. Every theory includes **assumptions,** which are beliefs that are taken for granted. For instance, our theory of failed Hollywood marriages might be based on the following assumptions: (a) Hollywood romances are fundamentally different from other romances, (b) Hollywood stars are more likely to cheat and to divorce their partners than regular people, and (c) marriages are supposed to last until "death do us part." Although some assumptions may be stated explicitly in a theory, others are merely implied. Because we take them for granted, we don't directly test our assumptions; instead, we either accept or reject them as a matter of principle.

Some of a theory's assumptions relate to its **focus,** which is the breadth of topics it covers. Communication theories can be quite broad in focus, pertaining to general communication processes such as storytelling in different kinds of relationships. Others are more narrowly focused on specific communication events, such as presidential rhetoric or jury deliberations. Likewise, theories include assumptions about their **scope,** which is the applicability of their coverage. Some communication theories apply across a variety of cultural and historical contexts, whereas others may address specific issues that emerged within particular periods of time or within specific cultural and societal conditions.

Besides their intellectual tradition and assumptions, theories also contain **concepts,** which are the abstract ideas that they discuss. Concepts represent specific ideas with explicit definitions attached to them. Some of the concepts in a theory about Hollywood marriage would include *marriage, Hollywood, divorce,* and *celebrity.* The theory would define each of those terms to prevent confusion about their meaning.

Scholars rarely invent a new concept every time they refer to a unique event. For example, we don't need a new definition of *marriage* whenever a Hollywood wedding occurs. If we want to distinguish between different kinds of marriages, we can create categories of weddings, such as elopements, Vegas weddings, church weddings, civil commitment ceremonies, and the like. It is important, however, for scholars to develop explicit definitions for the concepts in their theories. Explicit definitions help us determine when a particular concept applies and when it does not apply. That ability is critical, given that a concept can mean only what people agree that it means when they study a particular aspect of the communication process.[16] When a theory's concepts are tested, as in a research study, they typically become variables. A **variable** is any concept whose properties can vary. If everyone in a research study is married, then marital status is not a variable, because it is the same for everyone—it doesn't vary. But if some spouses are more satisfied with their marriages than others, then marital satisfaction is a variable, because it differs from person to person.

After defining a set of concepts, a theory identifies how those concepts relate to each other. A theory's **claims** are its declarative statements about how its concepts fit together. If you think of concepts as the building blocks of a theory, then claims are the binding mortar or glue that holds them together. Claims can take a variety of forms.

1. Some claims comprise "if, then" statements: *If* a Hollywood actress discovers that her spouse has been unfaithful, *then* she will file for divorce.
2. Other claims propose cause-and-effect relationships: Celebrity divorces are *caused by* the intense stress and pressure of the movie industry.
3. Still other claims articulate general principles that help us understand a phenomenon: Hollywood divorces are much more common today than 50 years ago because celebrities today hold more liberal views of marriage.

Whatever form they take, claims constitute the heart of a communication theory. They provide the explanations that tie together the concepts and give coherence to the explanation.

To summarize, communication theories represent an intellectual tradition, include a set of assumptions about their focus and scope, define their key concepts, and offer claims that tie the concepts together into an explanation of some communication process. Check out "Legos: A Learning Metaphor for the Parts of a Theory" to review the four parts of a communication theory.

▲ ▲ ▲

Legos: A Learning Metaphor for the Parts of a Theory

In December 2010, Legoland re-opened at the Mall of America in Minneapolis, Minnesota with a blue robot standing two stories high and a giant helicopter, both made of Legos. Although both are a sight to see, did you know that the process of building those amazing toys illustrates how scholars use different parts of a theory to build an explanation of communication? Every package of Legos contains identifiable parts similar to the parts of a theory. For example, the individual Legos represent the building blocks (or *concepts*) that are used to build the blue robot. Each has a specific size, color, shape, and purpose within the larger object that appears once the Legos are pieced together. The instructions (or *claims*) provide a series of statements that guide and direct us in putting together the Legos so as to create the blue robot. We assume that the Legos have been manufactured to precise specifications so that they snap together and hold each other in place as we build our robot. And we assume that our Legos won't snap together with building blocks that have been manufactured by other companies (a set of *focus and scope assumptions*). Finally, did you know that Legos were invented by Ole Kirk Christiansen and his son Godtfred Kirk in 1932 in the village of Billund, Denmark? Ole was a master carpenter who founded his carpentry business to make stepladders, ironing boards, and wooden toys. The wooden toys became his most successful product, and in 1934, his company adopted the name LEGO, which is formed from the Danish words "LEg GOdt" meaning "play well." By 1955, the company launched the "LEGO System of Play" with 28 sets and 8 vehicles.[17] Today, LEGO is the fourth largest manufacturer of play materials, with 9,000 employees and products in 130 countries around the world (an *intellectual tradition*).

So the next time you see a robot made of Legos standing two stories tall, or a young child playing with a new Lego set on Christmas morning, remember that each set of Legos consists of identifiable parts that help us better understand the different parts of every communication theory.

▲ ▲ ▲

COMMUNICATION PARADIGMS

In this book, we address three paradigms that encompass the vast majority of theories in the communication field. Those are the post-positivist paradigm, the interpretive paradigm, and the critical paradigm. Each one functions as a lens, bringing some aspects of the world into focus while leaving others out of view. Each lens gives us a different look at reality because the paradigms vary in their underlying beliefs about what is true and how truth can be known. More specifically, each paradigm embodies a unique ontology and epistemology.

Ontology is the study of existence and reality. It raises the question of whether reality exists "out there" as a set of concrete, material facts or is created in the processes of social interaction. **Epistemology** is the study of knowledge. All of the knowledge you can find in books, databases, and Wikipedia had to come from somewhere. Epistemology raises the question of where that somewhere is.

Epistemological discussions cause us to ask ourselves how we know what we know, and what we consider to be knowledge. If ontology and epistemology sound rather philosophical, that's because they are both branches of the philosophy of knowledge. By understanding their functions, you're in a better position to decide when and how to use a particular lens to examine your own life and experiences.

We'll take a closer look at each paradigm in this section. First, we will describe a research project conducted within the framework of that paradigm. Then, we'll identify the goal of the research, the ontology and epistemology reflected in the work, and the roles played by the researchers and by communication itself. As you read, focus your attention not only on how the paradigms differ but also on where they agree.

THE POST-POSITIVIST PARADIGM

In a recent study, one of us (P.S.) examined the relationships among parents' communication behaviors and their children's feelings of "being caught" between parents in the context of family conflict and divorce.[18] In that study, the researchers used family systems theory and social-cognitive models of marital conflict to predict how specific communication behaviors would influence children's experiences of family conflict. After surveying over 500 participants, the researchers discovered four important results:

1. Mothers' messages of value and respect for their children protected the children from feeling caught between their parents.

2. Mothers' positive communication predicts their children's satisfaction more strongly in divorced families than in intact families.

3. Fathers' positive communication predicts their children's satisfaction more strongly in intact families than in divorced families.

4. Children are least satisfied when they feel caught between their parents *and* their fathers use little positive
   communication.

Studies such as that one can provide scientifically proven knowledge that helps us to manage our relationships and improve our relational outcomes. Scholars working in the post-positivist paradigm
use the tools and methods of the natural sciences as a model for
developing communication or social science knowledge. Although
communication scientists recognize that they usually aren't identifying "laws" like those found in physics or chemistry, they work toward developing rigorous, reliable and claims about communication
behavior.

Goal: Explain, predict, and control. The goal of post-positivist
scholarship in our field is to explain, predict, and control communication behavior. Scholars do that by discovering regularities and
cause-and-effect relationships between communication variables
and their outcomes. The results of the study describe above can
help parents in both divorced and intact families to predict how
their communication behaviors will influence their children and to
control or manage the family system.

▲ ▲ ▲

Consider This
Think about a communication problem you have recently encountered. What communication behaviors (your own or those of those
of others) do you wish you could predict and control better? Why?
Do you think human beings are predictable—or are they too individual for general claims to be useful?

▲ ▲ ▲

Ontology: Realist. Post-positivists typically adopt a *realist* ontology that assumes that the world—its inhabitants, ideas, and social structures—is "out there" waiting to be discovered, known, and explored. In the study describe above, the researchers used surveys to measure particular communication behaviors and consequences because they believe those behaviors are real, measurable things.

Epistemology: Objectivist. Post-positivists adopt an *objectivist* epistemology, which means they believe only in what can be directly observed or experienced with the senses (empirical data) or explained rationally or analytically. From that perspective, if we can measure a communication behavior, then we know it is "real." If we cannot measure it or otherwise empirically observe it, then it is not real. In the study of parental confirmation and family satisfaction, the researchers used survey items that had been validated (or proven) by the scientific community to empirically measure the relationship between communication behaviors and relational outcomes.

Researcher role: Knowledge discoverer. In the post-positivist paradigm, researchers strive to maintain an objective, value-neutral position when studying social behavior. Their goal is to discover knowledge about the social world, so they try not to let that discovery be tainted by their own values, hopes, and biases.

Communication role: Representational. In the post-positivist paradigm, communication functions to represent a pre-existing social world or an idea, thought, or feeling. Conceiving of communication as *representational* suggests that communication is a tool or vehicle used to convey information across time and space.

THE INTERPRETIVE PARADIGM

Another of your authors (A.T.) adopted an interpretive approach when she and a colleague studied how firefighters socially construct—and subsequently respond to—risks in the contexts of their jobs.[19] Rather than assuming that work hazards and risks are concrete, measurable things that already existed in the world, the researchers explored how firefighters used their interactions to *construct* the very risks and hazards that they encounter on the job. Firefighters socially construct risks and hazards in ways that align closely with their preferred identities as professionals who want nothing more than to "get it on" with fire. The trouble is that firefighters spend most of their time responding to paramedic calls for people who have been hurt in traffic accidents or are experiencing difficulty breathing—not fighting fires. In fact, fighting fires accounts for less than 10% of the firefighters' on-the-job activity. Despite that, firefighters talk in ways that amplify the risks connected to fire while downplaying other equally real job risks, such as health hazards and traffic accidents. In other words, firefighters tended to dismiss the risks they encounter most frequently, leading to potentially dangerous on-the-job situations. Studies like that can help firefighters and organizational leaders better understand firefighter culture.

Goal: Understand. Scholars who adopt an interpretive perspective are interested in how members of relationships, organizations, and communities make sense of their worlds in and through communication. Their goal is to reveal deep and rich insights into how we, as social beings, use symbols to create and recreate our social worlds and in the implications of those constructions on our everyday lives. In the study described above, the researchers were interested in determining how firefighters' understanding of their own identities affected their risky behaviors.

Ontology: Social constructionist. The interpretive paradigm assumes that the world we live in is a world of our own making. This *social constructionist* ontology implies that we bring our world into being through our thoughts, actions and communication, and we then maintain and experience that world as real.[20] The researchers in the study described above did not begin their project by identifying objective risks faced by firefighters. Instead, they were interested in the risks that firefighters constructed by naming and responding to them as risks.

Epistemology: Subjectivist. In the interpretive paradigm, knowledge is considered to be subjective. In other words, there are no objective truths that exist separate from our experience. We cannot make a distinction between knowledge seekers and the knowledge they find because how and why they seek that knowledge will affect what is found. In other words, a *subjectivist* epistemology assumes that we come to know the world through our own unique points of views and positions. Through open and reasoned dialogue, we can come to a collective agreement about what the world means. In the study described above, the firefighters' understandings of risk, as articulated in interviews, in everyday conversations, and in organizational safety training documents, all "counted" as legitimate data or knowledge.

Researcher role: Knowledge creator. The role of the interpretive researcher is to create knowledge. Through dialogue with others—including other scholars and the people being studied (such as firefighters)—researchers come to understand the world anew. As an interpretive scholar writes about a culture, group, or entity, he or she brings it to life. Research is a method for creating knowledge, understanding, and realities.

Communication role: Constitutive. Communication is the primary building block or medium of our social worlds. Scholars use the phrase "communication is constitutive" to capture the idea that communication is that which creates, composes, and enacts our experience.

THE CRITICAL PARADIGM

Four scholars—Rebecca Meisenbach, Robyn Remke, Patrice Buzzanell, and Meina Liu—have been working in the critical paradigm for quite some time. As feminists, these researchers are interested in the patriarchal power that organizations have over their employees. In particular, they are curious about the ways in which organizations determine how and when employees can navigate the boundaries between work and family life.

In a recent research project, these researchers explored how the possibilities for maternity leave are produced and reproduced by examining organizational policies, workplace interactions, and interviews with women who have experienced maternity leave.[21] Their study indicated that 75% of women will get pregnant as employees, but women are taking less time off from work and feeling less satisfied with how work-life policies are developed and implemented. Consequently, the research team was interested in exploring how pregnant workers, through their communication interactions, both create and cut off possibilities for renegotiating maternity leave policies.

They found that workers typically reproduced organizational power by describing maternity leave as a process set up by human resources departments and governed by written policies within bureaucratic organizations that control the maternity leave. The researchers were also interested in how workers' talk and actions might transform organizational systems and empower employees. For example, workers could describe maternity leave as a practice that is arranged by mothers—in conjunction with organizational representatives—to support the needs of mothers, their families, and the organization. The authors recognize that reframing family leave policy in that way can be challenge. As critical scholars, however, they are committed to questioning how current policies constrain workers (perhaps unfairly) and finding alternatives that may lead to more empowering policies and practices.

Goal: Empower. Scholars who adopt a critical paradigm assume that power relations influence our everyday experience in a variety of ways. More specifically, critical scholars believe that power—whether in personal relationships, the workplace, or our larger culture—tends to inhibit our ability to experience our full human-ity. In other words, power is an oppressive force. Thus, the goal of the critical paradigm is to critique existing power structures, to offer alternatives, and to work toward human empowerment.

Ontology: Realist/social constructionist. The critical para-digm is perhaps the least unified of the paradigms in communi-cation. Although critical scholars are united in their interest in empowerment, they find oppression in both socially constructed discourses and material structures.[22] For example, one might argue that through ongoing communication practices, women and wom-en's work have been devalued compared to men and men's work in organizational contexts. The "care work" that nurses, teachers, social workers, and day care providers do tends to be less valued than the "real work" that engineers, doctors, and lawyers do. That socially constructed valuation of work is also seen in material and structural differences; for instance, engineers make more money and have more prestige than day care workers do. In other words, socially constructed realities become cemented in real material structures.[23]

Epistemology: Subjectivist. Scholars in the critical paradigm question taken-for-granted notions about what counts and knowl-edge and who has the authority to be a knower. In particular, criti-cal scholars explore why the knowledge claims of socially dominant groups are preferred over those of socially marginalized groups. Critical theorists, then, tend to adopt a subjectivist epistemology. They believe that certain ways of knowing and being are not neces-sarily "more true" than others, even though they have a more privi-leged position in our everyday life. In the study cited above, the researchers recognized the privileged position of the knowledge claims of organizational leaders, as represented in organizational policy. Importantly, however, they also listened to and valued the knowledge claims of pregnant female workers and their potentially empowering vision of work-life balance.

Researcher role: Advocate. In the critical paradigm, researchers operate more as advocates for social change than as detached observers of the social world. The scholars describe above are committed to conducting scholarship that represents and forwards feminist values of equity and social justice. They invest their scholarship with those values and use theory and research as a vehicle for social change.

Communication role: Power-laden. Communication works to reinforce, transform, or resist ongoing systems of power. From a critical perspective, there is no such thing as a neutral or power-free message. All communication reflects the values and interests of those who are using it. In the maternity leave study described above, many of the employees adopted the perspectives, language, and policies of the organizations for which they worked. By doing so, they reinforced and reproduced the power of those organizations to define the rules of the work-life game. The critical paradigm assumes that when we communicate, we are invoking power, whether we intend to or not.

▲ ▲ ▲

Test Your Understanding

Years ago, Karl Weick, an interpretive management theorist, made a distinction between a realist and social constructionist ontology through a clever account of two baseball umpires.[24] When asked how he differentiated between balls and strikes, the first umpire said, "I call them as I see them." The second umpire replied, "I call them as they are." Which paradigm do you think the first umpire would endorse? How about the second umpire? Why? Can you imagine how a third umpire from the critical paradigm might respond to Weick's question?

▲ ▲ ▲

Although we have presented the paradigms as mutually exclusive and distinct, they have similarities as well as differences. As we will point out in later chapters, some theories—particularly interpretive and critical theories—cross the divisions we have outlined here. Table 2.1 provides a glance at the various characteristics of the three communication paradigms.

Table 2.1 Communication Paradigms at a Glance

	Post-Positive	Interpretive	Critical
Goal	Explain, predict, control	Understand	Empower
Ontology	Realist	Social constructionist	Realist/social constructionist
Epistemology	Objective	Subjective	Subjective
Researcher role	Discoverer	Creator	Advocate
Communication role	Representational	Constitutive	Power-laden

Let's Discuss

1. What untested assumptions do you have about the communication process?
2. As you've seen, each paradigm promotes a specific goal or goals. Which of these goals do you see as must useful? Why?

FUNCTIONS AND PURPOSES OF COMMUNICATION THEORY

Thus far in this chapter, we have clarified the scope of theory and described the three paradigms in detail, but some important questions remain unanswered. How is communication theory useful?

What values and purposes do communication theories serve? How do they function? Why are they important?

Questions such as those ask you to consider how theories help us understand our social world. We will address those questions in this section by focusing on three general functions and seven specific purposes of communication theory. **General functions** are the tasks that all good theories—regardless of their subject matter—perform for the people who use them. General functions are *what theories do for us,* and they are largely the same for theories about gravity, political science, sexuality, literature, and communication. In contrast, **specific purposes** are the tasks we perform with theories—that is, *what we do with theories.* You may find it useful to think about the functions and purposes of communication theory as overlapping spheres; they are each distinct but interrelated.

The first general function of communication theory is knowledge elaboration. **Knowledge elaboration** means that communication theories organize, anticipate, summarize, and extend our knowledge about communication principles, practices, and experiences.[25] Good theories, that is, produce or create new knowledge.[26] Whereas epistemology addresses our assumptions about knowledge and how we can prove or validate claims, the knowledge function of theory asks you to consider what new insights, practices, or principles were learned. For example, after reading John Gottman's interaction theory of marital conflict, you will have learned that repeated criticism of your romantic partner leads to contempt and defensiveness, which has long-term negative consequences for marital happiness.[27]

The second general function of communication theory is **research stimulation,** which means encouraging people to study the ways to change and improve communication practices.[28] In the late 1970s and early 1980s, for instance, British theorist Anthony Giddens developed structuration theory to explain how organizations endure over time (see Chapter 7).[29] Since that time, communication scholars have adapted key ideas from structuration theory and applied its core concepts to the use of information technology in organizational groups.[30] One of the authors of this textbook (P.S.) has applied concepts from structuration theory to family communication.[31] For more than 40 years, structuration theory has continued to stimulate new research in a variety of communication, group, and organizational contexts.

The third general function of communication theory is **organization,** which means theories help us classify data, understand concepts and relationships, and arrange human communication experiences.[32] In other words, the organization function of theory helps us make sense of the knowledge we gain when we test and apply the theory. Imagine that you have been promoted to a leadership position at work and you are wondering about the qualities of great leaders. You know that your manager expects you to create new programs and significantly change workplace practices in your department, but how do you know which type of leadership is best suited to you and your assigned tasks? Different leadership theories help organize and explain different kinds of experiences and challenges in the workplace, and your understanding of their conclusions and usefulness will help you discover the most appropriate leadership approach.

Now that we've examined what theories do for us, let's look at what we do with theories—that is, their specific purposes. Unlike general functions, which apply to all theories, specific purposes vary somewhat from theory to theory. Not all theories have the same specific purposes, but we can describe at least seven specific purposes that theories can have: a) prediction, b) explanation, c) control, d) description, e) insight, f) emancipation, and g) praxis and problem-solving.

The first specific purpose of communication theory is prediction. **Prediction** is the practice of anticipating future events. The scientific paradigm is the approach most closely associated with the predictive function of communication theory. In our relationships with others, the ability to predict their behavior helps us successfully manage communication. Writing about attribution theory, communication scholar Valerie Manusov indicated that "people attempt to make sense of one another's actions (i.e., create attributions) as part of a general need to control and predict the world around us."[33] Indeed, imagine how difficult a relationship would be if you never knew what the other person was going to say or do next.

The second specific purpose of communication theory is **explanation,** which is the process of communicating why something occurs. Sometimes we can predict *what* others will do even if we don't know *why* they do it. An explanation identifies the reasons, motives, and interests that underlie behavior. A good example of the explanation function of theory is the use of evolutionary theory in communication research. One of us (K.F.) has applied evolutionary principles to family communication, noting that "The evolutionary approach to human behavior is exceedingly broad in the range of family relationships and behavior it can *explain*" (emphasis added).[34] Another good example of explanation is found in human needs theory.[35] Communication scholars use human needs theory to explain how people communicate to fulfill specific needs. For example, in a job interview we may negotiate for a higher salary or better benefits to fulfill the human need of *security.*[36]

The third specific purpose of communication theory is **control,** which is the ability to influence and manage the outcomes a theory predicts.[37] For example, public relations personnel frequently create messages with the intention of influencing public opinion, improving an organizational image, or selling a product.[38] Rhetorical communication scholars often focus on the nature of persuasive messages in political and civic contexts to determine the effectiveness or influence of a speaker on a given audience. Communication scholar Stephen Littlejohn suggests that the control function "grows out of value questions, in which the theorist seeks to judge the effectiveness and propriety of certain behaviors."[39] The control function also has implications for your specific communication behavior; after taking communication courses, can you utilize your new knowledge and skills to improve your communication in relationships, at work, and in public dialogue?

The fourth specific purpose of communication theory is **description,** which means mapping the conditions, experiences, events, and stories that are reflected in communication contexts. The descriptive function is most closely associated with representation: In what way does the theorist represent or describe the phenomenon in question? How closely does the description represent what it is intended to describe?

The fifth specific purpose of communication theory is **insight,** which is an understanding of the subjective experiences of others. Also called illumination, insight is a type of description that reveals the "life worlds" of people in multiple contexts with multiple interpretations of their experiences. Communication scholar Leslie Baxter has argued that an important theoretical function of relational dialectics theory in family contexts is the insight it can create into how family members experience their relationships and communicative lives.[40]

The sixth specific purpose of communication theory is **emancipation,** the act of freeing people from oppression. As you read, many theories (especially those in the critical paradigm) focus on injustices, power imbalances, and the oppression of individuals and groups.[41] Thus, emancipation draws our attention to the ways communication and language can change the social circumstances of the marginalized or less privileged. As we explained above, critical theories assume that power and authority are real, and that people enact power in specific ways.[42] Critical theories can therefore encourage us to ask which communication behaviors will empower those with less authority and privilege.

The final specific purpose of communication theory is **praxis and problem-solving,** which means using theoretical ideas and research practices to solve real-world problems. The central idea is that theory and research can serve a positive social and community function. The praxis and problem-solving function encourages researchers and community members to collaborate on theories of social and civic change. The application of theory is useful to the extent that it can make a positive difference in people's lives.

In this section we have discussed both general and specific functions and purposes of communication theory. As you may have noticed, many of the functions overlap. When you learn about specific communication theories, revisit the questions we posed earlier: How is communication theory useful? What values and purposes do communication theories serve? How do they function? Why are they important? For each theory you discuss in class, identify its functions and ask how its assumptions, findings, and insights can improve communication in your life.

FOR FURTHER DISCUSSION

1. We began this chapter by considering many possible reasons why Hollywood marriages don't seem to last. Which explanations resonated the most with you? Which ones seemed unlikely, or even ridiculous? What assumptions do you have that lead you to favor certain explanations over others?

2. Which of the three paradigms—post-positivist, interpretivist, or critical—best reflects the way you see the world? Why? Which aspects of the other two paradigms do you agree with nonetheless?

3. As functions of a theory, how are prediction and explanation similar? How do they differ?

KEY TERMS

Assumptions
Claims
Concepts
Conceptual framework
Control
Description
Emancipation
Epistemology
Explanation
Focus
General functions
Insight
Intellectual tradition
Knowledge elaboration
Model
Ontology
Organization
Paradigm
Praxis and problem-solving
Prediction
Research stimulation
Schools of thought
Scope
Specific purposes
Theory
Variable

3

Communication Theory
and Research

How Do We Come to Know What We Know?

Each of us wonders about something. You might have lofty questions, such as where life exists in the universe or what happens to you when you die. You may also wonder about more everyday issues, such as how your smart phone works or why it's hard to understand people from other cultures. Humans have pondered the mysteries of life—both the lofty and the mundane—since the beginning of time. The experience of wonder is common, but it isn't satisfying enough for most of us. We don't just want *questions*, in other words...we also want *answers*.

Our questions motivate us to learn about something, that is. Suppose you wonder what is the most effective way to handle conflict in a close relationship. How could you come to know more about that topic? If you want, you can speculate about the nature of conflict and come up with your own theory about how to manage it successfully. You could ask your friends in happy marriages to share their secrets. You may consult blogs and websites, read books, or e-mail psychologists for advice. Perhaps Siri knows. You might also distribute questionnaires to people in relationships or conduct experiments in which you observe their conflict directly.

In truth, there are many ways you could come to know more about handling conflict. All of these strategies would produce knowledge, but they would not necessarily lead you to the same conclusions. Your theory might say one thing about managing conflict successfully, but your happily married friends might say something else. Your experiment could support one idea, but the blog you're reading may disagree. With all these various sources of knowledge saying different things, how will you know which to trust and which to ignore? Which one is the *truth?*

Saying we want to know about something usually means we want to learn what's true about it...but getting at truth is often complicated. As you'll discover in this chapter, that's partly because people have differing ideas about what knowledge and truth are in the first place. It's also because there are multiple methods of identifying knowledge and truth. In the study of communication—as in many disciplines—those methods use a combination of theory and research.

We begin this chapter by exploring the relationship between theory and research. We'll discover the nature of knowledge and learn about the goals and processes of scholarly research, such as the research you read about in communication textbooks. Next, we'll revisit the purposes of theory and learn how to tell good theories apart from bad ones. We'll then dive deeper into various research methods, investigating the similarities and differences between quantitative, qualitative, and critical approaches. Finally, we'll learn how to evaluate research by applying the criteria for good scholarship.

THEORY AND RESEARCH: TWO SIDES OF THE SAME COIN

Read about teen pregnancy and you'll discover that it has a variety of negative effects on millions of American families. Two thirds of families started by an unmarried teen mother are poor.[1] Only 4 in 10 teenage mothers ever finish high school, and less than 2 percent finish college by their 30th birthday.[2] In social discourse, teenage mothers are frequently described in terms of welfare dependency and social exclusion, neither of which casts them in a positive light.[3] Moreover, children born to teen mothers are at elevated risk of being homeless, being incarcerated, and becoming teen parents themselves.[4] In all, the effects of teenage pregnancy on health care, foster care, and lost tax revenue cost U.S. taxpayers at least $10.9 billion a year.[5]

As interesting as all that is, it's fair to ask how we know these things. After all, these facts didn't materialize out of thin air. They didn't come to a wise man in a dream, nor were they discovered by someone reading tea leaves or interpreting the lines on your palm. All of these facts were identified through **research,** which is the systematic process of generating knowledge. To understand what research is, therefore, we first need to consider what knowledge is. We can then examine the nature and process of research, and explore its connection to theory. As we do, we'll discover that research and theory are really two sides of the same coin, in that they both serve our quest for understanding.

THE FOUNDATIONS OF KNOWLEDGE

Think of something that you *know* to be true. Perhaps it's that the earth is round, or that smoking causes lung cancer. Maybe it's that you have two siblings, or that your roommate's name is Chris. No matter the specifics, we can all think of many things that we know for certain are true. Now, consider this question: *How do you know those things?* Indeed, how do you come to know anything?

When you consider that question, you are thinking about *epistemology*. As we discussed in the last chapter, epistemology is the branch of philosophy that addresses the nature of knowledge. And, as we'll see, the nature of knowledge is not a simple matter.

Your **knowledge**—that is, your understanding of the information, facts, or skills related to some topic—is a complex collection of influences and inputs. To appreciate how complex, let's suppose you said that you know the following things:

1. God is real.
2. You're in danger right now.
3. Driving a car with a manual transmission is more fun than driving an automatic.
4. Sound travels faster in water than in air.

To say that you know these things means that you believe these statements to be true. If you consider *why* you believe these statements, however, you'll likely realize that you believe them for different reasons. Even though they are all knowledge claims, in other words, these statements reflect different forms of knowledge. Specifically, they represent knowledge by authority, intuition, experience, and research.

Some knowledge comes from authority. One way to learn the answer to a question is to ask someone who ought to know. You want to find out whether you have the flu, so you consult a doctor. Not sure what's wrong with your truck? Ask a mechanic. Perhaps you wonder about the existence and nature of God or the divine, so you discuss the issue with a member of the clergy. In each of these instances, you are asking an **authority**—a source whose education, background, or wisdom makes him or her knowledgeable on the topic of your question. Knowledge from authority is also called *expert knowledge,* and it includes much of what you learn from your professors, legal and financial professionals, medical providers, religious practitioners, and even your parents. When you ask questions from people whose authority makes them likely to know the answer—and then accept their answer as true—you are gaining knowledge by authority.

Importantly, a given source is an authority only on some issues, not all issues. No one is an expert on everything—so when you seek knowledge by authority, the qualifications of the source are important to know. You probably wouldn't trust a mechanic to diagnose your flu any more than you'd trust a doctor to diagnose your car problems...and in reality, you shouldn't. Expertise is context-specific, so although you gain knowledge by authority when you ask a doctor about your health, you would not gain knowledge by authority if you asked the doctor about your car. That doesn't necessarily mean the doctor's perspective on your car would be wrong—it just wouldn't be expert knowledge.

Some knowledge comes from intuition. You can probably recall an occasion when you knew something was true but you couldn't explain exactly *how* you knew it. In such cases, your knowledge comes from **intuition**, which is a form of understanding that doesn't rely on logic or conscious reasoning. Let's say your birthday is coming up and you suspect that your friends are planning to throw you a surprise party, even though no one has said anything to you about it. When you come home from work on the day of your birthday, a houseful of people yells "Surprise!" Later, you confide to one of your friends that you knew the party was going to occur. "I don't know *how* I knew it," you confess; "I just did."

In this case, your knowledge wasn't based on your conscious cognitive processing or your evaluation of evidence. You simply had a feeling that the party would happen, and you were right. Like many of us, you probably use your intuition to make sense of the world. Perhaps you "just know" where you can find a good parking spot or when your best friend is upset about something. You don't need an authority to tell you these things—they are simply evident to you. That's knowledge by intuition.

Some knowledge comes from experience. Suppose you decide to rent a car during your vacation in Europe. While at the rental counter, you discover that the only cars available to you have manual transmissions. "Can you drive a stick shift?" your travel companion asks. You reply that you can, and that it's much more fun than driving an automatic. "How do you know?" your companion inquires. "Because I've driven one before," you say. In this case, your knowledge comes from **experience**—that is, your previous exposure to or involvement with the activity.

Like intuition, most of us use our experience constantly to make sense of the world. A baseball player gains knowledge about how to hit a curve ball not just by asking experts or relying on intuition, but by actually trying to hit curve balls. Through direct experience, the player learns which ways of swinging the bat work better than others. Over time, he uses that knowledge to become better at hitting curve balls. Likewise, you know which checkout line is fastest at the grocery store, what time your mail will be delivered, and how to log into your Facebook page because you have experience with each of these things, and you have gained knowledge from that experience.

Some knowledge comes from research. Imagine a scientist who wants to know which of two medications is more effective for the treatment of depression. Never having been depressed herself, she can't answer that question by experience. There's no authority figure to consult, because no one knows which medication is better, and she certainly doesn't trust her intuition to settle the matter. What is the scientist to do?

To answer her question, she performs *research*—the systematic collection and evaluation of evidence. In this case, she recruits patients who are suffering from depression, giving some patients one medication and other patients the other medication. She then tracks their symptoms over time to see if one group improves more than the other one does. If so, then she has gained evidence that one medication is more effective than the other. After repeating the experiment several times with different patients, the scientist claims to know—on the basis of her evidence—which medication is better.

All forms of knowledge are not equal. By now, it's clear that when we say we know something, that statement can mean a variety of things. Most of us use knowledge from authority, intuition, experience, *and* research rather seamlessly, which can make it seem as though all forms of knowledge are equally reliable. But is that true?

A form of knowledge is *reliable* to the extent that it accurately reflects reality most of the time. Many of us recognize that any form of knowledge—authority, intuition, experience, and research—can be wrong. You might not have the flu, even though your doctor said you did. You might not get a surprise party, even though you felt you would. Both experience and research lead us astray at times, too. Just because all forms of knowledge can be wrong, however, that doesn't mean they are *equally likely* to be wrong.

The most reliable form of knowledge—the one least likely to be wrong—is knowledge from research. The primary reason why is simple: compared to research, the other forms of knowledge usually don't receive much scrutiny. To apply **scrutiny** to a knowledge claim—to *scrutinize* it—means to examine the claim carefully for any mistakes. Most of us don't scrutinize claims of knowledge from authority, intuition, or experience very much. When a mechanic says our carburetor is faulty, we don't usually spend a lot of time and effort trying to determine whether that knowledge claim is accurate. When we know from experience that taking the freeway home is faster than taking surface streets, we don't typically look for all the reasons why that claim could be wrong. In both cases, we simply accept and use the knowledge we have.

In comparison, however, knowledge claims produced by research are heavily scrutinized. As you'll discover in this chapter, researchers must define their concepts carefully and specifically, and they must evaluate their evidence systematically to determine whether their knowledge claims are supported. In most instances, the results of research are closely critiqued by other researchers in the same field—a process called *peer review*—before they can be published in a scholarly journal or book. As is the case in many disciplines, the best scholarly journals in communication reject for publication upwards of 90% of the research submitted to them, usually because the reviewers have identified problems that cast doubt on the knowledge claims being made.

We don't submit knowledge claims based on authority, intuition, or experience to scrutiny that is anywhere near as rigorous as what research-based claims receive. As a result, it is reasonable to have much higher confidence in the reliability of knowledge produced by research, as opposed to the other forms. Of course, research can be—and sometimes is—wrong. Because research is more rigorous and heavily scrutinized than authority, intuition, or experience, however, its claims are *more likely to be true* than claims based on other forms of knowledge.

What exactly do we mean when we use the term *research?* Let's explore what research is and what sets scholarly research apart.

▲ ▲ ▲

Let's Discuss

1. When do you rely on knowledge that comes from authority or intuition? Are there times when you trust your experience more than you trust research?

2. There are specific processes in place to scrutinize knowledge from research. In your own life, how do you scrutinize what you know from authority, intuition, or experience?

▲ ▲ ▲

THE NATURE OF RESEARCH

You do research all the time. To find out what time a movie starts, you call the theater or look it up on your smart phone. To see what your friends have planned for the weekend, you ask them. To choose the college you now attend, you might have scanned its website, visited the campus, and talked to other students about their experiences. All of those activities constitute research. Here's why: in each case, you began with a question and then you collected information—rather than relying on experience, authority, or intuition—to answer that question.

The research you do on an everyday basis is certainly useful, insofar as it helps you navigate your way through your daily life. How does your everyday research differ from that done by professional scholars, though? At a fundamental level, it doesn't—research of all types involves collecting information to answer questions. *Scholarly research* does differ from everyday research with respect to its quality and precision, however, in some particular ways.

Scholarly research is more systematic. Suppose you think, as many people do, that using Bluetooth or another hands-free device is safer than holding a cell phone while driving. It seems logical to you that if drivers keep their hands on the steering wheel, instead of trying to hold onto a phone while they drive, they are less likely to get into accidents. You decide to do an informal survey to test this idea, and you ask everyone you work with about their experiences. Several people admit to driving with hand-held phones, and most of them have been in an accident before. Case closed!

Scholarly researchers would recognize some potential problems with your approach. For one, the group you surveyed may not be a good representation of drivers in general. As a group, they might be better drivers than average—or worse—which affects their likelihood of having accidents in the first place. Second, you may have asked your question in a way that led people to associate cell phone use with car accidents, causing them to forget or ignore all the times they held a phone without having an accident or had an accident without holding a phone. Finally, although you found that many drivers who use hand-held phones have had collisions, that finding doesn't confirm your idea by itself. How many drivers have had collisions while using a hands-free device—or while using no phone at all? Is it substantially fewer?

Compared to your informal survey, a scholarly research study of the same topic would be more *systematic,* meaning that it uses a more ordered method. It would try to recruit people who represent more of a cross-section of drivers, and it would take into account factors such as how long they had been driving, how often they drive and where, and what their cell phone habits are. It would formulate questions in a neutral way so that people aren't encouraged to give the answers the researchers want. It would also account for all groups—those who have and haven't had accidents; those who drive while using hand-held phones, hands-free devices, or no devices whatsoever—and it would compare all of those groups before drawing a conclusion. These are all examples of how methodical and systematic scholarly research aims to be.

Scholarly research is more precise. Another problem with surveying people informally in this case is that they might have different ideas about what constitutes an accident. They may even have different ideas about what counts as a hands-free device. Unless you specifically define the important terms in your question, these differences can make your findings unreliable.

Scholarly researchers aim to make the concepts in their studies precise, so that everyone understands and interprets them in the same way. In this example, researchers might say "an accident is any collision caused by driver error and resulting in significant physical or financial harm to people or property." Researchers may quibble over the specifics of the definition, but they try to make the meaning of their questions as clear and concrete as possible for the people in their studies.

Scholarly research considers multiple possibilities. Perhaps you believe that using hands-free devices is safer because it allows drivers to keep their hands on the steering wheel. When you discover that accidents are more common for drivers who use hand-held devices, you feel confident that your explanation has been supported.

In comparison, scholarly researchers recognize that there may be more than one explanation for what they find, and they try to control for that possibility by comparing competing explanations. Holding a phone while driving might lead to collisions *because the driver's hands aren't on the wheel,* but it might also lead to collisions *because the driver is distracted from talking on the phone.* Those are competing explanations, and scholarly researchers would try to determine which one is correct instead of assuming that they know.

In this case, they might look to see how much accident rates vary between three groups of drivers: 1) those who use hand-held phones, 2) those who use hands-free devices, and 3) those who don't use cell phones at all. If the first group has substantially more accidents than the second or third groups, that's consistent with the explanation blaming the lack of hands on the steering wheel. Suppose, though, that groups 1 and 2 were both more likely than group 3 to have accidents. That is consistent with the explanation that it is distraction—not the lack of hands on the wheel—that is the culprit.

Scholarly research is more scrutinized. Based on your informal survey of co-workers, you can make whatever claim seems warranted to you. As described above, however, the claims of scholarly research aren't made public (usually by being published) until they are heavily scrutinized by other scholars in the same area of study. The scrutiny usually focuses less on *what the findings are* than on *how the findings were produced.* In other words, reviewers don't evaluate research based on whether they like the results, but rather on whether they can trust the results, given what the research method was. If the method isn't systematic and precise, then there is little reason to accept the knowledge claims, regardless of what they are.

As you can see, scholarly research is held to a much higher standard than the everyday research most of us do constantly. How do researchers meet this standard? Let's find out by exploring the process of conducting and interpreting scholarly research.

THE PROCESS OF SCHOLARLY RESEARCH

A large part of what makes scholarly research a reliable source of knowledge is that it follows a standard, agreed-upon process. No matter what researchers want to study—whether it's the role of microbes in animal digestion, the function of gravity in planetary orbits, or the symbolic meaning of marriage across human cultures—they employ a *research method* to do so. As you'll discover later in this chapter, scholars have a variety of research methods to choose from, and not every method follows the same exact process. Nevertheless, the basic process of research involves several specific steps.

1. Formulate a question and/or prediction. Regardless of the specific research method, the process of research always begins with a problem to be solved or a question to be answered. The point of doing research is to learn something, so the researcher must know what he or she wants to learn before embarking on a study.

In some cases, that question—which is called a **research question**—is what guides the study. In those situations, the researcher doesn't try to test any specific prediction, but instead focuses on answering a question about the world and communication's role in it. Whatever the answer is, that's what the researcher will report. At other times, researchers formulate specific predictions—called **hypotheses**—for the study to test. In that case, they report whether or not each hypothesis is supported by the results. Studies can include only hypotheses, only research questions, or a combination. Regardless, however, the process can't begin until there is something the researcher wants to know.

2. Define variables and sensitizing concepts. As you learned in Chapter 2, a *variable* is any concept whose values or properties can vary. Consider age, for instance. In a group of people whose ages vary, age is a variable. If everyone in the group were the same age, though, age would be a **constant**—that is, a value that does not vary. Instead of using variables, some critical and interpretive studies instead incorporate **sensitizing concepts,** which are theoretical tools that help orient researchers to a particular research problem. For instance, one of us (A.T.) has been interested in "discipline" as a concept to help solve the problem of women's identity in the context of work. Discipline may be enacted in very different ways, but the assumption is that it is a feature of the world of work. The objective of this research is to see how it operates in a specific context.

Variables and sensitizing concepts are important for answering a researcher's question. Imagine a post-positivist study exploring how age affects the tendency to gossip. In that study, age and gossip are two important variables; therefore, the researchers must define them precisely. You might assume that "everyone knows what age means and what gossip is," but scholars can't presume that. Rather, they would first generate a **conceptual definition**—an explanation of what the variables mean. They would then generate an **operational definition**—a determination of how they will be observed or measured.

For example, a conceptual definition of age might be "the amount of time that has passed since an individual's birth." That conceptual definition seems fairly straightforward, but the researcher must then determine how to measure that concept. Most of us measure our age by the number of years that have elapsed since our birth (e.g., "Frank is 37 years old"), but that isn't the only option. In fact, we can measure age using any unit of time, such as number of months since birth, number of days, or number of minutes. We can also measure age in categories, such as "20-30" and "31 or above," or "adolescent" and "middle-aged." The point is that researchers must decide how to measure age and every other variable in their study, and the method of measurement is called the operational definition.

In critical and interpretive traditions, scholars may be less concerned with measuring specific variables and more concerned with understanding how participants make sense of the concept of age.

Assuming, for example, that the sensitizing concept used to understand age is that it is a social construction, rather than a biological fact, those interpretive or critical scholars might ask, what does age mean to individuals and groups? How are age and aging bodies valued or devalued in a particular context?

3. Identify data. Once researchers know what they are interested in, they begin the process of *collecting data,* with **data** being the specific points of information the researchers want to know. Some pieces of data are **quantitative,** meaning that they are expressed as numbers. Age, for instance, is usually measured quantitatively, in that each participant reports a number (usually in years) that represents his or her age. Other pieces of data are **qualitative,** meaning that they are expressed as descriptions of a quality or characteristic, rather than as a number. In communication research, qualitative data are often in the form of words, such as the words a participant uses in an interview to describe his or her experience, opinions, or understanding of an issue. Qualitative data may also comprise a researcher's observations, artifacts, or other pieces of information that can be interpreted and assessed.

Many studies collect pieces of data that are only quantitative or only qualitative, but some studies include both types. You'll discover more about quantitative and qualitative research methods later in this chapter. In most instances, researchers collect multiple pieces of data in a single study. They may also collect the same pieces of data at more than one point in time, to see how those data change over time (that type of study is called a *longitudinal study*).

4. Analyze and interpret data. Suppose a researcher has collected data on age and gossip behavior from, say, 300 people. Simply having the data isn't sufficient for answering the question of whether age and gossip are related. Instead, the researcher must *analyze* the data and then *interpret* the results of the analysis.

To analyze data means to examine it methodically to understand its underlying structure and determine how various points of data relate to each other (if at all). Researchers choose the appropriate method of analysis to use based on two issues: 1) what problem, question or prediction they are examining, and 2) what form of data they are working with. If the method of analysis is inappropriate for the research question or hypothesis, then the question won't be answered or the hypothesis won't be properly tested. Beyond that, different methods of analysis are appropriate for quantitative and qualitative data, so researchers must consider which type of data they have.

After analyzing data, researchers interpret—or assign meaning to—the result. Let's say there appears to be a strong relationship between age and gossip behavior, such that as people get older, they gossip more often. That's what researchers know from the analysis, but what does it mean? Is the relationship strong enough to conclude that age and gossip really *are* related? Or, is the "relationship" researchers are seeing just a fluke, or just a product of the specific group of people they looked at? Interpretive or critical researchers might examine about how meanings for gossip change as individuals move across the life span or how gossip functions as a mode of social control in some communities. These are all questions of interpretation. Importantly, it is not the data themselves that are being interpreted, but rather the researchers' analyses of the data.

5. Report research findings. Most scholars don't do their research only to hide the results in a file drawer. Instead, they want to report their results—their **findings**—to audiences who will be interested in them. In the field of communication, researchers have several options for reporting their findings to others. They may ask to present their findings at a scholarly conference, such as the conference of the National Communication Association. They may publish their findings in a book or on a blog. Most often, though, they submit their findings for publication in a scholarly journal.

The communication discipline publishes multiple scholarly journals. Some cater to research on specific topics, such as *Communication Education* for research on education-related issues and *Journal of International and Intercultural Communication* for research about cultural and cross-cultural communication. Other journals, such as *Communication Research* and *Communication Monographs,* publish findings on a broad range of topics. Some journals are published by scholarly associations, such as the National Communication Association and International Communication Association, whereas others are published by private publishing companies.

6. Invite and respond to scrutiny. When researchers submit their findings to a conference or journal, their work will be scrutinized before it is accepted. In most instances, the people reviewing and scrutinizing the research are other researchers who study the same or similar topics. When reviewing research for presentation at a conference, reviewers usually express their evaluations in the form of a simple decision—that is, whether or not to accept the paper for presentation. When reviewing a submission to a journal, however, reviewers usually generate detailed written evaluations of the work, which include their opinion of whether or not it should be published.

Recall from our discussion above that most good journals reject around 90% of the research submitted to them. That means only the top 10% or so gets published. Reviewers may have multiple reasons for concluding that a specific research report should be rejected for publication. They may find that the study's method was inadequate, for instance, or that not enough people were included. They may disagree with the researchers' approach to analyzing the data or interpreting the results.

On some occasions, the journal simply rejects the research report based on the reviewers' critique. Sometimes, however, the reviewers identify problems with the report that are fixable, so the journal may invite the researchers to *revise and resubmit* their report. If the researchers do so, they are responding to the reviewers' scrutiny in the form of their revised report. The revised report is then scrutinized again, usually by the same reviewers who evaluated the original submission. In the end, the report is either published or rejected for publication.

The goal of this type of evaluation is for reviewers to scrutinize the research itself. Their opinions should not be based on how they personally feel about the researchers. To discourage the process from becoming personal, most journals use a *double-blind* review in which the identity of the researchers is concealed from the reviewers and vice versa. In such cases, only the editor of the journal knows the identities of everyone involved in the process.

7. Replicate the study. If a research report passes the scrutiny of reviewers, it is published, making its findings available to a public audience. For some types of research, however, the process doesn't end there. Instead, a final step in the process is to *replicate*, or reproduce, the study.

Suppose a report about age and gossip is published in a communication journal. Even though that study showed that age and gossip are related, its findings were based only on the people who were included in the study. What if a different group of people were studied? Would age and gossip still be related? The only way to answer that question is to replicate the study—that is, to do it again with different people. If the study is replicated and the same finding is produced, then the public can have greater confidence that the finding is real. Sometimes, the researchers who conducted the original study are the same ones who conduct the replication; on other occasions, it's a different group of researchers who replicates the study.

Replication is relevant primarily to quantitative research. The reason is that most quantitative studies seek to make claims that are **generalizable**—that is, applicable to people beyond just those who were in the study. The more often a finding is replicated, the more generalizable it is. On the contrary, qualitative studies typically do not claim that their findings generalize to other groups of people, making replication less relevant. Qualitative researchers, however, may take special care to show how their results are **transferable**—or relatable to other contexts. By documenting how they collected data and interpreted the results, qualitative researchers can aid other scholars in assessing how likely the findings are to apply to contexts beyond the one that was studied.

As this description makes clear, the process of research involves many inter-related steps. Table 3.1 summarizes what those steps are and what they mean. What role does theory play in this process? We examine that question in the next section.

Table 3.1 Steps in the Research Process

Step	Description
Formulate a question/prediction	Determine what question the study will answer or what predictions it will test
Define variables and sensitizing concepts	Decide what each variable and sensitizing concept means conceptually, and if relevant, how it will be measured
Identify data	Collect the relevant points of quantitative and/or qualitative data from each participant in the study
Analyze and interpret data	Evaluate the data methodically to determine structures and patterns, and then give meaning to the analysis
Report research findings	Generate a research report and submit it to a scholarly conference, journal, book, blog, or other forum
Invite and respond to scrutiny	Read the evaluations of anonymous reviewers and respond to their critiques of the research
Replicate the study	If necessary, run the study again to determine whether it produces the same findings

▲ ▲ ▲

Let's Discuss

1. Have you ever read a study and disagreed with its conclusions? Which aspects of the study led you to question it?
2. Why do you think it's important for researchers to replicate their studies?

▲ ▲ ▲

CONNECTING RESEARCH TO THEORY

Recall that we described theory and research as "two sides of the same coin." That description suggests that theory and research are closely related to each other—but what is the nature of their relationship? The answer to that question depends largely on which scholarly paradigm—critical, interpretivist, or post-positivist—you adopt. In many studies conducted within the critical and interpretivist paradigms, for instance, the theory and the research method are essentially one and the same. In the post-positivist tradition, however, theories and methods are separate but interconnected entities. As we describe the relationship between research and theory, bear in mind that some points are more applicable to certain paradigms than to others.

Epistemology guides questions and methods. Each of us—whether we are a scholar or not—has an epistemology, or an orientation toward knowledge. Our epistemology guides our perceptions of what truth is and what is required to demonstrate truth. Some of us perceive that certain claims are objectively true, regardless of whether people believe them. Others perceive that the very concept of truth is a cultural phenomenon to begin with, meaning that truth depends on the individual. Still others believe that some truths are objective—that is, true regardless of what people think or feel—whereas other truths are "constructed" socially and culturally.

The epistemological position an individual scholar takes is important, because it helps to determine the questions he or she asks and the methods he or she uses to answer them. If you don't believe that objective truth exists separately from social and cultural interaction, you would be unlikely to ask questions that presume an objective reality. Instead, your questions would probably focus on what is real to the people you intend to study. Moreover, you would likely not use research methods that try to uncover ordered, patterned behavior reflective of an objective reality. Rather, you would focus on describing and understanding your participants' own constructions of reality—that is, what messages and symbols mean to them. As these examples illustrate, your individual theory about the nature of truth plays a role in determining not only the research methods you use, but also the very questions you ask.

Theories predict and explain. The fundamental purpose of a theory is to explain something. Recall that an important step in the research process is interpretation, the point at which researchers attach meaning and significance to their analyses of the data. The act of interpreting—and therefore, understanding—the research results is often guided by theory. By providing an explanation of a phenomenon, a theory helps scholars understand what their findings mean and why they matter.

Especially in post-positivist research, scholars also use theories to generate predictions to test in their studies. This process is called *deriving hypotheses* from a theory. To derive hypotheses, researchers consider the explanation of a phenomenon that their theory provides. They then ask themselves, "If this explanation is true, then what else is also likely to be true?" In other words, they consider what the explanation implies, and formulate predictions about what they will find when they conduct their studies. Recall that when a study has hypotheses, the researcher is testing them to determine whether they are supported by the data or not.

Research can generate theory. The approach of deriving hypotheses from theory and then testing them in a study is called a **deductive approach,** because the researcher has deduced his or her hypotheses before testing them. Whereas a deductive approach begins with theory and gathers data to test the theory, an inductive approach begins with data and develops a theory to make sense of those data. Researchers can also take an **inductive approach,** meaning that they conduct studies, see what they find, and then generate theories or broader claims on the basis of their data. A formal theory that is created inductively is called a **grounded theory.** Figure 3.1 illustrates the deductive and inductive approaches to theory and research.

Figure 3.1 Deductive and Inductive Processes

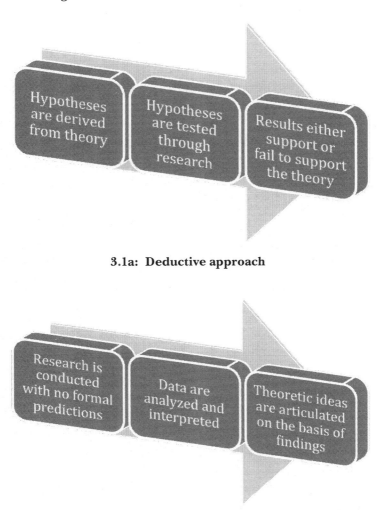

3.1a: Deductive approach

3.1b: Inductive approach

So far in this chapter, we have focused on the relationship between theory and research by exploring the various forms of knowledge, investigating the nature of research, examining the research

process, and considering the ways in which theory and research inform each other. Let's now turn our attention to what may be an even more fundamental question: What makes a theory a good theory?

CRITERIA FOR GOOD THEORY

Each of us probably recognizes that some of our ideas are better than others. As a college student, you probably have a good understanding of why you get good grades in some courses and worse grades in others. Your explanation probably points out that some classes are easier, require less work, and are more familiar and more fun to you than others, so that's why you get better grades in those classes. In comparison, you may not have a good understanding of how the price of tuition gets determined. To you, it might seem arbitrary—as if the school just draws a number out of a hat—or it may seem inflated every year only so the college president can get a raise. It's easy to understand why students might feel these ways about the cost of tuition, but most serious people would recognize that these are not very good explanations for how a college sets the tuition price.

In the same vein, some theories are better than others. In this context, "better" means more effective at fulfilling designated functions. Recall from Chapter 2 that theories have both general functions—extending knowledge, stimulating research, and organizing data and concepts—and specific purposes—prediction, explanation, control, description, insight, emancipation, and problem-solving. Remember, too, that some of these functions and purposes are more relevant in certain paradigms than in others.

With this in mind, we can say that a theory is *good* to the extent that it accomplishes the functions and purposes that are relevant to it. Beyond that general statement, however, some additional criteria for good theories are worth exploring. These criteria relate to a theory's scope, verifiability, heuristic value, and parsimony. Their relevance also varies according to the paradigm a researcher uses, as we see below.

GOOD THEORIES HAVE AN APPROPRIATE SCOPE

Recall from the last chapter that a theory's scope is the applicability of its coverage. A good theory provides an explanation for a phenomenon that is appropriate to its purpose. With respect to scope, theorists often distinguish between three types of theories:

1. **Grand theories** are those that seek to provide comprehensive, global explanations covering broad ranges of phenomena. Examples include Sigmund Freud's psychoanalytic theory, Charles Darwin's theory of natural selection, and Anthony Giddens's theory of structuration.

2. **Middle-range theories** are explanations of specific categories of phenomena. They are called *middle-range* because they do not try to explain multiple phenomena at once (as grand theories do), but they seek to explain more than just one or two aspects of a phenomenon (as narrow theories do). Examples are Murray Bowen's family systems theory and Judee Burgoon and David Buller's interpersonal deception theory.

3. **Narrow theories** are theories that explain specific aspects of a phenomenon, such as one or two recurring patterns of behavior. Examples include Beth Le Poire's inconsistent nurturing as control theory and Kory Floyd's affection exchange theory.

None of these types of theories is any more useful or important than the others. Calling some theories *grand* and others *narrow* does not imply any judgment of their relative value. Rather, each type of theory has a specific objective—and part of what makes a theory good is that it meets its objective. In the social sciences, good grand theories provide explanations for broad phenomena or groups of phenomena without trying to produce specific predictions about this or that social behavior. Good narrow theories provide precise, testable predictions about specific patterns of behavior without trying to explain broader phenomena, and good middle-range theories strike a balance between those approaches. Therefore, whichever objective a theory has, meeting that objective effectively is part of what makes the theory a good one.

GOOD THEORIES REFLECT REALITY

We've already seen that researchers have different perceptions of the nature of reality. Some believe in an objective reality that exists separately from human social and cultural experience, and others believe that all experiences of reality reflect the social and cultural interactions of humans. Researchers' conceptions of reality are part of what guides their choices of theories to use in their work.

For theories that assume an objective reality, an important criterion for goodness is that they lead to predictions that are both verifiable and falsifiable. A **verifiable** prediction is one that can be proven true, whereas a **falsifiable** prediction is one that can be proven false. At first glance, it may seem as though any prediction that is verifiable is also falsifiable, and vice versa. In fact, they are independent characteristics. To understand how, consider the following prediction: *Everyone either does or does not love chocolate.* That hypothesis can certainly be proven true—you can collect data from people to find out if they either 1) love chocolate or 2) don't love chocolate.

Although the hypothesis is verifiable, however, it is not falsifiable. The reason is that every possibility is contained in the prediction. Everyone is either "X" or "not X." Thus, no matter what you found when you surveyed people, your results would support the prediction; it is logically impossible to falsify. (*How about people who just* like *chocolate,* you ask? If they don't love it, they're in the second group, and if they love it, they're in the first. There are no other possibilities.)

If a theory assumes an objective reality, then a non-falsifiable prediction is useless, because we learn nothing by testing it. Good theories produce hypotheses that are both verifiable and falsifiable.

GOOD THEORIES GENERATE GOOD QUESTIONS

As you learned in Chapter 2, one of the general functions of all theories is to stimulate research. You'll recall from our discussion above that research always begins with a question. Thus, we can say that good theories are those that help researchers formulate interesting, worthwhile questions. This characteristic of a theory is called its **heuristic value.**

Theories with good heuristic value provide explanations that generate useful questions and predictions for researchers to explore. They may also imply questions or predictions that are novel or counterintuitive, leading researchers to make discoveries they would not likely have made without the benefit of those theories. Or, they may help people to better understand their experience by providing new ways of "seeing" or "being." In contrast, theories with poor heuristic value don't generate interesting or useful questions beyond those they are already designed to answer.

GOOD THEORIES ARE SIMPLE

Some researchers also believe that the best theories are the simplest ones. If my theory requires multiple arguments to explain a given phenomenon, but your theory requires only two, then yours is considered a better theory, all other things being equal. In other words, researchers generally prefer that theories be as simple as possible without being simpler than necessary. Researchers use the term **parsimony** to refer to a theory's simplicity.

The practice of valuing parsimony dates back to the 14th century to a principle called *Occam's razor.* William of Occam, a Franciscan friar and philosopher, argued that when there are competing explanations for a finding, the explanation with the fewest assumptions should be preferred. The analogy of the *razor* reflects the idea that this principle gets rid of unnecessary assumptions, just as a razor gets rid of unnecessary hair. As an example, suppose you come across two trees that have fallen to the ground during a windy night, and you wonder why they have fallen. One explanation is that the wind has blown them down. Another is that each tree was taken down by a meteorite that fell to the Earth and then left no trace of itself on the ground.[6] According to Occam's razor, the more parsimonious explanation is favored.

Identifying the more parsimonious explanation isn't a matter of asking yourself which one you believe more. Rather, it's a question of which explanation requires you to assume the least. The second explanation requires you to assume that meteorites can hit the Earth while leaving no trace of themselves—no marks on the tree, no meteoric debris on the ground, nothing. It also requires you to assume that meteorites hit the ground regularly enough to take out two trees in the same forest on the same night. In comparison, the first explanation requires you to assume only that it is possible for trees to be toppled by wind. The first explanation is therefore more parsimonious.

Scope, verifiability, heuristic value, and parsimony aren't the only criteria for good theories, but they are among those most commonly used by social scientists. Table 3.2 recaps each criterion and its meaning.

Earlier in this chapter, we discussed the difference between qualitative and quantitative research. Besides those, a third method often used to study social behavior is the critical method. As you'll discover next, those three methods differ from each other in terms of both their practices and the assumptions they entail.

Table 3.2 Criteria for a Good Theory

Criterion	Meaning
Appropriate scope	Good theories propose explanations that are appropriate in range to their objectives (whether grand, middle-range, or narrow)
Reflection of reality	Good theories reflect the perception of reality used by the researcher; if they assume an objective reality, they produce hypotheses that are both verifiable and falsifiable
Heuristic value	Good theories stimulate research by leading to useful (and perhaps novel and/or counterintuitive) questions and predictions
Parsimony	Good theories provide the simplest explanation possible, requiring the fewest possible assumptions

▲ ▲ ▲

Test Your Understanding

Can you tell if a prediction is verifiable and falsifiable? Consider the following hypotheses:

Hypothesis 1: Men are more talkative than women.

Hypothesis 2: Men are either more talkative than women, or they aren't.

Hypothesis 3: Compared to women, men are not more talkative, less talkative, or equally talkative.

The first hypothesis is **both verifiable and falsifiable**.[7] If your data show that men talk more than women do, then you have shown the prediction to be true. However, if your results show that women talk more than men do, or that women and men are equally talkative, then you have shown the prediction to be false. The second hypothesis is **verifiable but not falsifiable**. No matter what data you collected, it would either show that men are more talkative than women or that they aren't. Every possibility is contained in the prediction, making it impossible to falsify. Finally, the third hypothesis is **falsifiable but**

not verifiable*.* The reason is that it dismisses every possible outcome. If you compare women and men, you will either find that men talk more, talk less, or are equally talkative—there are no other possibilities. No matter what you found, therefore, it would be impossible to verify the prediction.

▲ ▲ ▲

Let's Discuss

1. What do you see as the strengths and weaknesses of the deductive approach to theorizing? How about the inductive approach?
2. Why do you suppose researchers value parsimony? Wouldn't elaborate theories be more useful than simple ones?

▲ ▲ ▲

QUANTITATIVE, QUALITATIVE, AND CRITICAL RESEARCH METHODS

As you learned above, research is the systematic collection and evaluation of evidence. Although that definition implies that *doing research* is a single, uniform activity, the truth is that researchers have diverse ideas about what evidence is and how it should be collected and evaluated. These diverse ideas give rise to three general research methods: quantitative, qualitative, and critical.

QUANTITATIVE RESEARCH METHODS

As you know, variables are quantitative if they are expressed as numbers. Quantitative research, therefore, is research in which all or most of the variables are numeric. Some variables, such as a person's age, height, or income, lend themselves naturally to being quantified. For other variables, such as a person's ethnicity or attitude about relationships, the researcher uses a number to represent the variable. One's ethnic or racial group, for instance, could be quantified in this way:

> 1 = African American
>
> 2 = Asian/Pacific Islander
>
> 3 = Hispanic or Latino/a
>
> 4 = Native American
>
> 5 = White/Caucasian
>
> 6 = Other

In this case, the number simply stands for the ethnic or racial group the participant identifies. It doesn't represent an amount of anything. An attitude can be quantified according to how strongly the participant feels it. For example:

How opposed are you to drilling for oil in the Alaska wildlife reserve?

1	2	3	4	5	6	7	8	9	10
Not at all									Very

In this situation, the number represents the amount of opposition that the participant feels.

Virtually any variable of interest to researchers can be expressed quantitatively if that is what the researchers choose. Researchers conducting quantitative studies have multiple options for collecting data. Three of the most common methods are surveys, experiments, and content analyses.

Some quantitative studies use surveys. One way to find out what people think or how they behave is to ask them. A **survey** is a method of collecting data by asking people for the data directly. Surveys therefore rely on what researchers call **self-report data**— that is, data about participants that is reported by the participants themselves.

There are many ways to conduct a survey. One option is to distribute a *questionnaire* for participants to fill out and return. Some questionnaires are printed on paper and handed out in person (such as in a large class), whereas others are posted online. A second option is to have participants keep a *diary* over a specified period of time. During a diary study, participants are instructed to write about specific experiences (e.g., how many times they experienced conflict with co-workers) on a regular basis. A third option for a survey is to conduct *interviews,* either face-to-face or through an electronically mediated channel (such as over the telephone or via Skype). Unlike questionnaires and diaries, interviews give the researcher the opportunity to ask a participant to elaborate on his or her answers.

Questionnaires, diaries, and interviews are all types of surveys because they each involve collecting data by asking people to provide it. Another method of quantitative research is to conduct an experiment.

Some quantitative studies use experiments. Although surveys are easy and efficient to conduct, there are limitations to what survey data can demonstrate. An important limitation is that survey data cannot determine whether one variable *causes* another. Only an **experiment,** a study in which one variable is manipulated by the researchers, can demonstrate a cause-and-effect relationship.

To manipulate a variable means to determine and control its values or types. In an experiment, one variable (called the *independent variable*) is manipulated in order to see what effect it has on another variable (called the *dependent variable*). Suppose a communication researcher is drafting a letter asking people to donate money to victims of the November 2013 typhoon in the Philippines and she wants to know whether including a photograph of a devastated family will make the appeal more persuasive. To find out, she conducts an experiment in which some people receive a letter without a photograph and others receive the letter with a photograph. After sending the letters, she records which group of recipients donated the most money. In this case, the presence of the photograph is the independent variable, which the researcher manipulated by including the photograph in some letters and not in others. The dependent variable is the amount of money donated.

Because they control some variables to determine their effects on others, experiments are the only method capable of identifying a cause-and-effect relationship. That isn't always the researcher's goal, however. Sometimes, the goal is to understand the substance of a message, which is the purpose of a content analysis.

Some quantitative studies use content analysis. Let's say that a communication researcher wants to understand the phenomenon of painting graffiti in public spaces. A useful method for that purpose is a **content analysis,** a quantitative method for summarizing and drawing inferences about the substance of a message. In content analyses, the message can be any piece of communication, from a book, e-mail message, or website to a law, a painting, or even graffiti painted across the side of a city bus.

According to political scientist Harold Lasswell, the goal of a content analysis is to answer the question "Who says what, to whom, why, to what extent, and with what effect?"[8] To address that multipart question, a researcher performing content analysis examines the message itself, the population from which it came, the context in which it was presented, and the receiver or receivers it targets, with one or more of the following goals in mind. First, the researcher may attempt to understand the *antecedents* of the message, such as its authors or purpose. Second, he or she may try to describe the *characteristics* of the message, such as what it means, what communication channels it uses, and to whom it is directed. Finally, the researcher may attempt to uncover the *consequences* of the message, such as the reactions it provokes.[9]

Although surveys, experiments, and content analyses are powerful tools, not every research question lends itself to a quantitative approach. As you'll see next, there are multiple methods available for studying issues that are better addressed qualitatively.

QUALITATIVE RESEARCH METHODS

Although most any variable *can* be quantified, not every variable *should* be. Some are much better understood by examining their qualities and characteristics than by converting them to numbers. The goal of qualitative research is to uncover patterns, themes, and insights by exploring the essential qualities of a phenomenon. Among the most common methods of collecting qualitative data in the communication field are participant observation and ethnography, focus groups, and qualitative interviewing.

Some qualitative studies use participant observation and ethnography. One way of learning about a social phenomenon is to observe it in its natural context. **Participant observation** is a method in which researchers learn about a social group or cultural phenomenon by becoming involved in it themselves. The goal of participant observation is for the researcher to "observe from within," either as a complete participant (one who joins the group being studied), a complete observer (one who gathers information as a bystander), or from a vantage point somewhere in between. **Ethnography** is a method of describing the culture and cultural practices of a group that makes use of participant observation and other forms of data collection, such as taking notes and conducting interviews.

Consider a young researcher interested in understanding what it is like to belong to a fraternity. Although he could ask fraternity members to complete a questionnaire or report in a diary about their experiences, the researcher wants to be able to understand and describe the experience himself. To do so, he joins a fraternity and keeps detailed notes about what he sees and hears. As a *participant,* he comes to know and understand the social beliefs and practices of the fraternity, and as an *observer,* he takes notes and keeps records of what he learns. When he later writes a research report of his study, he uses his data to provide a "native" or insider's perspective on the experience of fraternity life. Instead of using numbers to represent his findings, he uses language to depict the fundamental themes of the fraternity experience.

Some qualitative studies use focus groups. Besides doing participant observation, another way to learn about groups and their patterns of interaction is to conduct focus groups. A **focus group** is a small collection of people who are asked to discuss their beliefs, attitudes, or perceptions with each other. Focus groups are commonly used in marketing research to discover how people think or feel about a product, service, or advertisement. Social science researchers conduct focus groups to understand how people perceive a concept and how they talk about it.

An example of using focus groups in communication research comes from a study about the problem of workplace bullying.[10] Researchers Sarah Tracy, Pamela Lutgen-Sandvik, and Jess Alberts conducted two focus groups with working adults. One focus group included eight participants and the other included nine. The researchers posed questions meant to encourage conversation about the participants' experiences of workplace bullying, such as "When did you first know something was wrong?" and "How has [workplace bullying] affected you, the organization, and your family?"[11] The groups' discussions were recorded and later transcribed, and the researchers analyzed the transcripts to identify the central themes present in participants' descriptions of their experiences.

Some qualitative studies use qualitative interviewing. A third way to collect qualitative data is to interview people. Recall from the discussion of quantitative methods that an interview is a type of survey, insofar as it asks people to report about their perceptions, behaviors, or experiences themselves. Whereas quantitative researchers assign numbers to represent what interviewees have to say, qualitative researchers analyze the words that interviewees use. Qualitative interviewing aims to produce what researchers call *thick description*—that is, descriptions that explain not only an experience but also its meaning, significance, and context.[12]

Qualitative interviews can have many purposes. Some ask people to reconstruct and describe events that happened in the past. Others inquire about personally significant experiences or rites of passage. Some ask participants to evaluate an event or program. Still others focus on the values, norms, and practices of a society or cultural group. In all cases, the researcher pays attention not only to what participants say but also how they say it. The goal is usually to understand participants' interpretations, rather than to identify facts.

All qualitative methods share a focus on appreciating the qualities and characteristics of a phenomenon, instead of representing the phenomenon with numbers. As you'll see below, this is also true of critical research methods.

CRITICAL RESEARCH METHODS

You learned in Chapter 2 that adopting a critical paradigm leads researchers to focus on issues of power and privilege in social structures and situations. In this context, the term *critical* stems from the idea of a "critique" of power and privilege. According to theorists

Gaile Cannella and Yvonna Lincoln, critical researchers share four important characteristics:

1. They work to illuminate hidden power structures, especially those that empower some people at the expense of others.
2. They focus on how language and discourse shape social experience.
3. They are heavily engaged with issues of gender, race, and socioeconomic status.
4. They approach their own relationship to power from a perspective of domination and subjugation.

Broadly speaking, the purpose of critical research is to identify and challenge taken-for-granted assumptions and norms about social power. Critical researchers seek to find those groups who are dominated or marginalized by existing power structures and to empower or emancipate such groups by challenging the legitimacy of those structures.

The methods by which critical researchers typically collect data are largely the same as those used by qualitative researchers. Like qualitative scholars, critical scholars seek to illuminate people's subjective experiences—that is, they try to understand someone's life the way he or she understands it. This goal often leads critical researchers to use participant observation, ethnography, and qualitative interviews as methods of gaining access to people's perceptions and experiences.

In practice, therefore, qualitative and critical researchers may appear to do the same thing. A key difference between qualitative and critical research, however, is their fundamental purpose. Whereas the qualitative researcher attempts to understand and describe participants' experiences, the critical researcher tries specifically to identify how participants are helped or hurt by existing power structures and then to empower those who are disenfranchised.

Although critical researchers tend to emphasize qualitative data—such as that gathered through ethnography or interviews—they can also make use of quantitative data when necessary. A large-scale survey identifying groups who are disadvantaged by a social program, for instance, would provide useful information for a critical researcher interested in understanding that group's experiences.

They may take different approaches, but the methods of quantitative, qualitative, and critical research all aim to improve researchers' understanding of the world around us. Just as there are criteria for good theories, however, there are also criteria for good research studies. We conclude this chapter by briefly examining the standards for good research.

CRITERIA FOR GOOD RESEARCH

All theories are not created equal, and neither are all research studies. To distinguish the good from the bad, researchers apply a variety of standards. Importantly, a study may fare well on some criteria but poorly on others—so the best studies are those that meet all the criteria relevant to them. As with the criteria for good theories, some are more applicable to particular epistemologies than to others. With those caveats in mind, let's consider the extent to which a study is trustworthy, reflects reality, provides insight, and leads to social change.

GOOD RESEARCH IS TRUSTWORTHY

A good study provides reason to trust its findings. Regardless of what the study reports, in other words, there should be reason to accept the findings as believable. Meeting this criterion is largely a function of the method. If the method for collecting and analyzing data is adequately designed and carried out, then the findings should be trustworthy even if they are surprising. In contrast, a poorly designed, unreliable method should not inspire confidence in the study's results, even if those results were expected. Although the standards for appropriate collection and analysis of data vary greatly depending on the approach being used (whether an experiment, an ethnography, etc.), a good study is one in which those methods are designed and carried out as reliably as possible and have been replicated if necessary.

GOOD RESEARCH REFLECTS REALITY

As you know, researchers vary widely in their perceptions of reality—and the research methods they use typically reflect their assumptions. A second criterion for good research, therefore, is that it reflects whatever concept of reality the researcher presumes. Scholars who assume an objective reality should produce findings they are able to generalize beyond the specific group of people in their study, because they believe those findings represent a reality that is larger than their individual sample. Scholars who believe in a socially constructed reality nonetheless aim to reflect the realities of their participants accurately, by examining participants' experiences in depth.

GOOD RESEARCH PROVIDES INSIGHT

No matter one's orientation to epistemology, there is little reason to do research unless it improves understanding of the phenomenon being studied. A good study is one whose findings teach researchers something they didn't already know about their topic or about the population they are examining. It provides insight, increases clarity, and even causes researchers to ask new questions they hadn't previously considered. In contrast, a poorly done study tells researchers nothing new, either because it produces no findings or because its findings were already known to be true. Regardless of its methodology, every study should be able to answer the "So What?" question: Why are the study's findings newsworthy, and to whom are they important?

GOOD RESEARCH LEADS TO SOCIAL CHANGE

A fourth criterion for good research, applicable primarily to critical research, is that it leads to social change. Recall that a fundamental goal of the critical approach is to challenge power structures that privilege some while disenfranchising others. Critical scholars aim to emancipate oppressed groups by encouraging change in social structures and practices. A good yardstick for the effectiveness of critical research, therefore, is the extent to which it contributes to actual social change. Does it indeed help to empower the disenfranchised? Does it lead organizations to examine and modify their ways of exercising power? Good critical research contributes to these goals.

As this chapter helps you appreciate, theory and research have a very interdependent relationship. Each has its specific functions and is accountable to its own criteria for quality, but in scholarly practice, neither is fully sufficient without the other. After reading the first three chapters, you now know what epistemology is, what theories do, and how theories and methods inform each other. Beginning in the next chapter, you will explore and learn to evaluate specific theories relevant to a variety of communication topics.

FOR FURTHER DISCUSSION

1. In what ways do you use knowledge from authority, intuition, experience, and research in your own life? Which forms of knowledge do you find most useful or most trustworthy? When have you experienced the limitations of each form of knowledge?
2. Suppose you wanted to understand the meaning or meanings that the U.S. flag has for newly naturalized U.S. citizens. Which type of method—quantitative, qualitative, or critical—do you think would serve you best? Why?
3. Why is simplicity—or parsimony—a criterion for a good theory? If communication is complex, shouldn't a good communication theory also be complex? Defend your answer.

Key Terms

Authority
Conceptual definition
Constant
Content analysis
Data
Deductive approach
Ethnography
Experience
Experiment
Falsifiable
Findings
Focus group
Generalizable
Grand theories
Grounded theory
Heuristic value
Hypotheses
Inductive approach
Intuition
Knowledge
Middle-range theories
Narrow theories
Operational definition
Parsimony
Participant observation
Qualitative
Quantitative
Research
Research question

Scrutiny
Self-report data
Sensitizing concepts
Survey
Transferable
Verifiable

4

SIGNS, SYMBOLS, AND SEMANTICS

HOW IS IT POSSIBLE TO EXPLAIN, INTERPRET, AND UNDERSTAND OUR SOCIAL WORLD?

HOW DO WE make sense of our surroundings? What does it mean to say that we *create meaning* and use signs and symbols to interpret our environment? To address these questions, take a quick look around your immediate surroundings. How would you describe this environment to someone you know? What forms of language can you use for your interpretations and descriptions? Language allows you to make statements such as "My study space is really great (or messy) and I have pillows and padded chairs that make this space comfortable." As social creatures, we have the ability to *name things*, and naming is possible because we possess the genetic capacity for language and are born into an existing system of signs and symbols. But what are signs and symbols and how do they work to advance human understanding and social interaction?

To understand signs, think of a strawberry. A strawberry is an object, and a word or image that represents a strawberry is a **sign**, a representation of the actual object. The sign is not the object itself, but it stands for the object. How humans use and understand signs is part of a larger theory of signs, referred to as semiotics. Many types of signs exist, but scholars regard three types of signs as primary.[1] The first type of sign is an *icon*, which is a sign that is similar to the object it represents. A photograph is a good example of an icon because it bears the image of the object it stands for. The second type of sign is an *index*, which connects one object or event with another. For example, a wedding ring is an index that represents not only the wedding ceremony but also a commitment to marriage. The third type of sign is a *symbol*, which has no necessary connection to the idea or object it represents. The choice of symbols is arbitrary. The word "strawberry" is a symbol for that fruit—but that's only because we choose to call it by that name. If we wanted to, we could call a strawberry an avalanche, and if we all agree that the tasty red fruit we pick from grandmother's garden is an avalanche, then we have created a different symbol for it. Signs are human artifacts that are used as tools in the meaning construction and interpretation process, usually referred to as semantics.

Semantics is the study of meaning and is regarded as a subfield of **semiotics**, the study of signs.[2] A meaning-centered approach to the study of communication draws our attention to the use of words, symbols, and language in human expression and experience. This approach leads us to ask questions about the nature of meaning, such as "How is meaning possible? To what extent is meaning created at the intersection of individuals and social others? How do we really know when we achieve mutual understanding?" These questions center on what is often called the *problematics of understanding*,[3] and reflect the fact that meaning-making involves a human act (an utterance or gesture), usually directed at another human (object or target), filtered through established language and culturally based meaning systems (an interpretive screen), with some hope of developing coordinated behaviors that may or may not achieve common goals. The primary purpose of this chapter is to illuminate three theories of human communication that helps us understand the challenges of meaning-making. Those theories are symbolic interactionism, dramatism, and coordinated management of meaning.

Symbolic Interactionism

The study of symbolic processes has a long history that is grounded in philosophy, rhetoric, humanism, and more recently, sociology and psychology. The interdisciplinary nature of human communication studies derives partly from the recognition that symbols constitute a critical feature of communicative action. Although the study of rhetoric is foundational to the communication discipline—especially the influences of Greek scholars such as Plato, Aristotle, Socrates, and others—Symbolic Interactionism (SI) should be considered foundational to contemporary human communication studies, especially for scholars who adopt an empirical, observational perspective on communication and social dynamics. Let's see how and why this might be true.

Intellectual Tradition of Symbolic Interactionism

The development of SI is generally attributed to the works of philosopher and sociologist George Herbert Mead, who was a professor at the University of Chicago. Mead studied the links between communication, interaction, and meaning in society. His students collected notes from his classes and publications, and in 1934 they published the book *Mind, Self, and Society,* which argued that human symbolic processes are central to all of social life. Mead and his students labeled this perspective *social behaviorism.* Mead's theory was influenced by a broad range of ideas, including Charles Darwin's theory of evolution, Charles Cooley and William James's perspectives on the development of self (identity theories), the works of pragmatist and friend John Dewey, and those of many other philosophers and scholars.[4]

One factor that distinguished Mead from other philosophical traditions is that he was concerned about solving *real* social problems in everyday life (as opposed to theoretical problems). To do so, Mead combined philosophical, educational, sociological, and psychological models of behaviorism in his perspective of social life. Thus, **symbolic interactionism** is a theory that explores the centrality of human symbolic processes and the deep interconnections among the mind, the self, and society. It has produced a proliferation of perspectives and interpretations of complex symbolic and social processes. Scholars who continued the work by Mead include his most renowned student, Herbert Blumer, as well as others from the Chicago and Iowa Schools of Sociology.

ASSUMPTIONS OF SYMBOLIC INTERACTIONISM

In the 1990's, one of us (L. E.) enrolled in a graduate sociology course with Carl Couch at the University of Iowa. Couch had been a student of Herbert Blumer at the Chicago School of Sociology. The classroom happened to have chairs that were bolted to the floor. When students asked about the chairs, Professor Couch explained that in the late 1960's, some students threw chairs out the windows of the second-floor classroom in protest of the Vietnam War. As students started to riot on the University of Iowa campus, Couch then picked up his notepad, left his building, and watched students march in protest, taking notes all the while. Professor Couch argued that his behavior, in the social setting of student protest, was a strong representation of what a good sociologist does: observe human interaction in social scenes.

SI did not emerge out of sociological thinking alone, however. Rather, it combined principles from many academic disciplines, and its development was strongly linked to social psychology. Mead and Blumer had the strongest influence on SI, and below we outline the assumptions of the theory as conceived by these two influential figures.

Mead Assumption 1: Individual experience and the development of mind take place through interaction with others in social scenes. Although Mead focused on how social processes influence individual development and cognition, he was quick to recognize the critical role of the internal processing of mind. When considering that fact that individuals demonstrate a level of consciousness (and reflectiveness) about the self, Mead noted:

> That which belongs (experientially) to the individual *qua* individual, and is accessible to him [sic] alone, is certainly included in the field of psychology....The psychological datum is best defined, therefore, in terms of accessibility. That which is accessible, in the experience of the individual, only to the individual himself [sic], is peculiarly psychological.[5]

One issue that captured Mead's attention was the idea of attitudes. Although an attitude might be considered an inner psychological process, Mead was interested in how attitudes were displayed or demonstrated in *observable ways* in social settings. That is, he wanted to understand how an individual acts in ways that reflect her or his attitudes about social experience.

Mead Assumption 2: The individual act can be understood only in terms of the social conduct of a group. Mead's first assumption clearly identifies the role of internal psychological processes, but the process by which an individual comes to possess certain attitudes is, for Mead, always interconnected with social groups. Mead argued:

> For social psychology, the whole (society) is prior to the part (the individual), not the part to the whole; and the part is explained in terms of the whole, and the whole in terms of the part or parts...The social act is not explained by building it up out of stimulus plus response [the dominant psychological model at the time]; it must be taken as a dynamic

whole—as something going on—no part of which can be considered or understood by itself.[6]

A significant theoretical premise in SI is that we perceive and reflect on our actions in relation to others. In social interaction, individuals are both the *subject* and the *object* of social actions. How others perceive us—that is, how we are "objectified" by others—strongly influences our identity development. Because we have the capacity to be both subject and object, we must also imagine the subjective/objective nature of the other.

Mead Assumption 3: Language is the vehicle that makes possible individual and collective acts, which help people organize and coordinate behavior. Mead noted that language use is instrumental in the development of mind *and* the understanding of social behavior. Unlike existing psychological models during the early 1900's, which focused largely on inner structures and characteristics of mind, Mead emphasized how language and gestures are used to coordinate activity:

> People get into a crowd and move this way, and that way; they adjust themselves to the people coming toward them, as we say, unconsciously. They move in an intelligent fashion with reference to each other, and perhaps all of them think of something entirely different, but they do find in the *gestures of others,* their attitudes and movements, adequate stimuli for different responses. This illustrates a *conversation of gestures in which there is co-operative activity* without any symbol that means the same thing to all.[7] [italics added]

People coordinate behavior in ways that rely on both linguistic (verbal) and non-linguistic symbols (gestures). In other words, behavior is coordinated from observable actions and is not necessarily based on strong symbolic agreement or mutual understanding.

Mead Assumption 4: The emergence of self and mind is only possible because of social interaction; thus, the behavior of all living things has a social aspect. Mead believed the social aspect of human development was the critical mechanism by which people develop a sense of self and the evolution of intelligence, of *mind*.

> There is no living organism of any kind whose nature and constitution is such that is could exist or maintain itself in complete isolation from all other living organisms, or such that certain relations to other living organisms (whether of its own or of other species)—relations which in the strict sense are social—do not play a necessary and indispensable part in its life.[8]

For Mead, social experience also includes the ways in which people create groups and organize their lives. He argued, for instance, that the family is the fundamental unit necessary for both reproduction and maintenance of the species.[9] Understanding the role of symbolic interaction therefore requires a focus on groups (including families), organizations, and institutions.

Regardless of how we might frame Mead's orientation to the human enterprise, his most famous student, Herbert Blumer, articulated elements of the theory in ways that were strongly influential. We briefly identify three primary assumptions about S.I. based on Blumer's interpretation of social behaviorism. All assumptions are quoted verbatim from Blumer and are interpretations and extensions of Mead's philosophies of social processes.

Blumer Assumption 1: "Humans act toward things on the basis of the meanings that things have for them."[10] According to Blumer, much of the work in social science in the early and mid-1900's ignored or downplayed meaning, treating it as a taken-for-granted aspect of human behavior. If meaning, communication, and interaction are not viewed as central to the construction of self and social order, then what is? Blumer argued that psychologists focus on issues such as attitudes, stimuli, motives, perception, and cognition, whereas sociologists study social roles, social status, norms and values, social pressure, and group affiliation. Neither of these traditions places meaning and meaning-making processes at the center of its perspectives or theories. Blumer noted, "To bypass the meaning in favor of factors alleged to produce the behavior is seen as a grievous neglect of the role of meaning in the formation of behavior"[11]

Blumer Assumption 2:"...the meaning of such things [social situations; individual interpretations of everyday life] is derived from, or arises out of, the social interaction that one has with one's fellows."[12] For symbolic interactionists, meaning is the most important idea in the theory. Meanings are social products, formed through the activities of people in everyday life. But what is meaning? And what does it mean to say that objects and social processes are endowed with meaning? Sources such as dictionary.com define meaning using such terms as *intention* and *full of significance*.[13] A Wikipedia search reveals that meaning can be explained as the relationship between human experience and truth (ontology), as the nature of human existence (philosophy), or intentional communication and the use of language.[14] In Mead's development of the theory, he was clearly concerned with intention, thought, language, and communication.

Blumer Assumption 3:"...meanings are handled in, and modified through, an interpretive process used by the person in dealing with the things he [sic] encounters."[15] If you were to ask the student next to you to distinguish between meaning and interpretation, what kind of response would you get? Blumer argued that people do not understand the world only through pre-existing ideas and processes—instead, they interpret experience and intention as a series of gestures and actions. In this sense, individuals select meaningful objects or symbols in the environment on which to act or respond. According to Blumer, "The actor [person] selects, checks, suspends, regroups, and transforms the meanings in the light of the situation in which he [she] is placed and the direction of his [her] action."[16] Interpretation reflects both existing meanings and the formation of meaning (new meanings, new processes, new understandings).

KEY CONCEPTS IN SYMBOLIC INTERACTIONISM

The seminal text in SI is *Mind, Self, and Society,* published in 1934 by Mead's students. The first key concept in the theory is **mind,** the collection of cognitive faculties that allows for consciousness, judgment, and perception. As noted earlier, Mead was strongly influenced by Darwin's theory of evolution, psychological perspectives on behavior (such as Watson's), and philosophical writings about identity (such as Dewey's).[17] In Mead's conceptual framework, understanding the mind involved both biological/evolutionary processes and individual and social dynamics. Mead argued that social experiences influence the development and existence of the mind, something that existing philosophies of mind did not account for.

Another key feature of mind is that the development of mind and intelligence involves both an internal and external feature of human social interaction. Although biology and physiology clearly play a role in the development of intelligence, scholars had largely ignored the possibility that social interaction, gestures, and behavior, also help to formulate mind and intelligence. Mead opened the door to ideas about the social construction of mind (and the social construction of meaning), which challenged the dominant model of the mind as internal (emerging out of psychological traditions).

The second key construct in symbolic interaction is **self,** which arises in social interaction, and is defined as the recognition that an individual has both subjective and objective dimensions of human experience. Unlike mind, the self is not biological and does not exist at birth; rather, it develops as a process of the *relationship of the individual to the social community.* This distinction helped differentiate humans from other animals: all animals have intelligence, but only humans have a self. This claim is based on the assumption that humans have both subjective experience and objective orientations. An objective orientation means that individuals have the ability to see themselves as objects, a condition that leads to the development of self-consciousness and reflexivity. To be reflexive, means that we can think critically about our actions but also imagine how others see us. Note the difference between mind and self: the mind is essentially biological in origin, whereas the self is essentially social in origin.

Mead's ideas of subjective and objective self indicate two critical features of a *theory of the self.* Each self is composed of an "I" and a "me." Mead defined the "I" as a form of consciousness. It is an experience of human sensation and responsiveness to a physical environment, and the self's subjective, inner experiences. He defined the "me" as the part of the self that can image how others view social actions. It is the part that is concerned with the reflection of the self in the eyes of others. Blumer pointed out, however, that the self as a process and not a structure, which means that who we are is open, fluid, and changing.

When we can imagine how others see us, we can also imagine what it is like to be the *other*; that is, we can take on the **role** of the other, or the other person's behaviors, rights, and obligations. Our ability to understand the roles that others play also gives us the ability to understand the attitudes of social groups or communities. That is, we have a general sense of appropriate social behavior based on group roles and norms, this is referred to as the **generalized other**. Mead asserted that, "The attitude of the generalized other is the attitude of the whole community."[18] Both the development of self and understanding of social circumstances require a coordination of attitudes (self and other) and social activities (what groups actually do together). Mead argued that the process individuals undertake, their assessment and interpretation of the action of self and other in social scenes for coordinated action, are necessary for "the fullest development of that individual's self."[19]

The third piece of the SI puzzle, after mind and self, is the influence of *social processes and structures* on the development of self and

KORY FLOYD, ET AL

other. **Society,** defined as a collection of individuals, groups, and organizations, is viewed as the primary mechanism by which the individual self and social structures *co-emerge*. Mead noted,

> Indeed, any psychological or philosophical treatment of human nature involves the assumption that the human individual belongs to an organized social community, and derives his [sic] human nature from his [sic] social interactions and relations with that community as a whole and with the other individual members of it.[20]

Remember that Mead and Blumer saw the self as aware, self-reflexive, and social. Based on the ability to be self-aware, individuals can imagine the roles of specific people (called *particular others*) and imagine what the larger group or society (called the *generalized other*) deems important for social action.

How is coordinated action possible? The answer is *communication*.[21] Communication is the process by which individuals coordinate action and accomplish social goals, develop the self and co-construct understanding, influence societies, and are influenced by societies. According to Mead, communication "requires the appearance of the other *in the self*, the identification of the other *with the self*, the reaching of self-consciousness through the other. This participation is made possible through the type of communication which the human animal is able to carry out..."[22] [italics added].

By arguing that communication is central to meaning in social scenes, Mead set the stage for researchers to examine how people co-construct and co-create their selves and lives in social situations. His ideas have spawned years of empirical, critical, rhetorical, and qualitative research. Rather than summarize specific claims from this work, we encourage you to do a search of communication studies using SI as the frame. We also suggest looking at the journal *Symbolic Interactionism*. These activities will help you understand how important the idea of communicative action is for multiple theories discussed in the following chapters.

▲ ▲ ▲

Test Your Understanding
In the theory of Symbolic Interactionism, Mead and others pointed out that understanding human interactive processes requires many different disciplines. However, the theory was strongly influenced by psychology and sociology. Given that both psychologists and sociologists are interested in human cognition and behavior, what are the similarities and differences between them? How would you explain how the disciplines of psychology, sociology, and communication differ from each other?

▲ ▲ ▲

DRAMATISM

Similar to Mead's perspective on the importance of symbols in social situations, Kenneth Burke's theory of dramatism focuses primarily on the relationship among thought, language, and action. Like Mead, Burke was concerned with language as a mode of action rather than as a means of conveying information.[23] Also like Mead, Burke was concerned with the different ways that humans use symbols in their social circumstances. Although there are some striking similarities between symbolic interactionism and dramatism, Burke apparently developed his theory independently of Mead.[24]

INTELLECTUAL TRADITION OF DRAMATISM

Burke was an eclectic scholar whose intellectual contributions covered multiple disciplines and a wide range of topics. For example, he wrote about topics such as ethics, magic, religion, war, and science.

Later in his career, in the afterword of the third printing of his book, *Permanence and Change*,[25] Burke framed his perspective on human relations with this formula "Bodies That Learn Language" and emphasized the fact that we also symbolize our relationships through music, painting, sculpture, dancing, and architecture.[26] However, Burke was clearly concerned about human intellectual development, linguistic systems, and social action. Two important philosophical foundations for Burke were logology and dramatism.

Logology is an epistemology, or a way of thinking about how humans acquire knowledge of non-symbolic experiences. As Burke noted, "Surrounding us wordy animals there is an infinite wordless universe out of which we have been gradually carving our universes of discourse since the time when our primordial ancestors added to their sensations *words* for sensations."[27] But this form of knowledge construction recognizes that the symbolic and non-symbolic realms are interrelated, that is, one influences the other. More importantly, Burke argued that when people experience nature and sensations in the physical world, they then create and use words to symbolize those sensations. For Burke, the basic form of human symbol use, beyond the word, is the story. The **story** is defined not only as a description of a particular experience unfolding over time, like what it is like to learn to drive a car for the first time, but also allows for evaluation, play, honesty, abstract explanations of cognition and behavior, and every other possible interpretive frame to explain our experiences.[28]

If logology is Burke's way of understanding the construction of knowledge, then **dramatism** is his approach to understanding human social action through an analysis of motives, stories, and language use. It was important to Burke differentiate dramatism from *behaviorism,* the theory that all behaviors are acquired through learning and conditioning. Burke believed that behaviorism cannot account for, or help us understand, the attitudes or motives that drive human symbol use.

ASSUMPTIONS OF DRAMATISM

Given the scope of Burke's scholarship, it is difficult to identify what Burke might consider the key assumptions of dramatism. However, scholars have generally agreed on the central ideas underlying Burke's theory of social life and the desire to understand language and human motivation. Dramatism relies heavily on a theatrical metaphor and is closely aligned with theories of narrative and performance. The issue of performance is key because Burke is clarifying the ways in which people actually engage each other in interaction; the performance is the enactment of a set of human drives and desires.

Assumption 1: Humans are symbol-using animals. Any student who takes a course in rhetoric or rhetorical criticism will come across this assumption. A focus on symbols, especially the use of words and language systems, reflects Burke's interest in how we *live* and how we *know* what we know. The use of symbols demonstrates human creative potential and the desire to understand how we *act together.* That is, words and language allow us to hurt, support, victimize, influence, inquire, define, entertain, and so forth. The use of words or symbols invites us to make claims about social life, to take a position, to assert truth, or to criticize. We are commenting on the substance of an idea or a thing, and we are making a statement about what *is.*

The fact that you have a vocabulary means you can also identify what something *is not,* which Burke might call *denial* or *creation of the negative.* For example, you can identify what you are, such as an independent person or an optimist, but you can also identify what you are not, such as a troubled student or a mentally deranged adult. Your meaning-making processes involve the interplay of both assertions and denials.

Assumption 2: Life is drama. One way to think about Burke's perspective is to consider dramatic stories and narratives. What is the role of the story in human experience? Burke argued that dramatism is more than a metaphor for life's stories; it constitutes a way to think about and critique human symbolic experiences. The purpose of drama is not simply to tell a story. The use of symbols and language allows people to engage in critical analysis of unfolding dramas. Language is not neutral but represents a tool by which we constitute our communities and ourselves. As you will note below, we can use the structure of drama to understand all types of discourse, stories, and human experiences.

Assumption 3: Symbols and language systems constitute a filter through which individuals experience life. Burke argued that when humans use symbols to act with intention, they filter their experience of social life through what Burke called **terministic screens**: "Terministic screens, in short, direct our attention toward a particular representation of reality and away from another."[29] Screens serve as filters through which individuals make sense of everyday interaction; each of us filters information and experiences to shape our interpretations of reality. Consider for example, some of the violence in universities, high schools, and movie theaters that has taken place in the United States over the past few years. Depending on who you are, you will filter and assess the reality of those situations differently. Imagine how a police officer or firefighter interprets the events surrounding the 2012 movie-theater shooting in Aurora, Colorado, and how his or her interpretations differ from those of the state's governor, a theater employee who had that night off from work, or you. We all see our experiences—and explain our experiences—through our particular filters.

Burke made an important distinction between motion and action. Mead believed that behavior is based on physiological stimulation but action is based on intentional symbol use. Not surprisingly, Burke drew a similar conclusion about motion and action: motion is physical movement, whereas action is intentional symbol use. In the 1930s, both Mead and Burke were considering the differences between animal and human behavior and trying to figure out what makes humans unique. They both developed extensive perspectives on the role of symbols in the creation and maintenance of individuals and their intersection with a broader social world. For Burke, *the act* was key to understanding what humans do and why they do it.

Assumption 4: Understanding human motivation is driven by situational influences and linguistic processes. That is, we have language to help us frame and symbolize human experience within social scenes. Burke's scholarship also focused on the exploration of **motivation**, that which *drives* humans in their understanding and critique of social circumstances. Understanding people's motives requires us to consider what drives their actions. According to Burke:

> We discern situational patterns by means of the particular vocabulary of the cultural group into which we are born. Our minds, our linguistic products, are composed of products (verbally molded) which select certain relationships as meaningful. Other groups may select other relationships as meaningful. These relationships are not realities, they are interpretations of reality—hence different frameworks of interpretation will lead to different conclusions of what reality is.[30]

What Burke means is that the meanings we make about social interactions are interpretations of interpretations! Although we can think of many motives for people's behavior, Burke emphasized that motives are derived from physiology, from language acquisition in infancy, and from the development and use of language in adulthood. As a critical tool for the analysis of motives, Burke relied on the *dramatistic pentad* as the centerpiece of his theory of language and social action.

KEY CONCEPTS IN DRAMATISM

The first and most important concept in dramatism is a broad analytic tool called the pentad. The **pentad** is a set of five interrelated concepts: the *act* (what happened?), the *scene* (when and where did the act occur?), the *agent* (who was the person acting?), *agency* (how was the act actually carried out?), and the *purpose* (why was the act performed?).[31]Any communication phenomenon can be analyzed using the five elements of the pentad. Burke noted:

> Men [sic] may violently disagree about the purposes of a given act, or about the character of the person who did it, or how he [sic] did it, or in what kind of situation he [sic] acted; or they may even insist upon totally different words to name the act itself. But...any statement about the motives will offer *some kind* of answers to these five questions what was done (act), when or where was it done (scene), who did it (agent), how he did it (agency), and why (purpose). [32][italics in original]

The pentad is an amazing heuristic device for exploring human communication. Importantly, each of its five elements may be more or less important in any given situation. For example, at times the issues of how a communication act was accomplished (agency) may be more important that who engaged in the act (agent). What Burke created was a model of interrelated constructs that help explain and explore human motivation and storytelling.

▲ ▲ ▲

Theory into Practice
Think of a recent interaction you have had with a close friend or family member, and use the pentad as a tool to understand what happened. What kinds of answers did you reach? How were the five elements of the pentad interrelated, and how did their inter-relationship help you understand your interaction? Try this process individually at first. Then, share the details of your interaction and

your analysis with a classmate, and have that person do the same with you.

▲   ▲   ▲

With the pentad, Burke laid the foundation for structured analysis of social action—but what is social about an individual acting with purpose in a social scene? The second key term in dramatism, consubstantiality, helps to explain the social dimension of action. **Consubstantiality** is Burke's term for the human desire to connect with others.[33] When we use symbols and rhetoric, we attempt to fulfill some need or desire, such as the desire to connect with other people. Burke argued that the drive toward consubstantiality is the product of unconscious human process. In this sense, rhetoric becomes essential for fulfilling human desires.

The idea of consubstantiality—literally, "sharing substance with another"—is that humans act together. Although our coordinated actions are never in perfect unison, the best we can hope for is a close approximation of, or identification with, another person. Thus, the third concept in dramatism, closely linked to consubstantiality, is identification. In his book, *A Rhetoric of Motives*, Burke defined **identification** as the process by which we attempt a sharing of symbols, perspective, and life.[34] However, consistent with Burke's framing of language, identification works alongside division. Burke believed that as we strive for perfect connection with the other, the best we can hope for is identification, and its cousin, division. Division includes all the ways in which we fail to connect, or fail to become consubstantial with the other.

The fourth concept that reflects deeper philosophical issues is guilt and its interrelated opposite, redemption. **Guilt** encompasses a constellation of human emotional states such as anxiety, disgust, and embarrassment. **Redemption** is the deliverance from guilt or negative action and making amends for sins.[35] Why would Burke be so concerned with guilt and redemption? One answer can be found in his view of human speech. Burke argued that speech is not neutral, but is "loaded with judgments. It is intensely moral—its names for objects contain the emotional overtones which give the cues as to how we should act toward these objects." [36] It is unclear whether Burke personally advocated for any religious belief system, but he clearly integrated ideas about guilt and redemption into his rhetorical and linguistic philosophy. Generally referred to as the *guilt-redemption cycle*, the idea that guilt serves as a primal motivation for human behavior is central to dramatism. Because humans have the capacity to use symbols, they are able to judge and moralize about human action. Moralizing human action leads to assessments and evaluation, and religious ideologies provide one of the strongest social frameworks for assessing morality.

However we might speculate about Burke's religious philosophy, it is clear that the guilt-redemption cycle was linked to two principles of dramatism that enjoin both religious and secular notions of motives and responsibility. The first is the *principle of the negative*, which states that whenever we identify what the substance or meaning of something *is*, we may also identify what it *is not*. Analysis of communicative action can involve both the affirmation and the negation of the thought or action. Imagine that you evaluate your communication theory instructor as "the best instructor ever." Your idea of "the best ever" is made possible though interdependence with its opposite, "the worst ever." Whenever we make a claim about what something is, we can also make a claim about what it is not.

The second reason for guilt in dramatism is the *principle of perfection*, which is reflected in a phrase you might have heard, "Humans are rotten with perfection." But what does this quote mean exactly? Communication scholar Edward Appel noted that perfection "requires the total absence of flaws and defects" and argued that Burke conceptualized perfection as the purpose of all social action. [37] By striving for perfection, people work toward an ideal that is, in some ways, always thwarted by the possibility failure, and thus, the likelihood of guilt. So, if it is true that humans strive for perfection, it is almost certain that we will fail—and because of our failure, have some guilt about why we did not perform better or communicate more effectively.

The problem of guilt triggers the guilt-redemption cycle. Here is how the cycle works: individuals act with a sense of motive generated by moral position, which leads to conflict and guilt, which then leads to "mortification, victimage, and redemptive envisioning." Therefore, as people strive for perfection, their substance and actions come into conflict with others, and the need for re-envisioning of perfection occurs.[38] Change is an outcome of immersion in the guilt-redemption cycle.

CLAIMS OF DRAMATISM

Unlike empirical theories of communication, dramatism does not predict outcomes from its central assumptions. Like symbolic interactionism, however, dramatism has influenced generations of scholars in their explorations of thought, language, action, and meaning. One of the most influential uses of Burke's theory is the application of the pentad to myriad situations; the possibilities for doing so are rather limitless. Let's take a look at some examples.

A classic example of a Burkean approach can be found in a 1987 article analyzing the rhetoric of Reverend Jerry Falwell, who is widely regarded as the central leader in the development of the Moral Majority during the 1980s. The author, Edward Appel, combined the pentad with the guilt/redemption cycle, and identified nine characteristics of Falwell's rhetoric: 1) the specific motives, 2) the dramatic action, 3) the heightened perspective of the speaker/agent (Falwell himself), 4) appeals to a larger social group, 5) conflict with evil forces, 6) punishment of the enemy, 7) the redemptive vision, and 8) the redemptive vision, and 9) the "threat of total ruin."[39] One important question from this type of analysis is "How well do the features of dramatism illuminate the motives and actions underlying human interaction?" Appel was identifying Falwell's rhetorical appeals as methods used to convince the public to join his crusade.

A second example of Burke's influence is found in the development of conversational dramatism.[40] Communication scholar Robert Hopper has used the elements of the pentad in the performance of everyday talk—that is, data collected from actual people in conversation. By asking students to engage in *live performances* of everyday talk, Hopper privileged issues of identification, play, and improvisation in interaction. Performing a life drama serves to illustrate the fluid and interpretative nature of social interaction, what Hopper calls "whole-body interaction-enacted discovery."[41] What student participants discover is both the fidelity (truth) to the actual conversations but also open and expanded interpretations of the meanings of those social dramas. Thus, dramatism serves as a heuristic device for exploring human stories in action.

A third approach to Burke's pentad is found in a rare empirical study that explored how members of a publication group negotiated and edited the contents of a user manual targeted for concrete manufacturers and contractors to explain why concrete cracks.[42] As the author noted:

> The *acts* of this drama were a series of meetings between the technical writers and the engineers. The *purpose* of this particular negotiation process was to quickly produce a shortened version of the original manual because the client who originally funded the manual...wanted some material evidence that his funding was producing results.[43]

In this study, the five elements of the pentad and terministic screens were used as analytic tools. Scholars from rhetorical and empirical traditions clearly find dramatism and the terms of order useful in exploring the motives, actions, and transformations that accompany human dramatic events.

COORDINATED MANAGEMENT OF MEANING

The third theory in this chapter addresses issues of language, thought, and meaning. In some ways, it is both an extension of SI and drama-tism and an elaboration of sociological and rhetorical approaches to human communication. Communication scholars Barnett Pearce and Vernon Cronen developed the **Coordinated Management of Meaning (CMM)**, which places communication processes and rules at the center of human communication theory. Interestingly, the authors also use the dramatic metaphor to explore human interaction and communi-cation in social circumstances, but they differ slightly from dramatism by emphasizing the improvisational nature of performance. Similar to the theories of Burke, Mead, and Blumer, this theory is based is on a philosophically grounded cultural analysis that is steeped in a strong understanding of the history of philosophy and communication.

INTELLECTUAL TRADITION OF COORDINATED MANAGEMENT OF MEANING

The opening sentence of *Communication, Action, and Meaning*, the central text for CMM, reads: "The most human of human charac-teristics is that of wondering, and the objects of wonder most char-acteristically human are human characteristics."[44] The book's first chapter is dedicated to *wonder* in the human enterprise. Humans are infinitely interested in and wonder about sensory experiences, how symbols are created and used, and the patterns and regularity with which we make sense of everyday experiences. Thinking about *won-der* in human life reminds us how much time and energy we spend thinking about ourselves, and the conditions under which we try to assign meaning to life.

An important part of meaning making, according to CMM, is the cultural influence on our symbolic and interpretive processes. Pearce and Cronen saw cultural influences as significant, whereas both Mead and Burke thought social processes were primary. Is this differ-ence between social and cultural superficial? Remember that Mead's theory was about how we *observe* human behavior and symbol use in everyday life, but a focus on culture asks different kinds of questions about symbol use. In CMM, Pearce and Cronin argued that culture is inextricably linked to ways of knowing (epistemology) and ways of being (ontology), and these processes are *deeply embedded* in the beliefs, philosophies, and practices of any given culture. When developing CMM, the authors examined the cultural roots and historical influences on contemporary culture, including links among primitive cultures, Eastern and Western cultures, and modern cultures (19th Century scientific). Each of these historical periods is relevant not only for exploring *knowing* and *being,* but also for influencing cultural views of ethics, aesthetics, politics, and communication.

By comparing cultural orientations to social life, CMM identifies different definitions of communication. Pearce and Cronin argued that the modernist view of communication (that of the 19th Century) was as an "odorless, colorless vehicle of thought and expression."[45] This orientation to communication is reflected in models that characterize communication as a channel for *transmitting information.* Such models have been intensely criticized for ignoring the role of meaning. By comparison, the primitive cultural perspective on communication was described in CMM as the concern with the sacred, with rituals, myths, and magic. From an Eastern philosophical tradition, communication is viewed as an extremely limited way of *knowing* human life. For example, one interpretation of Eastern philosophy is that words serve as barriers to *oneness* with the universe, and that language is inherently flawed because it results in the human refusal or denial of what *is.* All three theories discussed in this chapter conceptualize communication as much more than the transmission of information. Specifically, they all place meaning-making, action, and symbol use as primary to human life.

Assumptions of Coordinated Management of Meaning

In CMM, Pearce and Cronen relied heavily on theories of communication, action, language, and meaning from multiple scholars across different disciplines. In some ways, the underlying assumptions of CMM represent a compilation of ideas from influential figures and perspectives: Aristotelian and Newtonian perspectives on empiricism, Wittgenstein's philosophy of language games, Malinowski's anthropological explanation of communication and culture, Freud's psychoanalytic theory of meaning creation, Campbell's cultural analysis of mythology, Bateson's anthropological assertion that meanings are important and necessary for socially learned behavior, and so forth.[46]

Assumption 1: Communication is a "form of human action by which persons co-create and co-maintain social reality" (according to Pearce and Cronen).[47] Social constructionists argue that meaning is the product of *language-in-use* in social and cultural circumstances, and therefore, communication helps create and maintain meanings in social systems. Like many social constructionist perspectives, CMM features communication as the central mechanism by which meaning making and action are possible. Thus, who you are and how you see the world are not based on predetermined biological factors but are influenced primarily by socially constructed and produced actions. Furthermore, you are not simply a bystander in social experience—rather, your actions, beliefs, and ideas help to construct, reflect, and maintain your interpretations of reality. For example, you are a student in an institution of higher learning, and although the larger university system has created a set of rules and meanings for you to follow, you engage in active sense-making of those rules and practices. You may also challenge the policies, change the practices, and influence how the system functions in the future. Thus, students actively communicate to co-create the social reality of the university system.

Assumption 2: The rules that guide human communicative action are constituted in people's meaning systems. According to Pearce and Cronen, *rules* "are descriptions of how persons process information."[48] Rules are cognitive, existing in people's minds. They help structure the way you think about social experience, including how you interpret what is acceptable and allowable in relationships. For instance, think about a close personal friend. You can probably identify the rules you have for appropriate behavior in that relationship. According to CMM, those rules help you understand which meanings, experiences, and behaviors are acceptable in your friendship.

Assumption 3: Meaning systems are embedded in hierarchically organized social systems. One goal of CMM was to integrate communicative action, social and cultural influences, and an understanding of how individuals and groups organize meaning. The primary focus here is on meaning systems: how they are possible, how they are structured, and how they function. Pearce and Cronen believed that organized systems of meaning imply "a mutual causal relationship between forms of communication that occur and the content and structure of social reality, necessitating a theory that locates communicators within larger social groups."[49] In this respect, a strong commonality exists among CMM, dramatism, and SI in their focus on social systems, social processes, and meaning.

KEY CONCEPTS IN COORDINATED MANAGEMENT OF MEANING

What does *coordinated management of meaning* mean? What is being coordinated? According to Pearce and Pearce, people engage in actions that focus on patterns of communication and joint performances (with others) to create rules that guide public discourse, social systems, and human beliefs.[50] The theory is designed to explore the myriad ways people organize meanings hierarchically in social interaction; the hierarchy suggests that some meanings and constructs are viewed as more or less important in any given interaction episode or social setting. Below we identify six key categories or levels of hierarchy within CMM.

The first category, a Level 1 concept (the "Level" designation helps to identify an ordering of concepts), is content, which also includes the key terms construction and construction systems. One way to think about **content** is the raw sensory data that we process at any given moment of wakefulness. Content is more than sensory input, however; it also includes perception and cognitive processing of information. Constructs or construction systems represent how the brain orders and clusters individual/social beliefs. The term **construct** has been widely used in both psychology and communication and refers to the attitudes and ideas that we have about our experiences. For example, each of you has an experience of family, and your interpretation of the experiences and events in the family have helped shaped your attitudes and beliefs (constructs) about how families work, what they mean, why they matter. These constructs are considered level 1 content in CMM.

The Level 2 concept is called speech acts, which highlight the role of speaking and action in social situations. **Speech acts** are the communication behaviors an individual enacts to achieve his or her goals. For example, if you say to someone "You are an incredibly smart and wonderful person," you are achieving the goal of declaring what you think of that person. Thus, speech acts allow us to navigate our relationships and social life by complimenting, insulting, giving advice, making threats, and so forth. According to Pearce and Cronen, speech acts are "the things one person does to another person by saying something."[51]

The Level 3 concept is relationships (also called **contracts**), which refers to the belief that relationships have particular, identifiable attributes that help explain the conditions under which they function. Any agreement between people is a *contract*—not a formal contract, but a reflection of how those people negotiate who is included in their relational system, how connected they are with each other, and what boundaries exist around their relationship. Our contracts guide what happens, and what should happen, in our relationships.

The Level 4 concept is the **episode**, which is a period of time in which communicators engage in meaningful interaction. Episodes can vary in length from very short to relatively long. They are part of a larger pattern of interaction that is key in understanding what people do together, what their relationship means, and how meaningful exchanges fit within social reality. What is interesting about episodes is that communication is always partial; rarely do individuals get to convey everything they want to say to a specific person. Thus, analyzing an episode of communication includes looking for what is said and perhaps also for what is unsaid.

The Level 5 concept is **life scripts**, which are also called *identity constructs*. Life scripts or identity constructs are the narrative of the self, or the overarching self-concept of an individual. Pearce and Cronen used the term "life scripts" because they thought that "self-concept" implied a static, rather than fluid, representation of self."[52] This key construct focuses on how your identity changes over time. Moreover, the authors claim that who you are is largely a by-product of those with whom you interact. The episodes you experience in your lifetime define your notion of self, which means that your identity can change based on how those episodes influence your meaning-making sensibilities.

▲ ▲ ▲

Theory into Practice
CMM has claimed that the life script is important for understanding how we co-create meanings in social life. Cronen and Pearce believed that the term "self-concept" leads to static views of who we are. Make a list of the qualities that defined who you were ten years ago. Then, list the aspects of your self-identity right now that were *not* on your list ten years ago. To what extent do these lists reflect your changing identity? Which identity characteristics do you think will still be on your list ten years from now? Are you comfortable sharing these identity features with other students? Why or why not?

▲ ▲ ▲

The Level 6 concept is archetypes, which is considered the highest level of the hierarchy of organized meanings. Pearce and Cronen explain **archetypes** in vague terms but suggest that all human share a world with common physical properties, common neurological structures, and common physiology. Thus, humans all have experiences of birth and death, development and maturation, hope and despair, joy and agony, and so forth.[53] Some scholars have replaced archetypes with the term culture in their analysis of CMM. However, Pearce and Cronen tried to identify a complex process of coordinated meaning making that transcended culture and focused on what humans have in common.

CLAIMS OF COORDINATED MANAGEMENT OF MEANING

Since its introduction, CMM has experienced three distinct lines of development. The first was the alignment of the theory with concepts from American pragmatist's language rules perspective and Wittgensteinian language analysis. The second was the exploration of theoretical constructs in different communication contexts, such as interpersonal communication, public and political communication, and rhetoric. Finally, the third line of development shifted the focus of CMM toward practical ways of solving real-world communication problems.[54] Because the first line of development is based on broad philosophies of action, thought, and meaning, we will described studies from the second and third lines of development that illustrate the wide appeal of CMM to communication studies.

CMM is not a predictive theory. Rather, it has been used to describe and illuminate how people make meaning in various social scenes. For example, communication scholars Mark Orbe and Sakile Camara studied the perceptions and communication behaviors of different cultural groups in various contexts concerning discrimination practices.[55] They chose CMM as a theoretical frame because it links culture, meaning, and intergroup dynamics. Based on the premise that discriminatory communication can damage relationships and groups, the authors concluded that discrimination was based exclusively on *perceptions of difference* (rather than both similarity and difference) between people. Specifically, they noted that those in power in a group (referred to as the majority membership) perceived discrimination as the enactment of a particular incident. In contrast, those in the minority perceived acts of discrimination as part of a larger life script that occurs in multiple situations across multiple generations. In this study, CMM encouraged exploration of communicative action across levels (content, speech acts, contracts, episodes, life scripts, and archetypes) as well as structural analysis of groups and social rules.

A second example of the application of CMM is a study in health communication exploring how individuals and families perceive and communicate issues of childhood obesity.[56] Although childhood obesity is often studied by examining diet, exercise, genetics, and the environment, this study explored how "communication within the family context is influenced by culture and how this communication may impact health-related behaviors and attitudes".[57] In particular, Bruss, Morris, Dannison, Orbe, and Quitugua used CMM as a way to understand how people behave, interpret, and derive meaning from regulative rules (those that guide what we do and say) and constitutive rules (those that shape our interpretations). Using focus groups, this study explored messages about health, diet, food, and obesity within Pearce and Cronen's six levels of analysis. The authors found that the family constitutes a strong cultural influence for communicative action and interpretation surrounding food. Caregivers, such as mothers, fathers, and in-laws, co-create meanings about food consumption and healthy lifestyles. As an example, consider how your family talks about food and health. How do you discuss different kinds of foods, such as vegetables, deserts, and meat? What are the rules that your family creates when it comes to what you eat, and when?

A third example of research using CMM focused on the intersection of family, culture, and war. Specifically, this study examined how family members make sense out of torture.[58] The author conducted in-depth interviews with 13 individuals from three Middle East families whose fathers had been detained and tortured. The interviews explored how families communicate (or fail to communicate) about: the torture experiences, the escape from the country where the torture occurred, and the role of story telling in living with the pain and aftermath of these terrible instances of abuse. The authors noted that the parents' decision to reveal the father's torture to children was a challenge in communication and story-telling—two of the three sets of parents revealed the torture experiences to their children and developed stories that helped explain those events. The author concluded by discussing the implications of the research for family therapists. In particular, they wanted therapists to recognize the communication dilemma associated with torture and acts of violence: if parents don't disclose the torture to their children, they may be isolating the traumatized person and forcing him or her to deal with the aftermath alone, but if they do disclose, they must consider how the needs of the children may differ from those of the parents or other family members. Children may respond in ways that create or reflect conflict, and they may have difficulties in their psychological responses to past events. The levels of CMM used in this study were speech acts, episodes, and cultural context, and clearly demonstrated the value of CMM for the study of communication and in real-life events.

SUMMARY AND CONCLUSION

The three theories described in this chapter focus on the interrelationship of thought, meaning, action, and communication. In some important ways, these theories are broad perspectives or commentaries on the challenge and complexities of studying communication action in everyday life. None of the theories is predictive—that is, they do not generate hypotheses or test predictions against specific outcomes. Nevertheless, their heuristic value is strong. These theories allow us to explore and describe the complexity of communication with people, in specific contexts, influenced by social and cultural belief systems, and moderated by individual sense-making and symbol use.

▲   ▲   ▲

Theory into Practice

Break into groups of three to five students. Within each group, choose two concepts from each of the three theories. Now choose a social scene, such as your campus, a coffee shop, a grocery store, or any scene that is familiar to you. Then, analyze that social scene using the six concepts you have chosen. Questions that can help you get started are: What types of symbols are used? Do people engage in dramatic action and story telling? If yes, what is the nature of the dramatic action? In what ways is the scene influenced by culture? Generate your own questions based on the six concepts as well. Report your findings to the rest of the class in a blog or an oral presentation.

▲   ▲   ▲

For Further Discussion

Symbolic Interactionism

1. Why is SI referred to as social behaviorism? How does the distinction between behavior and action help you understand meaning and communication?
2. Mead has argued that your social circumstances are central to the development of your identity. Do you agree? Why or

why not? How can you determine how much influence a society has on your communication behavior?

3. Why do Mead and Blumer place so much emphasis on the reflective self? What does that mean exactly and what does it have to do with social others? (Hint: think about their ideas of particular others and the generalized other.)

DRAMATISM

1. What does it mean to say that humans are challenged by consubstantiality? How are identification and consubstantiality different?

2. Do you agree with Burke that humans are motivated by guilt, and that guilt leads to the need for redemption? What do guilt and redemption have to do with Burke's idea of the human striving for perfection?

3. What is a terministic screen and how is it related to communicative action? Can you think about particular screens or filters you use in everyday life that might limit your interpretation of other people or events? How does the concept of a terministic screen expand your understanding of the motives you assign to others?

COORDINATED MANAGEMENT OF MEANING

1. Do you think colleges and universities focus on *wonder* in human communication and social life? How would you define wonder and explain how it relates to the study of human communication? (Hint: Wonder might have something to do with the idea that humans are inquisitive and curious about life.)

2. Suppose your school developed a course called *Communication and Magic*. What do you think could be included in the

course content that would count as magic? Is the idea of magic metaphorically useful? Why or why not?

3. How does CMM help explain your communication in everyday life? What key ideas do you find most useful when explaining the significant influences on your beliefs about family, school, and social life?

KEY TERMS

Act
Agency
Agent
Archetypes
Construct
Consubstantiality
Content
Contracts
Episodes
Generalized Other
Guilt
Identification
Life Scripts
Mind
Pentad
Principle of Perfection
Principle of the Negative
Redemption
Self
Semantics
Sign
Society
Speech Acts

5

ORGANIZING AND SENDING MESSAGES

HOW DO I COMFORT A HURTING FRIEND WHO HAS JUST HURT ME?

YOU AND BLAKE have been friends for years. Lately, though, he's been acting strange and distant. You have tried on several occasions to reach out to him and to ask what's going on, but he responds each time by acting as if nothing is wrong. Clearly, something's up— but you decide to respect his privacy, figuring that he'll tell you when he's ready.

Then one day, you check your Facebook and discover a post from Blake telling everyone that he has cancer. Immediately, you feel a flood of emotions: sadness for Blake, fear for his health, confusion over why he didn't tell you sooner, hurt over why he told you on Facebook rather than in person.

How would you make sense of Blake's decision to disclose his diagnosis via Facebook? What would you say to him? Perhaps you might try to comfort him in his time of need and ignore your own feelings of hurt and frustration. Or, perhaps you would feel a need to address how much you were hurt by his decision not to tell you in person. What implications would his decision have for your friendship, if any?

In this chapter, we address three theories that help us understand how people make sense of their own experiences and behaviors, as well as the experiences and behaviors of others. We start by discussing schema theory, which explains how individuals organize their perceptions of others and use their interpretations of others to guide their communication. Next, we examine constructivism, a theory that explores how people vary in their abilities to accomplish their goals effectively and appropriately. Finally, we explore planning theory, which describes how individuals produce words and actions that enable them to accomplish their everyday goals. As we did in Chapter 4, we will identify the intellectual tradition behind each theory and examine its assumptions and key concepts before analyzing its claims. Learning about theories related to organizing and sending messages will help you understand how we interpret other people's behaviors and respond to them effectively.

SCHEMA THEORY

Have you ever seen a set of blueprints for a house or an office building? Architects and engineers use blueprints to outline the various steps taken to build a structure. Blueprints provide a plan of action that enables construction workers to piece together a variety of materials to create something new. In a similar fashion, each of us has cognitive "blueprints" that organize our personal experiences and help us accomplish our communication goals. Those blueprints—which researchers call *schemas*—are organized knowledge structures that we develop and use to make sense of different phenomena. Schemas help us organize information from our environment and provide guidelines for understanding others and social interaction. Scholars developed schema theory to explain the process of schema formation and identify the different types of schemas people use to organize and send messages.

INTELLECTUAL TRADITION OF SCHEMA THEORY

Schema theory emerges from the social scientific side of the communication discipline. It was originally developed and tested in the fields of cognitive psychology and social psychology, but has since been widely used by theorists in the field of communication. For example, Susan Fiske and Shelley Taylor's work on social cognition,[1] as well as Roger Schank's work on dynamic memory and the processes by which people learn,[2] laid the groundwork for scholars to study how schemas influence the communication process. Some communication scholars have studied how schemas influence the ways in which we make sense of interpersonal conversations. For instance, Kathy Kellermann and her colleagues have looked at how memory organization packets (MOPs), which are organized sequences of interaction, help organize "scenes" and "scripts" that enable us to accomplish our everyday goals.[3] For example, a MOP of "staying in a hotel" might organize the scenes of "checking in," "ordering room service," and "checking out." The scene of "checking out," in turn, could contain any number of scripts, such as asking for the hotel bill, paying for the stay, and requesting a cab to the airport.

Other scholars, such as James Honeycutt and his colleagues, have examined how our expectations of our relationships influence our communication behavior.[4] Still others have used schema theory to understand why we choose various forms of media: "What makes us read one magazine article rather than another?" or "Why do we pay attention to particular items on the evening news while 'tuning out' others?"[5] As you can see, schema theory provides a useful lens for examining a host of communication issues. Let's briefly review some of the underlying assumptions of schema theory before turning our attention to its key concepts.

ASSUMPTIONS OF SCHEMA THEORY

Assumption 1: We are consistency-seekers. Most people feel comfortable when their attitudes, beliefs, and values fit together—and they feel anxious when their attitudes, beliefs, and values are challenged. As a result, many of us tend to surround ourselves with others who reinforced how we think. Someone who is politically liberal might choose to watch CNN instead of Fox News because the viewpoints expressed on CNN are more consistent with his or her beliefs. People who are deeply religious may choose to date and eventually marry only someone who holds a similar religious viewpoint. In general, research shows that we're more likely to form social relationships with people who are similar to, rather than different from, ourselves.[6] Seeking consistency in our attitudes, values, and behaviors helps us reduce the anxiety and confusion associated with uncertainty. Thus, schema theory assumes that when inconsistency is present, people feel discomfort and will work to restore consistency.

Assumption 2: We are naïve scientists. In everyday life, people like to have explanations for what is happening in the world around them. In other words, we all want to know *why* things happen the way that they do. Perhaps you received a strange text message from a friend and wondered what it meant. Maybe you're wondering why your instructor gave you a particular grade on an assignment. When you read the story at the beginning of this chapter, you might have wondered why Blake disclosed his diagnosis to you on Facebook rather than face-to-face. Whatever the circumstances may be, schema theory assumes that we are motivated to explain our own and other people's actions, and that we use our schemas to help form our explanations.

Assumption 3: We are cognitive misers. In our efforts to understand the world around us, we encounter far more information than we can possibly use. Instead of trying to make sense of everything we learn, we are motivated to organize that information efficiently, so that we don't waste time and energy trying to process it. As an example, consider how you might use folders to organize new email messages in your inbox. Rather than allowing new messages to pile up endlessly, you can use different folders to classify messages and make responding to them more manageable. Similarly, schemas help us organize and interpret new pieces of information as efficiently as possible, allowing us to conserve our mental energy.

To summarize, schema theory assumes that we seek explanations for our own and other people's behaviors, that we strive to maintain consistency in our attitudes, beliefs, and values, and that we organize information from the environment as efficiently as possible to make everyday life more manageable. Remember that assumptions represent ideas or beliefs that are taken for granted by theorists, and that not all theorists agree about a given set of assumptions. Before we turn our attention to some of the key concepts in schema theory, then, let's take a moment to consider some alternative perspectives to the idea of schemas and their role in the communication process.

▲ ▲ ▲

Perspective Checking

One consequence of seeking consistency in our attitudes, beliefs, and values, and doing so as efficiently as possible, is that we tend to develop perceptual sets. A **perceptual set** is a predisposition to perceive only what we want or expect to perceive.[7] For instance, people who are highly homophobic are more likely than others to perceive affectionate behavior between men as sexual in nature.[8] Schema theory assumes that perceptual sets are real cognitive structures that predict how we make sense of the world around us. Recall from Chapter 2, however, that not all communication scholars believe in an objective reality or in the importance of prediction as a theoretical goal. How might an interpretive scholar think about and explore issues of interpretation in the communication process? An interpretive scholar will almost always be concerned about the subjective experiences and interpretations of peoples' everyday lives. Although interpretive scholars may not necessarily agree or disagree with "objective reality" per se, they are concerned with subjective reality, or the interior spaces of the individuals they study. The data from such a study would emphasize the variability and uniqueness across participants rather than making generalizable statements about similar populations.

How might a critical scholar approach questions of perception and bias as they relate to the communication process? From a critical perspective, a perceptual set may be conceived as a discursively constructed worldview or ideology that tends to privilege dominant interests rather than an objected cognitive structure. A critical scholar might ask whether perceptual sets are a feature of "nature" or whether have they been "nurtured" over time to support meaning structures that tend to perpetuate the status quo. Recall that one of the functions of ideology is to smooth over or obscure possible contradictory meanings. Indeed, for those who support the "status quo," it may make sense to reinforce schemas or perceptual sets that discourage people from questioning contradictions or inconsistences. Critical theorists, in fact, may work to disrupt schemas, to invite uncertainty in an effort to create new meanings and new ways of being.

▲　▲　▲

KEY CONCEPTS IN SCHEMA THEORY

Fiske and Taylor identified four types of frames that we use to make sense of the world around us. First, **person schemas** represent an understanding of the psychology of typical or specific individuals. You might believe, for example, that "People are generally good-willed" and that "Children are innocent." Some people believe that "Professors live in ivory towers" and have no understanding of what really takes place in the "real world." We also possess schemas for specific individuals in our lives, such as family members and friends (e.g., "Dad is a workaholic" or "Jim is always running late").

Whereas person schemas are frames we use to understand other individuals, **self schemas** represent concepts we apply to ourselves.

Self schemas provide the frames that constitute your **self-concept**, or those stable ideas about who you are. Statements such as "I am not a morning person," "I am a very private individual," and "I work well under pressure" are all examples of self schemas that reflect insight into how you see yourself.

The third type of frame we use to make sense of people's behaviors are **role schemas**. Role schemas provide an understanding of the appropriate norms and behaviors for social categories (based on race, sex, age, occupation, and so forth). For example, when someone says that "Waiters should be kind and courteous," that "Flight attendants should be calm and helpful," or that "Parents should discipline their children out of love," such statements reflect role schemas that guide that person's interpretations of how waiters, flight attendants, and parents should act. In an interview with ESPN radio on August 10, 2011, Texas Rangers President Nolan Ryan was asked if he would use a new pitcher who was recently acquired in a trade to replace one of the all-star pitchers who had performed poorly the night before. Nolan responded by saying that such a decision was not his to make in his role as president of the club. Rather, his manager, Ron Washington, would decide how best to use the pitchers currently on the team's roster. In other words, Ryan used the role schemas of "president" and "manager" to make important distinctions between the expectations that fans should have for his manager and him.

Closely related to the concept of role schemas are **stereotypes**, which reflect our expectations about people based on their membership in a particular group.[9] The process of stereotyping someone includes identifying a group we believe another person belongs to ("you are a republican"), recalling some generalization others often make about the people in that group ("republicans don't care about working people"), and applying that generalization to the person ("therefore, you must not care about working people"). Although many people find stereotyping to be unethical or distasteful, perceptions about an individual made on the basis of a stereotype are not always inaccurate.[10] Perhaps the most productive way of dealing with stereotypes, then, is to become more aware of the stereotypical perceptions we make, to set them aside when getting to know other people, and to let our perceptions of others be guided by what we learn about them as individuals.

The fourth and final type of frame we use to make sense of the world is an **event schema**. Event schemas describe the typical sequences of events in standard social occasions. For instance, you might have been taught that when meeting someone for the first time, you should shake the person's hand and look him or her in the eyes as you provide your name. Perhaps you've learned that it's courteous to send a thank-you note after you've completing a job interview. Those are examples of event schemas. In many ways, event schemas are similar to **social scripts**, which are guides to appropriate social action. For example, have you ever attended a wedding that was weird or strange in some way? Why was it strange? More important, how did your perceptions of the people change, if at all, as a function of the differences you noticed in their wedding ceremony? One of us (P.S.) once attended a wedding in which the groom wore a white tuxedo, the bride wore a black dress, and the couple exchanged vows and performed the ceremony without the assistance of a minister or judge. How might you have reacted to such a wedding ceremony? Would you have considered it to be novel and progressive? Or might you have reacted the way your author did and look for the hidden cameras? This example illustrates how easily we take our event schemas for granted, questioning them only when we notice behavior that contradicts the standard social script we hold for a particular event.

Now that we have briefly reviewed the assumptions of schema theory and identified some of its key concepts, let's examine some of the central claims researchers have used to frame their investigations of the communication process.

CLAIMS OF SCHEMA THEORY

Schema activation. According to schema theory, schemas begin when an individual encounters a new idea or concept for the first time. The schema then becomes more complex as a person grows and matures.[11] For instance, think about the process a young child goes through as she learns to speak English. When she first encounters an automobile, she learns the word "car" and uses the word "car" to describe any type of car, truck, or moving vehicle that she sees on the road. As she grows, she begins to make distinctions between a "car," a "truck," and a "motorcycle." She then begins to distinguish between "sports cars" and "luxury sedans," between "pickup trucks" and "eighteen wheelers," and between "dirt bikes" and "cruisers." As she continues to grow, her schemas for different forms of road transportation become more diverse and complex.

Even when adults experience something for the first time, we develop a schema to help organize our perceptions of what we have observed. For instance, think about the first time you heard a man refer to himself or to someone else as a "stay-at-home dad." What were your immediate reactions to the idea of a stay-at-home dad? And how, if at all, have your perceptions changed over time of men who choose to be stay-at-home dads? Better yet, how would your schema influence your communication with a stay-at-home dad and his spouse when meeting them for the first time? This is just one example of the kinds of questions scholars might explore using the idea of schema activation.

Schema change. Think about all the different kinds of schemas you hold about different kinds of people, relationships, families, occupations, and so forth. How have your schemas changed over time? Schemas can change in a variety of ways, and schema theorists have identified three different models for describing how. First, the *bookkeeping model* suggests that we change our schemas gradually as we encounter information that doesn't fit them. Have you ever developed a friendship with someone that you initially didn't like? Suppose your first impression of that person was that he was self-centered and rude. As you had opportunities to observe him in social settings, however, you noticed that he was actually a thoughtful, friendly, and humorous person. In other words, you encountered information about your friend that was discrepant with your first impression of him. As a result, you changed your schema over time, eventually thinking of him as a friend.

The second model of how schemas change is the *conversion model*. Here, an intense encounter with discrepant information may radically change an existing schema. Perhaps you know someone who experienced a dramatic religious conversion after facing death due to a horrific accident. Such a religious conversion could change that person's schemas about a wide range of moral issues and behaviors. In another example, discovering an act of betrayal by a loved one can completely alter an existing schema that you hold about that person (e.g., that he or she can be trusted).

The final model describing how schemas change is the *subtyping model*, wherein we form subcategories of an overall schema to deal with new and discrepant information. For example, a football fan who has grown up watching the NFL his entire life might change his schema for "football" after watching his first season of arena football. Although traditional football and arena football share some characteristics, the latter is played on a different field, with a smaller number of players, and by a different set of rules. To account for those differences, the fan might divide his schema for "football" into subcategories for "traditional football" and "arena football."

The bookkeeping, conversion, and subtyping models explain schema change in different ways. Each theory may be accurate some of the time, although the subtyping model has received the most empirical support from researchers.[12] It is important to note, however, that once schemas are formed, highly evolved and abstract schemas (e.g., schemas for "family" or "career success") are much more difficult to change than are simple, concrete schemas (e.g., schemas for "chair" or "house").

Levels of expertise. As people develop expertise in a topic, their schemas for that topic grow in complexity, in abstraction, and in what researchers call compactness. A *compact schema* is one that is highly developed and relatively unwavering. Consider, for instance, what it means to be in love with someone. A person who is involved in a romantic relationship for the very first time may confuse feelings of attraction, infatuation, or lust with the experience of being in love. However, with growth and maturity, as well as experiences in other romantic relationships, a person's schema for "being in love" is likely to become more developed and stable. It is not uncommon for people to look back on their earlier romantic relationships and realize they didn't understand love at the time. As another example, consider how you have increased your understanding of the communication process simply by reading the first few chapters of this textbook. As you continue your study of communication theory, your schema for "human communication" will become more complex, abstract, and compact.

Assimilation and accommodation. Finally, schema theory advances two claims regarding the interpretation of information in light of an existing schema. First, **assimilation** refers to absorbing new pieces of information into an existing schema. A good example of assimilation is the process of learning. College professors vary in their abilities to teach, but really good teachers stand out because they relate to their students and help them connect with the material. In other words, they facilitate learning by drawing our attention to something we already know and then connecting the new material to our knowledge. The process of assimilating information into an existing schema tends to reinforce that schema, making this an effective way to learn.

Second, *accommodation* refers to the process of either initiating a new schema or giving up attempts to interpret the information at all. Imagine taking a class that you know ahead of time will be difficult.

As an example, one of us (P.S.) attempted to learn German in college. As the vocabulary and grammar grew more and more difficult, however, he eventually gave up his efforts to understand German and switched his foreign language course to Spanish. Because he was unable to assimilate, in other words, he accommodated. Through assimilation and accommodation processes, schema theory helps us better understand how we manage new information in light of our existing schemas.

Now that we have discussed the intellectual tradition, assumptions, key concepts, and claims of schema theory, let's compare our levels of expertise for an event schema that most college students have experienced.

▲ ▲ ▲

Test Your Understanding
Think of a typical first date. On a sheet of paper, identify the steps required to have a *successful first date*. Be as specific as possible and be sure to include all of the important steps that must be taken to ensure that both relational partners enjoy the first date. Of course, be sure that they are ordered in time from the beginning of the date (e.g., the request or "asking out" on a date) to the end of the date (e.g., a hug, a kiss). How many steps does your social script for a first date include? How many of them are tied to your own personal expectations of appropriate behavior for first dates? How many are tied more generally to popular culture and social norms? And how has your script changed over time as a function of going on several first dates? Have you become more (or perhaps less) of an "expert" on dating and romantic relationships, and how *compact* is your social script for first dates?

▲ ▲ ▲

CONSTRUCTIVISM THEORY

Have you ever noticed that some friends are better at providing comfort and social support than others? Or that some friends just "get you" better than others? What explains those differences? Can we identify the skills required to sympathize with others and communicate in understanding and helpful ways? If so, could we use those skill sets to teach people how to become more competent communicators? In this next section, we will examine constructivism, a theory that was developed to address questions such as these. Whereas schema theory was designed to help us understand how people perceive, organize, and interpret information from their social environments, constructivism goes a step further to explain people's abilities to communicate skillfully in social contexts based on individual differences in how they perceive and interpret other people's actions.

INTELLECTUAL TRADITION OF CONSTRUCTIVISM

Some people probably seem better than others at listening, persuading, comforting, informing, selling, or entertaining those around them. Constructivism is a social scientific theory that explains how individual differences in social cognition and message production enable people to communicate in more or less skillful ways. In other words, constructivism helps us understand what our differences in communication skills are, why they exist, where they come from, and why they matter. It was developed by Jesse Delia and his colleagues at the University of Illinois in the late 1970s, and it originally focused on explaining the development of interpersonal competence during childhood. In the last 30 years, however, it has expanded to address differences in communication skills across a variety of contexts, including business, education, health care, political, and intercultural communication.[13]

Building from Delia's research, for example, Brant Burleson and his colleagues at Purdue University have explained how people generate and interpret supportive messages. Specifically, Burleson used some of the concepts in constructivism to examine **comfort-ing communication**, which includes messages that seek to lessen the emotional distress experienced by others. He and his colleagues developed a related but distinct theory of supportive messages that extends some of the ideas presented in constructivism, including *person-centered communication* and *interpersonal cognitive complexity*.[14] Before we turn our attention to these concepts and others contained within constructivism, let's briefly review some of the assumptions made by constructivist researchers.

ASSUMPTIONS OF CONSTRUCTIVISM

Assumption1: Humans actively interpret the world and construct meaningful understandings of it. Before we can understand other people's behaviors, we must first understand how people interpret and make sense of their experiences. According to George Kelly, people make sense of the world using **personal constructs**, which are groupings of events based on similarities and differences (e.g., intelligent or unintelligent, kind or unkind, attractive or unattract-ive).[15] Constructivism theory assumes that each of us develops and uses a variety of personal constructs. For instance, you might have a system of constructs that applies to country music, another to de-signer clothes, another to sports, another to types of cars, and so on. According to Burleson, each construct system develops as a function of your interaction with the objects in a particular domain. More de-veloped systems of constructs are more *differentiated* (or numerically larger), more *abstract* (focusing on more central and less superficial qualities), and more *organized* and interconnected.[16] Thus, construc-tivism theory assumes that our personal constructs are real cogni-tive structures (or schemas) that enable us to organize and interpret our own and other people's actions.

Assumption 2: People make sense of their experiences in pat-terned ways. Therefore, once we understand an individual's personal constructs, we can make predictions about how skillfully that person will respond to different communication events. Constructivist scholars believe people's interpretations of their experiences inform their communication behaviors and that people act on the basis of their interpretations. Consequently, people vary tremendously in terms of their *functional communication competence*, which is their ability to communicate in ways that meet their goals. With these assumptions in mind, let's look more closely at the key concepts that constructivist scholars use to study communication.

KEY CONCEPTS IN CONSTRUCTIVISM

Interpersonal constructs. Each of us develops a set of constructs related to people. These *interpersonal constructs* consist of opposing terms that we use to make sense of others. For instance, you probably formed an initial impression of your communication instructor based on how attractive-unattractive, fair-unfair, kind-unkind, and intelligent-unintelligent he or she seemed to be. We use interpersonal constructs to organize our perceptions of other people's appearances (tall versus short), behaviors (tense versus relaxed), roles (doctor versus patient), attitudes (optimistic versus pessimistic), and traits (extraverted versus introverted). These initial perceptions, and the constructs we use to form them, set the tone for all future interactions.[17] If you initially thought your instructor was kind, intelligent, caring, and humorous, for example, you might be motivated to attend class and participate in discussions. Your motivation might be low, however, if you saw your instructor as unkind, unintelligent, uncaring, and a bore. Constructivism focuses our attention on the importance of interpersonal constructs and the degree to which they influence our interpretations of other people's actions.

Cognitive complexity. People who develop complex systems of interpersonal constructs are said to have high levels of **cognitive complexity.** Individuals who are cognitively complex are highly skilled when it comes to understanding people, relationships, and social interaction. They are good at storing, retrieving, organizing, and generating information about others as they interact with them in social situations. This skill, in turn, enables cognitively complex people to form diverse and accurate explanations of other people's behaviors. Researchers use a survey called the Role Category Questionnaire (RCQ) to measure an individual's cognitive complexity.

▲ ▲ ▲

Theory into Practice

Think of people about your own age whom you know well. Select one person you like and one you dislike. Take a moment to mentally compare and contrast them in terms of personality, habits, beliefs, and the way they treat others. Don't limit yourself to similarities and differences between the two; rather, consider all the qualities that make them who they are.

On a separate sheet of paper, take about five minutes to describe the person you like so that a stranger would have an accurate picture of him or her. Don't describe physical characteristics, but do list all of the attributes, mannerisms, and reactions to others that identify the person. Use phrases and single words to describe the person; full-sentence descriptions aren't necessary.

When you're finished describing the person you like, do the same thing for the person you dislike. Again, try to spend the same amount of time (5 minutes or so) to write down all of the personal characteristics or actions that accurately describe this person.

To determine your level of cognitive complexity, researchers would examine the descriptions you generated for both people and would count the number of distinct constructs contained within each description. That is, they would analyze the level of *differentiation* in your perceptions of a liked and disliked peer by counting the number of separate constructs you used to describe each person. The more constructs you used, the greater your cognitive complexity. According to Brant Burleson, after combining the total number of constructs used to describe both peers, scores on the RCQ that exceed 25 suggest high cognitive complexity.[18]

▲　▲　▲

Person-centered messages. Constructivism theory links individual differences in social perception and cognition to the use of person-centered communication. **Person-centered messages** are messages that recognize and adapt to the emotional, subjective, and relational characteristics of the situation. As Burleson noted, person-centered messages are responsive, tailored to conversational partners, and attentive to conversational goals. For instance, how might you respond to a close friend who comes to you after just discovering that his romantic partner has cheated on him? To use a highly person-centered message, you might say "I am so sorry to hear about that. I can only imagine how angry and hurt you must feel. I remember when one of my former exes cheated on me, and the complete shock I felt over the betrayal. I hope you know that I'm here for you . . . you know, if you need to vent or if you simply want to go hang out." On the other hand, a low person-centered message might include "Man . . . that sucks! I wouldn't be too upset about it, though. There are other 'fish in the sea,' right? To be honest with you, I'm not that surprised. I mean, don't get me wrong, but you're kinda hard to be around sometimes . . . I'm just being 'real' with you." Clearly, the first message is more supportive, more responsive, and more person-centered than the second message.

Although highly person-centered messages are unnecessary for many everyday communication tasks, such as asking a stranger for the time or telling a roommate where you left your keys, they represent skilled ways of communicating in more complicated situations. For instance, highly person-centered messages are especially useful when resolving a dispute with a loved one, supporting a friend who has just lost a job, or comforting family members in their time of need.[19] Competent communicators know when and how to use person-centered messages, and constructivism explains how using person-centered messages is tied to a person's cognitive complexity. Consequently, the following claims help tie together the key concepts of constructivism theory so as to provide one explanation for individual differences in communication competence.

CLAIMS OF CONSTRUCTIVISM

Constructivism makes a number of claims linking social perception and cognitive ability to communication skills. First, *cognitively complex people are more skillful communicators.* Compared to those with low cognitive complexity, the cognitively complex are better able to form and remember rich impressions of others. They are quicker to learn complex social information, more skilled at taking another person's perspective, and better at making sense of inconsistent information. For example, have you ever had a friend forget to return your call? What was your initial reaction? Did you take immediate offense at your friend's forgetfulness, or did you think about possible reasons why he or she might have forgotten to call you back? According to constructivism, your cognitive complexity reflects your ability to make sense of inconsistent information about others—in this case, the information that your friend forgot to call you back even though he or she usually does. Measuring someone's cognitive complexity therefore provides an overall index of that person's social perception skill.

Second, constructivism theory claims that *people who are cognitively complex and skilled at social perception are likely to produce person-centered messages.* Communicators with complex interpersonal constructs are better equipped to make accurate perceptions of people and situations. That enables them to understand social situations in sophisticated ways and to adapt to them. The theory also suggests that *cognitive complexity is associated with a person's ability to generate multiple goals for social situations and to use person-centered messages to accomplish those goals.* For instance, a cognitively complex person would identify a number of goals when responding to the situation we described at the beginning of this chapter, from expressing support and care for your friend's cancer diagnosis to conveying sensitively your disappointment at how the diagnosis was communicated. Meeting multiple goals at once requires tremendous skill, and constructivism theory predicts that *the availability of message plans contributes to the use of highly person-centered messages.* In other words, people who have many ideas about how to accomplish communication goals are more likely to use person-centered messages when they are pursuing those goals.

Finally, constructivism theory underscores the importance of motivation. Specifically, *people are more likely to use person-centered messages when they really want to achieve a certain outcome, believe they are capable of achieving that outcome, and believe it is appropriate for them to use person-centered communication.* Let's illustrate this final principle by considering the following scenario.

▲ ▲ ▲

Using Person-Centered Messages

Imagine you accidentally slept in and missed an important exam in one of your classes. Since the test is essential to your grade, you meet with your professor to ask about taking a make-up exam. Which of the following messages would you use to persuade your instructor?

Message 1: Professor, about the exam that I missed this morning, well, I really wanted to be there but I've been so stressed lately that I completely forgot to set my alarm! I've had some major projects in some of my other classes, and of course, my job has been taking up a lot of my time. I think

I've been doing a fairly good job of balancing it all, but then a project came up last week at work that prevented me from studying for this exam. I really need to do well on your test in order to keep my 'B' in your class, so could I *please* take the exam later this week? It would be really helpful to have a day or two to collect my thoughts and study for the test.

Message 2: Professor, about the exam that I missed this morning, well, I wanted to apologize for missing it. I've been so stressed lately that I completely forgot to set my alarm, but I accept full responsibility. I know our syllabus indicates that no make-up exams will be allowed unless authorized by you in advance, and I understand the issues of fairness involved in a class this size. However, I also know how important it is to you that we do our absolute best on all assignments and exams. I have been studying quite a bit for your test and I am eager to show you how much I've learned over the past few weeks. I know I don't deserve the opportunity, but if you would re-consider the policy in this case and allow me to take the exam, I would be eternally grateful.

Most of us would probably use the second message, but why? The reason is that Message 1 demonstrates low person-centeredness, whereas Message 2 demonstrates high person-centeredness. Although the goal of both messages is to persuade your instructor, Message 2 is more sensitive and adapted to the goals of your conversational partner (i.e., your professor). Rather than simply providing excuses for missing the exam and emphasizing your own need to take it (as in

Message 1), Message 2 accepts responsibility, emphasizes the importance of the test and the class, and acknowledges that granting an
opportunity to take the exam would represent an act of mercy on
behalf of your professor. Message 2 is therefore a more skillful attempt at persuading your instructor than Message 1 because it reflects an awareness of the situation and an adaptation to the goals
of the recipient.

▲ ▲ ▲

In sum, constructivism theory views communication as an intentional, strategic process in which people convey their ideas, beliefs, and
attitudes to others in an effort to accomplish goals. It extends some
of the basic ideas in schema theory by tying our interpersonal constructs (which are one type of schema) to the use of person-centered
messages. The use of such messages, however, is likely to change as a
function of our conversational goals. To accomplish different kinds
of goals, we need a variety of plans. Therefore, in the final section
of this chapter, we explore a third theory that helps us understand
how plans and planning processes enable us to accomplish our communication goals.

Planning Theory of Communication

Have you ever experienced a divorce in your family, or do you know
someone who has? One of the greatest challenges facing parents
who decide to divorce is knowing *when* to tell their children, *what* to
tell their children, and *how best* to tell them about the divorce. Some
parents put a lot of thought into deciding how best to communicate
their decision. Unfortunately, others simply abandon their families
with very little explanation for the divorce, leaving only pain and
confusion in their wake. The difference between these approaches
often depends on the parents' abilities to generate plans of action

that safeguard the children's well-being while simultaneously dissolving the marriage. Divorce is just one example of many life events that necessitate planning if they are to be handled appropriately. Scholars have developed planning theory to explain how we generate effective communication plans.

INTELLECTUAL TRADITION OF PLANNING THEORY

People use both words and actions to accomplish their goals, such as to inform, persuade, comfort, and entertain others. Goals identify the "destination" for our communication activities—they tell us where we want to go in a practical sense. To accomplish our goals efficiently and effectively, we need a set of directions, or action steps. The action steps we develop to accomplish our communication goals are known as *plans.*

Charles Berger and his colleagues at the University of California at Davis have explored how plans are created, how plans vary in terms of their complexity and sophistication, and how social actors respond to the thwarting of plans. Berger has also studied how plans influence people's emotions. His research led to the development of planning theory, which is a social-cognitive theory that explains how mental plans influence communication.[20] Like the first two theories that we covered in this chapter, planning theory is a social scientific theory grounded in the post-positivist paradigm. Specifically, Berger's theory emerged from the tradition of *cognitive realism,* which describes cognitive structures and processes that facilitate or inhibit the communication process. Consistent with this tradition, planning theory assumes that the cognitive structures and processes that facilitate human communication are real.[21] In other words, our schemas, communication goals, and plans exist independent of our abilities to identify them, label them, and talk about them. With this general assumption in mind, let's briefly review some of the remaining assumptions behind planning theory before examining its key concepts.

ASSUMPTIONS OF PLANNING THEORY

Berger outlines five fundamental assumptions that undergird a plan-based approach to strategic communication.[22]

Assumption1: Our actions are based on our interpretations of behaviors, not on the behaviors themselves. In other words, observations provide information that must be interpreted before they can become useful for determining future courses of action. For instance, in the movie *Father of the Bride*, Steve Martin plays George Banks, a befuddled father who has a hard time letting go of his young daughter Annie when she unexpectedly announces her plans to wed. Days before the wedding takes place, George comes home one afternoon to find Annie crying in her bedroom and telling him that the wedding is off. When he asks why, she shows him a blender that her fiancée Brian had given her as an early wedding gift. Although George is confused by her reaction, Annie explains how Brian's gift scared her about what his "expectations" might be for marriage: "What is this, 1958? Let's give the little wife a blender?" In an effort to bring them back together, George takes his future son-in-law for a drink and discovers that Brian had given the blender as a gift simply because Annie likes to make milkshakes. When George returns home with Brian by his side, he explains to Annie what Brian meant by the gift, after which Annie and Brian make up and decide to go through with the wedding. In this example, it was Annie's *interpretation* of Brian's gift—rather than the giving of the gift itself—that nearly led to the end of their engagement.

Assumption 2: The process of interpreting our observations is largely subconscious. For instance, we often form our initial impressions of others based on how we subconsciously process their nonverbal behaviors. Those nonverbal cues may then lead us to develop certain judgments about people, even if we're unaware of doing so.[23]

Assumption 3: Our knowledge of goals and plans (a) enables us to understand the actions of others, and (b) is used to guide our actions. Consider, for example, a mother who wants to teach her young son to use proper manners at the dinner table. When her son simply gets up from the table and heads for the living room, the mother may instruct him to say, "May I please be excused?" when he has finished his meal. Her understanding of her son's initial action is guided by her own knowledge of proper dinner etiquette. Given her goal to instill good manners, she guides his future actions by teaching him the proper words to say.

Assumption 4: The knowledge structures we use to guide our actions come from both mediated and unmediated experiences. Part of the knowledge we use to accomplish our goals is learned through personal experience. For instance, you may have developed certain study habits by learning what works and does not work for you in certain classes. Or perhaps you grew up watching an older sibling make various mistakes with your parents and you learned from observing those mistakes what to do to please your parents. People may also use mediated sources of information to generate knowledge for use in future interactions. For example, the self-help book industry has thrived by providing information on everything from attracting the ideal spouse to landing the perfect job or becoming a better parent. Websites and talk shows provide personal success stories by those who participate on them, and people often learn valuable lessons from these stories. Thus, mediated information can also be useful for building knowledge structures.

Assumption 5: Accomplishing goals requires both the plans and the skills necessary for producing effective social action. People may possess all manner of knowledge on a particular subject, but if they lack the skills needed to put such knowledge into practice, they will be ineffective at accomplishing their goals. If you have taken a public speaking class, you know there are many ways of introducing a topic, organizing what you want to say, and providing evidence to support your claims depending on the goals of your speech. Actually delivering an effective speech that accomplishes your goals, however, is another matter altogether. Some people experience a tremendous public speaking anxiety that no amount of preparation can fully overcome, whereas others are naturally gifted speakers who simply lack the appropriate training necessary for delivering a quality speech. Although planning theory focuses primarily on how plans influence the communication process, the theory assumes that skills are equally important for accomplishing communication goals. With those assumptions in mind, let's examine some key concepts and claims that explain how plans and planning processes influence our interactions with others.

KEY CONCEPTS IN PLANNING THEORY

Goals, plans, and planning. Before we can understand how plans facilitate or thwart the communication process, we must first define the concepts of *goals*, *plans*, and *planning*.[24] **Goals** are desired end states that an individual is committed to achieving or maintaining. They answer the basic question, "*What* do I want to accomplish?" For example, if you need more money but want to work less so you can concentrate more on school, your goal might be to persuade your parents to provide more financial assistance each month. To accomplish your goal, you need a plan. **Plans** are cognitive representations of action sequences that enable people to achieve their goals. Plans address the question, "*How* will I accomplish it?" In many ways, plans are scripts that guide us through a series of steps necessary for fulfilling our goals. To persuade your parents, you might plan out exactly what you want to say, how to say it, and when to make your appeal. You might wait until you have earned a high grade in one of your classes and your parents are in a good mood before describing your situation, for example.

Goals motivate social action, but plans guide that action. Thus, **planning** is the process we go through to produce a plan. It includes assessing the social situation, deciding what goals to pursue, creating or retrieving plans, and enacting them. Recall schema theory's claim that we develop expertise on a topic as our schemas grow and change. By learning what kinds of persuasive appeals have worked with your parents in the past, you may have developed a repository of plans (i.e., expertise with a given set of schemas) from which to draw.

Plan complexity and action fluidity. A key dimension of plans is their degree of **complexity**. According to Berger, plans are more or less complex depending on two factors. First, plans vary in their *specificity*. Some are quite abstract, identifying only general goals, whereas others are very concrete, including specific behaviors to enact. In the above example, you may have a very general plan of persuading your parents to give you money by promising to do well in school. A more concrete plan, however, would specify what "doing well in school" means: for instance, earning a certain grade point average or graduating in a specified time frame. Not surprisingly, research shows that plans with concrete actions are more effective than highly abstract or vague plans.[25]

Second, plans differ in their *action contingencies*. Some include an alternative action—a "Plan B"—to try if the initial plans don't pan out. Others have no such contingencies. To identify contingencies for your plan, you might role-play your conversation with your parents and practice responding to what they might say. How would you reply, for example, if your parents decided to give you money only if you moved back home? Would you meet that demand, or would you modify your request? Rather than insisting that your parents meet your initial request of an extra $400 a month, you might counter by asking for only $200 a month and offering to come home one additional weekend each month. The greater the number of contingencies your plan includes, the more complex the plan.

In addition to complexity, planning theory defines a plan's **action fluidity,** which refers to the fluency with which that plan is enacted. This concept answers the question, "How smoothly did the plan go?" The concept of action fluidity helps us understand how different plans and plan contingencies influence the effectiveness of verbal and nonverbal behaviors in helping social actors accomplish their goals. A student who spends little time planning how to ask her parents for money may stammer and pause when they ask her to move back home, revealing her frustrations and reducing her likelihood of success. Conversely, a student who spends a lot of time planning may respond smoothly with a counter offer, thus increasing her chances of success.

The hierarchy principle. A final concept in planning theory is the hierarchy principle. According to Berger, the **hierarchy principle** explains that changing plans at specific levels is easier than changing plans at abstract levels.[26] In other words, when our plans falter, we find it easier to alter their concrete features (e.g., the timing of our action or the words we'll use) rather than their abstract ones (e.g., the fundamental goals we're trying to accomplish). As an example, Berger has found that when communicators feel misunderstood, they tend to repeat themselves in a louder voice (i.e., to alter a concrete aspect of their plan), even though the other person may have heard them the first time. That's because they find it easier simply to repeat themselves than, say, to change their line of reasoning or alter other abstract aspects of their plan.

Considered as a whole, planning theory provides a number of key concepts that tell us what plans are, how they vary in terms of their complexity, and how we make changes to existing plans when we experience plan failure. With those concepts in mind, let's turn our attention to the claims advanced by planning theory.

CLAIMS OF PLANNING THEORY

Unlike the first two theories that we covered within this chapter, planning theory advances specific claims that are tied to the key concepts outlined above, as well as more general claims about planning as a process.[27]

Claims about goals, plans, and planning. Planning theory provides two claims related to goals and the planning process. First, *when developing plans to accomplish our goals, we check our long-term memory to see if we have any pre-formulated (or "stock") plans available for use.* For example, if you discovered that a close friend had lost a loved one, you would probably plan how best to express your sympathies and provide comfort in his time of need. To do so, however, you would first consider whether you had previously comforted someone who was grieving. If you had—and if your comfort was well received—you would most likely access and follow a similar plan for providing the same kind of comfort to your friend.

Second, *when our plans are successful, we feel positive emotions such as happiness, satisfaction, and pride. When our plans are thwarted, however, we feel negative emotions such as frustration, anxiety, and stress.* This claim is evident when you experience interpersonal conflict with someone. Conflict typically occurs when we perceive that someone is standing in the way of us accomplishing some goal. Regardless of how well you typically handle your disagreements with others, even the most competent communicator usually experiences some level of frustration, anxiety, and stress during conflict. Resolving that conflict tends to make us happier and more satisfied, however.

Claims about plan complexity and action fluidity. Planning theory also makes claims about people's motivation to achieve goals, the amount of knowledge they possess, the complexity of their plans, and action fluidity.[28] For instance, the theory predicts that *as the motivation to reach a social goal increases, the complexity of plans tends to increase as well.* Have you ever had something really important you wanted to say to your romantic partner? If so, you may have spent lots of time planning the conversation and thinking through different ways of expressing your feelings. You may also have thought about the various ways your partner might respond. In this case, your motivation to reach a particular goal (telling your partner something very important) was high; thus, you formed a complex plan for achieving it.

Planning theory also predicts that *the more strategic knowledge and specific knowledge a person possesses on a particular topic, the more likely that person is use to complex plans. Strategic* knowledge includes our knowledge about changing other people's opinions in general; *specific* knowledge includes facts and arguments relevant to the particular issue facing you at the time. Planning theory suggests that the level of strategic and specific knowledge you have affects the relationship between your motivation and your plan complexity. A high level of motivation combined with high levels of knowledge produces more complex plans. Low or high levels of motivation combined with low levels of knowledge tend to produce less complex plans.

The theory also addresses the degree to which politeness and other contextual cues change the kinds of plans we use to accomplish our goals. Specifically, *the more concerned you are about efficiency, the less complex your plans will be.* Remember that complex plans require more cognitive effort and energy to enact than simple ones. When efficiency is more important than politeness—such as in an emergency situation—people tend to communicate in simple ways that emphasize clarity more than tact, such as saying "Call 911!" instead of "Would you mind calling 911 for me? Thanks, I really appreciate it."

In terms of action fluidity, planning theory argues that *when we fail to accomplish our immediate goal, our actions are more fluid if we have a small number of contingent actions than if we have too many or too few.* Communicators who pursue goals with no planned alternatives may not be able to respond rapidly if their sole plan fails. At the same time, those who have too many alternative plans to choose from may also have difficulty responding in a timely manner. Have you ever witnessed someone "freezing up" because he or she had not thought through how to respond to a difficult situation? Perhaps you have seen someone experience "analysis paralysis" because there were so many options to choose from that the person was simply unable to make a decision. In either case, we are better prepared to respond to unexpected turns of events when we have a small number of alternatives.

Claims about the hierarchy principle. In many ways, the hierarchy principle represents both a concept and a claim of planning theory. When we are thwarted in our attempts to accomplish a particular goal, our first response typically includes low-level plan alterations (e.g., slowing down, repeating what we just said, raising our volume). Continued failure results in more abstract alterations to our communication plans (e.g., using different forms of evidence, changing our line of reasoning, pursuing a different goal altogether). At the same time, planning theory predicts that *repeated interruption or thwarting of plans will lead to the use of progressively less socially appropriate plans.* Again, you may have experienced this when one of your disagreements with a friend spiraled out of control: As the conversation got more heated, you acted in less appropriate ways. For many of us, the emotional flooding that occurs during interpersonal conflict heightens the degree to which we feel we are failing to make ourselves understood by our partner (thus, failing to accomplish the goal).[29] What begins as a relatively calm "discussion" gradually becomes more and more intense until both partners are angry, frustrated, and behaving in unhealthy or inappropriate ways. In fact, planning theory claims that *repeated thwarting over time, combined with higher levels of negative emotion, produces increasingly less complex plans.* Thus, the theory helps us understand not only why we tend to make simple, low-level changes when our plans are first interrupted, but also why our communication becomes less competent over time when we encounter repeated failures.

General claims of planning theory. The final set of claims detailed within planning theory deals more generally with plans and the planning process. For instance, *communicators who anticipate their partners' responses are more effective than those who do not.* That isn't to say we should try to put words into the mouths of our conversational partners. Rather, when we think through what we want to say, we can increase our chances of success by considering how our partners might respond and what we would say in each case. It is also important to remember that *no matter how effective the plan, it is likely to fail if communicators do not have the necessary performance skills to carry it out.*

Consequently, planning theory ultimately teaches us a very important lesson about strategic communication. When we fail to reach our social interaction goals, the problem may lie in our use of faulty plans, the fact that we lack important skills necessary for enacting our plans, or both.

SUMMARY AND CONCLUSION

In this chapter, we discussed three theories that start with social cognition and the idea that our schemas influence our communication with other people. Schema theory encourages us to consider how different types of schemas organize our perceptions of people and their behaviors, as well as how our schemas provide expectations of social interaction that guide our own communication behaviors. Constructivism goes a step further by tying a specific type of schema—our level of cognitive complexity—to our communication skills and abilities to generate person-centered messages. Finally, planning theory provides a detailed explanation of how we develop action sequences that enable us to accomplish our goals. It also helps us understand the relationships between goals, plans, and strategic communication. With these theories in mind, let's return to the challenging situation from the start of the chapter to see what we've learned.

FOR FURTHER DISCUSSION

Thinking back to the opening scenario, use the three theories discussed in this chapter to craft some potential responses to your friend.

SCHEMA THEORY

1. What are your expectations of a "close friend" (i.e., a person schema), and how are your expectations of what it means to

be a close friend tied to your understanding of how best to communicate bad news to others (i.e., a social script)? To what degree are your friend's actions inconsistent with your schema for how a close friend should handle bad news?

2. How might your reactions to your close friend change as a function of having had other friends go through similar circumstances? In other words, might you respond differently to your friend if this was the first time you had had a close friend who was diagnosed with cancer? Or might your response be different if you had already gone through this type of situation with other close friends (i.e., levels of expertise)?

3. What kinds of information are appropriate for disclosure through Facebook and other forms of social media? What kinds of information are inappropriate to disclose? And how might your interpretations of your friend's behavior change as a function of your event schemas for disclosing personal information through mediated forms of technology?

CONSTRUCTIVISM

1. What are some possible explanations for your friend's decision to disclose his news through Facebook? Why not tell you his news in person? Based on the number of answers you come up with to these two questions, what would constructivism theory have to say about your level of cognitive complexity?

2. Now, construct a highly person-centered message that comforts your friend in light of his recent diagnosis. How, if at all, would your message balance your competing desires to provide social support and comfort while also addressing your disappointment (or confusion) over his decision to tell you his news through Facebook?

PLANNING THEORY

1. What goals would you hope to accomplish the next time you talk to your friend? Would you simply seek to comfort him and lend him social support? Or would you also want to convey your disappointment in finding out the news through Facebook?

2. Once you've decided what you want to say, how would you go about saying it? What action steps would your plan include? How complex would your plan be? Would you call him first or try to see him in person? Or would you first respond to his Facebook posting and see how he responds to your post, if at all? More importantly, what exactly would you say?

3. If you decided to let go of your initial confusion or disappointment over his behavior and simply comfort him in his time of need, and he responded by acting even more distant and withdrawn, how would you respond? On the other hand, let's say that you decided to both comfort him and communicate to him that how he chose to tell you his news hurt your feelings. If he responds defensively and/or fails to understand what you are saying, how might you adapt or change your plans in response to his reaction?

4. To what extent would you anticipate your friend's reactions to what you are going to say? And how might his reactions, whatever they may be, influence the degree to which you are able to fully convey what it is you want to say in the moment?

KEY TERMS

Action fluidity
Assimilation
Comforting communication
Event schema
Goals
Hierarchy principle
Perceptual set
Personal constructs
Planning
Plans
Role schemas
Self schemas
Self-concept
Social scripts
Stereotypes

6

EXPLAINING AND UNDERSTANDING
HUMAN BEHAVIOR

WHY DO PEOPLE BEHAVE AS THEY DO?

SINCE GRADUATING COLLEGE together two years ago, Amira, Jackson, Naomi, and Carlton have been the closest of friends. Saturday night, one of their crazier college professors—a bit of an environmental nut who taught a wilderness communication course during their final semester—was having a reunion party at her house. Upon arriving, Naomi said "This is going to be weird, so I don't want to stay too long." Jackson looked at Naomi with a puzzled look and said, "I thought you were looking forward to the party. Let's just have a few drinks, eat, and then leave early and hit the clubs!" Amira looked at the two and said, "I'm not sure what your problems are, but I loved our last wilderness class; I definitely want to stay for a while." Although members of the group had various levels of enthusiasm, they finally agreed that staying at the party was probably the best idea.

The professor and her former students sat in the living room drinking and talking for the first hour and then the professor announced that it was time to get the food on the grill. After she left,

Carlton stood up and said, "You know what, I'm going to the bath-room for a short meditation." Grabbing her phone, Amira said, "Well, this looks like a great time call my mom, so I'll just leave you all while you get wasted," and then walked out of the room. Jackson headed for the professor's bedroom, saying "I know she has a bottle of 50-year-old scotch hidden somewhere and I am dying for a shot!" After everyone else had left, Naomi thought to herself, *I knew this was going to be weird, why did I even come in the first place?*

Have you ever wondered why people do what they do? Can you remember a time when a friend or relative behaved in a way that seemed troubling or contrary to their normal, everyday behavior? How did you respond? What reasons or explanations did you de-velop about *why* they acted as they did? In the party scenario above, how might we understand why Carlton went to the *bathroom* for medi-tation? If he were your close friend, what type of explanation could you offer? To figure it out, you might consider whether this behavior is typical for Carlton or not. Does he meditate on a regular basis? Have the two of you ever meditated together? We might also wonder Carlton would choose the bathroom for his meditation. Maybe he was seeking privacy and figured that the bathroom is the quietest place at the party. Perhaps the professor suggested that he experi-ment with unusual locations and times to meditate.

Similarly, we can seek explanations for Amira's decision to call her mother during the party. To explain her behavior, we could ask whether she calls her mother everyday, or whether this was unusu-al. Perhaps they had a serious conflict before the party and Amira was calling to make amends. Also, why did she make the remark about the rest of the friends getting wasted? Is there a long-standing conflict between Amira and her friends who party too much? What other factors might we consider when explaining her untimely and seemingly insensitive behavior at the party?

Now, consider Jackson. Why would he go snooping through his professor's bedroom? Do they have a special relationship that his other friends don't know about? Does he have a weakness for expensive scotch? Did his professor ask him to go to her room and retrieve the bottle?

Finally, what led to Naomi's belief that the party was going to be a weird experience? What aspects of the party did she perceive as weird, exactly? Has she had similar experiences with these friends in the past?

This chapter considers what you know about other people and how you understand their behavior. In some ways, this chapter is a commentary on the epistemological foundations of interpersonal interaction and communication. Remember that epistemology is the study of knowledge, what we know, and how we come to know what we know. We interpret events every day, using our knowledge both to explain and to evaluate other people's actions. The focus on this chapter is on two theories that provide a systematic way for understanding why individuals behave as they do. These theories address broad interpretive frameworks and examine behaviors that we anticipate and expect of others. They also describe how we create meaning when we interact with people who violate our expectations.

The first theory, attribution theory, is a philosophy and practice that seeks to understand the causes of human behavior. When you consider why Amira, Jackson, Naomi, and Carlton behaved as they did, two broad explanations might occur to you. The first is that their actions reflect their personalities. This is called an *internal attribution* because it attributes their behavior to personal, internal qualities. The second is that something in the situation caused them to behave as they did. That type of explanation is called an *external attribution* because it locates the cause for behavior in the environment.

The second theory, expectancy violations theory, describes how people react when other people's behaviors surprise them. To illustrate, one of the authors (L.E.) conducted a study that examined how individuals responded to receiving unexpected attacks from others—an act known as "being blindsided." Blindsided experiences were described as those situations when a person is attacked seemingly "out of the blue." Each conflict story described an interaction in which expectations were violated; none of the participants in the study expected to be attacked or criticized by the other party. Expectancy violations theory helps us understand how people respond to that type of unexpected behavior. Both attribution theory and expectancy violations theory therefore aid our understanding of why individuals act in the ways they do.

ATTRIBUTION THEORY

Questions of human behavior, meaning, and communication have been the focus of much study and research since the 1950's. Attribution theory was developed as a *common-sense* approach to the social psychology of human interpersonal relations. Psychologist Fritz Heider based attribution theory on the following premises: 1) we humans are quite competent at understanding their interaction with others, 2) we have relatively sophisticated cognitive explanations for human behavior, and 3) we are good at explaining why others do what they do, based on intimate knowledge of the self and others and a strong understanding of social circumstances. Let's explore the details of attribution theory and consider how it helps us interpret social behaviors and make competent communicative choices.

INTELLECTUAL TRADITION OF ATTRIBUTION THEORY

Heider developed attribution theory in the mid- and late 1940's but articulated the theory in greatest detail in his 1958 book *The Psychology of Interpersonal Relations.*[1] Unlike emerging scientific approaches to the study of individual behavior and interpersonal relationships, which were strongly based on predictions and explorations of deeper psychological structures affecting perception, cognition, and behavior, Heider sought to develop an approach to interpersonal relations that focused on the individual's *perception* of the causes of human behavior. In Heider's language, he argued for the importance of *naïve psychology*, favoring the everyday person's interpretation and explanation of behavior over more formal scientific explanations. Thus, the intellectual tradition is strongly influenced by psychological theories and research in perception, social cognition (how an individual thinks about social events, social scenes, and social others), and social psychology. As a result, you might wonder what attribution theory can tell us about communication. The answer can, in part, be found in Heider's explanation and concern for language use and symbolism in interpersonal relations. Heider argued that language was a conceptual tool for perceiving and understanding one's own and other people's behaviors. Thus, communication as a symbolic and meaning-making activity is central to attributions about human behavior.

For Heider, the central problem or challenge in a *common-sense* theory of psychology was the perceptual relationship between one person (*p*) and another person (*o*). Heider explained the challenge this way:

> Obviously, the existence of the other person, *o*, as an object with not only physical and spatial properties, must be mediated in some way to the subject, that is perceived by *p*, if *o* is to feature in *p's* thinking, feelings, and actions. Likewise, if *p* is to influence *o*, he [sic] must create changes that in some way can be perceived by *o*....The nature of this perception, in particular the principles that underlie the coordination between the stimulus conditions outside the person and his [sic] experience or phenomenal representation of them, is the topic to which we will address ourselves here.[2]

In this quote, Heider highlighted the essential relationship between *p* and *o*, explaining that the perception and behavior of *p* and *o* are influenced by the character and content of the *social environment*.

The perceptual challenge described above can be further clarified by understanding the role of perception and the personal and environmental stimuli that influence human behavior. Perceptual processes play at least two distinct roles in human interaction.[3] The first process is **phenomenal perception,** which represents both the nature of the contact between people (who they are to each other, how long they interact, what they say) and the environment in which they communicate. The second process is **causal perception** or causal analysis, which encompasses the various stimuli to which persons choose to *focus their attention.* These two perceptual processes lead us to think about a phenomenon (behavior, action, situation) and the way humans assign cause to the event or experience.

A central question for each of us is: "What precisely do we notice in the environment with respect to other people?" We can identify at least two types of stimuli that are relevant to the attribution process. The **distal stimulus** is an object in the social environment that is "outside the person's skin,"[4] such as a car, a violin, or another person. Distal stimuli are properties of the environment that everyone can generally agree exist. In comparison, the **proximal stimulus** is anything that directly affects the sensory experiences of the person, such as the taste of an apple, the sound of a car stereo, or one's feelings of concern for someone else. Because proximal stimuli are unique to each person, we don't necessarily expect everyone in the environment to agree on their existence. These two types of perceptual stimuli are interconnected. Most of us don't distinguish between noticing objects in the environment and having sensory experiences of those objects. However, according to psychologist Miles Hewstone, "What is psychologically important is the proximal stimulus, the way the object *appears* [italics added] to the perceiver."[5]

The intellectual foundations of attribution theory reflect a psychology of interaction that focuses on common-sense perceptions and interpretations of the *causes* of human behavior. We assign causes to our own behavior as well as the behaviors we encounter in a variety of social environments. Since Heider's attribution theory was developed in the mid 1900's, numerous theorists—including Harold Kelley, Edward Jones, Miles Hewstone, and Bernard Weiner—have extended its ideas.[6] We will describe some of those extensions later in the chapter.

Attribution theory has been used by scholars in multiple disciplines, including communication. Before outlining the key principles and concepts in this theory, let's briefly explore its five key assumptions.

ASSUMPTIONS OF ATTRIBUTION THEORY

Heider believed that individuals are naturally curious about human relations and what happens on an everyday basis. This somewhat "ordinary" view of individual psychology challenged the more scientific approach to actual, rather than perceived, causes of behavior in interpersonal interaction. You may also notice some resonance with ideas from Mead and Burke (described in Chapter 4), especially those processes designed to elaborate on human meaning-making capabilities.

Assumption 1: Common-sense psychology is a guide for understanding how people interact with each other. With this assumption, Heider is commenting on the degree of knowledge we each possess about human behavior and the kinds of explanations about self and others that seem to make sense. Although the human psyche is more complex than we can observe at a surface level, Heider was intentionally concerned with "'surface' matters, the events that occur in everyday life on a *conscious level*, rather than with the unconscious processes studied by psycho-analysis in 'depth' psychology."[7] Thus, you do not need a degree in social psychology to assign causes to human behavior. Rather, Heider believed that you engage the attribution process as a part of normal, everyday interaction.

Assumption 2: Common-sense psychology is of value because it contains truths about human behavior. The truths identified by Heider are commentaries on the knowledge we possess about

ourselves and others. Psychologists and sociologists have long speculated on the "stocks" of psychological, cultural, and/or social knowledge individuals have,[8] and Heider is weighing in on this question:

> Though the full significance of man's [sic] relation to man
> [sic] may not be directly evident, the complexity of feelings
> and actions that can be understood at a glance is surpris-
> ingly great...."Intuitive" psychology may be remarkably pen-
> etrating and can go a long way toward the understanding of
> human behavior, whereas in the physical sciences such com-
> mon-sense knowledge is relatively primitive....*the ordinary per-*
> *son has a great and profound understanding of himself [sic] and*
> *of other people,* which though unformulated or only vaguely
> conceived, enables him [sic] to interact with others in more
> or less adaptive ways.[9] [italics added]

The truths are what each of us can glean from our interaction with
others, the meaning we derive from interaction, and the intuitive
process by which we come to understand why people behave as they
do.

▲ ▲ ▲

Let's Discuss

1. When it comes to understanding and explaining communication behavior, how reliable is "common sense"? Is naïve
   psychology superior to scientific psychology?
2. How can we identify the cause or causes of another person's
   communication behaviors? Can we ever really know why people act as they do?

▲ ▲ ▲

Assumption 3: Common-sense psychology is based in the naïve analysis of action. Heider was interested in examining how the actions of others—especially the action sequence (an individual who is trying to engage in some action, and/or has the ability to engage in action, and/or intends to engage in action)—are understood in interpersonal relations. The naïve analysis of action "deals with how observable behavior is linked to unobservable causes. It is a fundamental activity that enables individuals to create organization from chaos and relate continuously changing stimuli to stable properties of the environment."[10] Thus, this form of behavioral analysis leads to a critical distinction between internal and external causes of action, which we address more completely below in Key Concepts.

Assumption 4: Language serves humans well for symbolizing social and physical environments. An approach to human behavior that relies on intuitive knowledge and everyday experience should be linked to the language of the common person.

> The fact that we are able to *describe ourselves and other people in everyday language* means that it embodies much of what we have called naïve psychology. This language serves us well, for it has an infinite flexibility and contains a great number of general concepts that *symbolize* experiences with the physical and social environment.[11] [italics added]

Heider was indicating a need to study the systematic use of language or the *language of attribution* and was interested in how language helps us understand experience. The language system proposed was not based in scientific principles; rather, it reflected the meaning of words and the meaning of situations from the individual sensemaker's perspective.

Assumption 5: Common-sense psychology is best expressed in everyday language. Heider was interested in the words people use to explain what they do. For example, he pointed out that the words *give*, *take, receive,* and *keep* are all transitive verbs that refer to some type of action, but they are not equivalent in meaning. In a relationship between *p* and *o,* the meaning of these action verbs varies according to who causes what outcome and the direction of action. The meaning of *take,* for instance, is not readily obvious. When a person offers something you want, you might say that you will *take* the item. On the other hand, *take* might also imply *steal,* as if you decided to *take* a textbook from another student. We may also say that you *take* advantage of an opportunity that presents itself. As this example illustrates, the conditions under which you *take* can vary. Thus, the words we use affect the attributions we make about human interaction.

Heider also wanted us to consider how additional words lend precision to our explanations. For example, in our exploration of *take, give, receive,* and *keep,* we might further the word analysis by adding concepts such as *lend, borrow, lose, beg, relinquish,* and so forth. To *give* something freely is different than to *relinquish* something reluctantly or through coercion. Whereas a scientist might be concerned with the technical meaning of a word or concept, Heider focused on everyday words as a way to understand the reality that lies beyond them. In this case, that reality consists of the reasons people give for their own and others' behaviors.

Throughout *The Psychology of Interpersonal Relations,* Heider makes repeated references to both the individual/psychological and social/environmental influences of causal attributions. The five assumptions are guides for understanding Heider's basic commonsense orientation to human perception and causal explanation of behavior. Next, we outline the key concepts in attribution theory, which are drawn primarily from the work of Heider, Harold Kelley, and Edward Jones.

KEY CONCEPTS IN ATTRIBUTION THEORY

Attribution is generally defined as the causal inferences people make about why people behave as they do. Almost all accounts of attribution theory start by distinguishing between personal and situational attributions for behavior. This difference is referred to as the **person-situation distinction**.[12] The person attribution, also called an **internal attribution**, "ascribes the causes of behavior to personal dispositions, traits, abilities, and feelings" (Weiten).[13] In other words, it explains people's behavior as a product of their personality, disposition, or other personal characteristics. Imagine that your friend Anna was supposed to meet you for a movie last night but did not show up. You wonder what caused her to miss your connection. Internal attributions include forgetfulness, meanness, aloofness, lack of interest, or any other explanations that are based on your perception of Anna's fundamental characteristics, preferences, or traits.

On the other hand, the situation attribution, also called an **external attribution,** "ascribes the causes of behavior to situational demands and environmental constraints" (Weiten)."[14] External explanations for Anna's behavior include her being called in to work unexpectedly, having an auto accident on the way to the theater, or other situational constraints that prevented her from showing up.

Identifying an internal cause for behavior involves considering a number of possible frames, or **dispositional properties**, that are linked to the depth of knowledge we have about another person. According to Fritz Heider, "Dispositional properties are the *invariances* that make possible a more or less stable, predictable, and controllable world" [italics added].[15] Attribution theory assumes there is some regularity and stability to the phenomenal world of persons and objects. When you make an attribution about someone's behavior, you might consider the *motives, intentions, character,* and *sentiments* of the person. Thus, your analysis might start with questions about intention, such as "What did the person intend or want to accomplish with his or her actions?" and "What motivates individuals to act in particular ways?" When we know people well, we believe we understand what motivates their actions because we have a sense of "who they are." Answering these questions may determine whether you see someone's behavior as relatively *stable* or not.

However, knowledge about the stable disposition of others does not, by itself, determine whether we assign internal or external attributions. Examples of stable dispositional qualities can include such constructs as achievement and ability. Let's assume that Mary is a student who gets good grades in all her classes. You might determine that Mary's intelligence leads to her high grades. Intelligence is a relatively permanent psychological characteristic that Mary possesses. However, you might also consider the influences of other, possibly less permanent dispositional qualities that contribute to Mary's high grades, such as her *achievement* or *motivation*. Compared with intelligence, motivation might be influenced by both Mary's interest in the subject or assessment of the teacher's competence. In this example, Mary's intelligence remains stable while her motivation might vary significantly.

In contrast to internal explanations, Heider argued that **environmental effects,** or external factors, influence attribution processes. Let's assume that our good student Mary takes a class in chemistry that she loves, but at the end of the semester receives a C in the course. Assuming she is both intelligent and motivated (stable dispositional qualities), how do we explain her lower grade? Heider would suggest that a number of environmental conditions could influence the outcome. For instance, Mary's lack of success might be attributed to *task difficulty* (perhaps the professor made the assignments too difficult). Maybe the laboratory assignments conflicted with her work schedule, meaning that Mary did not have the same *opportunity* for a good grade that other students had. A third possibility is that Mary was simply *unlucky*. Attribution theory might lead us to consider any or all of these explanations for Mary's poor grade.

Although the person-situation distinction is critical to attribution theory, scholars have identified additional principles and key concepts as well. In the best-known elaboration of the theory, Harold

Kelley offered a set of rules or principles about the roles and social dynamics of causal behavior.[16] First, the **covariation principle** states, "An effect is attributed to one of its possible causes with which, over time, it covaries."[17] This suggests that, in social interaction, people make attributions at *successive points in time*. For example, if you have a roommate who goes out and parties every Friday night, you have multiple time points from which to make attributions about that behavior.

Second, the **discounting principle** argues that "The role of a given cause in producing a given effect is discounted if other plausible causes are also present."[18] When there are multiple ways to explain a specific behavior, in other words, the discounting principle suggests that we are less confident that the behavior is due to any *single* cause, internal or external. What if your roommate decides NOT to go out this Friday? You might determine that work schedule, a school project, new love interest, illness, or bad mood are all possible reasons. Thus, you will discount any single cause as the reason for the change in your roommate's behavior.

Third, the **augmentation principle** holds that "When a given behavior occurs in spite of pressure against it, we feel more certain that it reveals something about the person."[19] For example, you have probably heard news stories about people who behave in altruistic ways, such as by running into a burning building to save others without any regard for their own personal safety. According to the augmentation principle, you are likely to believe that such actions reflect their character. Thus, you would probably make internal attributions for their behavior—for instance, they act in selfless ways because they are good, altruistic people.

When we're trying to figure out the reason behind someone's behavior, Kelley argued that we ask ourselves three critical questions. First, we ask about **consensus**: is the behavior unique to this person (low consensus), or do many others do it as well (high consensus)?[20] Consensus essentially frames our expectancies for other people.[21] That is, it causes us to question whether a given behavior is in line with how we expect most people to behave or is idiosyncratic to the person. Second, we ask about **distinctiveness:** how normal is this behavior in this situation? Behaviors of low distinctiveness are common and expected, given the situation. A highly distinct behavior is one we do not normally expect in that situation. Finally, we ask about **consistency:** how typical is this behavior for this person? If the action is common for the person, then it has high consistency; if the person rarely behaves in that way, then the action is low in consistency.[22]

These three questions are interdependent, meaning that our answer to each question affects our answers to the others. The following hypothetical vignette by psychologist Edward Jones nicely illustrates the interconnectedness of these three constructs in attribution assessments.

Joan tells us that she just read a wonderful book called *The Moviegoer,* by Walker Percy. Shortly thereafter, we see a copy in a bookstore and try to decide whether we should buy it. A relevant question is whether Joan's response is simply an example of her idiosyncratic taste or her predilection to praise everything she's read, or whether it was specifically occasioned by the excellence of the book in question. In order to decide whether it is Joan (the person [dispositional attribution]) or the book (the entity [external attribution]) we might review in our minds Joan's comments about other books. These comments might be high in *distinctiveness*—this is the only book we have ever heard her praise—or low in *distinctiveness*—she is always gushing over everything she reads. We might also have checked with others who may have read the book. Joan's comments may reflect high *consensus* (many others agree with her) or a lack thereof [low consensus]. If Joan's praise of the book is high in both distinctiveness and consensus, we should be well on the way toward an entity attribution: We should be pretty confident that *The Moviegoer* is indeed a good book. This would especially be the case if the next time we saw Joan she again praised the book, or if she also praised the movie adaptation because of its fidelity to the book. We would have evidence of *consistency* over time and over modality.[23]

This vignette not only exemplifies the three key questions but also illustrates some additional features of Kelley's model. In this case, the attribution process starts with a *judgment* by the perceiver, which is an attempt to understand the book in question. The perceiver's response could range from developing an independent opinion about the book to experiencing an emotional reaction. Finally, it is entirely possible that attributions can be made about *both* the person and the book. For example, the perceiver may determine that Joan is an indiscriminate book lover, but everyone else likes *The Moviegoer*, too.[24] Such an attribution identifies both personal and environmental causes.

▲ ▲ ▲

Consider This
Social psychologist Miles Hewstone has raised serious questions about the amount of time and energy people put into attribution processes. *How much thinking does the average person do when trying to explain behavior?*[25] An underlying assumption of attribution theory is that we are rational information processors, but that our processing is subject to limitations that make our assessments fallible. **Questions to consider**: How much time and energy do you invest in your attributions about other people's behaviors? Suppose you sought out more information about a person or situation, or spent more time

considering alternative explanations for any given behavior. Would doing so change the attributions you make? Why or why not?

▲   ▲   ▲

BIASES AND ERRORS IN ATTRIBUTION PROCESSES

Most of us act in ways we believe are beneficial to who we are and what we want. This process is called the **egocentric bias**. According to Edward Jones, we view the world from our own perspective and have a limited ability to understand the world from other points of view.[26] Thus, we have sensitivity to those events or experiences that are relevant to our personal development and welfare, and we engage in wishful thinking about who we are.[27] In this section we briefly outline two biases, the self-reference bias and the self-serving bias, as well as a fundamental challenge in attribution assessments, known as the fundamental attribution error. All three types of biases below are elaborations of the general principle of the egocentric bias.

First, the **self-reference bias** is our tendency to see ourselves as the focus of other people's behaviors.[28] Psychologists Keith Davis and Edward Jones introduced the concept of *hedonic relevance* to explain those situations that make us feel better or worse about who we are.[29] Their argument is that we tend interpret experiences that make use feel better or worse as *intentional acts*. That is, we assume that people behave in ways that either help us or hurt us. For example, let's assume that a close friend and you are having a conversation but the friend suddenly turns around and walks away. There might be any number of reasons for this change in behavior, but hedonic relevance suggests that you will take your friend's behavior personally, as an intentional act meant to hurt or disrespect you. This bias reflects our tendency to see the world from our own point of view.

Second, the **self-serving bias** is the idea that we form attributions for our own behavior that paint us in the most positive light possible[30]

To support our self-esteem, we like to take credit for what we do well but distance ourselves from our failures. Thus, when Andrew performs well on an assignment, he attributes his success to his hard work. When he performs poorly, however, he claims that the assignment was too hard or the professor was unreasonable. In Andrew's mind, his successes are deserved but his failures are not his fault.[31]

The self-reference and self-serving biases both relate to attributions we make for our own behaviors. In contrast, the **fundamental attribution error** clouds our judgments about other people's actions. Based on research from social psychologist Lee Ross in the 1970s, the fundamental attribution error says we tend to emphasize the internal causes of behavior at the expense of possible external or situational causes.[32] As an example, consider what you think when another driver cuts you off in traffic. Most of us wouldn't spend time trying to figure out what caused that behavior (Is the driver late for an important business appointment or distracted by a car full of noisy children?). Instead, we'd say "What a jerk!" thereby attributing the driver's behavior to his or her personality.

Psychologist Edward Jones believes the fundamental attribution error is part of what he calls **correspondence bias,** which is the tendency to make inferences about someone's personality from behaviors that may have situational causes. According to Jones, "Observers are handicapped in their attempt to perceive the situation from the actor's point of view. Although people are intellectually aware that situations influence and in some cases determine behavior, there is much more perceptual immediacy to the connection between act and actor."[33] The correspondence bias reminds us that we have a limited ability to understand the situational factors that cause behavior. Even if we recognize situational influences, we are still likely to see others as ultimately responsible for their action, and assign internal, dispositional causes to their behavior.

Now that we understand its key concepts, let's identify and describe some of the notable claims and findings of attribution theory.

RESEARCH IN ATTRIBUTION THEORY

Research using attribution theory has been instrumental in linking behavioral explanations to a number of interpersonal and social challenges. We peruse the findings of that research in this section.

Researchers have used attribution theory to study a number of phenomena related to social psychology and human action. For example, Bernard Weiner and colleagues have explored the ways in which people explain their successes and failures.[34] According to their research, individuals generally attribute their successes to their abilities and efforts, but explain their failures as the result of task difficulty or bad luck. Questions that arise from these investigations include the degree or extent to which individuals have free choice and control over their social environments, as well as an exploration of achievement, motivation, persistence, and assessments of risk. For example, if you believe in free will, you will tend to believe that your intentions and actions are more within your control than if you believe you are subject to social forces outside your control. The more strongly you believe in free will, the more likely you will take responsibility for your successes and failures. Obviously there are numerous factors that moderate the level of responsibility individuals take for their successes and failures.

Another interesting body of research from the field of developmental social psychology explores attributions about action and emotion.[35] This research finds that people make an important distinction between action and emotion. Specifically, action is regarded as purposeful, intentional, and under our control, whereas emotion is seen as reactive, biological, and less subject to willful control. In fact, Lalljee, Watson, and White found that across age groups in children, "Actions are explained primarily in terms of goals and in terms of personal characteristics, while emotions are explained in terms of the current situation or in terms of past events."[36] The authors noted that 5-year-old children clearly differentiate goal-based attributions from emotion-based attributions, but cautioned that the relationship between action-based and emotion-based attributions is complex. For our purposes, it is somewhat straightforward to understand how emotions like fear and anger can be driven by situations outside our control. For example, if you are out late at night walking alone and a stranger starts running toward you—fear is an understandable response that occurs from the perceived threat from the stranger. However, we might also consider the degree to which the emotional response of happiness occurs because of the fulfillment of a goal (intentional act) or because of a pleasant surprise from a friend or loved one (situational event).

Communication scholars have also used attribution theory to explore such issues as the use of profanity during conflict,[37] attributional support and recipient emotions,[38] and perceptual and attributional challenges for Alzheimer family member caregivers.[39] Kory Floyd (one of our authors) and colleagues studied mutual attributions for nonverbal behaviors in romantic couples, finding that: a) couples were more likely to notice negative behaviors than positive behaviors, b) relational satisfaction influenced the likelihood that partners would notice positive behaviors, and c) individuals and their partners often explained the individual's behaviors differently. The authors noted, "Particularly for males, there was a strong tendency to view one's own negative behaviors as more external, specific, uncontrollable, and unintentional, and due less to personal responsibility than their partners viewed their behavior."[40]

▲ ▲ ▲

Let's Discuss

1. In what ways is your own behavior affected by a self-serving bias?
2. In close relationships, do you think a tendency to notice negative behaviors more than positive behaviors is common?

If so, why? What effects might that have on the quality of a relationship?

▲ ▲ ▲

In general, research supports the distinction between internal and external causes for behavior, but with some variation depending on study focus, methodology, and contextual factors. For students wanting to read a broad range of attribution research applications we recommend the book *Attributions in Action*.[41] The authors not only provide a step-by-step guide for researching attribution theory, but identify key research areas of interest, including attributions in clinical settings (depression, distressed adult relationships, therapeutic intervention, and clinical interviews), attributions in organizations, and attributions in consumer beliefs and behaviors.

▲ ▲ ▲

Test Your Understanding
Each of you has had experiences in classrooms that can be used to analyze attribution processes. Working in groups of 4 to 6 students, your first task is to think about an interaction with a professor in a classroom (*not* your communication theory instructor!) in which some behavior resulted in either a positive or negative assessment. For example, you your professor may have given you a grade you found unfair or assigned a paper that was not in the syllabus. You may also have seen your professor communicate in ways that were unusual or surprising. Once you have a situation in mind, write down the attributions you made about the professor's behavior. Did you make an internal or external attribution? Did you see the behavior as consistent and relatively stable or as an "anomaly"? Might you have even called the professor "crazy?" Next, ask each student to share his or her individual experience and attributions with the

rest of the group. Finally, as a group, discuss what possible biases might have affected your assessments. How did you evaluate the professor's explanation for his or her behavior (if an explanation was given)? What do you think you have learned about attribution processes from this discussion? Do you think your future attributions may change as a result of your knowledge about attribution theory? Have you been subject to attribution biases in your assessment of your own and others' behaviors?

▲   ▲   ▲

EXPECTANCY VIOLATIONS THEORY

When one of the authors (Larry) lived in Santa Fe, New Mexico, his neighbor was unhappy about the RV he had parked in his driveway for about 6 weeks one summer. The local homeowners' association allowed RVs in the development, but the neighbor complained to other neighbors that the RV created an imbalance in her property's feng shui. Instead of approaching Larry or his wife directly, she hired someone to erect four 10-foot posts sporting Buddhist prayer flags on Larry's property, even after the RV had been removed. As you might image, Larry and his wife were shocked that their neighbor had engaged in this violation of expectations about privacy and personal property rights. After the homeowners' association compliance officer spoke with the neighbor, she claimed that the prayer flags were on her property but said she would hire a surveyor to be sure. Although Larry never confronted his neighbor directly, the poles and flags were removed a few days later.

As this story illustrates, both Larry and his neighbor had expectations about acceptable and unacceptable neighborhood behaviors. The neighbor apparently expected that her view should be unobstructed, and Larry expected that neighbors should not intrude on his property. Just as with neighborly behaviors, we have expectations for people's communication behaviors. The second theory in this chapter, expectancy violations theory (EVT), was developed by communication scholar Judee Burgoon as a way to explain what happens when people communicate in ways that violate expectations for normative social behavior.[42] Let's see what this means for the analysis of everyday communication behaviors.

INTELLECTUAL TRADITION OF EXPECTANCY VIOLATIONS THEORY

The original version of this theory was called **nonverbal expectancy violations theory** because it focused on the expectations people have about nonverbal behaviors such as eye gaze and physical proximity (distance). The theory was later modified to include expectations and violations of both *verbal* and *nonverbal communication.* The intellectual history of this theory is grounded in a number of philosophies and theories, including a brief nod to attribution theory. Below we briefly examine these influences on the development of EVT.

EVT is an empirical model that seeks to *explain* and *predict* violations and confirmations of expectancies in interpersonal relationships.[43] In many ways, the theory is a commentary on how individuals anticipate the interpersonal behaviors of others, and what happens when those behaviors are unexpected. As a basic premise, EVT assumes that individuals have clear ideas about social rules and norms that help determine the kinds of behaviors that are appropriate or inappropriate, or acceptable and unacceptable. Thus, social norms are based, in part, on a set of common understandings and rules about interpersonal interaction. Burgoon argued that *expectancies* (anticipation of others' behaviors) "derived from data become the foundation for further inferentially based expectancies through such *attributional processes* [italics added] as correspondence bias."[44] That is, we seek some understanding of the relationship between act and actor in social settings.

Another important influence on EVT was the theoretical work of Irving Goffman, and in particular, his notion of framing devices.[45]

A *frame* is a particular way of making sense of a social situation and placing that understanding into some type of organizing scheme. According to EVT, "People plan and adapt their own communication according to the kind of encounter and communication style they anticipate from another actor. At the same time, expectancies serve as perceptual filters, significantly influencing how social information is processed."[46] Thus, your expectations for the behavior of others are framed within social norms, rules, and understandings. EVT proposes a broad interpersonal/social frame as a backdrop against which violations of our expectations for behavior occur. Finally, besides drawing from social psychology (attribution theory, social meaning theory,[47] and Goffman's social theory[48]), EVT incorporates ideas about human arousal, information processing, and affective states from cognitive psychology and psychophysiology. EVT helps us understand situations in which behavior elicits responses that we notice—responses that are out of the ordinary and that activate cognitive processing.

ASSUMPTIONS OF EXPECTANCY VIOLATIONS THEORY

As an overview, EVT posits that we have expectations about the verbal and nonverbal behavior of other people. When another person violates one of our expectations, a change in our cognitive/emotional state is triggered (called an *arousal response*), which causes us to focus attention on the communication behaviors of the other party. Whether we view the violation as positive or negative depends on a host of factors, including the nature of the behavior itself, our feelings about the communicator, and our evaluations of the situation in which the violation occurred. These assessments lead us to assign a **valence** to the violation—that is, to see the violation as positive or negative. According to EVT, the valence we assign influences our subsequent communication acts.[48] Before examining each of the key concepts in this process, we first examine key assumptions of the theory.

Assumption 1: According to Burgoon and Hale, "in interpersonal encounters, interactants develop expectancies and preferences about the nonverbal [and verbal] behavior of others."[50] The source of our expectations may be cognitive, affective, and or behavioral. Psychologist George Kelly argued that the natural state of the person is one of anticipation, and that motivation is an inner characteristic that applies to all individuals—in other words, we are always in *movement*.[51] Thus, scholars have long examined individual and socio-cultural explanations for our anticipations and expectations of human communication and interaction.

Assumption 2: Burgoon and Hale explained that "if one's interaction partner conforms to expectancies, the expectancies themselves and the nonverbal behaviors they govern should operate largely out of awareness."[52] Thus, when people act as we expect them to, we don't pay much attention to their behavior. Most of the time, people do behave in expected, appropriate ways, so their behavior doesn't stand out to us.

Assumption 3: As Burgoon and Hale described, "There are circumstances under which the violations of social norms and expectations may be a superior strategy to conformity."[53] EVT challenges the conventional wisdom that it's always best to behave in expected ways. Violations of expectations for social behavior are often viewed negatively, but they can also produce positive effects. For instance, having someone stand closer to you than expected might make you uncomfortable—but if the person is especially attractive, you might enjoy the proximity. In fact, you may actually *prefer* that he or she stand unusually close to you, rather than maintaining a normal distance. In that situation, the person has produced a more positive outcome by violating your expectations than by conforming to them.

KEY CONCEPTS IN EXPECTANCY VIOLATIONS THEORY

Expectancy. An **expectancy** is an enduring or regularized pattern of behavior. Similar to a basic concepts of generalized and particularized others (See Symbolic Interactionism, chapter 4), EVT identifies both *general expectancies,* those patterns of communication that characterize a group or community, and *specific expectancies,* those patterns or communicative qualities that characterize a particular person. Social norms and rules largely determine our general expectancies. We rely on our general expectancies especially when we don't know the people we are communicating with. On the contrary, our specific expectancies are based on our knowledge of a particular person, his or her communication behaviors and patterns, and his or her unique interaction style. We rely more on our specific expectancies when interacting with friends, co-workers, relatives, and others we know well.

We can therefore say that our expectancies are influenced by three sets of factors: a) *communicator characteristics*, which include demographic factors (age, sex, ethnicity), unique personality traits, and communication styles; b) *relationship factors*, such as attraction, similarity, familiarity, relative status, and mutual support; and, c) *context characteristics*, such as the degree of privacy, formality, and task orientation in the situation. Judee Burgoon argued that, "The confluence of all these factors dictates the expectancies in a given encounter."[54] EVT also asserts that the experience of expectancy violations is cross-cultural, even though the content of some expectancies is unique to particular cultures.

Expectancy violations and arousal. Expectancy violations occur when people act in unanticipated ways. According to Burgoon, noticing a violation produces **arousal,** an increase in physical energy and attention. When a violation occurs, individuals engage in a two-step process of *interpreting* the meaning of the violation and *evaluating* its desirability. This process results in an assessment of the violation as either positive or negative. EVT predicts that two factors, in particular, influence the positivity of a violation: communicator reward valence and violation valence.

Communicator reward valence. **Communicator reward valence** is the reward value of the person who commits the violation—in other words, the extent to which that person is perceived as desirable to interact with. When the meaning of a violation (such as a personal space violation) is not immediately clear, EVT predicts that we consider the reward valence of the person who committed it. As Burgoon explained, many factors determine the reward valence of an individual:

> *Reward* is a function of all those static and initial, or pre-interactional, communicator and relationship characteristics (such as gender, personality, physical attractiveness, reputation, status, and anticipated future interaction) and all those derived, interactional behaviors (such as possessing tangible rewards, having an amusing communication style, or giving positive feedback) that cause the communicator to be perceived, on balance, as someone with whom it is *desirable* to interact.[55] [italics added]

EVT provides that we make more favorable evaluations of violations committed by high-reward communicators than by low-reward communicators. Therefore, the source of the violation is one important factor in our overall assessment of a violation's positivity.

Violation valence. We don't consider the reward value of only the communicator, however. We also determine the **violation valence,** or the extent to which we perceive the unexpected behavior itself to be positive or negative. Some behaviors are likely to be judged negatively regardless of who does them. For instance, most people wouldn't enjoy being yelled at and embarrassed in front of their peers, no matter how rewarding the person who did the yelling. Other behaviors could be evaluated positively or negatively, depending on the circumstances. An unexpected hug from a friend may feel good when we're feeling lonely but bad when we're suffering a sunburn. We would assign a positive valence to the violating behavior (a hug) in the former situation but a negative valence in the latter.

▲ ▲ ▲

Theory into Practice

Many empirical tests of EVT have focused on nonverbal behaviors and the extent to which different types of nonverbal actions are considered violations. For example, multiple studies indicate that when a highly regarded male engages in continuous eye contact, the behavior is interpreted as dominant, but when a highly regarded female exhibits the same level of eye gaze, the act is viewed as submissive.[56] Similarly, when an attractive same-sex partner has an open and relaxed body posture, his or her behavior is considered dominant, but that posture is considered submissive with an unattractive same-sex partner. The same holds true for assessments of an "arm around the waist"; the more attractive the partner, the more likely his or her behavior is viewed as dominant. Various forms of touch are also evaluated differently depending on the attractiveness of the communicator *and* his or her perceived status.

Working in groups of three to four students, discuss why you think these kinds of differences exist? What is the role of communicator reward value in these findings? Ask each individual in the group to identify situations in which touch (or other nonverbal behaviors) is a positive violation and situations when touch is a negative violation. In your discussion, elaborate on the influences of context, relationship, social norms, and forms of touch.

▲ ▲ ▲

CLAIMS OF EXPECTANCY VIOLATIONS THEORY

EVT has been extensively tested through empirical studies and continues to provide insight into interpersonal interaction. In this section we identify and discuss four claims that are relevant to our continued discussion of verbal and nonverbal behavior. Each claim is quoted verbatim from a 1998 paper by Judee Burgoon and Jerold Hale.

Claim 1: "Violations are arousing and distracting."[57] Central to EVT is the claim that violations result in arousal, distracting us from our normal routines. We typically experience cognitive arousal first, by recognizing that something in the environment merits our attention, and then experience physiological arousal through increases in heart rate, breathing rate, pupil dilation, perspiration, and stress hormones.[58]

Claim 2: "Interactants develop expectations about the distancing and immediacy behavior of others."[59] When interacting with others, most of us prefer intermediate levels of conversational distance, eye gaze, and sensory involvement rather than very high or very low levels.[60] Because we usually anticipate pleasant interaction (unless we have a reason not to), these preferences become our expectations when we interact with other people. Therefore, when people enact very high or very low distance, gaze, or involvement, our expectations are violated. Although early tests of this idea focused on interaction in the laboratory, more current studies have examined violations in numerous contexts, including online environments. For example, communicating on Facebook comes with its own set of social norms and expectations. In one study, McLaughlin and Vitak suggested that, "norm violations can occur based on simply annoying behaviors or posts that can negatively impact an individual's self-presentation goals."[61] That study found that most expectancy violations on Facebook were positive and occurred between positively valenced individuals. For negatively valenced individuals, the victim of the violation usually either ignored the violator or removed that person from his or her account.

Claim 3: "Communicator behaviors and characteristics that contribute to interpersonal rewards mediate communication outcomes."[62] Behaviors and characteristics we generally find rewarding in others include physical attractiveness, smiling, head nodding, positive and negative feedback, competence, attitudinal similarity, and wealth.[63] According to EVT, these and similar features influence our assessments of an expectancy violation. For example, one study focused on swearing in work settings examined multiple factors that might influence people's evaluations. These included the sex and status of the speaker, the formality of the situation, and the content of the verbal message.[64] Results indicated that swearing was more unexpected in formal settings than at social gatherings, and that some types of expressions were considered more unexpected than others (e.g., the F-word, compared with "that sucks"). Interestingly, the authors did not find differences in speaker sex or status, speculating that over time, social expectations for sex based differences may have changed.

▲   ▲   ▲

Let's Discuss

1. What does it mean to say that a behavior is "expected"? Does it mean you think the behavior *will happen,* or does it mean you think the behavior *should happen?*

2. In your own interactions with people, what leads you to consider someone a high-reward communicator? How about a low-reward communicator? In what ways do you interact with high- and low-reward communicators differently?

▲   ▲   ▲

Claim 4: Communicator reward valence moderates assessments of positive and negative violation valence. Not surprisingly, how we think about others influences the way we feel when they violate our expectations. As noted above, for instance, we generally dislike it when people violate our expectations for personal space—but when the violator is highly rewarding, we often *prefer* that he or she violate our personal space. Non-rewarding communicators, however, are judged most positively when they conform to expectations for personal space.[65] In a recent study of computer-mediated communication, researchers examined the amount of time it takes people to respond to e-mail messages. In the study, participants expected rewarding communicators to reply to messages within one day. When rewarding communicators took two weeks to respond—or never responded—their behavior violated expectations. On the contrary, participants showed no preference for response times from non-rewarding communicators. Apparently, when it comes to the timing of e-mail responses, our expectations are strongly affected by the respondent's reward level.

EVT provides a strong theoretically driven framework for exploring violations of individual expectations and social norms. The application of EVT has expanded to include numerous topics of interest to students and scholars in communication. For example, interpersonal relationship scholars have examined expectancy violations in the areas of forgiveness and forgiving in dating relationship,[66] attributions of deception,[67] and responses to hurtful events.[68] Another valuable program of research applies EVT in educational settings. For example, one study examined how violations of instructor communication relate to student motivation and learning.[69] The author assessed perceptions of instructor verbal and nonverbal immediacy behaviors, clarity in communication, and affinity-seeking behaviors. According to the results, violations of clarity were negatively valenced, and students received less classroom guidance and explanation than desired. The findings also indicated that when instructors engaged in more affinity-seeking behavior than desired, students were less motivated and less able to learn.

Expectancy violations theory is an excellent example of an empirically testable theory (see chapter 3). It provides insight into social norms and into the communication behaviors that violate or challenge those norms. As a student of communication, you should be acutely aware of how communication theories raise questions about interaction, meaning, and understanding in your everyday life. This chapter provides an important summary for thinking about both the routine and taken-for-granted ways of communicating with others. It also highlights the value of nonverbal communication. Most communication theories are based on symbolic or verbal communication; EVT is a reminder that interpretations of communication behavior involve the interplay between nonverbal, contextually driven interaction and verbal behavior.

SUMMARY AND CONCLUSION

In this chapter, we discussed two theories that focus on the explanation for the causes of communicative behavior. These theories seek to examine *why* we do what we do and to predict the cognitive and behavioral responses to surprising and unexpected behavior and events. Attribution theory and expectancy violations theory are both commentaries on the intersection between cognition and communication that help focus our attention on processes that are often unconscious or routine. Considering the intellectual history of each theory, take note of the importance of social meaning, social context, and the role of communication in meaning creation and evaluation. Consider that both theories reflect how communication can create connection and separation simultaneously. Positive assessments of other people and their motives and intentions reinforce the value of our relationships. Negative experiences and assessments, although potentially painful and difficult, can also reinforce our uniqueness and difference from others, an important identity function.

FOR FURTHER DISCUSSION

Think about two memorable conflicts you have had with other people over the past few weeks, months, or years. What was memorable about the conflict? How do you explain the communicative choices that you and the other person made during the interaction? Working in groups of 3 to 5 people, analyze how attribution theory might be used to evaluate conflict behavior. What kinds of attributions were made about your own and the other party's role in the conflict? Do you think you or the other party engaged in faulty attribution processes? If so, did that influence your future interactions? Consider also whether or not the conflict was exacerbated by violations of expectations. To what extent do you think conflicts are created by faulty attributions or reflected in unresolved violation of expectations? Finally, engage in a dialogue with group members about how an analysis of conflict and these two theories might lead to more competent communication for future interpersonal interactions.

ATTRIBUTION THEORY

1. Do you agree with Fritz Heider that people are generally very good at understanding human behavior? Why or why not? Do you think attribution theory helps explain communication behaviors? Explain.
2. To what extent do you think people oversimplify attributions as either internal (dispositional) or external (situational)? How often do you think communication is influenced by *both* internal *and* external forces? Describe an instance when

you have explained someone's behavior by referencing both internal and external factors.

3. Attribution theories have identified the fundamental attribution error as a significant limitation in assessments of human behavior. What is the fundamental attribution error, and how do you think people can reduce their chance of committing it?

EXPECTANCY VIOLATIONS THEORY

1. EVT asserts that we often evaluate expectancy violations positively when the other person is considered high in reward valence. What does it mean to say that communicators have a high or low reward valence? What factors influence the reward valence of an individual?

2. Explain the role of cognitive arousal in EVT. What is arousal, and how does it influence our communication with other people? Why is the concept of arousal so central to EVT?

3. EVT is based, in part, on human attributional processes. What similarities and differences do you see between EVT and attribution theory?

KEY TERMS

Arousal

Attribution

Augmentation principle

Causal perception

Communicator reward valence

Consensus

Consistency

Correspondence bias

Covariation principle

Discounting principle

Dispositional properties

Distal stimulus

Distinctiveness

Environmental effects

Expectancy

Expectancy violations

External attribution

Fundamental attribution error

Internal attribution

Nonverbal expectancy violations theory

Person-situation distinction

Phenomenal perception

Proximal stimulus

Self-reference bias

Self-serving bias

Valence

Violation valence

7

DISCOURSE AND CHANGE

HOW CAN LANGUAGE CONTRIBUTE TO SOCIAL CHANGE?

THINK ABOUT A time when something in your life changed, in either a minor or major way. What do you think "triggered" that change? To what extent was it a result of conversations you had with other people, something you read, or ideas that you have been thinking about? Change is a fact of life not only for individuals but also for groups, organizations, and societies. This chapter describes the role of communication and discourse in personal, group, organizational, and social change. **Discourse** is considered *language in use*—that is, the way people talk and use texts (such as published books or the Internet) in social interaction.[1]

Specifically, this chapter explores three theories that address different dimensions of change, discourse, and communication in context. In *structuration theory* (ST), Anthony Giddens advances the idea that communication behaviors and social practices help produce and reproduce organizational structures and systems over time. A modified version of ST, called *adaptive structuration theory*, applies to group decision-making processes. In *diffusion of innovations theory* (DI), Everett Rogers identifies the role of persuasion and communication in people's decisions to adopt new innovations. The diffusion or adoption of new ideas, new technologies, and new practices reflects innovations that change how a person engages with the social world. Finally, in *communication accommodation theory* (CAT), Howard Giles explores how people use communication to increase or decrease their connectedness to others. Each of these three theories emphasizes discourse and change in different ways, but all of these theories are concerned with the role of communication in the development of change in society.

STRUCTURATION THEORY/ADAPTIVE STRUCTURATION THEORY

British theorist Anthony Giddens developed **structuration theory** (ST) as a way to understand how *practical* and *discursive* practices help people produce and reproduce organizational structures and systems over time. Giddens was concerned about the relationship between influential actors and social systems, and the extent to which their discourse behaviors affect social system change. Communication scholar Marshall Scott Poole and business professor Geraldine DeSanctis adapted Giddens's theory to study group dynamics and the use of Group Decision Support Systems (GDSS). Poole and DeSanctis called their theory **adaptive structuration theory** (AST). A basic assumption in AST is that specific communication practices organize group processes related to both group tasks and social systems.[2] Below we elaborate on the historical influences, assumptions, and key concepts of ST, and later identify the role of AST in research in group decision processes. As you read about ST, notice the interplay between the *knowledgeable actor* and the production and reproduction of the social systems, as well as the relationship between communicative actions and the continuation (or discontinuation) of social, organizational, and institutional systems.

INTELLECTUAL TRADITION OF STRUCTURATION THEORY

Through the 1960's and 1970's, Giddens argued that social theory privileged organizational system and structural analysis, while paying less attention to how individual actors affected social systems. Individuals were viewed as pawns of larger social system forces and therefore were not considered instrumental in organizational change. Giddens claimed that social theory lacked a clear and appropriate "theory of the actor" that would account for the knowledge and influence that actors bring to social circumstances. In contrast, both American and British philosophers had articulated a well-developed *philosophy of action* addressing reasons, purposes, and motives for action, but had not paid much attention to institutional analysis, power, or social change. ST was intended to address the limitations of social theory by elaborating on the important role of individuals within systems, and to addresses the limitations of action philosophies by developing a clear model for analyzing institutions, change, and power. ST has its historical roots in social theory, hermeneutics (sometimes referred to as interpretive sociology), and structuralism/functionalism.

Although structuralism and functionalism were dominant social theories during the early years of Giddens's focus on structuration processes, he was quick to critique *and* embrace ideas from these and other theoretical perspectives, including Karl Marx's theory of societal evolution and social class, Ferdinand de Saussure's structural linguistics, Talcott Parsons's functional theory, Claude Lévi-Strauss's structural anthropology, Ludwig Wittgenstein's philosophy of discourse and language, and Martin Heidegger's philosophy of being and time. Giddens's goal was to create a theory of action that included a clear explanation of human agency and recognized the importance of situating action in time and space. Giddens defined **human agency** as the *continuous flow of conduct*—that is, how individuals act in social circumstances over time. Likewise, he defined **action**—that is, human behavior—as a "stream of actual or contemplated causal interventions of corporeal beings in the ongoing process of events-in-the-world."[3]

Moreover, Giddens wanted to emphasize that an understanding of social systems cannot be achieved with "snapshot" assessments of a system at *a given point in time*. A thorough understanding of organizational systems and structures needs to consider the situational and contextual factors that influence organizing structures and systems *over time*. According to Giddens, "to study the structuration of social systems is to study the conditions governing their continuity, change or dissolution."[4] Let's now turn our attention to key assumptions in ST.

Assumptions of Structuration Theory

Although Giddens himself did not identify formal assumptions of ST, it is clear from his work that his theory is strongly grounded in beliefs about how people and institutions collide in social development. The four assumptions elaborated below are essential in framing how he understood both a philosophy of action and a philosophy of social institutions.

Assumption 1: Every person has a great deal of knowledge about the conditions (practices and actions) that reproduce society.[5] Unlike social theories that frame the actor as a socially unaware, Giddens believed that each of us has a great deal of knowledge in the production and reproduction of social systems. These *stocks of knowledge* are the source of the motivations and reasons for our actions. Giddens thought of individuals as active and influential agents in social conduct, but he recognized that that are also constrained by the systems they inhabit. For example, consider what you know about your college or university. You probably have knowledge about enrollment practices, department curricula, social clubs, student services, and so on. Gidden's assumes that we are not social dupes or powerless in the face of social forces that influence our behavior; individuals as active and influential agents in social conduct, but with a recognition that we are also simultaneously constrained by the systems we inhabit.

Assumption 2: All people have some degree of discursive penetration (understanding about the language and practices) of the systems to which they contribute.[6] *Discursive penetration*, defined as the knowledge individuals have and are able to express through language of social systems, is one of three forms of knowledge or consciousness that social agents possess. The second type of knowledge that has an influence on actor practices comes from the *unconscious*. Although Giddens does not elaborate on unconscious processes, he is clearly referencing the significant theoretical works of psychiatrist Sigmund Freud and others.[7] The third type of knowledge is called *practical consciousness*, which Giddens defined as "tacit knowledge" that is skillfully applied by people in their everyday social conduct, but which they are not able to explain through language.[8] Tacit knowledge is also referred to as practical knowledge or consciousness and involves those things you know how to do, but would have difficulty explaining to others. For example, can you verbally explain how to ride a bicycle? The ability to ride a bicycle involves practical knowledge, but the ability to *explain how to ride* one is discursive knowledge. Discursive consciousness or knowledge is important because it is through discourse that we give *accounts* of our practices and actions. In other words, we justify what we do through our explanations.[9]

Assumption 3: However fast social change occurs, social traditions and routine practices of institutions must be recognized as influential on long-term social processes.[10] Two features of this assumption are important. First, the social reproduction of organizations and institutions involves the interplay of stability and change. Second, social development over time is influenced by the strong traditions of social life. That is, institutional traditions are relatively enduring or "sedimented" into social structure. This assumption runs contrary to structuralism (which asks about how parts are related to wholes) and functionalism (which asks about how systems function).

Assumption 4: Any discussion about social or organizational reproduction must account for time and space.[11] Giddens believed that both structuralism and functionalism largely ignored the question of how systems and structures are reproduced *through time.* Accordingly, he argued that "there are three intersecting planes of temporality involved in every moment of social reproduction."[12] The first element of time, called the "temporality of immediate experience," focuses on the ongoing flow of *daily life activity.* The second element of time is the life-cycle of the group or organization. This idea is that each organism (including a group or organization) has a natural life cycle that includes its birth, development, maturation, and death. The third element of time is referred to as the *longue duree,* or long-term understanding of structures and systems in institutions. Giddens argued that all three are interrelated and that even the most mundane conversations can affect the long duration (survival and ongoing development) of institutions. The four assumptions identified here are central to Giddens's critique of social theory and development of ST, but an elaboration of key concepts is necessary for a fuller understanding of the theory.

KEY CONCEPTS IN STRUCTURATION THEORY

Giddens argued that social theorists conceived of structure and system as interchangeable concepts, and although they are interdependent concepts, the differences between the two are important to ST. The first key concept is the **system,** defined as the interdependence of action and patterns of relations between and among actors. System thinking helps us understand the relationship of parts to the whole, and the interrelationship of all members of a social group or institution. Giddens noted that systems "are composed of

patterns and relationships between actors and collectivities reproduced across time and space."[13] For instance, think about a group
project you have completed with other students. Giddens would argue that students maintain the system by *regular social practices* and
patterns of interaction, which might include holding regular meetings,
setting agendas and assignments, and planning for deadlines. If
group members do not engage each other in system interaction, the
reproduction of the group will end.

The second key concept is **structure**, defined as the *rules* and *resources* used in the social reproduction of a system over time.[14] Think
about your communication theory class—what types of rules help
your instructor manage the class over the course of the term? How
does he or she use resources—such as money, classroom materials, and other tangible and intangible assets—to create an effective
learning environment? These rules and resources are examples of
the structure that helps maintain the production and reproduction
of your class.

Moreover, rules and resources can be used within a system as
forms of domination. **Domination** is defined as the extent to which
people exercise control over other people, control over organizational rules, or control over institutional resources. Rules and resources have **legitimacy** when they are perceived as beneficial, and
they help to regulate normal and acceptable practices in a system.
Giddens suggests that we look for those practices or rules that are
contested or challenged within organizations and institutions to determine how domination is exercised. Undesired or *contested* allocation of resources and challenges to existing rules and policies are
indicators of possible domination practices; *rules as domination* indicate control or power over the *social world*, and *resource allocation as
domination* indicates control or power over the *material world*. We will
revisit the issues of domination and legitimation later in this section
when we discuss power in structuration.

The third key concept, **duality of structure,** refers to the recursive nature of social practices. As Giddens explained,

> By the duality of structure I mean that the structural properties of social systems are both the medium and the outcome of the practices that constitute those systems....structure is both enabling and constraining, and it is one of the specific tasks of social theory to study the conditions in organization of social systems that govern the interconnections between the two.[15]

In other words, patterns of interaction and the effective use of rules and resources keep systems going, but the seeds of change exist in each moment of a system's reproduction. Every semester when students come to class, receive a passing grade, and continue a program of study, the structuration of higher education is achieved. The specific discourse and educational practices of each student contribute to the effective production and continuation of the social system.

The fourth key concept is called the stratification model of action. Earlier we noted that individuals engage in social practices, that is, *intentional actions* that influence social system production and reproduction. Any action you take in any social system constitutes a choice among possible courses of action; thus, choosing to take a specific action means choosing not to take a different action.[16] The meanings we assign to action are therefore connected to particular social circumstances. Engaging in intentional action is a *process* that is moderated by your ability to understand how your action relates to larger patterns of interaction and to the rules and resources of social systems. Giddens developed the **stratification model of action** as a representation of three interrelated modes of action.

The first mode of action, **reflexive monitoring of action,** describes how we can both reflect on our actions and also monitor the environment conditions that influence interaction.[17] Monitoring our behavior helps us determine if our actions are competent for the social setting or whether they challenge its rules and practices.[18] The second mode of action, **rationalisation of action**, refers to the reasons we give for our actions in the context of daily life. Giddens noted that our explanations are limited by practical knowledge (those things we can do but may not be able to explain) and by how much others share our understanding of common social scenes, the role of unconscious processes, and mutual knowledge. The third mode of action, **motivation of action**, refers to a person's wants and needs, both conscious and unconscious.[19] Considered together, the three modes of action inform us about reflective capacity, accounts, and motives for action within social systems.

The fifth key concept is called **principles of integration**. Although the concepts of system, structure, and duality of structure are presented as somewhat separate ideas, Giddens stressed the interdependence of action. **Integration** is defined as the regular and ongoing relationships and "*reciprocity of practices* among actors and collectivities."[20] ST identifies two types of integration. The first type, **social integration**, examines reciprocity and interaction between actors. The second type, **system integration**, explores how groups and organizations reciprocate action. In both types of integration, Giddens believed that a tension exists between autonomy versus dependence. That is, people seek some level of independence in their social actions, but they are simultaneously dependent on others. For example, consider your experience in a group project for class. Were you able to do whatever you wanted, or did the assignment or the behavior of other students constrain you in particular ways? You were probably able to exert some influence on the group—that is, you had a certain degree of autonomy. However, you probably also had to work with other students to accomplish your goals—that is, you had a certain degree of dependence.

The sixth key concept is *knowledge,* which is defined by Giddens as both the shared beliefs among individuals (mutual knowledge) and individual practical and discursive practices and beliefs. Knowledge is not about only what an individual knows, however. In fact, ST identifies two key issues related to the boundaries of knowledge. The first issue is the **unacknowledged conditions of action**, which means that we cannot know how our unconscious drives and desires influence our actions. As a result, we cannot truly explain the motives that drive our action. The second issue is the **unintended consequence of action**, which means that we do not necessarily control the direction of ongoing system reproduction, despite our best intentions for action and/or change in a system.

The seventh key concept is **power**, defined as the relation between autonomy and dependence.[21] Think about power as the *degree to which* you have freedom to do want you want *versus* the *degree to which* you are controlled or constrained by others. Giddens noted that institutions use power not only to control the actions of their members but also to accomplish strategic objectives. The *power of one's actions* is, in part, determined by the ability to achieve purposeful outcomes. Recognizing the relationship between power and agency, Giddens noted:

> Power relations are always two-way; that is to say, however subordinate an actor may be in a social relationship, the very fact of involvement in that relationship gives him or her a certain amount of power over the other. Those in subordinate positions in social systems are frequently adept at converting whatever resources they possess to some degree of control of conditions of reproduction of those social systems.[22]

The use of power also determines how actors in social systems are able to advocate certain practices over others (*legitimization*), constrain or control others (*domination*), and use language and symbols effectively (*signification*).

The eighth key concept is **contradiction,** which is considered a structural feature of social systems, and occurs when principles negate one another, so that enacting one principle makes it impossible to enact another.[23] According to social psychologist Irwin Altman, a contradiction is the interplay of two opposition ideas or concepts.[24] For example, happiness and sadness are opposites, yet one concept is necessary for defining the other. Understanding happiness requires understanding sadness. Giddens was especially interested in the contradictions in capitalist systems. For example, there is a contradiction between the wealth accumulation of the rich (the basis of capitalism) and the social programs that advocate equitable distribution of wealth (the basis of socialism). Another contradiction exists between private property and collectively shared spaces such as National Parks.

Importantly, the interplay of two oppositional forces often results in conflict, the ninth key concept. **Conflict** is the active struggle in social practices between actors or between groups (such as organizations, institutions).[25] Conflict might be based on contradictions, such as the tension between freedom and constraint, but the mere existence of a contradiction does not constitute conflict. Rather, conflict requires an *active struggle* or *interference* between parties. For example, conflict occurs when private homeowners clash with the government over land use rights. Parties in conflict are in a state of *antagonism*, which means they are on opposite sides of an issue.

Power, contradiction, and conflict intersect in what Giddens calls the *dialectic of control*. Control over actors in social systems occurs when domination and power are successfully used. Conflict often emerges in the struggle for control of social systems—a prime example is the ongoing conflict in Congress between republicans and democrats. Neither political party is able to exercise complete control over the other, but their differences are often based on strong oppositional beliefs that result in conflict over their influence on the state.

ADAPTIVE STRUCTURATION THEORY AND RESEARCH

Communication scholars were quick to embrace ST in the 1980's and later, in part because of the central role played by *agency* and *communication* in the production and reproduction of social systems. Small group researchers such as Marshall Scott Poole, Gerry DeSanctis, Robert McPhee, and others modified ST, using its basic theoretical principles to study decision-making behaviors in groups. Their modification of ST is called adaptive structuration theory, and we will describe its key ideas and explore research about group decision making.[26] It is worth noting, however, that communication scholars have applied ST to explore a variety of communication contexts, such as coworker relationships and informal communication in telecommuting,[27] communication technologies and work-life relationships,[28] public participation in organizing environmental control,[29] and coparenting relationships in stepfamilies.[30] Additionally, Poole and McPhee reported in 2005 that there were literally hundreds of studies in the field of organizational studies and over 50 in organizational communication research that were informed by ST.[31] In their overview, the authors grouped ST studies into four domains: 1) individual-level and organizational identification, 2) group-level analysis and the development of AST, 3) organizational levels and structure, and 4) inter-organizational power and meaning. We will focus our attention here on AST and group research.

The adaptation of ST applies to groups, and in particular the relationship between group decision making and communication technologies.[32] In 1985, communication scholars Poole, McPhee, and David Seibold applied ST to group decision-making practices, combining group decision-making theory and research with key concepts from ST. They argued that group decisions are an important element in the production and reproduction of systems; group interactions create and reflect the interpretive schemes of their members; the rules for decision making in groups constituted *normative structures*; and, communication and power structures are key in facilitating group decisions.[33]

In the early 1990's, however, Poole and DeSanctis applied AST specifically to information technologies known as group support systems (GSSs), and task-oriented groups.[34] As they argued,

> Group support systems combine communication, computer, and decision technologies to support meetings, decision-making, and related group activities. In a typical GSS, members are provided with a networked PC that allows them to enter data and control the operation of the system. The GSS offers a range of procedures, such as agenda setting, idea recording, and voting routines. Specialized decision modeling or structured group methods such as multi-criteria solution evaluation and brainstorming are usually available. Often there is also a large display screen for common group information, such as list of ideas of tabulation of votes.[35]

The use of GSS with AST focused on two broad lines of research.[36] The first explored how interaction produces and reproduces group and organizational structures. The second focused on general patterns of structuration that characterize a decision or series of decisions.[37]

ST and AST both focus on the role of action and communication in the production and reproduction of social systems. Communication is considered a key feature of ST, partly because social practices involve both interpretive and meaning-making sensibilities, and language is linked to significant and meaningful symbols and mutual knowledge. In fact, Giddens argued that the communication of meaning was a process of interaction that considers "what went before" and anticipates "what will come next."[38] His concern for meaning is central to the theory of action, which focuses on what actors *mean* to say or do.

Consider how ST and AST might apply to your everyday lives. For example, think about any group (organization) to which you belong. What sorts of rules and resources help sustain and reproduce that group? How do the practices of individual members reinforce existing rules and structures? To what extent does your knowledge of group practices influence what you do and say? Hopefully our brief overview of ST will get you thinking about the part you play in maintaining social systems of all kinds.

▲ ▲ ▲

Test Your Understanding

Given the complexity of ST, the role of discourse in Giddens's theory may not be immediately obvious. Working in groups of 4 to 5 students, discuss the following questions: What does Giddens mean by *discursive consciousness*? What kinds of knowledge do you possess that fit into the category of *practical consciousness*? As a group, think of at least two extended examples of practical consciousness that we have not already discussed in the chapter. What do you know how to do but would find difficult to explain to others?

▲ ▲ ▲

DIFFUSION OF INNOVATIONS THEORY

When one of the authors (L.E.) was young, he worked for 12 summers and holidays on his grandfather's farm. During the summers, his grandfather told stories about when the family got indoor plumbing, bought their first automobile, and first installed electricity and indoor lighting. Each of these events is an example of *adopting an innovation*. Communication scholar Everett Rogers created **diffusion of innovation theory** (DI) to explain how new ideas and technologies spread through societies. Rogers defined an **innovation** as "the idea, practice, or object that is perceived as new by an individual or other unit of adoption."[39] Innovations are more than objects such as iPads; they can also be ideas or practices, such as new leadership approaches that are developed and then used (adopted) by managers or organizational members. DI has been used in a variety of settings and research traditions since the turn of the last century. As you read about elements of this theory, consider how innovations change people, groups, and societies. In addition, think about the innovations (ideas and technologies) that you have adopted during your life, and how they have changed the way you think and interact with others in your culture (both positively and negatively).

INTELLECTUAL TRADITION OF DIFFUSION OF INNOVATIONS THEORY

The origins of DI can be traced to European social science and, in particular, to the French lawyer and judge, Gabriel Tarde.[40] Although Tarde used the term *imitation* instead of *innovation*, he explored both the process of diffusion (how an innovation spreads through a culture) and the reasons why most innovations fail. His interests included diffusion and adoption of mythological beliefs, industrial processes, and certain words in legal cases. Rogers, who considered Tarde a "sociological pioneer," contributed to research that explored the adoption and rejection conditions of innovations.[41] Tarde thought that the diffusion of innovations was a fundamental dimension of *human behavior change.*

After Tarde, diffusion research spread to British and German-Austrian researchers and was called *diffusionism.*[42] Diffusionism was an anthropological project that focused on the ways societies change (and especially on innovations that moved from one society to another). Eventually, diffusion research was seen in at least ten different disciplines, including anthropology, early sociology, rural sociology, education, public health and medical sociology, communication, marketing and management, geography, general sociology, and general economics.[43]

Among the most influential diffusion research conducted in the United States was that of Bryce Ryan and Neal Goss, both professors at Iowa State University.[44] In 1928, one of the newest agricultural technologies was hybrid corn seed. Hybrid corn seed represented a significant improvement over conventional corn seed and was strongly promoted by Iowa agricultural officials. Ryan and Goss examined the spread and rate of adoption of the hybrid corn seed. Their work identified one of the most important principles of how adoption actually works. Specifically, they found that interpersonal networks and social modeling between adopters and potential adopters were the most important factors in the decision to adopt an innovation. That is, *social processes of communication and interaction are key to the adoption of innovations.* By the mid-1900's, communication scholars had assumed a central role in diffusion research, especially because many diffusion studies examined the role of media as the vehicle for innovation adoption influence on a mass scale.

ASSUMPTIONS OF DIFFUSION OF INNOVATIONS THEORY

Communication scholar Everett Rogers has arguably been the most visible and productive U.S. scholar to study the diffusion of innovations. In 1962, Rogers examined 506 diffusion studies and developed a theoretical framework based on commonalities across these studies.[45] Although Rogers did not articulate specific assumptions or theoretical foundations of DI, we can identify several assumptions that are central to his theory.

Assumption 1: Adoption of innovations is an index of social change. As noted in Chapter 4, symbolic interactionism scholar Carl Couch argued that all good sociology involves the *observation* of human social experience. Early diffusionists believed that all social change could be explained through DI, and that the spread of innovations could be observed and documented as the source of change. Contemporary scholars have since modified the idea that all social change results from innovation, but clearly, innovations are one transparent *site* of change. For example, if you own a smart phone, consider how adopting that innovation has changed the ways in which you communicate with others.

Assumption 2: Changes that stem from innovation adoption occur primarily through communication processes and channels. Communication plays the central role in the creation of knowledge and decisions to adopt innovations. In one study, communication scholars Michael Papa, Arvind Singhal, and Wendy Papa worked with the Vietnamese government to help families adopt healthier eating habits.[46] In the study, one community of rice farmers was significantly healthier than rice farmers in nearby communities. The researchers discovered that the unhealthy rice farmers were throwing away small shrimp that thrived in the rice fields, seeing them as invasive to the crops. Conversely, the healthy families incorporated the shrimp into their diets. The researchers asked the healthier farmers to communicate their dietary behaviors to other families, which ultimately improved the nutritional habits of the malnourished farmers. In this instance, the adoption of new rice-harvesting practices created a positive social change, and this occurred because of the communication between individuals in different groups.

Assumption 3: The diffusion of any innovation is a time-consuming process. Recall from our discussion of structuration theory that Giddens was critical of sociology that ignored time. ST and DI are similar in that they incorporate communication, action, and change over time. In fact, the very concept of **diffusion** represents the process by which members of a social community convey information about innovations over time.[47] The adoption of innovations does not necessarily occur immediately or quickly; many innovations aren't adopted for years, and the constraints on any given community may make adoption impossible even if it is desirable. For example, over one billion people globally lack regular access to electricity and the opportunity to purchase many technological products enjoyed by Americans.[48] When, how, and why individuals make decisions to adopt or not adopt innovations can be more fully explained by the theory's key concepts.

KEY CONCEPTS IN DIFFUSION OF INNOVATIONS THEORY

We have already defined two key constructs in the theory, *diffusion* and *innovation*. The heart of DI is the idea that different types of innovations (ideas and objects) are diffused across individuals, groups, and societies through communication. Rogers defined communication as "a process in which participants create and share information with one another in order to reach a mutual understanding."[49] He stressed that communication is a two-way process in which people move toward *convergence* (toward each other) or *divergence* (apart from each other). He viewed diffusion as a "special type of communication" that focuses on messages and interaction about *new ideas.*[50] To understand the theory's key concepts, we explore two broad organizing categories: elements of DI (four central ideas), and types of innovation decisions.

Four main elements of diffusion of innovations. The four main elements of DI are innovation, communication channels, time, and the social system. Although we defined *innovation* above, Rogers stressed the fact that innovation is an individual perception, not an objective reality. According to Rogers, "If the idea seems new to the individual, it is an innovation."[51] People perceive the newness of an innovation based on their knowledge about it, their openness to persuasion from others about its usefulness or desirability, and their eventual decision whether or not to adopt it. In 2005, for example, the World Health Organization estimated that 1.1 billion people lack access to quality water resources.[52] Organizations such as Waves for Water, founded by the Brazilian soccer star Neymer Jr., have distributed water filters in developing countries to reduce water-borne disease and to increase the availability of drinkable water.[53] The goal of such organizations is to convince community members and villagers to *adopt* the use of water filters to improve their health. This process occurs through conducting educational campaigns that increase knowledge, persuading people about the benefits of adoption by addressing their doubts and concerns, and moving toward a favorable decision to adopt.

Three additional concepts help explain the innovation process: technological innovations, information, and uncertainty. According to Rogers, a technological innovation "is a design for instrumental action that reduces uncertainty in the cause-effect relationships involved in achieving a desired outcome."[54] In the Water for Waves example, villagers needed more **information,** or usable knowledge, about both water-filtering processes and the health benefits associated with using water filters. Communication and education help reduce **uncertainty,** or doubt, about the innovation; increased certainty about the value and benefits of an innovation increases the probability of adoption. In addition to these key processes in adoption, Rogers also stressed that several *characteristics of innovations* help explain why different innovations have *different rates* of adoption.

The five characteristics of innovations are relative advantage, compatibility, complexity, trialability, and observability. **Relative advantage** is "the degree to which an innovation" is perceived as superior to alternatives. "The *greater the perceived relative advantage* of an innovation, *the more rapid the rate of adoption will be* (italics added)."[55] For example, a smart phone has some distinct advantages over older flip phones. **Compatibility** is a characteristic that links innovations with past experiences, needs, and values of potential adopters.[56] Thus, if a new innovation is introduced to a group or community, unless its adoption posses challenges to existing needs and values, the likelihood of adoption increases. **Complexity** is defined as both the difficulty in understanding the innovation and difficulty in use.[57]

Trialability is defined as "the degree to which an innovation may be experimented with on a limited basis."[58] One of the rather "cool" developments advocated by Apple was the opening of numerous stores throughout the United States and the rest of the world. Customers have the opportunity to come and play with devices, ask questions, and try out the product before purchase. **Observability** is defined as the extent to which the outcomes of an innovation are *visible to others*. How many times has another person shown you some new app or some new technology before you even knew it existed? Overall, these five characteristics of innovations help determine how *quickly people will adopt an innovation*.

The second main element of DI is **communication channels**, which are simply the means by which people exchange messages.[59] Two channels in particular—*interpersonal* (face-to-face interaction) and *mass media* (radio, television, internet, etc.) —are important to adoption considerations. Mass media are effective at raising awareness and knowledge of innovations on a grand scale, whereas interpersonal interactions are effective at persuading individuals to adopt an innovation. Regardless of which channel is used, Rogers pointed out that people are most persuaded by those they perceive as similar to themselves, as opposed to dissimilar others.

The third main element of DI is *time,* which is explained as the concern with how diffusion is measured over a given period. In DI, time highlights the innovation-decision process, described as an individual moving through a) initial knowledge, b) attitude formation about the innovation, c) the decision to reject or adopt, d) the implementation and use of the innovation, and e) confirmation that the right decision was reached. Time also indexes the rate of adoption in a system, defined as the number of people who adopt a innovation in a given time period.[60] As an illustration, consider the adoption of smart phones in the United States. Do you think most Americans have already adopted smart phones, or does less than a majority have them? In June 2013, the Pew Research Center found that 56% of Americans own smart phones, which means that smart phone adoption is in the early majority phase.[61]

The final main element of DI is the **social system**, comprising those interrelated units (which can be individuals, informal groups, organizations, or other subsystems) that engage in joint problem solving.[62] Rogers recognized that social systems could either help or hurt the decisions to adopt innovations. Specifically, certain influential individuals within a social system—known as *opinion* leaders—play a key role in other people's decisions about whether or not to adopt an innovation.[63]

Types of innovation decisions. Social systems influence, and are influenced by, three types of innovation decisions.[64] One type, the *optional* innovative-decision, refers to an individual's adoption or rejection decisions that are independent, that is, unaffected by the decisions of others. Although norms and interpersonal networks can influence a decision maker, an optimal decision is not based on social pressures or the will of the majority. A second type is the *collective* innovative-decision, which reflects an agreement by consensus of group members to adopt an innovation. The final type, the *authority* innovative-decision, is an adoption decision made by relatively few individuals who possess technical expertise, power, and/or social status. Decisions about adoption can reflect only one of these types, or they can be based on a combination of two or three.

CLAIMS OF DIFFUSION OF INNOVATIONS RESEARCH

Literally thousands of studies have been conducted on the diffusion of innovations, making it virtually impossible to summarize the claims of DI comprehensively. However, based on Rogers's years of scholarship, we will briefly identify claims and findings in three areas: 1) classification of adopter categories and the development of the S-curve, 2) adopter categories as ideal types, and 3) characteristics of adopters.

Rogers argued that in the early days of DI research, numerous classification schemes were devised for adoption at various points in time. Figure 7.1 depicts a typical S-curve of adoption showing the slow initial rate of adoption that occurs as a limited few (early adopters) embrace the innovation. As communication and knowledge about the innovation increase, the rate of adoption increases dramatically (the sharp upward curve depicts the early and late majority). Those individuals who wait to adopt well after the majority are known as laggards. The S-curve is useful for describing successful innovations, but may not be a good representation of innovations that are less successful or fail altogether.

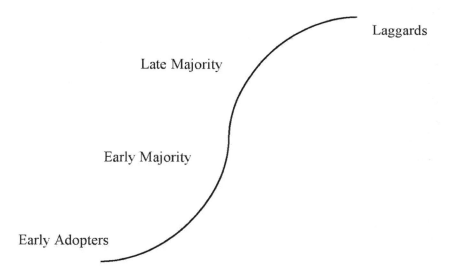

Figure 7.1 Example of a Diffusion S-Curve

Rogers claimed that each adopter represents one of five ideal types: innovators, early adopters, early majority, late majority, and laggards.[65] Innovators are adventurous people who often have substantial financial resources, and ability to understand complex technical knowledge, and an ability to cope with high levels of uncertainty. In the second type, *early adopters* (first individuals to adopt), individuals tend to be more integrated into social systems, have stronger local connections, and are composed of more opinion leaders than all other groups. The early adopter is also skilled at communicating ideas to peers by increasing knowledge and decreasing uncertainty about an innovation. They have the *respect* of their colleagues. The *early majority* comprises deliberate decision makers who adopt an innovation after the early adopters do. Members of the *late majority* are skeptical of an innovation, often adopting it as a result of increasing social pressures. Finally, *laggards* are the slowest to adopt an innovation because they tend to be suspicious of innovations and opinion leaders. They follow a lengthy adoption decision process and lag behind all the other groups in awareness and knowledge of an innovation.

Specific characteristics of adopters have a key influence on their decisions: socioeconomic status, personality variables, and communication behavior. Early and later adopters differ from each other on several dimensions of these characteristics. See Table 7.1 for a summary of these differences.

Table 7.1 Differences between Early and Later Adopters

	Compared to later adopters, early adopters...
Economic status	• Have more years of formal education
	• Have higher social status
	• Enjoy greater upward mobility
	• Have higher literacy
Personality	• Are more empathic
	• Are less dogmatic
	• Have a stronger capacity to cope with abstraction
	• Are more rational
	• Have more favorable attitudes toward change
	• Are less fatalistic
	• Have more pro-science views
Communication	• Participate in more social interaction
	• Are more strongly connected to interpersonal networks
	• Have more contact with opinion leaders
	• Seek more information about innovations
	• Experience more exposure to mass media

▲ ▲ ▲

Examining "Personal Uses" of Innovation Adoption

Early in the chapter we discussed Tarde's interest in innovation failures. He estimated that about one new innovation in ten is successful. Working individually, create two lists. In the first, identify ideas or innovations that you have adopted over the last year or two. In the second, identify ideas or innovations that you have *considered adopting.* Try to include three to five items on each list—then, work with other students to address the following questions: 1) Are there innovations you adopted that you now reject or no longer use? 2) If so, what are the reasons why you stopped using the innovation? 3) Do you or other students in your group use technologies in any negative or destructive ways? 4) How can you determine whether the benefits of a technology outweigh its costs?

▲ ▲ ▲

COMMUNICATION ACCOMMODATION THEORY

Communication scholar Howard Giles and his colleagues developed **communication accommodation theory** (CAT) to explore the communication strategies people use to increase or decrease their *social distance* from one another. At the heart of the theory are questions about how individuals communicate in ways that create *convergence* or *divergence* with others in interpersonal relationships. Giles and colleague Philip Smith originally defined **convergence** as "the processes whereby individuals shift their speech styles to become more like that of those with whom they are interacting."[66] Later, Giles, Coupland, and Coupland clarified that convergence occurs when people adapt to each other's verbal or nonverbal behaviors, including speech rate, speech duration, smiling, and eye contact.[67] In contrast, **divergence** is the process of using verbal or nonverbal behavior to differentiate oneself from others.[68] CAT draws attention to the ways in which people accommodate to others using communication. Accommodation behaviors such as convergence can create and encourage continued interaction, result in favorable assessments, increase identification, and decrease perceived differences between people and groups. As you read more about CAT, think about the role of communication in both divergence and convergence.

INTELLECTUAL TRADITION OF COMMUNICATION ACCOMMODATION THEORY

CAT emerged out of research and theory in social psychology and sociolinguistics and is focused primarily on the relationship between language behavior and social context. The theory was originally called *speech accommodation theory* (SAT) because of its focus on the convergence of speech variables such as rate of speech, speech styles (what we say and how we say it), and listening.[69] SAT examined how people adjust their talk or discourse in social scenes by attempting to identify the rules and norms that govern language.[70]

When developing CAT, Giles drew on four social psychological theories. The first was Donn Byrne's *similarity-attraction paradigm,* which proposes that similarity in attitudes and beliefs leads to attraction.[71] According to CAT, speech convergence is *one of the ways* in which individuals increase similarity and attraction. Convergence can also reflect a speaker's desire for approval from others—thus, the greater one's need for approval, the more he or she attempts to converge with others. The second theoretical influence on CAT was *social exchange theory* (see chapter 8), which recognized that convergence can incur costs as well as benefits. For instance, speakers who converge their speech patterns with those of others can suffer a loss of personal identity or be perceived as lacking individual integrity.[72] Although convergence was originally thought to be consistently positive, social exchange theory illuminated its potential risks.

The third theory to influence CAT was Fritz Heider's *attribution theory* (see chapter 6), which focuses on the dispositional and situational influences on human behavior. Giles and Smith argued that although people usually judge convergence positively and divergence negatively, "the extent to which this holds true will undoubtedly be influenced by the listener's attributions of the speaker's intent."[73] Suppose you notice someone donating her time to a food shelter. Would you automatically assume that she is kind and generous? Before drawing that conclusion, you might want to consider the reasons for her behavior. What if you learned that her volunteering was court-ordered? How about if you discovered she was a researcher collecting data on the homeless? Would those circumstances change your opinion of her?

The final theoretical influence on CAT was Henri Tajfel's *theory of intergroup relations,* which explains that people tend to judge out-group members (those from social groups other than their own) more negatively than in-group members, especially with respect to values, attributes, and abilities. For example, when communicating with someone with a different social or cultural background, we are more likely to question his motives for convergence than we are to question a member of our own culture or social group. We may possess unfavorable stereotypes about out-group members, believing that their intentions are devious or their cooperation has an ulterior motive. In contrast, communicating with in-group members strengthens our social identity by making us feel distinctive or unique compared to others.[74] CAT is a complex theory that pays attention to convergence and divergence in communication and takes into account the psychological characteristics of communicators (linguistic and psychological accommodations, motives, intentions, and dispositional qualities).

Assumptions of Communication Accommodation Theory

The important question in CAT is not "Do individuals converge or diverge in an interaction?" Rather, it is "*To what extent* do individuals converge or diverge?" According to Giles, the goal of CAT is to develop evidence-based communication practices that focus on both interpersonal and intergroup contexts.[75] Below we identify three assumptions of CAT that help us understand its foundations.

Assumption 1: Communication accommodation comprises the range of strategies wherein speakers "attune" their talk to characteristics of the other.[76] *Attuning*, or adaptating to interaction styles, can be achieved through strategies of discourse management (talk in everyday interaction) and interpersonal control (anticipating and responding to a partner's conversational needs).[77] Coupland, Coupland, and Giles argued that,

> The sociolinguistic heart of CAT is this focus on processes
> of *communicative attuning*, adaptive and strategic moves made
> by interactants to increase and decrease social and sociolin-
> guistic distance. Because it specifies processes of perception
> and evaluation, the model is useful to explain various forms
> of intentional and unintentional *mis*matches in communica-
> tion styles.[78]

Attuning communication for convergence and divergence involves a host of verbal and nonverbal strategies related to identity development and broader socialization processes within and between groups and communities.

Assumption 2: Communication is influenced by people's orientations to interactions and the socio-historical contexts in which they are embedded.[79] One's degree of convergence and management of social distance are determined not only by a specific conversation but also by the social and historical context governing appropriate social behavior, including the person's cultural norms and ideologies. Similar to symbolic interactionism (see chapter 4), CAT incorporates elements of individual identity, intentional action, and social systems knowledge to reveal how individuals achieve connection and closeness (or disconnection and distance) with others. For instance, spouses' convergence in a given conversation is based on their individual motives and attitudes, their relational quality and history, family system dynamics, and their specific goals for that conversation.

Assumption 3: Through communication, people not only exchange facts, ideas, and emotions; they also negotiate their memberships in various social categories.[80] This assumption recognizes that communication is embedded within organizations and communities. We inhabit different types of groups, or *speech communities,* that come together around similar ways of talking and being. These speech communities reinforce the identity and values of the individual and the group. There are times, however, when membership in different groups creates tensions or boundaries that are difficult to negotiate. Imagine an American of Middle-Eastern descent who must simultaneously negotiate two identities: that of and American citizen and that of a person with Middle-Eastern ancestry. In any given interaction, the individual might embrace American identity and values over competing ethnic identity beliefs and values, or vice-versa. CAT not only examines the specific behaviors of individuals in their interaction with others, but also recognizes that group membership plays an important role in *the explanation* for convergence and divergence in interpersonal interaction.

KEY CONCEPTS IN COMMUNICATION ACCOMMODATION THEORY

Nikolas Coupland and colleagues developed a general model of accommodation focused on processes and communication practices that influence convergence and divergence in interpersonal interaction.[81] Their model recognizes the strong influence of context (social and historical influences) and communicators' cognitive, affective, behavioral, and somatic states on behavior strategies and choices. The degree of convergence or divergence is influenced by the social and psychological orientations of speakers, and also by their evaluation of each other's communicative performances.

Earlier we identified two master concepts that are central to CAT: *convergence,* the process whereby people adjust their communication behavior to create connections with others; and *divergence,* the process by which people create distance or accentuate differences from others. Giles and colleagues acknowledged that not all interactions involve convergence or divergence; sometime people seek to maintain their current degree of connectedness to one another. Thus, **maintenance** is the third key concept and is defined as the process in which a person persists in the use of his or her original communication style, regardless of the communication behaviors of the other person.[82] Of the three concepts, convergence is generally regarded as more favorable for people because it implies communication efficiency and cooperation in interaction.

Other key concepts that bear directly on CAT are accommodation, under-accommodation, over-accommodation, and non-accommodation. First, **accommodation** is the process by which individuals vary their behavior for the purposes of convergence and divergence. According to Giles and colleagues, "An accommodative climate is one in which conversational partners listen to one another, take the other's views into account, and explain things in ways that 'sit right' with their partner."[83] Accommodation also implies that interactions are characterized by pleasantness, politeness, and respect. Second, **under-accommodation** is the process whereby people believe that others do not engage in appropriate accommodation to their needs, goals, and desires.[84] For example, research has shown that in conversations between young people and their elders, young people view older people as under-accommodating because of their negative stereotypes about youths and their lack of concern for youth needs.[85] Moreover, young people view elders as "overly verbose about the 'good old days,'" yet also as inclined to "talk excessively about painful past events, such as illness and bereavements."[86]

Third, **over-accommodation** is the process wherein people appear to condescend to others because they are trying too hard to increase social connection. For instance, research shows that older people often feel "talked down to" by younger people, who address them with terms such as "my dear" and "sweetie."[87] Fourth, **non-accommodation** is the strategy of making no attempt to converge or diverge from others in particular interactions. According to Giles, "non-accommodating messages can be interpreted by targets as suggesting that they are not worthy of the sender's respect or positive regard."[88]

Altogether, CAT addresses the role of communicative behaviors that lead to convergence, divergence, or maintenance of social distance. Successful convergence is signaled through communication strategies such as explicit and clear talk, referred to as *comprehensibility strategies.*[89] Additionally, *discourse management strategies* include choices about conversational topic selection and focus, managing talk sequences, and respect for face needs. And finally, *interpersonal control strategies* can include actions such as interruptions, topic deflection, and other behavioral choices that *protect the identity of self.*[90]

▲　▲　▲

Theory into Practice

We would like you to engage in a communication accommodation experiment. Your instructor may provide assignment guidelines for this exercise or you may undertake our recommendations on your own. First, think about the ways in which you demonstrate convergence with others. Second, find someone you know relatively well and think about convergence behaviors that might bring you closer together. Third, identify the specific behaviors you want to use in your interaction with that person. Consider converging with behaviors such as eye contact, body posture, speech rate, turn taking, pitch, volume, and topic matching. Fourth, interact with the person and consciously focus on matching behaviors that will increase your convergence. Pay particular attention to the reaction of the other person as you increase your convergence behaviors. How did he or she respond? Was there a sense of connectedness that you have not noticed in previous interactions? Do you think the person was aware of your specific intentions? Write down your observations of the experiment and report your findings back to class.

▲ ▲ ▲

CLAIMS OF COMMUNICATION ACCOMMODATION THEORY

CAT has been applied in a variety of domains, including mass media, courtroom interactions, medical consultations, psychotherapy, second-language interactions, inter-ethnic communication, family settings, health care settings, and law enforcement.[91] Based on that work, we can identify some central claims of the theory.

First, *individuals engage in numerous strategies that maintain, increase, or decrease social distance in interpersonal settings.* The elegance of CAT is found in its application of specific communication behaviors to the process of relationship development. For example, researchers David Huffaker, Roderick Swaab, and Daniel Diermeier found that in online multi-party negotiations, partners with higher agreement displayed higher levels of language convergence than those who were unable to reach agreements.[92] The authors argued that language convergence likely fosters stability and unity in coalitions.

Second, *communicative convergence is important for individual and group identity development and social approval.* Convergence has valuable benefits for individual and social development at both the psychological and sociological levels. Giles and colleagues noted that "the identity maintenance function of communication serves to fulfill emotional needs of participants as they attend to speech markers and nonverbal features that positively reinforce their egos."[93] Self-esteem and identity needs are supported in convergent experiences with others; that is, we feel good when we make connections with others.

Finally, *accommodation behavior represents the ability to adapt to socially and contextually driven demands of everyday life*. One of the ways we adapt to our changing world is by creating order from the uncertainty of interaction. Another is by considering the social rules and norms that provide a framework for communicative action and competence. Through accommodation, we align our individual beliefs, motives, and ways of being, and we recognize that others play an important role in our continued adaptation to social circumstances.

Summary and Conclusion

In this chapter, we have focused on three theories that address discourse and change in a variety of ways. Structuration theory is valuable for the analysis of organizational systems and structures, explaining how knowledgeable actors and communication practices help produce and reproduce organizations and institutions over time. Anthony Giddens's goal was to provide a structure that adequately accounted for the role of time in human organizing. Diffusion of innovations theory addresses how and when people are open to change via the adoption of new practices/ideas and new technologies. Everett Rogers stressed the fact that our adoption of new ideas and technologies creates and reflects various types of changes at individual, organizational, and social levels. Finally, communication accommodation theory explores modes of adaptation that demonstrate our sensitivity to others in social interaction. Giles and his colleagues address issues of linguistic competence and the fulfillment of individual and social connection needs. These three theories represent a valuable introduction to the influence of discourse and change in our everyday lives, and to how we cope with the intersection between our individual needs and goals and those of others in society.

FOR FURTHER DISCUSSION

STRUCTURATION THEORY

1. What is the difference between structures and systems? In what ways are they interdependent?
2. How useful is the concept of practical consciousness? Do you agree or disagree with Giddens that actors possess a great deal of social knowledge? Defend your answer.
3. How does Giddens define power? Why is it central to structuration theory, and what is its role in the production and reproduction of organizational and institutional systems?

DIFFUSION OF INNOVATIONS THEORY

1. Diffusionists argued that the adoption of innovation is the primary way that social change occurs. Do you agree? If not, describe other ways in which individuals and societies change?
2. How has the adoption of technologies changed your life over the past few years? To what extent do you believe that access and availability of technologies is beneficial to your culture?
3. Rogers discusses two sources of significant influence on adoption decisions: interpersonal relationships and mass media. How effective do you think the media are in knowledge distribution, persuasive messages, and strategy development with respect to technological innovations? In your own life, do you tend to be persuaded more by friends or by media sources?

COMMUNICATION ACCOMMODATION THEORY

1. What level of awareness do you think people have about their communication convergence behaviors? To what extent do you think communication convergence is based on subconscious or practical knowledge rather than specific overt strategies?

2. How does group membership affect people's desire and ability to converge with out-group members? Do you think rivalries between members of different groups are healthy for communication? Explain.

3. Think about an interaction with someone who either over-accommodated or under-accommodated in his or her communication behavior with you. How did you respond? What roles do you think over- and under-accommodation play in our assessments of the communication competence of others?

Key Terms

Accommodation
Adaptive structuration theory
Communication accommodation theory
Communication channels
Conflict
Contradiction
Convergence
Diffusion
Diffusion of innovation theory
Discourse
Divergence
Domination
Duality of structure
Human agency
Information
Innovation
Integration
Maintenance
Motivation of action
Non-accommodation
Over-accommodation
Power
Rationalisation of action
Reflective monitoring of action
Social integration
Social system
Stratification model of action
Structuration theory
Structure
System integration

Systems
Unacknowledged conditions of action
Uncertainty
Under-accommodation
Unintended consequences of action

8

Communication in Developing Relationships

How Do You Decide if a Relationship Is Worth the Effort?

Micaela had never been more excited or more confused. Earlier in the day, she had attended her first-year student orientation class at Midwestern State where she met a good-looking guy named Alex.

> "Hey, how's it going?" Alex asked.
> "Good, and you?" Micaela replied with a smile.
> "I'm Alex . . . I hope I'm in the right place for orientation."
> "I think so! I'm Micaela."
> "So where're you from?"

Over the next two hours, Micaela and Alex exchanged small talk as they endured the orientation session. They chatted about their impressions of the orientation coordinator, their experiences with their new hall directors, and their families and hometowns.

Their conversation flowed smoothly and they both enjoyed meeting someone new. After orientation, Alex invited Micaela to join his friends and him at a coffee shop near campus. Although she wanted to go, Micaela hesitated and said she had to run errands but would try to stop by later. Alex said he understood and that he hoped to see her again.

What Micaela really had to do that day was call Jamal to talk about the changes she was noticing in their relationship. Jamal and Micaela had been together since their sophomore year in high school. Although they cared about each other, Micaela noticed Jamal being more withdrawn and less open with her on the phone since they each left home to attend different colleges. Before leaving for school, she felt confident that she and Jamal could make a long-distance relationship work—but now she wasn't so sure. She began to question Jamal's commitment to their relationship, given his recent behavior. And now, she found herself wanting to spend time with Alex rather than having a difficult conversation with Jamal.

Like Micaela, many of us have experienced the exciting opportunities and unique challenges that emerge as we seek to develop and maintain personal relationships. From the uncertainties we experience as meet new people, to the information we share about ourselves with others, to the ways we balance competing demands on our time and emotional resources, relationships provide us with some of our most rewarding—and at times, most painful—life experiences.

In this chapter, we explore three theories that help us understand how communication facilitates the development of personal relationships. First, we examine uncertainty reduction theory and recent research on relational uncertainty, both of which explain how we communicate when we are unsure about others. We then discuss social exchange theory, which details how self-disclosure helps build and sustain intimacy in relationships. Finally, we explore social exchange theories, which explains why we seek out and maintain some relationships but not others. By learning about how the communication process works in developing relationships, we hope you'll appreciate why we seek personal connections with others and how they come to be.

Uncertainty Reduction Theory

Life is filled with uncertainty. As one of us (P.S.) was working on this chapter, for example, he met a new colleague and formed his initial impressions of what it would be like to work with this person. Immediately afterward, his best friend of 30 years called to say that he and his family were moving away, leaving him to wonder how the move might change their friendship. Later that same day, he received a text message from a close family member saying she had just been diagnosed with breast cancer. Clearly, life and the relationships that give our lives meaning are rife with uncertainty. Just as Micaela experienced the uncertainty of attending college for the first time, meeting Alex, and managing the changes in her relationship with Jamal, we also face life transitions, opportunities to meet new people, and new challenges to our existing relationships. To help us understand how uncertainty influences our initial interactions with others, as well as how we communicate in established relationships, scholars have developed uncertainty reduction theory.

Intellectual Tradition of Uncertainty Reduction Theory

The scholar primarily responsible for advancing uncertainty reduction theory (URT) is Charles R. Berger, Professor Emeritus of Communication at the University of California – Davis. Berger and his colleagues developed URT in the late 1970s and early 1980s to explain and predict how uncertainty influences communication when people first meet. URT was one of the first theories to originate in the field of interpersonal communication, and it laid the foundation for later generations of communication scholars to test, refine, challenge, and extend its claims.[1] You may recall from Chapter 5 that Berger and his colleagues were also responsible for planning theory. In many ways, URT was a theoretical ancestor of planning theory. It should come as no surprise, then, that URT (like planning theory) is a social scientific theory grounded in the post-positivist paradigm. It focuses on helping us understand how uncertainty works as a causal force that influences our communication behavior.[2]

Originally, URT explained how people communicate when they meet each other for the first time. With time, William Gudykunst and his colleagues extended URT to examine the anxiety and uncertainty that arises when people of different cultures communicate.[3] Other scholars, such as Leanne Knobloch and Denise Solomon, moved beyond first meetings to see how relational uncertainty influences communication in established relationships.[4] Despite differences in their focus, each of these programs of research assumes that uncertainty is a fundamental characteristic of communication in relationships. It is, in essence, a fact of relational life. With this general assumption in mind, let's briefly review some of the remaining assumptions of URT before examining its key concepts.

Assumptions of Uncertainty Reduction Theory

Three key assumptions inform uncertainty reduction theory.

Assumption 1: According to Berger, when strangers meet, "their primary concern is one of uncertainty reduction or increasing predictability about the behavior of both themselves and others in the interaction."[5] In other words, people try to gain certainty so they can understand the world around them. When you meet people for the first time, you may know little about who they are, where they are from, how they will act toward you, and how the conversation will go. This lack of data generates a sense of uneasiness or anxiety that prompts you to seek out information. As you ask questions and make small talk, you learn about people and become able to predict how they will behave. Getting to know people reduces the uneasiness and anxiety associated with your uncertainty.

Assumption 2: People are especially eager to reduce uncertainty under certain circumstances.[6] First, we are motivated to reduce uncertainty about people when we *anticipate future interaction* with them—that is, when we believe we will see them again. For instance, a father may be particularly motivated to reduce uncertainty about his daughter's boyfriend when meeting him for the first time because he anticipates interacting with him again in the future. Second, we typically feel motivated to alleviate uncertainty when an individual possesses resources we desire (i.e., that person has *incentive value*). In other words, we seek additional information to reduce our uncertainty about someone who can determine the rewards and costs we will receive. New employees are usually motivated to learn more information about their supervisors as people, including their expectations and professional goals, because they perceive their supervisors as possessing the power to determine their own job security and opportunities for promotion.

Assumption 3: We become curious about another's behavior when that person violates our expectations. Our curiosity about that individual's *deviation* from the social norm, in turn, motivates us to reduce uncertainty about the person.

Besides specifying conditions that enhance our uncertainty about others, Berger also provided a series of axioms in URT. An **axiom** is a plausible assumption or an untestable claim about the relationship between two concepts contained within a theory. In URT, Berger proposed seven axioms that emphasize the correspondence between uncertainty and communication. In subsequent research, communication scholars Malcolm Parks and Mara Adelman added an eighth axiom related to shared communication networks.[7] The axioms appear in Table 8.1.

Table 8.1 Axioms of Uncertainty Reduction Theory

Axiom 1:	Uncertainty is negatively associated with verbal communication.
Axiom 2:	Uncertainty is negatively associated with nonverbal affiliative expressiveness (i.e., those nonverbal behaviors that create a connection with another person, such as smiles, head nods, eye contact).
Axiom 3:	Uncertainty is positively associated with information-seeking behavior.
Axiom 4:	Uncertainty is negatively associated with the intimacy of communication content (i.e., self-disclosure).
Axiom 5:	Uncertainty is positively associated with reciprocity rate (i.e., the degree to which one person self-discloses similar amounts and levels of information that he or she is receiving from the other person).
Axiom 6:	Uncertainty is negatively associated with the degree of similarity between partners.
Axiom 7:	Uncertainty is negatively associated with liking (i.e., we are less likely to like someone we are uncertain about).
Axiom 8:	Uncertainty is negatively associated with shared communication networks between partners (i.e., the more people we know in common, the less uncertain we are about each other).

To illustrate how these axioms work together, let's return to our opening scenario from the beginning of this chapter. Micaela and Alex are strangers when they first meet at their student orientation session at Midwestern State. After their initial greeting, they talk about superficial topics such as their initial impressions of the session coordinator (Axiom 4), exchange self-disclosures about their personal experiences with their new hall directors (Axiom 5), and ask questions about each other's hometown, families, and background (Axiom 3). The more they talk, the less uncertainty they experience (Axiom 1), the more they smile, engage in eye contact, and use head nods to indicate understanding (Axiom 2), and the more they like each other (Axiom 7). Their uncertainty is further reduced when they discover that they both enjoy coffee (Axiom 6), which leads to Alex's invitation for Micaela to join him and his friends at a local coffee shop across from campus. Had Micaela accepted Alex's invitation, her uncertainty about Alex might have been further reduced when she discovered that Alex is a friend of Julie, who happens to be her new suite mate (Axiom 8).[8]

As evident from the example above, many events occur when two people meet for the first time. Berger and his colleagues provided these axioms so that researchers could derive theorems, or predictions about relationships between variables. These theorems could then be tested to determine if URT needed to be modified or if the axioms behind URT needed to be abandoned. For example, by combining Axiom 1 with Axiom 6, we can create the theorem that "Verbal communication is positively associated with perceived similarities between conversational partners." By connecting the various axioms to each other, communication scholars have tested, challenged, and refined the fundamental assumptions behind URT, providing meaningful extensions to this early theory of interpersonal communication.[9]

KEY CONCEPTS IN UNCERTAINTY REDUCTION THEORY

Unlike some of the other theories we have read about thus far (such as schema theory or constructivism in Chapter 5), URT focuses more on axioms and theorems and less on the development of key terms. That being said, it is important that we establish a common definition for uncertainty. According to Berger, *uncertainty* is a lack of knowledge about what is inevitable, and it is a function of the number and likelihood of alternatives that may occur in a particular context. Uncertainty is high when several outcomes are equally likely to occur, and it is low when only one outcome is likely to occur.[10] As Leanne Knobloch explains, "uncertainty is a subjective experience that stems from people's awareness of ambiguity."[11] URT describes two types of uncertainty that emerge in initial interactions: *cognitive uncertainty* refers to the doubts people have about their own beliefs and the beliefs of others, whereas *behavioral uncertainty* references the questions people have about their own actions and the actions of others. With this key concept in mind, URT provides a series of claims related to the communication process as people respond to (or cope with) both forms of uncertainty.

CLAIMS OF UNCERTAINTY REDUCTION THEORY
URT provides a number of claims that tie our experiences of uncertainty to the communication process. First, URT suggests that *communication can be both a cause and an effect of uncertainty*.[12] For instance, suppose you spent a lot of time planning and preparing an expensive date for your romantic partner. Although you both enjoyed the date and you both had a good time, your partner never says "thank you" or expresses any appreciation for the time and effort you put into planning the evening. After dropping your partner off and driving back home, you may find yourself asking "What's going on here?" or "Why didn't she say 'thank you'?" or "What, if anything, should I do about this?" In this instance, your partner's communication behavior *produced uncertainty* in your relationship. On the other hand, when meeting someone new for the first time, uncertainty may prompt us to ask and answer general questions ("Where are you from? What's your major?"), pay particular attention to nonverbal cues ("She must be a shy person because she's hardly looking at me"), and learn information from disclosures ("I had no idea that you liked jazz!"). In these moments, uncertainty *produced our communication behavior*.

A second and perhaps more notable claim of URT is that *individuals must find ways to cope with uncertainty and produce messages under*

conditions of uncertainty.[13] Specifically, Berger and his colleagues identified three coping strategies people use to manage uncertainty:
(a) seeking information, (b) planning, and (c) hedging. Consistent
with the belief that communication helps us reduce uncertainty by
acquiring information, URT describes three information-seeking
behaviors. First, *passive strategies* involve observing the person from
a distance. Examples include gathering information about the person through social media such as Facebook, subtly watching how
the person reacts to others, and observing how the person acts in
an informal setting. Although passive strategies tend to be low-risk
strategies that minimize the potential for embarrassment, they may
not produce the kinds of information you seek. Thus, URT suggests
that you might choose instead to use *active strategies*, which include
any actions you take to gather information about someone without
directly talking to the person. Rather than talk directly to someone
you're are attracted to, for instance, you might ask others for information about the person. Asking others may bring you information that you could not obtain through the use of passive strategies,
but it carries the added risk that someone will tell the person you
are asking questions about him or her. Finally, you might use *interactive strategies* by communicating directly with the target person.
Asking questions allows us to gather information about others and
discover similarities, although most of us are sensitive to norms of
politeness that limit the number of questions we may ask and the
explicitness of questions that most people consider to be appropriate.[14] We might also self-disclose information about ourselves in the
hope that the person will reciprocate and disclose something in
return. Or perhaps we might try relaxing the person, as people are
generally more likely to disclose information when they are at ease.
Regardless of the strategy we choose, interactive strategies provide
the most direct method for reducing uncertainty, yet they possess
the greatest potential for producing anxiety, discomfort, and awk-
wardness as well.

Besides information-seeking behaviors, Berger also identifies *planning* as a useful strategy for coping with uncertainty. As we discussed in Chapter 5 (under Berger's planning theory), a *plan* is a cognitive representation of action sequences that we can take to accomplish a communication goal. URT suggests that individuals may cope with uncertainty by planning before and during social interaction. The plans we create to respond to uncertainty, however, must be designed at the right level of complexity. Plans that are too simple tend to be ineffective, and overly complicated plans tend to prevent us from being flexible in how we respond to unexpected circumstances.[15] Thus, individuals are most successful at responding to uncertainty when they are able to create, enact, and alter their plans so they're ready for however a conversation unfolds.

URT offers a third strategy for coping with uncertainty, namely, *hedging* against the negative outcomes that could occur when communicating under conditions of uncertainty.[16] To illustrate, consider what you might say when asking one of your instructors for an extra-credit opportunity. According to Berger, you might use humor to soften the request ("I bet you're really losing sleep over which extra credit opportunity to provide") or you might use ambiguous messages to hide your true intent ("Are all of the points that we can earn this semester outlined in the syllabus?"). You might also use a disclaimer to prevent negative impressions ("Please don't think less of me for asking, but will we have opportunities to earn extra credit in this class?"), or attempt to control the floor while gaining information from the other person ("Since my other professors provide extra credit, can you tell me what kinds of extra credit opportunities you provide?"). When compared to information-seeking and planning strategies, hedging strategies allow us to manage our uncertainty and gather information while avoiding the embarrassment that often comes with the other strategies mentioned above.

Taken together, URT makes claims about the various strategies individuals can take when attempting to cope with uncertainty.

Embedded in those claims is the general assumption that we usually try to *reduce* our uncertainty so as to improve our abilities to predict and explain what other people think and how they will behave. As we have noted in earlier chapters, however, theorists don't always agree about all of the assumptions embedded within a particular theory, such as URT. Before we turn our attention to more recent theoretical developments on this topic, let's take a moment to consider what interpretive and critical scholars might say about uncertainty and the communication process.

▲   ▲   ▲

Perspective Checking

In a recent anthology on uncertainty and information management, Leslie Baxter and Dawn Braithwaite challenged some of the traditional assumptions of URT, which tend to favor certainty and treat uncertainty as problematic. They suggested that uncertainty is an important and *positive* process through which meaning is created between people. They argued that privileging certainty over uncertainty can potentially extinguish creativeness by relational partners.[17] It is probably safe to classify the dialectical study of certainty and uncertainty as a constructionist/interpretive perspective. Why? In much work on dialectical theory scholars seek to explore individual enactments and explanations for communication in developing relationships. Dialectical theorists often examine the subjective (internal) and inter-subjective (how two or more people make sense of their interactions) experiences of communicators and would probably not argue that the primary role of communication is uncertainty reduction; they would argue that communication simultaneously invokes the interplay and both certainty and uncertainty in developing relationships.

▲   ▲   ▲

RELATIONAL UNCERTAINTY AND COMMUNICATION IN ESTABLISHED RELATIONSHIPS

Although URT originally focused on initial interactions between strangers, Berger and his colleagues readily acknowledged that, "in order for a relationship to continue, it is important that the persons involved in the relationship consistently update their fund of knowledge about themselves, their relational partner and their relationship."[18] In other words, questions of uncertainty are likely to emerge again long after two individuals get to know each other and develop a more intimate relationship. Building on this idea from URT, Leanne Knobloch, Denise Solomon, and their colleagues developed a program of research examining *relational uncertainty,* which they define as the degree of confidence people have in their perceptions of involvement within interpersonal relationships.[19] Although their ideas are similar to URT in many ways, the study of relational uncertainty shifts our focus from thinking about how well we can predict our partner's thoughts and behaviors, to thinking about relationship involvement issues.[20] Let's briefly examine the key concepts behind relational uncertainty before discussing some of the claims advanced by Knobloch and her colleagues.

▲ ▲ ▲

Let's Discuss

1. Why do we often dislike feeling uncertain about other people? When, if ever, can uncertainty be a benefit?
2. Early theorists claimed that reducing uncertainty about a person would lead to increased liking for that person. Is that usually true, in your experience? How much does it matter what you learn about the person?

▲ ▲ ▲

KEY CONCEPTS OF RELATIONAL UNCERTAINTY

According to Knobloch and Solomon, relational uncertainty stems from three sources: the self, the partner, and the relationship.[21] **Self uncertainty** includes the questions people have about their own participation in a relationship. For example, when thinking about Micaela's relationship with Jamal, Micaela might have been asking herself such questions as "How certain am I about my feelings for Jamal?" or "Do I really want to continue to pursue a long-distance relationship with him?" Given Jamal's recent behavior, Micaela might also have been experiencing **partner uncertainty**, which includes the doubts people have about their partner's participation in a relationship. She may have been asking herself "How committed is Jamal to our relationship?" or "Is he really going to do what it takes to maintain our relationship?" Both self and partner uncertainties focus on the individuals in a relationship, but according to Knobloch and Solomon, people may also experience a third source of uncertainty: the relationship itself. **Relationship uncertainty** describes the ambiguity people experience about their relationships, above and beyond either self or partner concerns. When romantic partners are wrestling with uncertainties about what they can and cannot say to each other, whether or not they both feel the same way about each other, the definition of their relationship, and/or the future of their relationship, they are experiencing relationship uncertainty. Thus, relational uncertainty captures the degree to which people experience doubts from self, partner, and relationship sources.[22]

In addition to the *sources* of relational uncertainty, Knobloch and her colleagues have also identified two *levels* of relational uncertainty. First, we experience relational uncertainty on a global level when we have a general sense of ambiguity about involvement in a relationship. Second, we can experience relational uncertainty on an episodic level as a result of a specific event that has occurred within a relationship. For instance, Micaela may experience global uncertainty in her relationship with Jamal that would have occurred regardless of any specific events that have transpired in their dating relationship. On the other hand, she may be experiencing relational uncertainty on an episodic level because of their recent decision to attend separate colleges and to begin a long-distance relationship. Many types of events can produce episodic uncertainty, including personality changes, competing relationships, acts of deception and infidelity, acts of aggression, and loss of contact.[23] With these two levels of relational uncertainty in mind, let's now turn our attention to two general categories of claims that tie relational uncertainty to the communication process.

Claims About Relational Uncertainty and Communication

The first set of claims advanced by Knobloch ties relational uncertainty to how individuals produce messages. First, Knobloch proposes that *relational uncertainty worsens the face threats that people experience when communicating with a partner.*[24] **Face** refers to the public image or identity people portray when communicating with others, and **face threats** occur when that preferred image is challenged, threatened, or criticized.[25] Researchers have found that romantic partners are less likely to confront each other about unexpected events,[26] and are less likely to discuss controversial or taboo topics, such as religion,[27] when they are experiencing relational uncertainty. This is due, in part, to the potential face threats associated with discussing difficult or controversial topics.

Second, *relational uncertainty increases the difficulty of planning messages.* That is, people experiencing relational uncertainty may lack confidence in their understanding of social situations, which undermines their abilities to construct and enact effective plans. Likewise, relational uncertainty makes it harder to craft appropriate and effective messages. For instance, Knobloch found that individuals produce less effective date request messages under conditions of relational uncertainty.[28]

Knobloch's third and final claim related to message production is that *relational uncertainty leads people to avoid communicating directly about sensitive issues.* By definition, individuals experiencing relational uncertainty lack confidence in the status of their relationship. As a result, they often avoid talking about sensitive issues because they are unsure of how their partners will respond. Research has shown, for instance, that people who are experiencing partner or relationship uncertainty are unwilling to tell their dating partners about behaviors that irritate them.[29] Scholars have also found that people are less likely to express feelings of jealousy when they are unsure about the state of their relationship.[30]

The second set of claims advanced by Knobloch ties relational uncertainty to how people interpret and process messages. Specifically, Knobloch suggests that relational uncertainty (a) *undermines people's abilities to draw accurate conclusions from their partner's messages,* (b) *erodes people's confidence in their ability to communicate with their partner,* and (c) *prompts individuals to view their partner and their relationship more negatively.*[31] In her program of research, for example, Knobloch has found that people coping with relational uncertainty evaluate irritating partner behavior more negatively.[32] They also describe unexpected events as more severe, more negative, and more emotionally upsetting.[33] Other scholars have found that dating partners are less confident in their abilities to discuss controversial topics (such as religion) under conditions of relational uncertainty.[34] Taken together, communication scholars have supported Knobloch's claims that relational uncertainty affects both message production and message processing in intimate relationships.

Now that we have briefly discussed the key concepts and claims associated with relational uncertainty, let's compare the three sources of relational uncertainty across different kinds of close relationships.

▲ ▲ ▲

Test Your Understanding

Listed below are several questions that often emerge when individuals experience self, partner, and relational uncertainty.[35] Although most of Knobloch's research has focused on romantic relationships, how might we study some of these questions in other kinds of close relationships? Review the questions below and see if you can identify which question of uncertainty within each source (i.e., self vs. partner vs. relationship) is likely to be the most salient (or prominent) in two types of interpersonal relationships: a *committed romantic relationship* and an *opposite-sex friendship*.

Self Uncertainty

1. How certain are you about your commitment to this relationship?
2. How certain are you about your feelings for this person?
3. How certain are you about how important this relationship is to you?
4. How certain are you about whether or not you want to maintain this relationship?
5. How certain are you about your goals for the future of the relationship?

Partner Uncertainty

1. How certain are you about how committed this person is to your relationship?
2. How certain are you about this person's feelings for you?
3. How certain are you about how important your relationship is to this person?

4. How certain are you about whether this person wants to maintain this relationship?
5. How certain are you about this person's goals for the future of the relationship?

Relationship Uncertainty

1. How certain are you about what you can and cannot say to each other in this relationship?
2. How certain are you about how you and this person view this relationship?
3. How certain are you about the state of the relationship at this time?
4. How certain are you about whether or not this is a romantic or platonic (non-romantic) relationship?
5. How certain are you about the future of the relationship?

▲ ˙▲ ▲

As you can see, each source of uncertainty carries with it a different set of questions that may or may not be relevant to every relationship. Once individuals move past their initial uncertainties, how do they develop a relationship? Why do some people remain casual acquaintances, whereas others become lifelong friends? We know that all relationships change over time, but how does this happen, exactly? To explore those questions, let's turn our attention to a theory that examines how relationships unfold through the process of self-disclosure.

SOCIAL PENETRATION THEORY

In the 2001 film *Shrek*, Donkey is walking through a field with Shrek and questioning him about his plans to defeat the dragon and save

Princess Fiona.[36] During their conversation, Donkey suggests that Shrek should simply pull some of that "ogre-stuff" and use stereotypical ogre-tactics to destroy his enemies. Shrek replies, "For your information, there's a lot more to ogres than people think."

Donkey: Example?
Shrek: Example? Okay, er . . . ogres . . . are . . . like onions.
Donkey *[Sniffs onion]:* They stink?
Shrek: Yes . . . NO!
Donkey: Or, they make you cry.
Shrek: No!
Donkey: Oh, you leave them out in the sun, they get all brown and start sproutin' little white hairs.
Shrek: NO!!! LAYERS! Onions have layers. OGRES have layers. Onions have layers . . . . you get it? We both have layers!
Donkey: Oh, you both have layers! Oh . . . you know, not everybody likes onions.

In this scene, Shrek is using the metaphor of an onion to communicate the idea that people have different layers to their personalities, and that the process of truly getting to know someone involves moving beyond our initial impressions of who that person is (similar to peeling back the layers of an onion). Little did the writers and directors of *Shrek* know that nearly 30 years prior to the release of their film, social psychologists were using the very same onion metaphor to describe how people develop intimate relationships through self-disclosure.

Intellectual Tradition of Social Penetration Theory
In the late 1960s and early 1970s, the social landscape in the United States began to change, as people began placing more emphasis on openness and relational freedom in their personal relationships.[37] In response to this cultural shift, scholars developed theories to

explore how openness and self-disclosure enhanced intimacy in re-lationships. The situational view of interpersonal communication, wherein interpersonal communication occurred whenever a small number of people were communicating face-to-face, was replaced by a developmental view. The new view was that the number of people and the physical environment were less important than *who* relation-al partners were to each other and *how* (and *what*) they communi-cated.[38] During this period, social psychologists Irwin Altman and Dalmas Taylor developed social penetration theory (SPT) to help us understand how self-disclosure facilitates intimacy and what stages individuals go through as they move from less intimate to more inti-mate relationships. Similar to uncertainty reduction theory, SPT is a social scientific theory from the post-positivist paradigm.

In their book, *Social Penetration: The Development of Interpersonal Relationships,* Altman and Taylor began with the central idea that relational development is a process, one that includes a series of stages that increase in intimacy as individuals learn more informa-tion about their partners.[39] A few years later, communication scholar Mark Knapp published a book titled *Social Intercourse: From Greeting to Goodbye,* in which he built upon some of Altman and Taylor's ideas to identify and describe the stages of coming together and coming apart that typically characterize intimate relationships. Although Knapp's work refined some of the ideas put forth in SPT, he read-ily agreed with Altman and Taylor that communication is central to relational development, as "relationships are created, sustained, moved, and killed by messages."[40] With this idea in mind, let's ex-plore some of the assumptions behind SPT before turning our atten-tion to the theory's concepts and claims.

ASSUMPTIONS OF SOCIAL PENETRATION THEORY

Assumption 1: Relational development is characterized by changes in interpersonal communication. Specifically, this theory assumes that relationships unfold and change over time as interpersonal

communication shifts from superficial forms of talk to more intimate and personal forms of talk. To illustrate this assumption,
Altman and Taylor used the metaphor of an onion to describe how
self-disclosure helps people learn more about others.[41] Just as an onion has layers, individuals have layers representing different facets of
who they are. Each layer varies in terms of the kinds of information
a person is willing to share, and each self-disclosure helps us learn
more and more about a person we're getting to know.

The outer, or surface, layer of the person contains information
that others can learn about you just by looking at you (such as your
sex, race, and approximate height). Just below the surface layer is
the "peripheral" layer, which contains information you would generally share at informal gatherings (such as your first name, hometown, and college major). Peeling the layers even further leads to the
"intermediate" layers of information, where most of us keep things
about ourselves that we share occasionally, but that we do not pur-
posively keep hidden (such as our religious and political views, or
feelings about our family and romantic relationships). Finally, when
we disclose information that we consider to be very private and personal (such as deeply held values, our private dreams, or our greatest fears and insecurities), we have reached the "central" or inner
core of the person.

Assumption 2: Relationships generally develop in a linear way
as partners move through stages of relational development. In other words, most of us experience a variety of personal relationships
that range in intimacy from "strangers," to "casual acquaintances,"
to "friends," to highly intimate relationships, such as "best friends,"
"romantic partners," and/or "spouses." What determines whether
or not someone we have just met will eventually become a friend,
close friend, or perhaps a romantic partner? According to SPT, it
is self-disclosure. Thus, an implicit assumption of SPT is that self-
disclosure enhances intimacy in relationships: The more information you share and the more information your friend or romantic

partner shares, the closer the two of you will become. Of course, this is not always the case, and Altman and his colleagues later revised this implicit assumption of SPT to acknowledge the role of privacy in intimate relationships.[42] Specifically, they recognized that the *content* of the disclosure and the *meaning* that partners assigned to it was more influential than the act itself in determining whether or not two people grew closer (or experienced more intimacy) as a result of self-disclosure. *does not explain*

Assumption 3: Relationships de-escalate and deteriorate in a process that is opposite of how they formed and developed in the first place. In other words, Altman and Taylor assumed that relationships dissolve in stages that are the mirror opposite of the stages partners go through when coming together. In essence, SPT views the waning of relationships as a process of social de-penetration, as partners withdraw intimate self-disclosure on an increasing number of topics over time. Now that we have briefly discussed three assumptions of SPT, let's examine its key concepts.

KEY CONCEPTS IN SOCIAL PENETRATION THEORY

As is evident from both the onion metaphor that Altman and Taylor use and the assumptions they make about how relationships develop and deteriorate over time, the central concept in SPT is self-disclosure. **Self-disclosure** is the act of intentionally giving others information about ourselves that we believe they do not already possess.[43] From highly intimate conversations with your parents about your hopes and dreams to mundane chats with a romantic partner about your day, self-disclosure involves sharing a part of yourself with someone else. According to SPT, self-disclosure can vary in terms of both the *breadth* of topics you discuss and the *depth* with which you discuss any one topic. **Breadth** describes the range of topics you talk about, whereas **depth** measures how personal or intimate your disclosures are. One way to view the different kinds of relationships you have is to analyze how much (or how little) you have self-disclosed to different people within your social circle. For instance, Micaela may have disclosed some information to Alex across a variety of relatively superficial topics. Based on the limited information we have about her relationship with Jamal, however, it is probably safe to assume that she has disclosed more information on a greater number of both superficial and intimate topics. Thus, SPT would predict that Micaela has a greater level of intimacy with Jamal than with Alex because of the greater breadth and depth of topics she has disclosed to Jamal.

A second but equally important concept in SPT is reciprocity. When applied to self-disclosure, the **norm of reciprocity** states that when an individual reveals something about himself or herself (e. g., hometown or academic major), the other person should respond by sharing similar information, both in terms of the amount of what was shared and in terms of the depth of what was shared.[44] Information is a resource, and when we disclose things to other people, we typically expect them to disclose things to us in return.[45] That being said, it is important for us to remember that reciprocity is a *norm*, not a *universal law*. Sometimes, partners in established relationships reciprocate at a later point in time.[46] At other times, we may be disclosing information to a physician or counselor in a context in which the norm of reciprocity no longer applies. Despite these exceptions, reciprocity remains a key concept in SPT, one that can be coupled with self-disclosure to form a series of claims about the social penetration process.

CLAIMS OF SOCIAL PENETRATION THEORY

The claims advanced by SPT can be grouped into two general types of claims: those related to stages of relational development and those related to self-disclosure and reciprocity. First, Altman and Taylor propose that relationships go through four sequential stages as they develop.[47] In the *orientation stage*, new acquaintances are cautious and tentative in their conversations as social conventions and norms provide general guidelines for interaction. These initial interactions involve very little personal sharing, and in many ways, they are most likely characterized by the question asking and small talk that we discussed in URT. For instance, when Alex first met Micaela, he asked her if he was in the right place for the orientation class. She answered his question, and then introduced herself.

As individuals begin to relax and move *[Breadth]* beyond making small talk, they enter the *exploratory affective exchange stage*. Here, conversational partners exchange mutual disclosures on a wider range of topics, although the content of what is being discussed typically remains at the peripheral and (occasionally) intermediate levels of information (remember the onion metaphor?). Suppose we could have followed the rest of Micaela and Alex's conversation during their orientation session. They might have discussed common areas of interest, personal hobbies, or other relatively "safe" forms of information about themselves that moved their initial acquaintance toward friendship.

Once conversational partners have established a greater level of *[depth]* openness between them, Altman and Taylor claim that they have reached the third stage of relational development, the *affective exchange stage*. This stage typically characterizes close friendships and romantic relationships, as partners use increasing amounts of disclosure at the intermediate and core areas of their personalities to unite them to each other.

According to SPT, the fourth and final stage of relational development is the *stable exchange stage*. Here, conversational partners understand each other very well and communication is open at all levels of the "onion" (i. e., surface, peripheral, intermediate, and core). In fact, so open is the communication in the stable exchange stage that partners often communicate using only nonverbal displays of meaning. They are likely to have access to nearly all information on all topics at all levels, indicating a relatively high level of intimacy.

Consequently, Altman and Taylor suggest that most of us reach the stable exchange stage with only a small number of people.

In addition to the four stages of relational development, SPT also advances claims about self-disclosure and reciprocity. Most notably, SPT claims that *self-disclosure typically begins with information that is public or peripheral and moves toward more personal forms of information as individuals get to know each other.* For instance, if Micaela were to change her mind and meet up with Alex and his friends at the coffee shop, SPT would predict that their conversations would include disclosures that gradually focused more and more on personal attitudes, beliefs, and values, especially if Alex and Micaela are attracted to each other. SPT also suggests that *the rate of exchange changes as partners move through relational stages.* In other words, during the early stages of the relationship, both people are disclosing information freely on public or social topics. As they continue to peel back the "layers of the onion" and reach intermediate levels of information, however, social norms and their reluctance to become more vulnerable will slow the process. Altman and Taylor claim that this reluctance helps explain why many relationships never move beyond the orientation or affective exploratory stages of development.

▲ ▲ ▲

Let's Discuss

1. When someone self-discloses to you, do you feel an expectation to reciprocate? Under what conditions would it be inappropriate or even unethical to do so?
2. Think about a relatively new friendship you have. Which of the four stages of relationship development best describes that friendship? How do you know?

▲ ▲ ▲

In sum, social penetration theory views self-disclosure as the main behavior that helps people learn more about each other and build intimacy in their relationship. It assumes that relationships grow in a relatively linear fashion through stages of development that reflect how much information partners have about each other. It also assumes that information is a resource that is exchanged between partners.

Information isn't the only resource that people exchange, however. For example, you might take your best friend out to dinner in exchange for helping you move, or your romantic partner might help you clean your apartment in exchange for helping her complete an important assignment. At the same time, we don't always seek information and desire similar levels of intimacy with everyone we know. What motivates us to develop intimate relationships with only a handful of people while maintaining more casual, superficial relationships with others? And what explains the decisions we make as we balance competing demands on our time and energy in different types of relationships? In the final section of this chapter, we explore theories that answer these questions and others that relate to communication in developing relationships.

Social Exchange Theories

Would you be willing to marry someone you didn't love for $100 million dollars? If your answer is "yes" or even "maybe," what if you could spend only one night apart each month? And what if your marriage had to last at least 10 years? And what if you had to have at least one child together within the first five years of your marriage? As comical as this proposal might sound, it is the decision facing Brooke Shields's character, Buckley, in the 1999 romantic comedy, *The Bachelor*. In the movie, Chris O'Donnell plays Jimmie Shannon, an unrepentant bachelor faced with the choice of either getting married within 24 hours or losing a $100 million inheritance from his recently deceased grandfather. Although Jimmie's girlfriend Anne (played by Renee Zellweger) loves him, she sees through his sudden proposal and refuses to go along. As a last resort, Jimmie turns to Buckley, a relatively cold-hearted and superficial cosmopolite who is willing to marry him for the inheritance until she learns about all the strings that are attached. In their "shotgun wedding" scene, Buckley grows increasingly anxious as she weighs the $100 million reward versus the costs of living with Jimmie for 10 years and having his child. Finally, she snaps and flees the scene.

Although Jimmie and Buckley's interaction is comical and fictitious, most of us can probably remember times when we had to weigh the rewards and costs of keeping a friendship or remaining in a romantic relationship. In those moments, what determined how satisfied and committed you were to those relationships? And how were your decisions related to fairness and reciprocity? To help us understand what we value in our relationships, and how we use those values to make decisions, we turn our attention to social exchange theories.

INTELLECTUAL TRADITION OF SOCIAL EXCHANGE THEORIES
The idea of a social exchange is not a singular theory, but rather a family of theories that all reflect an economic approach to personal relationships. The guiding principle behind social exchange theories is that people want to maintain relationships in which their benefits outweigh their costs. In other words, people attempt to maximize their rewards and minimize their costs in relationships with others based on a fair exchange of resources. Although different fields have exchange theories of their own, most communication scholars who adopt a social exchange perspective use the *interdependence theory* of psychologists John Thibaut and Harold Kelley,[48] as well as the *equity theory* of social psychologists George Homans,[49] Elaine Walster, Ellen Berscheid, and William Walster.[50] Each theory helps explain why people seek, maintain, and end personal relationships

through an understanding of costs and rewards. Social exchange theories are social scientific theories operating from the post-positivist paradigm.

In the communication discipline, Michael Roloff is a Professor at Northwestern University who published one of the first books in the early 1980s applying exchange principles to interpersonal communication.[51] According to Roloff, an **exchange** is simply a transfer of something in return for something else. Unlike economic exchanges that involve legal obligations, explanations of the rewards and costs for both parties, and typically short time frames, **social exchanges** are voluntary transfers of resources that rely on trust and goodwill. They seldom involve explicit negotiations, they are more likely to be individualized, and they are more likely to include an undetermined and flexible time frame.[52] With this in mind, communication scholars Daniel Canary and Laura Stafford have used social exchange theories to explore how people maintain their marriages and romantic relationships.[53] Other communication scholars, including one of your authors (P.S.), have used interdependence theory to examine how communication between parents affects the relationships of ex-spouses in stepfamilies.[54] Regardless of the specific type of relationship under investigation, all social exchange theories share a common set of focus and scope assumptions.

ASSUMPTIONS OF SOCIAL EXCHANGE THEORIES

The first assumption of social exchange theories is that *humans are motivated by self-interest*. In other words, social exchange theorists believe that humans are driven primarily to pursue activities and relationships that benefit them in some way.[55] Motivation is what prompts a person to act. If we can understand an individual's interests or values, then we can predict and understand their behavior, as their interests and values provide the motivation for their actions. Thus, social exchange theories assume that individuals seek activities and relationships they regard as beneficial for themselves.[56]

Second, social exchange theories assume that *humans are rational.* That is, people use logic and reason when making decisions about a particular course of action. This assumption stems from *utilitarianism,* which is the idea that people rationally weigh the rewards and costs associated with their behaviors. These theories also assume that the logical process of calculating rewards and costs is the same for all individuals.

Taken together, then, social exchange theories assume that individuals are rational and motivated by self-interest. Remember that not all theorists agree with the assumptions behind a particular theory, however. For example, people who believe in altruistic behavior may question whether or not humans are *primarily* motivated by self-interest. For example, are there times when we act self-sacrificially for the betterment of our partners, families, or local and national communities? Still others may disagree with the assumption that people make rational decisions when weighing the costs and rewards of a committed relationship. For instance, do we always act in rational, logical ways when it comes to love, trust, and forgiveness in a romantic relationship?

As you might imagine, the assumptions of social exchange theories often invite criticism, especially from communication scholars who work outside of the post-positivist paradigm. Nevertheless, social exchange theories assume that humans act primarily out of a self-interested motivation to maximize their own benefits and minimize their own costs. With this in mind, let's turn our attention to some of the key concepts and claims advanced by social exchange theories.

KEY CONCEPTS IN SOCIAL EXCHANGE THEORIES

To understand a social exchange, we must begin by defining rewards, costs, and relational outcomes. Put simply, a **reward** is anything that a person values or perceives as being beneficial. In personal relationships, examples of rewards include love, trust, acceptance, social approval, respect, information, and power. On the other hand, **costs** are benefits that we give up as part of the exchange process. They may include those things that are perceived as not being beneficial to an individual's self-interest (such as giving up a job promotion so that your partner doesn't have to move), or things that are missed or sacrificed for the sake of the relationship (such as no longer working out as often at the gym so that you can spend more time together in the evenings). Social exchange theories predict that **relational outcomes** can be determined by subtracting the costs of a relationship from the rewards. In other words, they are defined as the solution to the following equation, $O = R - C$, or *outcomes = rewards* minus *costs*.

Returning to Micaela's relationship with Jamal, some of the rewards of remaining in a relationship with Jamal may be the love, trust, and companionship they have developed over their two years of being together. The potential costs of having a long-distance relationship, however, may exceed the rewards that she's received in the past. For example, the geographic distance between them may lead to fewer opportunities to be together face-to-face, which in turn increases the financial costs of talking on the phone and traveling to see each other on the weekends. This, in turn, may raise questions about their level of commitment and involvement in the relationship (i. e., relational uncertainty), particularly as they meet other people at their respective campuses and develop new friendships. At some point, Micaela may find herself weighing the rewards of love, trust, and companionship with the costs of having a long-distance relationship to determine the outcome of dating Jamal.

Identifying the rewards and costs of a relationship is useful, but social exchange theories go even further to help us understand how our assessments of relational outcomes influence our communication behaviors and decision-making in relationships. Specifically, Thibaut and Kelley's *interdependence theory* provides two additional concepts that help us make predictions about relational satisfaction and stability. First, your **comparison level** (or CL) is your realistic expectation of what you want and think you deserve from a relationship. In many ways, your CL represents your "standards" for a relationship, which are based on both your experiences and the prevailing cultural norms for such relationships. For example, many of us expect our romantic relationships to be monogamous. You might also expect a close friend to be loyal, considerate, and helpful in times of need. Perhaps you expect your father or mother to love you unconditionally and to accept you for who you are. Each of these sets of expectations reflects your CL for that type of relationship. As we examine below, your CL guides your assessments of how satisfied you are in a relationship.

In addition to your CL, interdependence theory says you also have a **comparison level for alternatives** (or CLalt). This is your assessment of how good or bad your current relationship is compared to your other options. In other words, we determine not only whether a relationship meets our expectations, but we also weigh the rewards and costs of that relationship relative to others that we could be involved in instead. Are you satisfied with your current roommates, for instance, or do you think you could find better roommates after your lease is up? Likewise, are you happy with your current friendships from high school, or do you think you'd be better off allowing those relationships to fade and finding new friends in college? Interdependence theory suggests that *we maintain relationships when we believe that doing so is better than our alternatives,* such as ending the relationships or investing in new ones. Later in this chapter, we'll discuss how our CLs and CLalts work together to influence relationship decisions.

Collectively, the CL and the CLalt help us understand some of the underlying factors that may motivate us to initiate, sustain, alter, or end different relationships. We sometimes make these decisions in the heat of the moment. According to *equity theory*, however, we are more likely to evaluate our ratio of rewards to costs over time. Equity theory is a social exchange approach that relies on the **principle of**

distributive justice, which suggests that whomever contributes the most to a relationship should receive the most benefits. It extends this principle, however, by suggesting that the best relationships are those in which your ratio of costs and rewards is equal to your partner's. When we receive less from our relationships than we invest in them, we are **under-benefited**. Conversely, when we receive more from our relationships than we put into them, we are **over-benefited**. Equity theory uses these concepts to advance claims about fairness and reciprocity in relationships.

Now that we have defined the key concepts behind both interdependence and equity theory, let's briefly explore the claims that both theories advance about satisfaction, stability, and perceptions of fairness in social and personal relationships.

CLAIMS OF SOCIAL EXCHANGE THEORIES

If we assume that humans are rational and motivated by self-interest, then it follows that individuals will generally seek to maximize their rewards and minimize their costs in personal relationships. Thus, the first claim of social exchange theories is that *when the perceived rewards of a relationship exceed the costs, people are motivated to develop and sustain the relationship.* Conversely, *when the perceived costs of a relationship exceed the rewards, people are motivated to change and/or end the relationship.* Think of your relationship with a roommate, for instance. There are costs involved in sharing a residence with someone, such as trusting her to pay her share of expenses, giving her access to your possessions, and relying on her to clean up after herself. If your roommate fails to do these things or betrays your trust, you may decide that the costs of rooming with her exceed the rewards she provides, such as being a likable, fun person and a good listener. According to social exchange theories, you weigh the rewards and costs to determine your relational outcome, which in turn motivates you to either continue your current living arrangement or seek a different roommate.

In addition to this general claim of social exchange theories, interdependence theory offers specific claims related to relational satisfaction and stability. First, your *CL predicts your satisfaction with a relationship*. That is, your relational satisfaction changes as a function of whether your partner or friend is meeting your expectations and standards for the relationship. For instance, you might believe that friends should care about your well-being, always keep your secrets, and make routine efforts to stay in touch. If one of your friends began treating you disrespectfully, interdependence theory predicts that you would feel less satisfied in your friendship.

Feeling less satisfied with your friend, however, may or may not lead you to end your friendship. To understand what actions you might take, we need to know what options you believe you have. Interdependence theory suggests that your *CL*alt *predicts your commitment to a relationship*. Whereas your CL influences how satisfied you are in a relationship, your CLalt influences whether you will stay in that relationship.

By combining your CL with your CLalt, interdependence theory suggests one of four possible outcomes. If your romantic partner is meeting your expectations for the relationship (CL is high) and you perceive no alternatives to the relationship (CLalt is low), you'll probably be satisfied with your relationship and you won't be likely to end it. On the other hand, if you become less satisfied with your partner because he or she is failing to meet your expectations (CL is low) and you perceive that you have some alternatives to this particular partner (CLalt is high), you'll likely look for opportunities to end the relationship.

Those two outcomes seem rather obvious and straightforward—what about more complicated situations? Have you ever had friends who seemed happy with their dating partners but chose to cheat on them or leave them for someone else? How about people who are miserable in their marriages but refuse to separate and divorce? Why do people maintain relationships that appear to be so costly?

Some individuals may have partners who meet or exceed their expectations (CL is high), but because they perceive a greater alternative in someone else (CLalt is high), they may choose to end an otherwise satisfying relationship. This may be the case in some instances of infidelity. Conversely, people who are quite dissatisfied with their current relationship (CL is low) may believe that they have no alternatives to their relationship (CLalt is low), and thus remain in a distressing or extremely dissatisfying relationship. This potential outcome may help explain why people stay in emotionally or physically abusive relationships for long periods of time.

▲ ▲ ▲

Let's Discuss

1. Social exchange theories assume that humans behave rationally. Do you share that assumption? Do you ever behave impulsively or on the basis of emotion? Are these ways of behaving "irrational"?
2. The comparison level for alternatives is sometimes used to help explain why people stay in dissatisfying or even abusive relationships. From the perspective of social exchange theories, what would make someone leave such a relationship?

▲ ▲ ▲

Finally, equity theory provides a different set of claims that tie our assessments of rewards and costs to our emotions and judgments of fairness. Specifically, equity theory suggests that if you and your partner receive the same level of benefits but your costs are greater than your partner's, you won't want to maintain the relationship. In effect, this creates a situation in which you are under-benefited, and *people who are under-benefited in relationships tend to experience anger, resentment, and sadness*. However, if your benefits or rewards are greater than your partner's, then you are over-benefited, and *people who are over-benefited in relationships tend to experience guilt*. Because most of us prefer not to feel angry and resentful toward our close ones, or guilty and uneasy about how invested they are in the relationship, equity theory predicts that *relational partners will seek to restore equity rather than remain in an inequitable relationship*. In essence, this theory suggests that equitable relationships are more satisfying than inequitable relationships. It is important to note, however, that partners weigh the rewards and costs in their relationships and assess equity *over time*. That is, we tend to evaluate how fair and equitable our relationships and friendships are in the long run, rather than on a moment-to-moment or day-by-day basis.

SUMMARY AND CONCLUSION

In this chapter, we explored theories that explain how the communication process works to help us initiate relationships, build intimacy, and make decisions about investing in relationships. Uncertainty reduction theory provides a framework for understanding how information and ambiguity influences our initial interactions with strangers and new acquaintances. Uncertainty does not cease to exist after we get to know someone, however. Thus, more recent theorizing about relational uncertainty helps us understand how people's confidence in relationships affects their abilities to produce and process messages. As the process of coping with uncertainty continues, social penetration theory explains how self-disclosure can enhance intimacy by allowing us to peel back the layers of other people's personalities. Finally, social exchange theories provide a vocabulary and a calculus for determining how satisfied and equitable our relationships are, as well as whether or not we are committed to them in the long run. With these theories in mind, let's return to the opening scenario at the beginning of this chapter and see if we can use the ideas contained within each theory to analyze Micaela's situation.

FOR FURTHER DISCUSSION

Thinking back to our opening scenario, use the three theories that we discussed in this chapter to analyze how Micaela might respond to her new friendship with Alex and her romantic relationship with Jamal.

UNCERTAINTY REDUCTION THEORY AND RELATIONAL UNCERTAINTY

1. Why are Alex and Micaela asking each other questions when they first meet during their student orientation session? If we could have listened to their conversation, what kinds of information do you think they shared with each other?

2. If Micaela wants to continue getting to know Alex, how might she go about doing so? Does she currently have cognitive uncertainty about Alex, behavioral uncertainty, or both? What kinds of information gathering strategies might she use? Should she use passive, active, or interactive strategies?

3. What sources of relational uncertainty might Micaela be experiencing right now in her relationship with Jamal? Which specific questions do you think she is asking herself? How might these sources of relational uncertainty be influencing her perceptions of Jamal's recent behavior? And how might these sources of relational uncertainty influence her phone conversation with Jamal later that night?

SOCIAL PENETRATION THEORY

1. Based on the information you have, which layers of the "onion" have Alex and Micaela peeled back thus far? If Micaela further pursues a friendship with Alex, what types of information do you think she will disclose to Alex the next time they talk?

2. What stage of relational development are Micaela and Alex currently experiencing? What stage are Micaela and Jamal

in? If their phone conversation does not go as well as Micaela hopes, what might happen to their levels of self-disclosure and their relationship?

3. If Micaela decides to further pursue a friendship with Alex, how long might it take for her to begin disclosing to Alex what's going on in her relationship with Jamal?

SOCIAL EXCHANGE THEORIES

1. Analyze Micaela's relationship with Jamal using what you know about the rewards and costs associated with having a long-distance romantic relationship. How might her current rewards and costs changes as a function of transitioning from a geographically-close relationship to a long-distance relationship?

2. Although you only have a limited amount of information about Micaela, can you speculate as to what some of her expectations and standards are for having a romantic relationship (i. e., her comparison level or CL)? For instance, how might Micaela feel about Jamal's frustrations with her for choosing to attend Midwestern State rather than Coastal College? And how might her expectations influence her current satisfaction with their relationship?

3. Does Micaela have a comparison level of alternatives when it comes to her relationship with Jamal? If so, how might her CLalt influence her commitment to Jamal?

4. In general, how equitable is Micaela and Jamal's relationship? If you believe there is inequity in their relationship, who is under-benefited and who is over-benefited? Finally, based on her CL and CLalt, what types of decisions do you think Micaela will make regarding her relationship with Jamal?

KEY TERMS

Axiom
Breadth
Comparison level
Comparison level for alternatives
Costs
Depth
Exchange
Face
Face threats
Norm of reciprocity
Over-benefited
Partner uncertainty
Principle of distributive justice
Relational outcomes
Relationship uncertainty
Reward
Self uncertainty
Self-disclosure
Social exchanges
Under-benefited

9

COMMUNICATION IN SUSTAINING RELATIONSHIPS

HOW DO YOU KEEP A RELATIONSHIP GOING?

I MAGINE YOU'VE BEEN in a romantic relationship for around ten months. You believe your partner is amazing and you're starting to think he or she may be "the one." About a month ago, though, you both went to a party where your partner made a racially insensitive comment to one of your friends. When you mentioned it afterward, your partner became defensive and the issue exploded into a fight. Your partner said your friend overreacted and didn't know how to take a joke. You finally decided the incident was one big misunderstanding.

Then it happened again at a work reception last night, when someone mentioned overhearing your partner tell a racially offensive joke. Now you're starting to wonder what this behavior really represents. Is your partner a racist, or does he or she just have a poor sense of social etiquette? Does this behavior occur only when alcohol is present? What other inappropriate behaviors can you expect? Understandably, those questions have you wondering whether your partner is as good a match for you as you thought. On one hand, you realize that nobody's perfect and that you'll have to learn to live with your partner's flaws if this relationship is going to work. On the other hand, you recognize that some issues are too important to ignore. In a way, you feel as though you're being pulled in two directions at once, both toward your partner and away from him or her. You wonder how—if at all—you should move forward with your relationship.

Tensions and concerns are common in developing relationships. This chapter looks at three theories that help us understand why that is the case and how we can manage. First, relational dialectics explores the challenges and tensions that exist in all types of interpersonal relationships. Second, communication privacy management theory addresses the tension between revealing and concealing private information. Third, interactional/systems theory examines how interconnections of complex systems and patterns of interaction may influence personal relationships.

DIALECTICAL THEORY

Research and intellectual pursuits in universities tend to be rational, systematic, and highly structured. But what about the experiences you have in life that are chaotic, uncertain, or confusing? How does contemporary communication theory help you understand the messiness of everyday life? A dialectical perspective seeks to explain the messiness, tensions, and contradictions that infiltrate human interpretation and experience.[57] Primarily an interpretive theory, dialectical theory illuminates the push and pull between interconnected yet opposing forces.[58] For example, a common dialectical tension or contradiction in personal relationships is *autonomy* versus *connection*. In relationships, individuals need separation or distance from their intimate partners, but at the same time, they also need connection and intimacy. Over the course of a relationship, people negotiate or struggle with the degree of their connection with, and their independence from, their relational partners. Dialectical contradictions, such as autonomy versus connection, constitute basic human needs, and the fulfillment of needs is instrumental in the development of healthy relationships.[59]

INTELLECTUAL TRADITION OF RELATIONAL DIALECTICS

Dialectical theories have a strong intellectual history in both Eastern and Western thought.[60] The Greek philosopher Aristotle explored opposition in argumentation and promoted the idea that an argument or claim (**thesis**) is in dialectical tension with its counter argument or counter claim (**antithesis**). A tension can be resolved either by the superiority of the better argument or by integrating the two arguments (**synthesis**). Similarly, the German philosopher Hegel examined the human struggle between **being**, the focus on who we are, versus **becoming**, the potential, dreams, or desires for who we want to be. Unlike Aristotle, Hegel did not see a resolution or synthesis to the life-long tension between being and becoming. On a more practical level, German philosopher Karl Marx highlighted the tension between *production* and *consumption* in capitalist economic systems. The more we consume (material products) the more we must produce (work) to pay for our consumption. Finally, Chinese philosopher Lao Tzu articulated a Taoist philosophy that included the meaning of *yin* and *yang*. According to communication scholars Leslie Baxter and Barbara Montgomery:

> The original meaning of the words yin and yang was that of the shady and sunny sides of a mountain, but yin and yang represent more generally two archetypal bipolarities of Taoist reality: yin, the condition of darkness, the receptive Earth, the complex intuitive mind, the state of stillness and rest, the female; yang, the condition of light, the creative Heaven, the rational mind, action, and motion, male.[61]

Eastern and Western philosophies have each elaborated some version of dialectical thinking that influenced more contemporary theories of dialectics.

Scholars have produced a variety of dialectical theories that focus on symbolic contradictions. For example, William Rawlins explores tensions in friendships over the life span,[62] using many assumptions found in Russian philosopher Mikhail Bakhtin's work on *dialogism*.[63] Richard Conville's conceptualization of dialectics is based on the structural-helical model that explores repeated patterns of behavior that occur as relationships move between different stages of relationship evolution and transformation.[64] Irving Altman and colleagues have developed a *transactional dialectics* that examines how tensions emerge at the intersection of interpersonal processes, physical and social environments, psychological and contextual influences, and temporal qualities (rhythms and cycles of change).[65] For purposes of this chapter, we will focus on the most prominent contemporary perspective, that of *relational dialectics*. Remember that all dialectical theories focus on the interplay of oppositional forces over time; thus, they are all theories of change.

Relational dialectics is based primarily on the intellectual contributions of Bakhtin and was introduced to the communication discipline by Leslie Baxter and colleagues in the late 1980's and early 1990's. Unlike argumentative, philosophical, or economic dialectical theories, relational dialectics focuses on symbolic contradictions. Issues such as autonomy (need for independence) and connection (coming together) are considered symbolically significant in developing and sustaining relationships. Baxter and Montgomery's (1996) groundbreaking text, *Relating: Dialogues & Dialectics*, was part of the communication discipline's efforts to develop a communication theory of dialectics. Let's explore the assumptions, key concepts, and types of relational contradictions in relational dialectics.

ASSUMPTIONS OF RELATIONAL DIALECTICS

Relational dialectics draws its beliefs about relationships and social life from Bakhtin's dialogism.[66] Dialogism is the idea that our thoughts, beliefs, and experiences are embedded in the ongoing conversations we have with people throughout our lives. In many ways, dialogism and dialectical theory are commentaries on relational change and how individuals and couples manage tensions over the course of the relationship's history. The five key assumptions of relational dialectics relate to issues of *centripetal/centrifugal forces, unfinalizability, authorship, prosaics,* and *chronotope.*[67] First, Bakhtin's social theory was founded on the interplay between centripetal forces versus centrifugal forces. **Centripetal forces** are those that bring people together and connect them with others, whereas **centrifugal forces** are those that separate and divide people (much like spinning a blood sample in a centrifuge separate the plasma from the red blood cells). Second, Bakhtin articulated a view of relationships and social life as **unfinalizable**; that is, the issues and tensions that relational partners encounter are never fully resolved. For example, managing the tension between stability and change usually occurs over the life of the relationship, not just for a short period.

Third, Bakhtin asserted that we all speak with the *voices of others* we have encountered in our lives. A central question, therefore, is "whose voice is speaking?" Bakhtin noted that we are all *multivocal,* meaning that our communication is strongly influenced by the voices of others or the multiple communicative influences on our ideas and beliefs (see "Test a Core Assumption" below). Each speech act or *act of communication* is infiltrated by the voices of influential and memorable people with whom we have interacted. Fourth, Bakhtinian scholars Morson and Emerson coined the term **prosaics** to emphasize the importance of understanding human experience at a practical level. According to these scholars, "Prosaics…is a form of thinking that presumes the importance of the everyday, the ordinary, the 'prosaic.'"[68]

Finally, influenced by Einstein's theory of relativity, Bakhtin argued that **chronotope**, literally translated as *space* and *time*, recognizes that "every dialogue is enacted in a concrete temporal-spatial context."[69] Chronotope acknowledges that dialogue occurs in actual situations in space and time that influence how meaning is created and how you connect with, and separate from, others in interaction.

KEY CONCEPTS IN RELATIONAL DIALECTICS

Based on Bakhtin's assumptions of dialogue, four key concepts provide a clear structure for understanding how scholars study relational dialectic processes. The first key concept is **contradiction**, defined by Baxter and Montgomery as "the dynamic interplay between unified opposites."[70] A unified opposite means that two ideas or concepts are interconnected opposites, such as: black versus white, up versus down, day versus night, or happy versus sad. Dynamic interplay means that two concepts are conceptually linked, so that we need one concept to help define the other. For example, without an experience of sadness you would have difficulty understanding happiness. The second key concept is **change**, which is the difference observed in a phenomenon over time. Although dialectical scholars disagree about how change works in relationships, many agree that it involves two different processes: movement to a different place or experience and/or repeated patterns of interaction. Because dialectics view human interaction as a process, dialectical theorists might be suspicious of theories that do not account for change over time.

The third central concept in dialectics is **praxis**, defined as the process by which you are enabled or constrained by previous communication actions.[71] When you interact with someone, what you say and do can influence your future interactions. Thus, previous communication acts cannot be undone or taken-back. If you say "I love you" to a new romantic interest, you might wish you had not spoken the words so early (or so late, or at all), but you would both find it hard to ignore the influence of that message on your future conversations.

Praxis also means, however, that we are free to create, invent, and modify messages over time. You might later say "I meant 'I love you' as a friend," or "I thought I loved you, sorry." The point is that each communication act can be modified by subsequent acts, creating what is called a *dialogue chain*. The fourth central concept is **totality**, which refers to the inseparability of phenomena. Baxter and Montgomery explain totality as "a way to think about the world as a process of relations or interdependencies."[72] Consider that your experience of contradictions involves not just one oppositional pair, but potentially multiple contradictions occurring at the same time that cannot be separated from one another. Relational dialectical scholars Baxter and Montgomery refer to the interconnection of contradictions as *knots*, entanglements of many different needs and processes playing out in roughly the same time periods.[73] For example, partners in developing relationships must negotiate how much time to spend together (integration) versus how much time to spend apart (separation). They must also manage the question of how or whether to communicate their needs to each other. In this case, at least two contradictions are at play—that between autonomy and connection and that between communicating or not communicating. Dialectical theory recognizes that the number of possible contradictions is vast, and proposes that we socially construct relevant categories of thinking and experience that might result in tensions between oppositional forces. In the next section we explore research that documents some of the most common dialectical contradictions.

COMMON TYPES OF RELATIONAL CONTRADICTIONS

Dialectical scholars have identified a significant number of contradictions that influence individuals, relationships, and social systems.[74] Although any single contradiction may be most important at any given time, dialectical theorists remind us that what an individual, couple, or social group might find important can vary a great deal. In the past 20 years, however, dialectical scholars have identified at least three contradictions for relational partners (e.g., dating partners, spouses, friends) that appear to be central for managing relationships. First, **stability versus change** is defined as the tension between sameness or permanence for individuals and relationships and allowing or creating change. Although we want our partner to be stable (predictable) in some ways, too much predictability can lead to stagnation and boredom. Change can be good, but if your partner changes too much or too often, he or she becomes unpredictable and can appear unreliable. One of the dilemmas faced by relational partners is how to negotiate that which is stable in relationships and that which should change, or needs to change. A relationship survives in part because relational partners create and experience both stable and changing dynamics over time.

Second, as noted earlier, **autonomy versus connection** refers to the ways in which people negotiate their competing needs for closeness and distance. Psychologists have long recognized that people need affection, love, and a sense of belongingness to thrive. In wedding ceremonies, for example, new spouses often light a unity candle to represent the idea that they are becoming "as one." But dialectical scholars argue that relational success also requires people to have a measure of independence from each other. Although connection is important, some level of autonomy is necessary to prevent "losing oneself" in the other person.

Third, **openness versus closedness**, reflects the tension between being open and communicative and being closed and non-disclosive. Scholars will often describe this communication challenge as the tension between expressiveness versus protectiveness (privacy).[75] This focuses on how we choose to communicate about our private, inner selves. Should you be 100% honest with others at all times, even if your honesty hurts them? Or, is it best to keep some information to yourself? We all make choices about what to tell our friends, relatives, romantic partners, and others. Being too closed and private isn't good in our close relationships—but perhaps being too open and expressive isn't either. How do you usually manage this tension?

The three central dialectics identified in this section illustrate the kinds of issues and challenges we face when communicating in developing and sustaining relationships.

Test Your Understanding
Relational dialectics recognizes an important tension between the *self* and *other*. According to Bakhtin, self-identity is a dialectical process—the idea of *self* is created in reference to various *others* throughout our lives. That means that who we are is, in large part, based on the influence of significant others in our lives. Here is one test: Have you ever had an idea that no one else in history has had? Have you ever had an idea that no one else in your class has had? If you believe so, talk with classmates to see if you're right, or check the Internet to see if anyone else has written about your idea. If your idea seems to be unique, congratulations...and if you have difficulty coming up with a unique idea, join the crowd! Now, consider these questions: Where do most of our ideas come from? Where do our values and beliefs come from? Where do our ideas about who we should be come from? A dialectical approach explains that most of our ideas, beliefs, and knowledge of self are created out of the communicative interplay between self and other(s). (FYI, a unique idea is not creating a unique object—like the Easter basket you made for your 98-year-old aunt that contained three chocolate bunnies with black dog collars, and a new set of dentures! Or the quilt you made with black, orange, and green images of your ten

hairless cats! After all, where do your ideas about color, quilts, and animals come from?)

▲ ▲ ▲

Relational dialectics was designed to illuminate the types of tensions that people experience in their relationships and to recognize that relational survival may well depend on managing change over time. Our next theory, communication privacy management theory, shares some important principles with relational dialectics, but is a more focused exploration of the tension that exists in the way we manage privacy issues. Pay close attention to the similarities and differences between these two theoretical approaches.

▲ ▲ ▲

Let's Discuss

1. In your own life, in what ways do you notice the difference between *being* and *becoming?* How about in the lives of others?
2. Besides the tensions between stability/change, autonomy/ connection, and openness/closedness, what other dialectical tensions do you experience in your own relationships?

▲ ▲ ▲

COMMUNICATION PRIVACY MANAGEMENT THEORY

INTELLECTUAL TRADITION OF COMMUNICATION PRIVACY MANAGEMENT THEORY

Communication privacy management (CPM) theory is a logical-empirical approach to the exploration of privacy and boundary management in relationships. Communication scholar Sandra

Petronio developed the theory in 1991 based on the importance of self-disclosure in relationship development.[76] Her ideas were influenced by Altman and Taylor's social penetration theory.[77] Altman and Taylor explored the role of self-disclosure in the development of intimacy and used two dimensions for determining how intimacy development works. The first, *breadth*, concerns the variety of topics that you might discuss with another person. The more of someone's interests, experiences, and goals we know about, the closer we tend to feel to that person. The second dimension, *depth*, refers to the level of detail that is shared. In an intimate relationship, we usually share deep, private information that we wouldn't share with casual acquaintances. Altman and Taylor argued that the combination of relational breadth and depth determined the degree of intimacy. This claim led Petronio to wonder how people make decisions about sharing private information, and what risks they encounter when doing so.

ASSUMPTIONS OF COMMUNICATION PRIVACY MANAGEMENT THEORY
The first assumption of CPM is that people have a need to manage **private information,** or data that one person prefers to keep secret. As Petronio noted, "To tell or not to tell is a condition that we frequently face, yet the question is complicated. The question is when to let other know our private side and when to let it stay confidential."[78] The balance of disclosure and privacy is central to the development of close relationships, but achieving balance often reflects a dialectical contradiction where uncertainty and ambiguity are present. How do *you* decide whether to disclose private information?

The second assumption is that **privacy boundaries** help us make decisions about disclosing private information.[79] You do not disclose everything about your life to everyone—instead, you consider your needs, the needs of the other person, and the nature of the situation. Then, you create privacy boundaries that help you distinguish between public and private information. For example, if you are dating someone but find you have romantic interest in another person, should you say something? Perhaps you have a romantic interest but do not decide to pursue the other party. Should you disclose your fleeting interest to your current partner? What factors help you decide?

The third assumption is that people have needs of **control and ownership** (or co-ownership) of private information.[80] When we disclose private information, we make ourselves vulnerable to others and may feel as though we're giving up some of our control over the information. Psychologists consider control to be a basic human need, so if that need is threatened by a disclosure of information, then it should come as no surprise that we experience tension as a result of that threat. Think about a time when a friend shared some personal news with you. Did your friend ask you to keep control over the news and not to share it with others? Or, was the information already known to many people, making your friend feel less vulnerable about your sharing it with others? Petronio believes that we each must manage the tension between vulnerability and control when we consider sharing information.

The fourth assumption of CPM is that the decision to disclose is guided by a **rule-based management system**. According to Petronio, "using rules is a meaningful way to understand different kinds of communicative interactions, including revealing and concealing."[81] Rules for privacy management are developed both personally (i.e., your own rules for disclosing) and collectively. Collective management implies a level of co-ownership of information we have shared or intend to share. The work place is a strong example of environments where revealing or concealing ideas can influence our communication activity. What do you consider a matter of privacy in the workplace? To what extent do you have a right to private thoughts when your ideas have an influence on other's work behaviors?

The fifth assumption of CPM is that privacy management is **dialectical.** In other words, we experience tension about whether to disclosure or conceal our private information.[82] Petronio focuses on the openness versus closedness dialectic as it relates to perceptions of disclosure and privacy. This assumption explores how individuals seek a balance between these to competing needs. How individuals achieve a balance is moderated by perceptions of privacy, privacy boundaries, control over information, and rules. Petronio would argue that CPM explores how individuals make assessments about whether to disclose, and once the decision has been made, the tension shifts from individual tension to collectively co-owned information.

KEY CONCEPTS IN COMMUNICATION PRIVACY MANAGEMENT THEORY

Before we discuss how CPM might influence your daily life, let's define three key concepts: disclosure, privacy, and rules. Disclosure is the act of sharing information that is considered private or semi-private. Disclosure may make us feel vulnerable by taking a chance that others may not protect our private information. **Privacy** refers to the belief of ownership, the right to control, and decisions about disclosure of information, our feelings, and our ideas. As Petronio noted, "making *private information* the content of disclosure allows us to explore the way privacy and intimacy are separate but related fundamentally to the act of disclosure."[83] In other words, one of the reasons we disclose private information is to establish and nurture intimacy and connectedness with others. Finally, **rules** are the formal or informal processes that guide human interaction. Rules help us distinguish between appropriate and inappropriate social behavior. CPM accounts not only for the attributes of rules, but also for their development and evolution. Below we explain four criteria for rule development in CPM: privacy rule foundations, privacy rule development, boundary coordination operations, and boundary turbulence.

Privacy rule foundations. A central question about privacy has to do with the *development* of rules. Petronio argues that some privacy

rules already exist in the general rules that govern individual behavior, family dynamics, and social situations. For example, families
often have rules that restrict a family member from sharing details
of family conflicts. Rules also get negotiated between and among
people. For example, although you may perceive there to be general
rules regarding dating relationships, couples may negotiate their
own rules, ones that reflect the unique features of their relationship. Thus, managing privacy means that both existing social rules
and newly created rules affect privacy management and disclosure.

A second dimension of rule foundations is that all rules have
attributes, which are qualities that help clarify how they function in
interaction. According to Petronio, privacy rule foundations have at
least four attributes:

1. rules may become routine and stabilize (used consistently
   over time)
2. rules may become permanent and form the basis of orientations to privacy (i.e., not just stable but a permanent part of
   disclosure rules)
3. rules may change as they are modified or negotiated over
   time
4. people develop sanctions (rewards/punishments) that control the use of rules

But how do individuals decide what types of rules govern decisions about disclosure and privacy? Let's look now at how new rules
are formulated.

Privacy rule development. Privacy rules are affected by at least
five factors, including culture, gender, motivation, context, and risk-
benefit ratios. First, *cultural* values help people decide what types
of rules are appropriate when concealing or revealing privacy information. Many people have strong needs for privacy, but culture
influences the degree to which privacy is valued. Individualistic

cultures tend to value privacy more than disclosure, whereas collectivistic cultures value privacy less and disclosure more. The point is that culture can have a significant influence on ideas, behaviors, and decisions about revealing and disclosing private information. Second, CPM includes *gender* among the influences on rule development, and suggests that gender may influence how men and women define privacy. Petronio argued that although some studies show that women tend to disclose more than men, other studies reveal the amount of disclosure of private information is equal. Perhaps the biggest difference between men and women is the expectation for disclosure; both men and women believe it is more appropriate for women to disclose private information than men.[84] Third, individuals make decision about rules based on their *motivation* for disclosure versus privacy. People's motivation for behavior is affected by their goals and needs, the type of relationship in which they are acting, and other influences. Fourth, the *context* of interaction has a strong influence on rule development and includes both the physical setting and the social environment. As Petronio explained, "In addition to marking territory, personal space, and issues of crowding, physical surroundings impact both our nonverbal behavior and our choices about revealing and concealing information."[85] Fifth, we tend to make judgments about what Petronio calls *risk-benefit ratio*—that is, the relative risks and benefits associated with disclosing and concealing. When a tension exists about whether to reveal or disclose private information, you may consider the risks or disadvantages of disclosing, and then decide if they outweigh the benefits of disclosing. All five influences on privacy rule development can affect our decisions about concealing and revealing. However, decisions about privacy are also based on individual and collective boundaries, as we see next.

Boundary coordination operations. Because the disclosure of private information creates potential vulnerability and risk, it is useful to consider how individuals coordinate their privacy boundaries.

Petronio identified four attributes of boundary coordination: linkage, ownership, permeability, and coordination patterns.[86] First,
boundary linkage refers to the strength and quality of connection
among people. The idea of linkage assumes that we are connected to other people based on a host of factors, including attraction,
status, gender, and education. Consider your relationship with a
good friend—what is the quality of the connection you have with
that person? What types of boundaries have you establish regarding
your willingness to disclose private information? Second, *boundary
ownership* refers to the control or co-control of private information.
Petronio argued that ownership is about "rights and privileges individuals perceive they have and other accord them as co-owners"
of private information.[87] The challenges of owning private information are not insignificant—when communicating with others, for instance, we may be unclear about whether information is considered
private or public. Without explicit agreements about ownership and
co-ownership, a great deal of uncertainty can exist because the status of ownership is unclear.

Third, *boundary permeability* refers to whether access to information is open (thin boundaries) or closed (thick boundaries).
According to Petronio, "CPM argues that when the boundaries
are closed and protection rules prevail, the information within the
borders is more likely to be considered secret."[88] In contrast, open
boundaries mean fewer restrictions on disclosure. Finally, the first
three boundary permeability conditions, linkage, ownership, and
permeability, taken together, constitute *collective coordination patterns*.
Coordinating your disclosures is thus a complex interplay of deciding whom the target person is, how much trust and risk are involved
in a disclosure, and how open or closed we want to be with others.

Boundary turbulence. A final issue in privacy boundary management is recognition of possible *turbulence* in the system. As Petronio
explains, "Boundaries may become turbulent when the level of permeability is not coordinated or when people create linkages that violate

ownership expectations. Boundary turbulence illustrates that boundary coordination is not always smooth and that boundary regulation is not a perfect system."[89] Sometimes there is boundary turbulence when relational partners have different expectations or rules for what is appropriate and inappropriate to disclose, and when. Turbulence occurs when one partner might expect access to more private information about the other, but the partner does not disclose or grant access to private information. For example, dating partners early in relationships negotiate boundaries about things like past dating history, or past sexual relationships. A rule-based management system helps us understand the logic and decision systems used to determine how and when to disclose private information. Below we summarize some of the research findings taken from CPM.

CLAIMS OF COMMUNICATION PRIVACY MANAGEMENT THEORY

One of the primary claims of CPM is that people experience dialectical tensions when deciding whether to disclose or conceal private information. Managing that tension is a complex and evolving process. Research using CPM has focused on a variety of personal and social problems related to communication practices. Below we discuss a sample of studies that illustrate the theory's practical applications.

Studies using CPM as a theoretical frame have explored a variety of issues, including the disclosure of HIV,[90] infertility,[91] friendships to romantic relationship progression,[92] and blogging.[93] When a tension exists between revealing or concealing private information, turbulence and conflict are likely.[94] When confronted with potential conflict about privacy information, you can choose either to discuss the issues or avoid the conflict. One study revealed that, on average, individuals in dating relationships withhold roughly 40% of all complaints about their relationship to their partners, meaning that partners negotiate the extent to which they are willing to reveal or disclose their relationship problems with their partners.[95]

▲ ▲ ▲

Let's Discuss

1. How do you know that you "own" a piece of information? What makes information *belong to you?*
2. People sometimes feel caught in an ethical dilemma when they are expected to keep information private that has the potential to harm others. How do you decide whether the benefit of sharing such information outweighs the benefit of keeping someone's confidence?

▲ ▲ ▲

Another example of communication privacy dilemmas is the decision of whether to disclose infidelity in marital relationships. Consider the challenges an individual faces when deciding whether to admit to having sex with someone outside the marriage. Why would a person choose to disclose an affair? Under what conditions would concealing the affair be beneficial, either to the individual or the couple?

▲ ▲ ▲

Theory into Practice

CPM claims that people decide whether to reveal private information, and to whom, based on perceived risks, ownership of the private information, and their needs for privacy. Think of a situation when you decided to reveal private information, and another situation when you decided not to. In each case, how did you feel about your decision? Did you have any regrets later? If so, what was the nature of those regrets? If you could turn back the clock, what would you do differently, if anything? What would you say you have learned about the tension between disclosure and privacy over the course of your relationships?

▲   ▲   ▲

In both relational dialectics and CPM, we are reminded of some of the challenges of navigating our individual needs and interests within relationships. Both theories consider not only personal relationships but also broader social networks of relatives, friends, coworkers, and other acquaintances. Thus, they are both theories of human communication and interaction within social systems. The third theory in this chapter addresses the importance of a "system perspective" for understanding human communication.

INTERACTIONAL/SYSTEMS THEORY

INTELLECTUAL TRADITION OF INTERACTIONAL/SYSTEMS THEORY
Interactional/systems theory is not one specific theory. Rather, interactional and system perspectives reflect a family of theories that share common themes and assumptions about communication processes. Most influential is the work done by the Palo Alto group,[96] which focused on interaction dynamics in human relationships and systems. Central to an interactional perspective on human communication is the idea that individuals both initiate communication with others and also respond to it with *feedback.*

Similarly, a system perspective reflects the need to understand the nature and complexity of systems in various contexts. A system perspective informs us about the process of *organizing.* All human systems—from families to corporations—represent some way in which people organize themselves. Systems represent sets of interrelated *parts* that form a unified *whole.*[97]

Most scholars identify General System Theory (GST) as having a significant influence on theorizing about systems.[98] Along with cybernetics and other system theories, GST has a strong foundation in biology and evolution and focuses on the function, structure, and nature of the complex, open, interactive parts and wholes of any given system. As economist Gareth Morgan explains, "The early development of systems theory was very much influenced by perspectives emphasizing equilibrium and homeostasis."[99] *Equilibrium* is the way a system maintains balance. Balance can be conceived in many ways, including balancing input and output, balancing profits and growth, and balancing health and illness within a system. Because all systems experience change over time, the issue of balance is related to the health of the system. *Homeostasis* refers to how the ways in which an organism or organization maintains stability in spite of external influences. Equilibrium is a broader more inclusive term since it includes balancing both internal and external system environments.

ASSUMPTIONS OF INTERACTIONAL/SYSTEMS THEORY

As a family of theories, the interactional/systems perspective has varying assumptions. However, we can identify five basic assumptions that we believe hold true across nearly all theories.

Assumption 1: Systems are maintained through communication and interaction. When people interact and give feedback, that allows a system to function and adapt to changing circumstances over time. Communication also allows members of systems to connect with each other and to understand the functioning, complexity, and variation of a system. Within families, for example, a system perspective leads you to consider not only the communication patterns among family members but also the role of communication in building and maintaining a healthy family system. To determine whether a specific family system is healthy, it's not enough to consider only the isolated interactions between specific family members. Instead, you would focus on the overall communication patterns of all family members.

Assumption 2: Systems are best conceptualized as wholes. Early models of communication focused on the basic, most foundational parts of the communication process. The goal of those models was to reduce the complex system of communication into more manageable units. Focusing on the "parts" of communication makes it difficult to understand how the whole process works, however. In contrast to that practice, most system theory scholars now embrace both a micro perspective (looking at parts) and a macro perspective (looking at the big picture). In families, for instance, communication scholars explore communication between two siblings (a micro approach), while also considering how that communication affects, and is affected by, the entire family system (a macro approach).

Assumption 3: All systems affect themselves through feedback. Interactional/system theory scholars recognize that understanding complex systems requires exploring the nature and quality of feedback within them. Feedback occurs when information about the structure, function, or health of a system is "fed back," or returned to the system. Feedback is critical for system members to assess how well their system functions, in terms of the quality and effectiveness of interaction, the needs of interested parties, the likelihood of continued system health, and other criteria. Feedback is critical to the process of creating meaning. It helps keep a system healthy and can invite attention when a system is in crisis or functioning poorly.

Assumption 4: Systems may be classified as open or closed. Open systems affect (and are affected by) their external environments. For example, a corporation is an open system because it must interact with customers. The corporation attempts to influence customers' buying behaviors, and the corporation is influenced by what consumers choose to buy. In contrast, closed systems have little to no interaction with their external environments, but are fully self-sufficient. The universe is a closed system, for instance, because by definition, there is nothing external to it. Scholars disagree as to whether any social system can truly be classified as closed. That's because social systems (such as families, schools, churches, hospitals, and other systems) interact with and depend on each other. They are interdependent, as we consider next.

Assumption 5: Systems exist in a state of interdependence with other systems. An extension of the idea of openness, interdependence exists when two or more entities influence each other. Nearly all systems are interdependent. Interdependence can exist within a system—as when employees of a bank influence each other—and outside the system—as when the bank interacts with customers or government agencies. For most social systems, the health and survival of the system and its members depends on its interactions with other systems. Recent work in environmental studies and communication focuses on an "integrated systems" perspective highlighting the intense interconnection among human, biological, chemical, psychological, and physical systems. This perspective recognizes that there is no clear or natural separation of complex systems—rather, systems of various types are all interdependent. For example, poor water quality affects not only different species and ecosystems, but human health as well. Environmentalists often argue that we need to see the world from a systems point of view, acknowledging that all systems in the environment influence and are influenced by each other.

KEY CONCEPTS IN INTERACTIONAL/SYSTEMS THEORY

The interactional/systems perspective has many key concepts, including *wholeness and interdependence, hierarchy, entropy, equifinality, requisite variety, system evolution,* and *homeostasis*. First, **wholeness and interdependence** refers both to the total system and to the connections between its parts. Any assessment of a system from an individual perspective is always limited, but considering how a system functions holistically helps us understand its challenges and relative health. You are likely to behave differently in families or organizations if you consider their entire structure and function, rather than focusing only on your place within those systems. Second, **hierarchy** represents the arrangement of power and authority from top to bottom in a system.[100] Hierarchy reflects how some individuals in a system are valued more than others. The chair of a university department is higher on the organizational chart than a professor, for instance, and the professor is higher on the chart than a student. Philosopher Ken Wilbur discusses two types of hierarchies. The first is the human-constructed ordering and priorities of people, such as that reflected in an organizational chart.[101] The second type is referred to as **holarchies**, which Wilbur defines as a natural nesting of parts within wholes:

> Each element [of a system] is a whole that is simultaneously a part of another whole: a whole atom is part of a whole molecule, a whole molecule is part of a whole cell, and a whole cell is part of a whole organism, and so forth. Each element is neither a whole nor a part, but a whole/part.[102]

Making a distinction between hierarchies that exist in nature and those that are human-made is important, because human-constructed hierarchies are more open to change, conflict, challenge, and power struggles.

Third, **entropy** is defined as the level of randomness and disorder of a system.[103] People try to control and regulate systems through policies, rules, and practices, which gives those systems some measure of stability. Regardless of those efforts, however, all systems experience some level of disorder (entropy) that influences their functioning. Fourth, **equifinality** is a process in which a system can reach the same final state in more than one way.[104]. This concept reinforces the fact that there is no single correct way for the system to function. The final state of a system is not always known or desirable, however. For that reason, some system theories focus on the accomplishment of system goals, rather than final states. In this way, equifinality allows us to consider many different options for managing system complexities.

Fifth, **requisite variety** means that a system needs a certain degree of diversity. According to Morgan:

> The principle of requisite variety, originally formulated by the English cybernetician W. Ross Ashby, suggests that the internal diversity of any self-regulating system must match the variety and complexity of its environment if it is to deal with the challenges posed by that environment.[105]

This means that system survival may depend on the extent to which diversity in the internal and external environment is similar. But how is this concept useful? In organization studies, Morgan argues: "If a team or unit is unable to recognize, absorb, and deal with the variations in its environment, it is unlikely to evolve and survive."[106] Sixth, **system evolution** refers to the capacity of a system "to move to more complex forms of differentiation and integration, and greater variety in the system facilitating its ability to deal with challenges and opportunities posed by the environment," according to Morgan.[107] Evolution is about the adaptation of the system; the more a system adapts to changes in internal and external environments, the more likely that system is to survive and thrive.

Finally, **homeostasis** is the ability of a system to regulate its function and maintain a "steady state." When you're sick, for example, your body's immune system attempts to correct the illness to achieve homeostasis. During the illness, your body is temporarily out of balance, so your immune system tries to return your body to a state of relative stability and balance.

CLAIMS OF INTERACTIONAL/SYSTEMS THEORY

Systems theory has long been regarded as an excellent frame for understanding interconnections in organizing. From the logical-empirical perspective, interactional/systems theory is difficult to test because the theory makes no predictions about communication phenomena per se. However, it has been useful for advancing a number of common claims. First, according to Morgan, all systems undergo flux and transformation. That is, within every system there is relative stability but also uncertainty and chaos. From a dialectical orientation, systems can be regarded as the interplay between various oppositional forces such as stability versus change. Second, British theorist Anthony Giddens, the author of structuration theory has argued that all social systems (as opposed to other types of systems, such as biological systems) exist only through their reproduction over time. People engage in system practices that reinforce and recreate their existing systems. Our communication behavior, in particular, serves to keep the system running, which helps reproduce the system, with some variation, over time.

A variation on structuration theory is found in the philosophy of Peter Senge and colleagues at the Sloan School of Management at the Massachusetts Institute of Technology.[108] With respect to environmental issues, organizations, political systems, and natural processes, Senge and colleagues developed six principles or claims of our current production and environmental crises:

1. The industrial system—what we make, buy, and use—sits within the larger system of nature. [Principle of system interdependencies]

2. This larger natural world includes living, regenerative resources such as forests, croplands, and fisheries. It also includes resources that do not regenerate, such as oil and minerals. [Principle of system resources and reproduction of systems]

3. The regenerative resources can sustain human activities indefinitely, so long as we do not "harvest" them more rapidly

than they replenish themselves. [Principle of healthy balance within and across systems]

4. The non-regenerative resources can only be depleted or "extracted." [Principle of system parts—and material resources]

5. In the process of extracting and harvesting resources to produce and use goods, the industrial system also generates waste. This waste comes from extracting and harvesting resources, and from how we produce, use, and eventually discard goods. [Principle of entropy]

6. The industrial system also sits within a larger social system of communities, families, schools, and culture. Just as overproduction and waste damage natural systems, they also cause anxiety, inequity, and stresses in our societies. [Principle of *nested* systems, i.e. "systems within systems"]

Systems theory is useful for integrating a wide variety of physical, biological, psychological, social, and communicative phenomena.[109] Effective systems analysis requires an understanding of observable patterns of interaction or system practices.[110]

▲ ▲ ▲

Consider This
Considering our opening scenario, how can each of the three theories described in this chapter inform your understanding of communication in relationships? If you were actually in the situation described at the beginning of the chapter, how would you respond? What would you do and say? Do you think this chapter provides helpful suggestions about challenges that couples face in romantic relationships? If so, what ideas do you find most useful?

▲ ▲ ▲

SUMMARY AND CONCLUSION

In this chapter, we discussed three theories that focus on processes that influence the development and maintenance of personal relationships. Relational dialectics reminds us that people often experience tensions over the course of their relationships, and that the management of these tensions reflects basic needs of both self and other. Communication privacy management theory extends work on dialectics by highlighting a central tension in the ways that individuals manage their privacy in all types of relationships. In both theories we should consider the fact that many tensions are ongoing, and are not meant to be solved or resolved per se, but reflect the fact that our communication behavior is a *relation* between push and pull forces. An important question for a dialectical orientation is how individuals respond to and manage the tensions. Finally, interactional/systems theory recognizes the role of communication and interaction in the management and continuation of influential social systems. Whereas relational dialectics and CPM focus on micro-level issues in personal relationships, a system perspective reminds us about macro-level issues and the complexity and scope of practices that influence our communication behavior.

▲ ▲ ▲

Theory into Practice

Thinking back to our opening scenario, use the three theories that we discussed in this chapter to craft some potential responses to your friend. Break into groups of no fewer than 6 people, and then divide each group into three subgroups. Within each group, have each subgroup choose a different theory and prepare a 3-to-5-minute presentation on its importance, value, and practical application. After each subgroup presents, members of the other subgroups should comment on possible weaknesses and limitations of the theory just discussed. After all three subgroups have presented their arguments; identify which theory your group found to be the most useful and practical. Prepare a short explanation to give to other groups in class.

Questions for Reflection: Did the class groups choose (by consensus) only one theory as the most practical over the other two theories? Were the groups divided over which theory was the most practical? If so, what accounts for the differences in perspectives of the different groups? What types of weaknesses or limitations of each theory were identified by groups?

▲ ▲ ▲

For Further Discussion

Relational Dialectics

1. Consider a past or current romantic relationship. What kinds of tensions did you experience in the relationship? When were you uncertain about whether you should communicate your thoughts, feelings, or perceptions, what happened? Did you eventually make a decision or is there still indecision? How did you manage the dialectical tension?

2. A relational dialectics orientation applies to more than just romantic relationships. Do you remember instances in family relationships when dialectical tensions were evident? If so, what were those tensions and how were they managed? What about possible dialectical tensions in the workplace? Can you think of tensions that created problems for you at work? Have you managed tensions differently at work than in personal relationships? If so, how?

COMMUNICATION PRIVACY MANAGEMENT THEORY

1. Why does Petronio (CPM) believe that tensions exist in whether to reveal or conceal private information? Under what conditions might you consider disclosure of private information to be risky? Do all privacy disclosures involve risk?
2. Take a few minutes to review the rules for privacy disclosure. Can you identify rules that you regularly follow when disclosing private information? Are there rules that you generally ignore? Do you have additional rules that you have created to govern your choices about privacy disclosures?
3. CPM claims that a tension exists between concealing and revealing private information. Does this mean that CPM is really a theory of dialectics? What are the similarities between relational dialectics and CPM? What are the differences?

INTERACTIONAL/SYSTEMS THEORY

1. Consider the ways in which system theory is useful for the study of human communication. How do we apply system theory principles to our communication practices? What lessons does systems theory offer for potentially improving our relationships with others?
2. How are open and closed systems different? Besides the universe, can you think of any closed systems? If not, what does that say about the concept of closed systems?

KEY TERMS

Antithesis
Autonomy versus connection
Becoming
Being
Centrifugal forces
Centripetal forces
Change
Chronotope
Contradiction
Control and ownership
Dialectical
Entropy
Equifinality
Expression versus protection
Hierarchy
Holarchies
Homeostasis
Other
Praxis
Privacy
Privacy boundaries
Private information
Prosaics
Requisite variety
Rule-based management system
Rules
Self
Stability versus change
Synthesis

System evolution
Thesis
Totality
Unfinalizable
Wholeness and interdependence

10

PROCESSES OF PERSUASION

HOW CAN I GET OTHERS TO DO WHAT I WANT?

L IKE MANY POLITICAL contests, the 2004 presidential campaign between democrat John Kerry and republican George W. Bush often got heated. Through speeches and television ads, each candidate criticized the other's experience, character, and suitability for the nation's highest office. Bush said that Kerry was "wrong on taxes, wrong on defense," whereas Kerry called Bush "a divider, not a uniter." Although many voters express displeasure at such negative tactics, they have been common in U.S. political campaigns for decades for one simple reason: They are often persuasive.[1]

In a presidential campaign, of course, a candidate's goal is to convince people to vote for him or her. To accomplish that goal, candidates communicate with voters in ways they hope will persuade those voters to support them. We can think of **persuasion** as the use of communication to influence someone's attitudes, beliefs, intentions, or behaviors. Most of us began practicing persuasion early in life, when we pleaded with playmates and caregivers to give us what we want. For many of us, those early experiences taught us that although *attempting persuasion* is relatively easy, *accomplishing persuasion* is much more challenging. Indeed, even seasoned professionals such as U.S. presidential candidates often find it difficult to persuade. What are the most effective ways to get people to think or do what we want? Three theories that address that question are cognitive dissonance theory, the elaboration likelihood model, and inoculation theory.

COGNITIVE DISSONANCE THEORY

The days leading up to December 21, 1954, were exhilarating for Dorothy Martin. The Chicago housewife had recently received a prophecy from the planet Clarion that the world would soon end in a great flood and that members of her group, the Seekers, were to be rescued by a flying saucer. Martin and her followers left their jobs and their spouses, gave away their money and possessions, and ceased contact with outsiders to prepare for their upcoming departure from Earth. As midnight on December 20 approached, members removed zippers, bra straps, and any other metallic items that might interfere with the arrival of the spacecraft. Midnight struck, according to one clock, yet no visitor from outer space appeared. Another clock sounded midnight a few minutes later, but still, no visitor materialized. By 4 a.m., the group had been sitting in stunned silence for several hours. Finally, at 4:45 a.m., Martin received a new prophecy informing her that, because of the group's efforts, the impending destruction of the world had been called off.

This event, chronicled in the 1956 book *When Prophecy Fails,* is notable for what occurred on December 21, but even more so for what happened afterward.[2] Imagine, for a moment, how Martin's followers must have felt after neither of her predictions—the catastrophic flood or their rescue on a flying saucer—came to pass. They had given up everything—their jobs, their marriages, their worldly possessions—to stand with Martin, yet *nothing happened.* If you put yourself in their shoes, you might think they would recognize Martin as a fraud and never believe her again. Quite to the contrary, though,

Martin's followers actually *increased their commitment to her and to the group*. Instead of abandoning their discredited beliefs—as one might expect—they started preaching and proselytizing with renewed conviction. What would persuade them to do so?

One of the people standing with Martin and her disciples on the morning of December 21, 1954, was a young psychologist named Leon Festinger. He and two other psychologists had infiltrated the Seekers in order to study its social dynamics. Once Martin's doomsday predictions came and went, Festinger was fascinated by how many of her followers not only accepted that outcome but actually became more committed to Martin as a result. Festinger realized there was a logical explanation for this seemingly illogical outcome, and he formalized that explanation in the form of cognitive dissonance theory (CDT).[3]

INTELLECTUAL TRADITION OF COGNITIVE DISSONANCE THEORY

Cognitive dissonance theory is a scientific theory that reflects the intellectual tradition of the discipline of social psychology (rather than the discipline of communication). Festinger, a child psychologist by training, later changed the focus of his research to social psychology, which is the study of how thoughts, emotions, and behaviors are affected by social interaction. Festinger followed the scientific method when conducting his research and interpreting his results—and for that reason, he crafted CDT to offer a scientific account of how people manage inconsistencies between their beliefs and their behaviors. As a scientific theory, CDT best reflects the post-positivist epistemology.

CDT assigns a central role to cognition. In other words, it assumes that people's actions are largely determined by their thoughts (as opposed to their emotions, their physiological processes, their environmental conditions, or other influences). Given that CDT originated in the field of psychology, the heavy focus on cognition is understandable—and it implies that affecting people's thoughts is an efficient way to affect their behaviors, which is a key insight for those attempting to persuade others.

Although CDT originated in an academic discipline other than communication, communication scholars have used it to create effective persuasive messages that lead people to think or act in specific ways. CDT is therefore a good example of a theory that communication researchers have *co-opted,* or applied in ways that go beyond the theory's original scope.

ASSUMPTIONS OF COGNITIVE DISSONANCE THEORY

Three basic assumptions are fundamental to the claims of CDT.

Assumption 1: Our beliefs are related to our actions in one of three ways. Each of us holds certain beliefs about what is true or false, good or bad, and right or wrong. A given belief can be irrelevant to, consistent with, or inconsistent with a given behavior. Suppose you believe the cultural adage that *honesty is the best policy*—that you should always be honest with other people. That belief can relate to your actions in one of three ways. First, your belief may be *irrelevant to* a particular action. If you're in charge of feeding your dog every day, that's certainly a useful behavior but it isn't really related to your belief in the value of honesty. Second, your belief may be *consistent with* your action. Let's say your boss asks you a difficult question and you answer honestly. Your behavior in that instance is in line with your belief in the importance of honesty. Finally, your belief can be *inconsistent with* your action. Perhaps you exaggerate certain pieces of information about yourself while creating an online dating profile. Although you may have reasons for doing so, that behavior goes against your belief in the value of honesty.

Assumption 2: We notice inconsistencies between our actions and beliefs. Most of us don't pay much attention to behaviors that are consistent with our beliefs, or to behaviors that are irrelevant to our beliefs. For the most part, such behaviors go unnoticed. An important assumption of CDT, however, is that we do pay attention to actions that are inconsistent with our beliefs. Suppose you haven't picked up a piece of dental floss in months, even though you believe that regular flossing improves the health of your teeth and gums. Your action of avoiding flossing is therefore inconsistent with your belief in its value. CDT doesn't assume that you dwell on this inconsistency 24/7. Let's say you see a container of dental floss on the shelf at the drug store, though. According to CDT, you'll be reminded not only of the importance of flossing but also of the inconsistency between your belief (flossing is good) and your behavior (rarely flossing).

Assumption 3: Recognition of inconsistency between actions and beliefs causes cognitive dissonance. When we acknowledge that our actions and beliefs are incongruent with each other, we experience **cognitive dissonance,** a mental state characterized by tension between competing attitudes and behaviors. Suppose you sometimes lie even though you value honesty, or you fail to floss even though you believe in its benefits. Recognizing these inconsistencies puts you in a state of cognitive dissonance—and CDT claims that you will find that state to be uncomfortable. According to Festinger, we generally prefer our actions to be seen as consistent with our values. In other words, we don't enjoy being perceived as hypocrites, those who say one thing yet do the opposite. When we do behave in ways that contradict our beliefs, therefore, we experience mental discomfort in the form of cognitive dissonance.

KEY CONCEPTS IN COGNITIVE DISSONANCE THEORY

The central concept in CDT is *cognitive dissonance.* As explained, people can experience cognitive dissonance when they hold beliefs ("Smoking is bad for you") that are inconsistent with their behaviors ("I sometimes smoke"). Not all cognitive dissonance is equally problematic, however. Rather, three variables in particular affect the magnitude of a person's cognitive dissonance.[4] First among those is the **perceived importance** of the issue, which is the significance attributed to an issue. Even when people behave inconsistently with their beliefs, they are unlikely to experience intense cognitive dissonance if the focus of their inconsistency seems trivial. For instance, many people believe it is wrong to waste resources, yet they occasionally leave on lights in rooms they no longer occupy. Although they would recognize the inconsistency between their belief and behavior in such an instance, they may not experience intense cognitive dissonance if conserving electricity seems unimportant to them (or if they believe they are wasting too little electricity to care). In contrast, people experience more intense cognitive dissonance when their behavior contradicts values that are important to them, such as committing marital infidelity or driving a car while intoxicated. If people believe strongly that these behaviors are destructive, then enacting such behaviors will produce a heightened sense of cognitive dissonance.

A second variable affecting the magnitude of cognitive dissonance is a person's **dissonance ratio,** which compares how many of the person's beliefs are consistent with, versus inconsistent with, his or her behaviors. All other things being equal, someone with multiple dissonant cognitions—that is, many beliefs that are inconsistent with the person's actions—will experience more intense cognitive dissonance than someone who has fewer dissonant cognitions.

Finally, the magnitude of cognitive dissonance is influenced by the ability to **rationalize** the dissonance, or to make excuses for it in one's own mind. Festinger himself once said that "humans are not a rational animal, but a rationalizing one," by which he meant that people do not always make logical decisions but they excel at the ability to justify their decisions in their own minds. One might presume, for instance, that Dorothy Martin's Seekers would have felt powerful cognitive dissonance after failing to experience the flood and rescue they believed would occur—especially given that the issue was obviously of high importance to them. After all, their belief ("I should commit myself only to trustworthy people, whose words I can count on") was in conflict with their behavior (being committed to Dorothy Martin). To resolve that conflict, they had to rationalize Martin's failure—such as by accepting her story that the group's efforts caused the destruction of the world to be cancelled. Once they could explain away the failed prediction, they could remain committed to the group—even become *more* committed—because their cognitive dissonance was resolved. Research on other doomsday groups—those predicting catastrophic, world-ending events—has found that members are likely to remain committed (or even to become more committed) to such groups following failed predictions *if* they can create mental stories that explain away the failures.[5]

As a modern example, many people expected the catastrophic end of modern life to occur on January 1, 2000, as a result of the "Y2K bug." In the weeks and months leading up to that date, several communities in the United States braced for massive failures in communication, transportation, finance, defense, and other vital systems due to the fact that the software programs controlling such systems were able to recognize dates with only two digits assigned to the year. The fear was that, when the year switched from "99" to "00" on January 1, 2000, computer systems across the country and around the world would assume that the date was actually January 1, 1900, causing system-wide software failures. Some even predicted that airplanes would fall from the sky at the stroke of midnight, their computer guidance systems having suddenly failed.

Consider a religious community that believed in the Y2K predictions and worked hard to prepare for the catastrophe. After failing to observe such events, members of that community would certainly experience cognitive dissonance—but their dissonance would not necessarily shake their faith in their community if they could rationalize the failure. For instance, they may decide that the predicted date was wrong, allowing for the possibility that the Y2K catastrophe may come to pass eventually. Alternatively, they may conclude that an all-powerful entity, such as God, decided to spare them the devastation. They may also tell themselves that their prediction actually did come to pass, just in ways that they don't yet recognize. Any of these narratives would explain away the apparently failed prediction, thereby reducing or eliminating cognitive dissonance and allowing members to remain committed to the group.[6]

Other key concepts in CDT relate to the mental strategies people use to manage cognitive dissonance. According to CDT, people experiencing cognitive dissonance perceive the specifics of their environment in selective, strategic ways that help to minimize their dissonance. Four selective-perception strategies are especially common. First, **selective exposure** means intentionally avoiding information that contradicts a person's behaviors or beliefs. Gun control advocates, for instance, may refuse to look at the website of the National Rifle Association (NRA), an organization that opposes gun control. If they do read the NRA website, they may engage in a second strategy, **selective attention,** which means paying attention only to information that supports their viewpoints—such as statistics about accidental gun deaths—while ignoring or discounting details that do not.

With a third strategy, **selective interpretation,** people make sense of ambiguous information in a way that supports their behaviors or beliefs. Consider the claim that countries with tight restrictions on private gun ownership have relatively low rates of violent crime.[7] A gun control advocate might interpret that observation as conclusive proof that private gun ownership causes violent crime. An opponent of gun control may disagree with that interpretation, pointing out that many variables affect rates of violence and that a correlation between gun restrictions and crime rates does not prove that one causes the other. Finally, people experiencing cognitive dissonance engage in **selective retention** by remembering only the details that support their points of view while more easily forgetting the information that does not.

▲ ▲ ▲

Let's Discuss

1. When are your actions inconsistent with your beliefs? How much cognitive dissonance do you experience as a result?
2. In what ways do you engage in selective exposure and selective attention? Are there specific issues for which you are particularly sensitive to opposing information?

▲ ▲ ▲

Festinger did not craft CDT to explain the process of persuasion, specifically. However, as we'll see below, researchers can use the principles of CDT to create messages and conditions that are favorable for persuasive efforts.

CLAIMS OF COGNITIVE DISSONANCE THEORY
CDT makes a number of specific claims. First, the discomfort of cognitive dissonance motivates efforts to reduce or eliminate it. Recall CDT's assumption that we generally find cognitive dissonance to be uncomfortable. According to the theory, our discomfort motivates us to act in ways that we believe will eliminate—or at least reduce—our cognitive dissonance. Imagine that you experience cognitive dissonance about the way you handle money. On one hand, you recognize that putting money into savings is important, not only so that you can make major purchases in the future (such as a car or house) but also so that you are prepared to respond to unforeseen expenses (such as a period of unemployment or an unexpected increase in your rent). On the other hand, saving money is not as much fun as spending it—and there are many things you like to buy. As a college student, you enjoy going out with your friends, planning trips for spring break, and having the latest smart phone...all of which cost

money. You recognize, therefore, that your spending behaviors are often at odds with your belief in the value of saving money. This inconsistency between your actions and beliefs creates cognitive dissonance, which CDT assumes you will find uncomfortable.

At times, your level of discomfort may be so mild that you are able to ignore it. Certain instances can make your cognitive dissonance quite uncomfortable, however. Suppose your closest friend gets laid off from work and is forced to drop out of college due to a lack of money. Seeing that happen, you are again reminded about the importance of saving and you suddenly feel very uncomfortable about your own spending behaviors. CDT claims that when the discomfort of your cognitive dissonance is noticeable, that discomfort motivates you take some type of action to resolve your cognitive dissonance, or at least reduce it.

A second claim of CDT is that dissonance can be reduced or resolved in one of three basic ways. When you experience inconsistency between your beliefs and your actions—leading to cognitive dissonance—you have three main options for responding to that inconsistency: You can change your beliefs, change your actions, or change your perception of your actions.

Consider Carli, who works full-time as a receptionist for an orthodontist. On occasion, Carli takes highlighters, Post-It notes, and handfuls of paper clips from her desk to use at home. She also believes, however, that stealing from others is morally wrong. The combination of her behavior of taking office supplies home and her belief about stealing creates uncomfortable cognitive dissonance, which she is motivated to eliminate or reduce. To do so, Carli can:

1. *Change her behavior.* Carli can modify her actions to make them consistent with her beliefs. Specifically, she could discontinue her practice of taking home her office supplies.
2. *Change her beliefs.* Another option is that Carli can alter her beliefs to make them consistent with her behaviors. In this

case, she could choose to believe that stealing isn't wrong after all.

3. *Change her perceptions of her behavior.* A third option for Carli is to change how she thinks of her actions so they are no longer in conflict with her beliefs. For example, she can *justify her behavior* by telling herself that although stealing is wrong, it is okay in this instance because she sometimes does work for her employer at home. She can also *exempt her behavior* from her beliefs by telling herself that although stealing is wrong, what she is doing doesn't qualify as stealing because her employer would be okay with it if he knew about it.

Adopting any of these strategies would increase the congruity between Carli's behavior and beliefs, thereby reducing her cognitive dissonance.

Third, communicators can persuade by appealing to cognitive dissonance. Knowing that cognitive dissonance is uncomfortable and that it motivates people to act, communicators can design persuasive messages that emphasize people's cognitive dissonance and then offer a way to resolve it. First, communicators generate an experience of cognitive dissonance by pointing out a way in which listeners' beliefs are inconsistent with their behaviors. Knowing that dissonance is uncomfortable, communicators then suggest an action that will eliminate or reduce listeners' cognitive dissonance. The idea is that, because the discomfort of dissonance motivates people to take action to resolve it, people are likely to take the action that communicators recommend.

Imagine that you are creating an advertising campaign to sell a new brand of all-natural, organic peanut butter. It is more expensive than other brands, so many cost-conscious consumers will be disinclined to consider buying it. How can you craft your advertising message in a way that will persuade people to buy?

Using the principles of CDT, you could point out that most consumers want what is best for their families, and that when they buy cheap brands with inferior ingredients, they are not giving their families their best. This statement may generate a sense of cognitive dissonance in people because it highlights a discrepancy between what they believe ("My family deserves the best") and what they do ("I don't give the best to my family"). To make your message persuasive, then, you could offer a way to resolve this cognitive dissonance: *Buy my peanut butter.*

The idea here is that listeners will be persuaded to buy your peanut butter as a way of reducing their cognitive dissonance. The effectiveness of your persuasive message would depend on two things: how successful you were at generating cognitive dissonance in the first place, and how easy it is to take the action you recommend. Not every listener would experience cognitive dissonance as a result of your message. Some listeners would disagree with your suggestion that they believe their families deserve the best products—they may believe, instead, that their families should simply be content with what they receive. Other listeners would agree that they want their families to have the best, but they would argue that the brands they buy are already superior. Listeners of either type would perceive no inconsistency between their beliefs and their behaviors, and would therefore experience no cognitive dissonance as a result of your message. Still other listeners would recognize that 1) they want their families to have the best, and 2) they don't buy the best peanut butter, but they may counter this observation with the thought that 3) they provide the best of other, more important things, such as shelter, clothing, and medical care, so peanut butter isn't important. Although such listeners may experience some cognitive dissonance as a result of your message, it probably wouldn't be enough to create discomfort.

The second element affecting the persuasive success of your message hinges on what you want listeners to do. Suppose that, for some part of the population, you have succeeded at generating enough cognitive dissonance to be uncomfortable. Changing their behavior isn't their only option for resolving that dissonance, however. Instead, they could change their beliefs by deciding that their families don't really deserve the best products. They could also change their perceptions of their behavior by making themselves believe they already provide their families with all the best products. Your suggestion to change the brand of peanut butter they buy is only one of multiple options, therefore. The trick is to suggest the easiest option for listeners to do. Compared to switching peanut butter brands, changing beliefs and changing perceptions are both more complicated. By suggesting that they simply buy a different brand of peanut butter, therefore, you have offered listeners the easiest way to reduce their dissonance, which should make your message more persuasive.

▲ ▲ ▲

Theory into Practice
Let's say you belong to a service organization at your school that decides to do a donation drive for a no-kill animal shelter in your community. You're in charge of creating an email message encouraging students to donate. As a student yourself, you recognize that most students don't have a lot of extra money to donate to charities. Still, you want to raise as much as you can to help the shelter. Craft a message that you believe will 1) create cognitive dissonance among listeners, and 2) suggest how they can resolve their dissonance by donating to your cause.

▲ ▲ ▲

ELABORATION LIKELIHOOD MODEL

Adam Levine has what most people would call a busy life. The Grammy-award-winning lead vocalist of Maroon 5 and judge on NBC's *The Voice* is also a songwriter, part-time actor, and entrepreneur with his own fragrance and clothing line. In 2013, *People*'s Sexiest Man Alive also began appearing as a celebrity spokesperson for the acne product Proactiv. Having suffered with acne as a teenager and adult, Levine speaks from personal experience in television commercials recommending Proactiv as an effective treatment.

By advocating Proactiv, Levine joins legions of other celebrities who lend their names and fame to endorse products. Olympic gold medalist Michael Phelps has done advertisements for Visa, AT&T, Kellogg, Nike, Subway, and Louis Vuitton. Actress Halle Berry has advertised Revlon and Versace; soccer star David Beckham has pitched Adidas and Armani; and socialite Kim Kardashian has appeared in commercials for the diet pill Quick Trim. Companies spend billions of dollars each year hiring top celebrities to endorse their products...and research confirms that such endorsements can pay big dividends in the form of increased sales and greater brand recognition.[8]

The question is: Why are celebrity endorsements persuasive? Suppose you're considering buying Proactiv. Would you investigate the data about its clinical effectiveness and weigh that information against its cost and side effects before deciding to buy? Or, would you be persuaded by its endorsement from Adam Levine (as well as singers Katy Perry and Justin Bieber and actresses Naya Rivera and Kaley Cuoco)? When considering making a purchase—or indeed, taking any action—millions of consumers find celebrity recommendations more persuasive than other data. Why would people rely on seemingly unimportant information (such as which singer or movie star is paid to endorse a product) instead of truly relevant facts (such as the product's safety, effectiveness, and value) when choosing to make a purchase? One explanation is proposed in the elaboration likelihood model.

INTELLECTUAL TRADITION OF THE ELABORATION LIKELIHOOD MODEL

The elaboration likelihood model (ELM) was developed by social psychologists Richard Petty and John Cacioppo. Like cognitive dissonance theory, ELM exemplifies an idea that took root in another academic discipline and has subsequently been used by communication scholars. This practice of co-opting theories established in other fields of study has been relatively common in the social sciences, becoming even more so in recent years as researchers in different disciplines have worked with each other more often.

ELM reflects a scientific, post-positivist view of human behavior. It doesn't predict that all people act in the same ways—even in the same situations—but it does assume that regularities exist in human behavior that can be discovered and understood using the scientific method. In this way, it is similar to cognitive dissonance theory. However, whereas CDT was not originally proposed as a *theory of persuasion,* per se, the ELM was specifically designed to explain and predict the persuasive process.

ASSUMPTIONS OF THE ELABORATION LIKELIHOOD MODEL

Several key assumptions underlie the elaboration likelihood model.

Assumption 1: People want to hold correct attitudes. Perhaps the most fundamental assumption of the ELM is that individuals are motivated to hold accurate, useful attitudes. In the language of psychology, an **attitude** is an enduring way of thinking or feeling about someone or something. Each of us has attitudes—either positive or negative—about many of the people, objects, or issues we encounter in our lives. As Petty and Cacioppo argued, people generally want their attitudes to be accurate.[9] When people hold incorrect attitudes—such as by thinking that something is positive when it is actually negative—they expose themselves to potential harm, because people's attitudes strongly affect their behaviors.[10] For example, suppose you think positively about a political candidate and your attitude leads you to donate money to his campaign. If your attitude is incorrect (because, say, he is a dishonest fraud), then the money you give him may be wasted, causing you financial harm. Similarly, if you have a negative attitude about a product such as Proactiv, when in fact it is a good product, then avoiding Proactiv can harm you by preventing you from using an effective treatment.

To avoid harm, therefore, you are motivated to ensure the accuracy of your attitudes. As Festinger (the theorist behind CDT) pointed out, people often gauge the correctness of their attitudes by comparing them to the attitudes of others.[11] In other words, you might pay attention to attitudes expressed by other people—such as your friends, your family members, or even your favorite celebrities—and then align your own attitudes with theirs, all in an effort to make sure your attitude are as correct and useful as possible.

Assumption 2: Persuasive messages change or reinforce attitudes by affecting listeners' thoughts. Before the ELM was developed, many researchers believed that persuasion would occur whenever people are exposed to ideas that they learn and remember. Consider a television commercial, however. Are you persuaded by every commercial you hear and remember? Probably not—in fact, you can likely think of some commercials you find *so annoying* that you are determined never to buy the product or service being advertised. In those instances, therefore, you have learned and remembered the ideas—but you have not been persuaded.

Unlike earlier perspectives, the ELM assumes that messages are persuasive only if they generate *favorable thoughts*.[12] Even if they are memorable, annoying television commercials are often unpersuasive because they generate unfavorable thoughts. People don't like them, so they don't find them persuasive. The ELM assumes that people are persuaded by messages that cause them to have favorable thoughts. In this way, ELM—like CDT—is a strongly cognitive theory.

Assumption 3: People's motivation and ability to process information varies. Not everyone is equally motivated—or even equally able—to think about messages, however. Both individual and situational factors affect people's motivation and ability to process information. One such factor is a listener's interest and involvement in the topic of the message. The more interesting, relevant, or important a message is to someone, the more likely that person is to think about the information in that message.[13] That doesn't necessarily mean the person's thoughts will be favorable...just that he or she is more likely to consider the message than someone who doesn't find it interesting.

Another factor is a listener's condition when he or she encounters a message. Someone who is tired, ill, distracted, or under the influence of drugs or alcohol will often find it more difficult than usual to process information. A third variable is the quality of the message itself. If it is confusing, hard to hear, or filled with unfamiliar jargon, then listeners will have a difficult time processing it.

KEY CONCEPTS IN THE ELABORATION LIKELIHOOD MODEL

As its name suggests, the elaboration likelihood model tries to explain the likelihood of *elaboration*. According to Petty and Cacioppo, **elaboration** is "the extent to which a person carefully thinks about issue-relevant information."[14] People's elaboration about a message ranges from high to low. High elaboration involves evaluating messages carefully and critically, weighing evidence and drawing conclusions based on data and logical reasoning. When elaboration is low, the information in a message is not considered carefully and thoughtfully. **Elaboration likelihood** is the probability that high elaboration will occur.

Let's say you're shopping for a car and your roommate recommends buying a gas-electric hybrid, a car that runs primarily on electricity stored in its rechargeable batteries. Having never driven a hybrid before, you have many questions about whether this is the right type of car for you. While searching online for information, you come across a website listing the "Top 10 Reasons Why You Should Buy a Toyota Prius." Knowing that the Prius is one of the best-selling hybrid models, you read on and find that many of the reasons on the list relate to the car's fuel efficiency, cost of ownership, high resale value, and low environmental impact. If you are able to understand and evaluate this data—and if you are motivated to make a well-informed decision—then the likelihood is high that you will engage in elaboration by thinking critically about the information and then weighing its merits before being persuaded by the list. On the other hand, if the statistics are too dense or the language is too complicated to understand—or if you really don't care about fuel efficiency or environmental impact—then your likelihood of engaging in elaboration is lower. That doesn't mean you won't eventually be persuaded to buy a Prius; it means only that this particular message probably won't be what persuades you.

According to the ELM, your likelihood of being persuaded by a particular message is also affected by various message qualities. One such quality is the **message source,** which is the entity producing the persuasive message. The entity might be a person, a company, a government agency, or some other organization. In any case, people generally evaluate the source of a message before deciding whether that message has merit. According to research, three qualities of a message source are especially influential: expertise, trustworthiness, and attractiveness.

Some messages come from sources whose education, experience, or abilities make them experts on the subject of the message. In general, we are less likely to think carefully and critically—that is, to engage in elaboration—when a message comes from an expert.[15] The reason is that we assume, whether consciously or subconsciously, that an expert knows what he or she is talking about. Therefore, we generally accept the expert's statements as true instead of generating negative thoughts about the accuracy of the message. In comparison, we are less likely to give a non-expert the benefit of the doubt, which leads us to question claims, generate counter-arguments, and produce negative thoughts about the message.[16] Importantly, research indicates that expertise affects persuasion only if we know before hearing the message that the source is an expert.[17] Learning about a source's expertise *after* hearing the message doesn't make the message more persuasive; likewise, finding out after hearing a message that the source *isn't* an expert doesn't decrease persuasion.

Sources are trustworthy to the extent that they appear objective and unbiased. A trustworthy source presents information as accurately and completely as possible without trying to lead listeners to form any specific conclusions. In contrast, messages from biased sources heavily favor information that supports a particular, predetermined conclusion, while omitting or downplaying information that contradicts that conclusion. Suppose you want to learn more about climate change. Which source is more trustworthy—a university study on global weather patterns funded by the National Science Foundation or the movie *An Inconvenient Truth,* starring former U.S. vice president Al Gore? Most people would probably find the university study to be a more trustworthy source. That's because scientific studies can only report what they find to be true, and their conclusions are heavily reviewed and scrutinized by other scientists. In comparison, Hollywood movies can say whatever they want—and when they intend to lead you to a specific conclusion (i.e., climate change is catastrophic and caused by humans), they can present information in ways that are biased toward that conclusion. That doesn't mean that messages from biased, non-objective sources are necessarily inaccurate or misleading, only that they are more likely to be than messages from trustworthy sources. As you might expect, messages from biased sources are generally less persuasive than those from trustworthy sources.[18] A message whose source appears biased is often persuasive only to people who already agree with it.

▲ ▲ ▲

Let's Discuss

1. When it comes to choosing products to buy, whose endorsements do you find most persuasive? Why? Whose endorsements would you find unpersuasive?
2. How do you judge the quality of a message source?

▲ ▲ ▲

Finally, the attractiveness of a source influences how persuasive his or her messages are. In general, physically attractive speakers are more persuasive than less-attractive speakers.[19] That is precisely why companies typically use good-looking models and celebrities—rather than ordinary-looking or unattractive folks—to advertise their products and services. Unlike with expertise, attractiveness is persuasive even when people discover the speaker's attractiveness *after* hearing the message.[20] Importantly, however, attractiveness has a stronger influence on persuasion under conditions of low elaboration than high elaboration.[21] The more carefully one thinks about a message, that is, the less important the attractiveness of the source is.

Besides the source of the message, two additional factors that affect the persuasiveness of an argument are the argument's quality and quantity. **Argument quality** is a measure of how solid and strong a persuasive message is. As you might expect, research has consistently shown that high-quality arguments generate more favorable thoughts, and are more persuasive, than low-quality arguments.[22] That is especially true when people are people listen to arguments about topics they find interesting and engaging.[23] **Argument quantity** is a measure of how many arguments a message contains. Several

studies have shown that messages containing more arguments generate greater persuasion than messages containing fewer arguments.[24]

CLAIMS OF THE ELABORATION LIKELIHOOD MODEL

ELM claims that different levels of elaboration lead to different ways
of thinking. The principal claim of the ELM is that people use one
of two methods to process a message, depending on their level of
elaboration. We might say, therefore, that there are "two routes to
persuasion": the central route and the peripheral route.[25] When
elaboration is high, people tend to use **central route processing,**
which means they carefully examine the information in a message,
scrutinize the arguments and evidence, and consider other relevant
details before being persuaded by that message.[26] However, when
elaboration is low, people tend to use **peripheral route processing,**
meaning that they don't scrutinize the argument or evidence but
instead pay attention to less-relevant factors.

To return to an earlier example, let's suppose that after seeing
a television commercial about Proactiv, you think about ordering it.
What aspects of the message—the commercial, in this case—would
persuade you to buy or not to buy? If you considered the message using central route processing, you might ask yourself whether the evidence for the product's effectiveness consists of high-quality scientific
data or simply the testimonials of a few users. You may also want to
know what credentials the product's creators had or how the product
compares to other, similarly priced treatments. These are the types
of message features that would persuade you either to buy Proactiv or
not to buy it. In comparison, if you considered the message using peripheral route processing, your attention would be on features other
than the strength of the argument and evidence. You might think
favorably about the product if you find Adam Levine—or another celebrity endorser—attractive. If the commercial contained images of
doctors in white lab coats, those images might persuade you that the

product works. You may also be persuaded if the message shows statistics about clinical effectiveness, even if you don't give any thought to what those statistics actually mean or how trustworthy they are. The point is that when you use peripheral route processing, you don't think critically about the quality of the argument and evidence, but find other features of the message more persuasive.

A second claim of ELM is that situational and personality factors influence which method of thought is used. Most people don't use either central or peripheral route processing exclusively—rather, they alternate between the two. Which route they employ at any given time depends on various characteristics of the situation and on their personalities. The situational characteristic most likely to influence the method of thought is probably relevance. When dealing with issues that have high personal relevance, people are more likely to process messages centrally rather than peripherally. That is, they will spend the extra energy to think critically about questions or issues that strongly affect them. In situations when the issues don't feel highly relevant, peripheral processing is more common because it doesn't require as much effort. Another situational characteristic that can affect the method of thought is distraction. When people are distracted by elements in the environment—such as noise, extreme temperatures, or excessive activity—their ability to pay attention to a message is decreased. As a result, they are more likely to use peripheral route processing because they lack the ability to focus on the message and its arguments.

Regardless of the situation, some people have a strong preference for one processing route or the other. A personality variable called **need for cognition** reflects a person's inclination toward effortful thought.[27] Those with a high need for cognition enjoy thinking carefully about things most of the time. In comparison, those with a low need for cognition prefer to spend less energy thinking. As you might imagine, people with a high need for cognition are more motivated to scrutinize messages carefully by employing central route processing, compared to people whose need for cognition is low.[28]

Third, stable attitude change is best achieved through central processing. When people change their attitudes as the result of a persuasive message, their new attitudes will be stronger if they used central processing as opposed to peripheral processing. Specifically, attitudes formed through central processing are more persistent over time (i.e., they last longer), more resistant to change/less susceptible to counter-arguments, and more predictive of future behavior than are attitudes formed through peripheral processing. In contrast, persuasive messages that induce peripheral processing are more likely to produce short-term attitude change.

As an example, imagine a non-profit group that wants to convince people of the importance of recycling. To do so, the group produces two 30-second online messages that it links to various community web pages. In a clear and understandable way, the first message explains three reasons why recycling is beneficial. The arguments for recycling are specific, concrete, and backed by solid evidence to encourage listeners to process the message centrally. In comparison, the second message features a basketball player from that community's professional team who says "Recycle—it's cool" while spinning a ball atop his index finger. This message encourages peripheral processing because it contains no solid arguments or evidence for listeners to process centrally. According to the ELM, both messages may change people's attitudes about recycling in the short term. However, for those who process it centrally, the first message will be more effective in creating attitudes that are changed for the long term and that actually predict increased recycling behavior.

Importantly, the central and peripheral routes do not differ in the *amount* of attitude change they produce, only in the *strength* of attitude change. In other words, central processing won't cause people to change more of their attitudes than peripheral process-ing. Central processing will only cause the attitudes that do change to be changed more strongly.

▲ ▲ ▲

Test Your Understanding

As you've read, a person's likelihood of engaging in high elaboration (and thus, central route processing) is influenced by that person's motivation and ability to do so. Motivation and ability are differ-ent factors, however. Your motivation is your *desire* to do something, whereas your ability is your *capacity* for doing it. Both are necessary for central processing to occur, and it is possible to have either with-out the other. For instance, you may want to think critically about a television ad, but if the ad is in a language you don't understand, you will lack the capacity to do so. Moreover, you may have the knowl-edge and ability to scrutinize a claim you hear from a politician, but you aren't likely to do so if you don't care about the issue. People who engage in central processing, therefore, are those who *can* and *want to* do so.

▲ ▲ ▲

INOCULATION THEORY

Few businesses spend as much on advertising as does the tobacco in-dustry. In the United States and abroad, tobacco companies spend billions of dollars each year to promote their products.[29] Largely in an effort to reduce the marketing of tobacco to children, many countries tightly control the advertising methods that manufacturers can use. For instance, U.S. law prohibits tobacco companies from marketing tobacco products on television or radio, forbids them from sponsoring sporting or entertainment events under the brand names of cigarettes, and limits the color and design they can use in product packaging and print advertisements.[30] Several government agencies and charitable organizations have also sponsored anti-smoking campaigns, some featuring graphic ads explaining the health risks of tobacco use. Despite these restrictions and campaigns, however, the U.S. Department of Health and Human Services reports that, each day, nearly 4,000 people under the age of 18 smoke a cigarette for the first time.[31]

Thus far in this chapter, we have discussed theories explaining how people can be persuaded. What if the goal were to help people *avoid* being persuaded? What could be done, for instance, to help children successfully resist the well-funded advertising efforts of tobacco companies, making them less likely to start smoking? These are the types of questions answered by inoculation theory.

INTELLECTUAL TRADITION OF INOCULATION THEORY

Inoculation theory was introduced in the early 1960s by social psychologist William McGuire.[32] His goal was to describe not only how people's attitudes and beliefs change, but more specifically, how people maintain their attitudes and beliefs in the face of persuasion attempts. In other words, inoculation theory explains how people resist persuasive messages.

This theory makes use of a medical inoculation metaphor. In health care, an inoculation is the injection of a vaccine or other substance into the body to increase immunity to specific diseases. **Inoculations**—which are also called *vaccinations* or *immunizations*—work by purposefully introducing a weak strain of the infection they are designed to prevent. In response, the body's immune system fights off the weak strain, thereby enhancing its ability to resist later, stronger strains of the same infection. As you'll see, inoculation theory uses the immunization process as an analogy for how people can be made to resist persuasion attempts.

Like CDT and the ELM, inoculation theory takes a post-positivist approach to explaining and predicting human behavior. It is also similar to CDT and the ELM in that it was developed in an academic discipline other than communication and has been used successfully by communication scholars to explain people's responses to persuasive messages.

ASSUMPTIONS OF INOCULATION THEORY

Inoculation theory is informed by two key assumptions.

Assumption 1: People can protect their attitudes and beliefs against counterarguments. Inoculation theory begins with the assumption that most people are able to defend their attitudes and beliefs when something threatens them. Let us imagine, for example, that you have a positive attitude toward corporal punishment—in other words, you believe that spanking is an effective form of child discipline. Now suppose you encounter a message that threatens that attitude, such as a magazine article claiming that spanking is ineffective and psychologically harmful to children. That message acts as a **counterargument,** a claim that contradicts something you already think or believe.

It is possible, of course, that reading the article would persuade you to think differently about corporal punishment. Perhaps your positive attitude toward spanking wasn't that strong to begin with, and the magazine article presented a strong enough argument to affect how you felt about it. In that case, the counterargument would have caused you to change your attitude. In most cases, however, inoculation theory presumes that you can and would defend your attitude in the face of the counterargument. In other words, you—like most people—have the ability to maintain your existing attitudes and beliefs even if others disagree with them.[33]

Assumption 2: Resistance to counterarguments can be enhanced. Your ability to resist counterarguments is important, because without it, you would change your attitudes and beliefs whenever you encounter someone who thinks differently. Inoculation theory assumes, however, that you can learn to increase your already-existing ability to defy counterarguments—just as getting a vaccination increases your body's naturally existing ability to resist disease. This assumption is important because the theory proposes that certain messages act as inoculations against future persuasion attempts. For instance, public health officials may design a message that is intended to help children resist the persuasiveness of cigarette ads. Such messages can be effective only if people's natural ability to resist counterarguments can be improved.

KEY CONCEPTS IN INOCULATION THEORY
According to the theory, the process of inoculating people against persuasive attempts begins with a **threat,** which is the perception that an existing attitude or belief is vulnerable to change. Threat serves as an individual's motivation for resistance. People are driven to resist persuasion, that is, when their attitudes or beliefs are threatened by counterarguments.

According to McGuire, threat can manifest itself in two forms. The first form, *explicit threat,* occurs when people are forewarned that their existing attitudes or beliefs are going to be challenged. Suppose you believe strongly in marriage equality for same-sex couples but you know you will shortly be listening to a political speech challenging your position. You would experience explicit threat in such a situation because you were aware that the attack on your belief was coming. The second form of threat, *implicit threat,* occurs when people contend with unexpected challenges to their positions. Regarding your belief in marriage equality, you would experience implicit threat if a friend began attacking your belief unexpectedly.

Perhaps the key element in inoculation theory is the **inoculation message,** which is sometimes also called the *inoculation pretreatment* because it is typically included at the early stages of an experiment. The inoculation message presents people with weak counterarguments against their positions, and then refutations of those arguments. According to the theory, receiving an inoculation message improves people's ability to resist later persuasive attempts.[34]

As an illustration, recall the question posed earlier about how to help young people resist the well-funded persuasive messages from tobacco companies encouraging them to take up smoking. Communication researchers Michael Pfau and Jong Geun Kang, along with education professor Steve Van Bockern, conducted just such a study in the early 1990s.[35] Their inoculation message, presented in the form of a short video shown to adolescents, consisted of two elements. The first element was a weak counterargument designed to generate threat against the belief that one shouldn't smoke. For the weak counterargument, Pfau and his colleagues used statements such as "smoking is socially 'cool,'" "experimental smoking won't result in regular smoking," and "smoking won't affect me."[36] In an inoculation message, weak counterarguments work like the weak strain of a virus in a vaccination, which are weak enough to avoid causing infection but strong enough to activate the person's resistance. Similarly, weak counterarguments are weak enough to avoid being persuasive but strong enough to elicit resistance from the receiver. The second element in Pfau and colleagues' inoculation message was the refutation, consisting of attacks on the counterarguments (e.g., explaining why experimental smoking does lead to regular smoking, or how taking up smoking will affect the adolescent). Pfau and colleagues found not only that the inoculation messages helped adolescents resist pressures to smoke, but also that some of the effects of the inoculation messages lasted for more than a year and a half.[37]

Presenting counterarguments and refutations at the same time is a process called **refutational preemption,** because the intention is to prevent later persuasive attempts from being effective. McGuire recognized two types of inoculation messages, which differed in how they achieved refutational preemption. *Refutational-same* messages present—and then refute—the same arguments for which they are trying to increase resistance. In contrast, *refutational-different* messages present and refute arguments that are different from those for which they are attempting to increase resistance. According to McGuire, the two types of inoculation messages should be equally effective at increasing resistance to persuasion attempts. For example, Pfau and colleagues Henry Kenski, Michael Nitz, and John Sorenson examined the ability of inoculation messages to increase resistance to political attack messages.[38] During the 1988 U.S. presidential campaign, republicans attacked democratic candidate Michael Dukakis for being "soft on crime." To enhance resistance to such attacks—that is, to make them less persuasive—the researchers created a refutational-same message arguing that Dukakis favored tough criminal sentences and increased funding for drug enforcement. Notice how this message raises and then refutes the very argument that the researchers were trying to weaken (i.e., Dukakis is soft on crime). They also created a refutational-different message arguing that, unlike his opponent, Dukakis believed the U.S. must do better to stop air and water pollution, provide health insurance for families, and expand economic opportunities for all. As you can see, this message addresses arguments that are different from the argument (Dukakis is soft on crime) that the authors tried to weaken. After presenting people with one or the other refutational messages, Pfau and his co-authors found that Dukakis supporters were less persuaded than people who received neither message by a later advertisement attacking Dukakis as soft on crime. As inoculation theory predicts, the refutational-same and refutational-different messages were equally effective.

CLAIMS OF INOCULATION THEORY

The first claim of inoculation theory is that people can be inoculated against persuasive messages. As explained, the inoculation process in persuasion works similarly to the inoculation process in medicine. The claim is that exposing people to arguments that weakly threaten their attitudes or beliefs, and the refuting those arguments, enhances people's own abilities to protect their attitudes or beliefs by refuting similar arguments in the future. In this way, people become "immune" to later attempts to persuade them.

Research has shown that inoculation is successful at protecting people from persuasive attempts on a wide range of issues, such as banning animal testing,[39] protecting against credit card abuse,[40] legalizing marijuana,[41] supporting U.S. involvement in the Iraq War,[42] resisting alcohol use,[43] and opposing challenges to condom use.[44] Similarly, companies can inoculate consumers against the effects of their competitors' advertising,[45] and political candidates can inoculate voters against the effects of their opponents' attacks.[46] Regardless of the issue, the basic goal of an inoculation message is the same: to increase the listener's own ability to protect his or her existing attitudes and beliefs against persuasive attempts to change them.

Second, the target attitude or belief must be in place before inoculation. Inoculation is a preventative strategy. It can help people protect their positions on issues, but only if those positions exist prior to inoculation.[47] Consider an inoculation message intended to protect a belief in free speech. The inoculation can present counterarguments to free speech and then refute them, thereby protecting listeners from later attacks on free speech, but this process assumes that listeners believe in free speech to begin with. In other words, inoculation can protect only attitudes or beliefs that are already in place.[48]

In the early days of inoculation research, many scholars focused their attention on *cultural truisms*; that is, attitudes or beliefs they considered so fundamental as to be virtually universal. A good example comes from one of McGuire's first studies of inoculation. In the aftermath of the Korean War, nine American prisoners of war, when given the opportunity, chose to remain with their North

Korean captors and to renounce the United States.[49] This action spurred Congressional hearings aimed at figuring out why the North Koreans' "brainwashing" techniques were effective and how they could be prevented in the future. Those questions sparked McGuire's initial research, based on the presumption that a belief in the value of freedom was a cultural truism.[50] McGuire believed, in other words, that a belief in the value of freedom could be assumed to exist.

Most contemporary researchers take a different approach. To ensure that listeners hold the attitudes or beliefs that their inoculation messages are intended to protect, they typically measure pre-inoculation attitudes or beliefs, and then account for them in their analyses.[51]

Finally, perceived involvement influences the effectiveness of inoculation messages. Recall that for inoculation to work, listeners must experience some level of threat. In other words, they must perceive that something—such as a counterargument—threatens their existing position on an issue. A certain level of threat is necessary to motivate people to resist a persuasion attempt, and threat is affected by people's perceived involvement with the issue in question. A person's *involvement* might be thought of as his or her vested interest in a position—and when it comes to involvement, it appears that a moderate level is best. Michael Pfau and colleagues explained that when involvement is too high, people aren't threatened by counterarguments, and when involvement is too low, they don't care enough to feel threat. As a result, both very high and very low levels of involvement can counter the effects of an inoculation. On the contrary, people with moderate involvement in an issue care enough—but not too much—to experience threat, making moderate involvement ideal for inoculation.[52]

▲ ▲ ▲

Inoculation at Work: The Vatican vs. *The Da Vinci Code*

The 2006 film *The Da Vinci Code,* based on a novel of the same name by Dan Brown, depicted the Roman Catholic Church in some unflattering ways. Among other controversies, the storyline suggested that the Church had actively suppressed the truth about Jesus' alleged marriage to Mary Magdalene for centuries, persecuting Mary to perpetuate the image of Jesus as celibate. For many Catholics, the movie appeared to mock and even attack some of their most fundamental beliefs. Believing that the film represented a threat to the Catholic faith, Catholic organizations, including the Vatican, issued statements prior to the film's release identifying the key claims in the storyline and then refuting them.[53] Such statements were intended as inoculations against the movie's potential persuasiveness. In the language of inoculation theory, the film's controversial claims were the counterarguments to a belief in Catholicism, and the Church's message presented and then refuted those counterarguments, constituting an inoculation.

▲ ▲ ▲

FOR FURTHER DISCUSSION

1. When do you experience cognitive dissonance? To what extent does it motivate you to change the way you think, feel, or act?

2. Do you sometimes buy products or services because someone you admire has endorsed them? Under what conditions is that likely, according to the ELM?

3. Think of an attitude or belief that you hold so strongly that you consider it unchangeable. If you were constructing an inoculation message to protect that attitude or belief in other people, what counterarguments would you use?

Key Terms

Argument quality
Argument quantity
Attitude
Central route processing
Cognitive dissonance
Counterargument
Dissonance ratio
Elaboration
Elaboration likelihood
Inoculation message
Inoculations
Message source
Need for cognition
Perceived importance
Peripheral route processing
Persuasion
Rationalize
Refutational preemption
Selective attention
Selective exposure
Selective interpretation
Selective retention
Threat

11

COMMUNICATION IN ORGANIZATIONS

HOW DO I GET ALONG WITH OTHERS IN ORGANIZATIONS?

RANDY PAYNE IS a middle-level manager in a financial services company located in the Midwestern United States. He has lived there his whole life and has built a web of meaningful friendships and community involvement. He has been eager to move up the organizational ladder to learn new skills and provide a better standard of living for his family. Recently, he was offered a promotion in his area, but the promotion would require relocating his family to the West coast. Ten years ago, he would have jumped at the opportunity without hesitation. Even five years ago, uprooting his young family for the promise of a better life would have been challenging but doable. Today, however, in addition to his partner and his children, his aging parents who live nearby complicate his decision. His parents have not amassed the nest egg they would have hoped for, and over the last few years, health care costs have depleted their savings. In short, Randy is worried that his parents may need his care over the next several years. Although his organization does have a family leave policy, the "movers and shakers" in the organization don't really use the policy.[1] He is equally worried that if he passes on the promotion opportunity, another one might not come along. He is struggling to make the right decision.

Randy's story highlights how organizations have become primary sites of meaning-making in our lives, how organizational cultures often require employees to signal loyalty by moving, and how "private" decisions made by organizations often have "public" consequences. Randy is challenged to make sense of his career, his place in his family, and his career's place in his family. His sense-making is influenced by his organization's culture, where being a team player and performing "face time" are important symbols of employee loyalty and commitment. He views his difficult decision as an individual problem requiring an individual solution. However, in his quiet moments, he has wondered whose interests are best served by decisions that put corporate goals ahead of personal, family, and community welfare.

In this chapter, we address four theories that help us understand how people make sense of their own and others' organizational lives. We are born into, spend our lives in, and die in the context of organizations. Increasingly, our identities, lifestyles, and national well being are significantly influenced by what happens in our organizational lives. To understand the role of communication in organization contexts, we will first explore Karl Weick's sense making theory, which explains how we bring organizations into being through communication. Second, we will investigate organizational culture approaches, which focus on how communication creates a "unique sense of place" in organizations. Third, we turn our attention to how organizational decision-making affects a variety of stakeholders through Deetz's multiple stakeholder model of organizational communication. Finally, we take up how power and control is perpetuated through everyday organizational communication through a discussion of Barker and Cheney's notion of unobtrusive control.

KARL WEICK'S SENSE MAKING TRADITION

INTELLECTUAL TRADITION OF SENSE MAKING THEORY

You might notice that this book is subtitled "Making Sense of Us." In many ways, Karl Weick was the theorist responsible for our discipline's focus on the process of sense-making as a communicative activity. Karl Weick is an organizational psychologist who is interested in how social worlds are made meaningful through interpretive processes. In that way, his work can be located firmly in the interpretive tradition that concerns itself with meaning making, naming, and interpretation. Like a good organizational scientist, however, Weick is also interested in refining his theoretical explanations—many of which are influenced by evolutionary biology and cybernetic systems thinking—and enhancing their reliability. These seemingly contradictory ontological goals are explained by some of Weick's claims. Weick has encouraged managers to act before thinking in his admonitions to "leap before you look," or "ready, fire, aim." This might sound a bit counterproductive at first. After you've been introduced to Weick's theory, it should "make sense."

Karl Weick published his first book, *The Social Psychology of Organizing*, in 1969 during a time of significant social change and uncertainty in the United States. Against a backdrop of social change, many organizational theorists were looking for theories that would provide more order and stability. Weick, however, embraced the ambiguity of social change and wrote a theory in which equivocality was viewed as a major resource for change and organizational growth and development. Indeed, long before the phrase "think outside the box" became popular, Weick was theorizing exactly that. Communication scholars conducted their first test of his theories in the 1970s.[2] Since then he has been a major contributor to the field of organizational communication and continues to be influential today.[3]

Assumptions of Sense Making Theory

Sense making theory rests on some fundamental assumptions:

Assumption 1: Humans organize to make complex environments meaningful. In other words, we organize our lives, our relationships, our communities, and our workplaces around the meanings that we assign to the equivocal "raw data" of our experience. The term *equivocal* refers to something that can be interpreted in more than one way. Our human experience is largely equivocal. We can act collectively or organize only once we have decided how to interpret that equivocal experience. Let's take nonverbal behavior as an example. If you are at a coffee shop and you see an attractive person simultaneously looking at you and rapidly raising and lowering one eyelid, you might interpret that equivocal behavior in the following ways:

1. The person has something irritating in his or her eye.
2. The person is squinting at the glaring sun.
3. The person has a tic.
4. The person is flirting with you.

You might assign any one of these equally plausible interpretations to the behavior. The behavior itself, argues Weick, isn't the critical determiner of your response. Instead, your interpretation of the behavior, your sense-making, is the critical factor. Once you have settled on an interpretation and believe that the other person shares that interpretation, you will begin to jointly organize your actions and future actions in response. You will proceed quite differently if you settle on the "flirting" interpretation rather than the "irritant" one. These sense-making—or what Wieck call "equivocality reducing"—encounters organize our social realities and bring them to life. In fact, Weick insists that the reason that organizations exist is to reduce an otherwise equivocal world.

Assumption 2: The social world is *enacted* or brought into being through equivocality-reducing communication. As we make sense of the raw data of our environment, we begin to build or create our social worlds. Interpreting someone's behavior as flirting may begin the process of "enacting" a romantic relationship, for instance.

Assumption 3: Sense making happens *retrospectively*. We assign meanings to events and interactions after the fact rather than prior to them. Weick's famous line, "How can I know what I think until I hear what I say?" summarizes retrospective sense making. It suggests that the very act of talking about our experience is the means through which we understand and create our worlds. To continue our example, if we describe to our friends the first encounter we had with our partner, we might explain how that first wink was the start of something big. Through our narration, we explain the present by making sense of the past, whether we are enacting interpersonal relationships, organizational cultures, or even national identities.

KEY CONCEPTS IN SENSE MAKING THEORY

Given his assumptions, three concepts are particularly important for Weick. Those concepts are organizing, equivocality, and the environment. Weick's emphasis on process propels him to focus his theory on *organizing* (the verb), rather than on *organizations* (the noun). Weick says if you look for an organization you won't find one; all you will find are processes, or "interlocked sets of behavior," including communication behavior.[4] In other words, the things we call organizations are really nothing more than ongoing sets of communicative behaviors or organizing. In much the same way that we build a relationship out of the raw data of a passing wink, we build organizations by making meaning of our *equivocal* environments.

If something (an idea, a message, a behavior) has **equivocality,** then it has more than one possible and plausible meaning. Most informational inputs in organizational systems are equivocal and require members to "consensually validate" one particular meaning in order to act. Weick says, "The basic raw materials on which organizations operate are informational inputs that are ambiguous, uncertain, equivocal."[5] As organizational members, we have to communicate to figure out how to interpret that data. Once we have an interpretation, we can organize around it, in much the same way that we might organize a relationship around an initial wink.

▲ ▲ ▲

Test Your Understanding

Organizational representatives often deliver equivocal messages to their stakeholder groups, often in the face of equivocal events. BP's response to the Deepwater Horizon explosion, which killed 11 people and subsequently released the largest crude oil spill of all time into the Gulf of Mexico in 2010, has been roundly criticized. Shortly after the explosion and before a full investigation of its cause, BP spokespersons said that while they were "totally responsible" for cleaning up the spill, they were not responsible for the accident, claiming, ""This was not our accident ... This was not our drilling rig ... This was Transocean's rig. Their systems. Their people. Their equipment." Only two weeks later, BP revealed that many organizations may have been involved, including BP. Just a little over a month after the accident, BP spokesperson, Tony Hayward made the following equivocal remark to a large group of reporters and local citizens, some of whom lost loved ones in the explosion and their livelihood as a result of the spill: "The first thing to say is I'm sorry. We're sorry for the massive disruption it's caused their lives. There's no one who wants this over more than I do. I would like my life back." How would you have interpreted that message? How might a message like that encourage BP to organize its activities in new ways? If you were a local resident, how might you have interpreted his message? Can you imagine how local residents might use that interpretation as a call to action?

▲ ▲ ▲

The process of organizing not only produces the entities we come to know as organizations—it also produces or enacts the environment. The **environment,** in Weick's view, is not something that exists independently of organizing, but is a result of organizing. When organizational actors attend to some aspect of the external world, that is the environment they see, respond to, and engage in. It is only by attending to a new market, a competitor, that we begin to communicate about and subsequently bring to fruition the environment. The environment, like the organization itself, is a product of our attention and action, not a pre-existing construct. "Organizations paint their own scenery, observe in through binoculars, and try to find a path through the landscape."[6]

CLAIMS OF SENSE MAKING THEORY
Organizations and environments are brought to life through a three-stage, evolutionary collective process. The stages of variation, selection, and retention are the centerpiece of Weick's theory. **Variation** refers to changes in otherwise stable aspects of the environment that demand or require our attention. Variations in the ongoing stream of experience offer important interpretive moments that require a response of some sort. A variation requires us to step out of our ongoing stream of experience and focus our attention on something new. It is impossible for individuals or groups to pay attention to every available stimulus; instead, we notice only a very small portion of all the available raw data of experience.

Once we have responded to a variation of something, the process of **selection** leads us to choose a potential meaning for it. Because experience is equivocal, rich with many plausible meanings, there is usually more than one way to make sense of it. Importantly, we typically engage in meaning selection with others through conversation.

Indeed, a group can reinforce and establish meanings that no one member is capable of producing on his or her own. It is by talking through and about experience that we collective settle on a potential meaning for that experience.

After we have selected a workable meaning, the process of **retention** leads us to preserve that meaning in our interpretive database or repertoire. If a particular meaning enables an organization to grow or develop, then the next time an organizational member encounters a similar experience, he or she will likely assign the same meaning to it. Weick reminds us, however, that retention systems are not fixed or static; instead; "they affect subsequent actions; they are frequently edited; they are protected in elaborate ways that may conflict with variation and selection; they are [partially] coercive . . . ; and they contain items that are frequently opposed to the self-interests of persons who must implement these items."[7]

This three-stage process accounts for how organizations change and adapt over time. Weick is careful to remind us, however, that we cannot become overly reliant on our retained meanings. He suggests that organizational members practice *heedful interrelating*. If organizations become complacent and use only stock interpretations, they may fail to enact the most potentially meaningful aspects of their environments. Greater heed better enables organizations to comprehend and respond to "unexpected events that evolve rapidly in unexpected ways."[8] In a study of firefighters' "near misses," Baran and Scott explored how leaders of firefighter teams managed to avoid potentially dangerous situations through heedful interrelating.[9] Communication strategies such as repeating directions, questioning assumptions, developing interpersonal trust and coordination, and assigning accountability to officers on the scene reflect heedful interrelating. Such strategies enable firefighters to organize in the face of life-threatening ambiguity. The authors explain, "heedful interrelating describes the process by which group members engage in sensemaking, not as a lone, cognitive act but rather as an interactive process through which they develop assumptions about the level of risk present in the situation. This process involves group members trying to fix meaning, or pinpoint what is going on, while recognizing that each action they take changes the rules of the game. As such, group members must pay close heed to how their actions may have unintended consequences."[10] This study makes clear routines or rules that worked in one context may no longer be appropriate in another.

Finally, Eisenberg suggests that heedful interrelating asks organizational members to "hold on loosely to their beliefs and remain open to hearing disparate perspectives from others. In this kind of world, people must not only be less certain, but also less certain about the value of certainty. To do otherwise, may invite disaster."[11] Karl Weick's sense making theory ushered in an era of interpretive theories in organizational communication scholarship. Building on the idea that we collectively create organizations through communication, scholars turned their attention to understanding how members create unique organizational cultures through rituals, language and symbols, and narratives.

CULTURAL APPROACHES

INTELLECTUAL TRADITION OF CULTURAL APPROACHES

Karl Weick, a management scholar, focused on sense making that provided organizational communication scholars new ways of understanding organizations and members' experiences of them. Drawing on the work of Weick and other interpretive scholars from disciplines such as anthropology, communication scholars began to focus their efforts on how members experience organizational life. This focus was sharpened at an academic conference in the Utah mountains in the early 1980s and captured in what soon became a foundational text in organizational communication, *Communication and Organizations: An Interpretive Approach.*

That book ushered in a robust interest in the theory and practice of organizational culture. This interpretive turn led to a focus on how members and managers could create culture, "unique sense of place," and a shared system of meanings and values that would guide members' behaviors.[12] Scholars were interested in how culture could be used as a vehicle for connecting members to something larger than themselves, that is, a shared sense of purpose.[13] Practitioners were interested primarily in how "strong cultures" could lead to enhanced organizational effectiveness.[14]

ASSUMPTIONS OF CULTURAL APPROACHES

According to Joanne Keyton, an organizational and group communication scholar, five assumptions provide the foundation of theories of organizational culture.[15]

Assumption 1: Members create cultures. Cultures are not the result of a leader's wishes or vision, nor do members simply react to or "fit into" a culture. Instead, cultures are the sum total of an organization's past and its present members' interactions. Like an ongoing storyline, members join cultures and then shape that culture into something else as they interact.

Assumption 2: Organizational cultures are dynamic and change over time. As new members join organizations and other members leave, or as leaders respond to new issues and opportunities or the broader social surround evolves, the unique sense of place in an organization may also change. Those changes may be incremental or dramatic.

Assumption 3: Cultures are often fragmented. Whereas some organizational cultures appear consistent and singular (e.g., Disneyland seems to be the "happiest place on Earth" for both its members and guests), cultures are often experienced differently depending upon one's position in the organization, one's identification with the culture, and many other factors. Indeed, studies have revealed that even at Disneyland, some ride operators created a subculture that sometimes contradicted and challenged the culture Disney management worked hard to uphold.[16]

Assumption 4: Cultures carry emotionally charged meanings. Members often identify with their work and their organizations. Consider the work lives of a kindergarten teacher, a corrections officer, and a surgeon. In each case, members express, or control, their emotions in specific ways to meet organizational or role expectations. Those emotional performances shape the culture and, in turn, the culture provides boundaries for appropriate emotional expression.

Assumption 5: Organizations provide the "foreground" and "background" of organizational life. Members make sense of current interactions and experiences in light of their understanding of the existing culture. However, those interactions then reinforce, tweak, or transform the culture, which then becomes the backdrop for future interactions. Thus, cultures are created and recreated continuously.

KEY CONCEPTS IN ORGANIZATIONAL CULTURE

One definition of organizational culture is "the unique sense of place" that characterizes an organization. A more precise definition is that provided by Keyton: "Organizational culture is the set(s) of artifacts, values, and assumptions that emerge from the interactions of organizational members."[17] This definition highlights how organizational culture is both an ongoing process as well as a product of organizational communication. This definition also contains several key components.

Artifacts are the stuff of organizational life. They are the tangible features of organizational experience that members can see, hear, touch, taste, smell, or otherwise encounter. When you walk into an organization such as your university, your grocery story, or your doctor's office, what do you see? In a classroom, you may see individual desks in row or several large tables with chairs distributed across the room. What does the furniture suggest to you about the teaching and learning that take place in each configuration? How might interactions in the different seating configurations influence the culture? When other students come to class, what are they wearing? What about the professor? How does the dress code, however informal, influence the interactions in the classroom? Office furniture, dress codes, surveillance cameras, norms for routine interactions, and stories about organizational heroes, successes, and significant events, as well as office gossip are all examples of artifacts. Of course, artifacts do not make cultures. Artifacts reflect and are interpreted in terms of cultural norms and values.

Organizational communication scholar Kathy Miller describes **values** as simply what "ought" to happen in an organization.[18] Celebrated organizational theorist Edgan Schein explains *espoused values* as the "articulated publicly announced principles and values that the group is trying to achieve."[19] Espoused values might include innovation, product quality, competitive pricing, or work-life wellness. Schein recognizes, however, that what organizations *say they ought to do* and what they *actually do* may sometimes differ. For example, an organization that claims to value teamwork might offer rewards and incentives only to individuals. Similarly, a company may claim on its website to embrace diversity but a quick look at its top management team may reveal a homogenous group. If an organization's espoused values are inconsistent with its enacted values, the culture may be less coherent and may be poised for an uncomfortable and unplanned cultural shift. When espoused values and enacted values are aligned, a culture is likely to be stronger and more coherent. In sum, values undergird a variety of organizational processes and practices, though they are not always explicitly articulated. Additionally, the values of some policies and practices may align, compete with, or contest the values of other organizational policies and practices.

If we drill down into a culture's core, what we find are guiding *assumptions,* which are deeply entrenched, rarely examined, and taken-for-granted beliefs about the nature of reality, knowledge, truth, humanity, work, and relationships.[20] Assumptions guide how we should think, feel, and act, and to do otherwise would not "make sense" to us. For example, if we assume that humans strive to be as productive as possible, then we will design workplaces that give workers autonomy, creativity, and self-direction.

In cultures that value individualism, such as the United States, people commonly organize their work lives and personal lives as very separate and compartmentalized spheres and link rewards directly to individual contributions. In other, collectively oriented cultures, the self is viewed as meaningful only in terms of the collective. Thus, the idea of separating work and personal life simply does not make sense and rewards and sacrifice are shared across the community. For example, Japanese organizations tend to provide organizational bonuses to all members and additional bonuses to members of high-performing teams. Additionally, seniority-based pay is common. These practices or artifacts reflect the cultural assumptions that family, the group, harmony, and commitment to the long term are the foundations for a good work life.[21] Although leaders and members may not verbalize the assumption that the self is a product of a collective, that assumption underlies many stated values (e.g., teamwork) and artifacts (e.g., bonuses for all).

▲　▲　▲

Test Your Understanding

According to the *Washington Post*, Google's philosophy assumes that "Generous, quirky perks keep employees happy and thinking in unconventional ways, helping Google innovate as it rapidly expands into new lines of business."[22] Which organizational values do you think drive each of the following cultural practices at Google? (see www.google.com/about/corporate/company/culture.html)

1. Local expressions of each location, from a mural in Buenos Aires to ski gondolas in Zurich, showcasing each office's region and personality.
2. Bicycles or scooters for efficient travel between meetings; dogs; lava lamps; massage chairs; large inflatable balls.
3. Googlers sharing cubes, yurts, and huddle rooms—and very few solo offices.
4. Laptops everywhere—standard issue for mobile coding, email on the go, and note-taking.
5. Foosball, pool tables, volleyball courts, assorted video games, pianos, ping pong tables, and gyms that offer yoga and dance classes.
6. Grassroots employee groups for all interests, like medication, film, wine tasting, and salsa dancing.
7. Health lunches and dinners for all employees at a variety of cafes.
8. Break rooms packed with a variety of snacks and drinks.

Can one practice be informed by more than one value? How would you know which value is most important in the organization's culture? What assumptions about "the nature of work," "knowledge," and "the nature of humanity" are reflected in these practices? Do you think these assumptions could serve as a foundation for other, perhaps more traditional, organizations?

⋏ ⋏ ⋏

Claims of Organizational Culture

Organizational communication scholars agree that culture is a useful conceptual tool for explaining how members create and recreate their social realities. They disagree, however, over the extent to which cultures can be manipulated, directed, or "engineered".[23] Some argue that CEOs, founders, and inspirational leaders can grow a particular culture by attending to the symbolic side of organizational life. By telling stories, staging rituals, promoting heroes, leveraging other important artifacts, and tying material rewards directly to the performance of key cultural values, some scholars believe that leaders or "symbolic managers" can influence a culture in significant and lasting ways.[24] Others suggest that culture "emerges" through everyday interaction and is not necessarily something that can be controlled by organizational leaders. "Leaders," says Martin, "don't create cultures; members of the culture do."[25] The truth likely lies somewhere in between these two positions.

If there is no general consensus on the degree to which culture can be managed, there is similarly no consensus on precisely how cultures should be studied. In other words, the strategies to discover an organization's culture vary. Because cultures are not always immediately observable owing to their grounding in unarticulated assumptions, culture scholars have to describe and interpret the culture in order to understand it. Culture scholars typically adopt ethnographic methods such as interviewing members, observing the everyday "goings on" in the organization, reading organizational documents, and participating in organizational life. Ethnographer Bud Goodall studied culture by following clues, like an organizational detective working to piece together the mystery—the cultural story of an organization and its members—to share with others.[26] *Ethnography,* after all, literally means writing culture. As texts, cultures can be interpreted in different ways, and thus there are often many tales to be told about the same culture.[27] Each tale helps us to understand and make sense of organizational life and our places within it.

DEETZ'S MULTIPLE STAKEHOLDER MODEL

INTELLECTUAL TRADITION OF THE MULTIPLE STAKEHOLDER MODEL

The interpretive turn, influenced as it was by Weick and organizational culture scholarship, provided an important moment for organizational communication theory. It centered our focus on understanding how members created their social worlds and moved us away from conceiving of organizational communication theory as a tool for managers to exact more productivity. The focus on shared meanings and strong cultures, however, tended to gloss over the power dynamics at work in cultures. Critical organizational communication scholars soon realized that one feature of organizing that was under-theorized in interpretive approaches was power. Deetz's multiple stakeholder model of communication addresses the often taken-for-granted power that organizations have to influence our lives, even as we may actively and consensually create these less-than-democratic cultures.[28] His model offers us a way out of corporate controlled cultures through a new way of conceiving and practicing organizational communication.

Stanley Deetz is an organizational communication scholar who has long been interested in how communication can either enhance or repress the democratic and participatory potential of organizations. Deetz's stakeholder theory comes out of the critical orientation, a tradition concerned with the power of organizations to control our lives at work and beyond. Deetz, in particular, is concerned with how corporations have become the primary site of the most fundamental social, economic, and political decision making of our day, thus eroding our ability to participate fully in our democratic process. In other words, the decisions that most powerfully influence our public and civic lives are being made in private corporate boardrooms without public representation, rather than in the public voting booth.

Decisions about where we work, how we work, how we raise our families, how we engage our communities, and even how we use or misuse natural resources are determined largely by corporate policies and practices. If, for example, an organizational culture prizes "face time," holds up "workaholics" as heroes, and rewards employees who come in early, stay late, and take home work on the weekends, then family life, leisure, and community service are likely to suffer. As Deetz and Putnam say, "we must ask fundamental questions about where significant decisions are made and how the process of making these decisions can be made more effective and democratic."[29]

Corporate decision-making also influences how different employees are valued. The common perception that the free market's demand is the sole determinant of an employee's worth is only part of the story, claims Deetz. Market demand is only one mechanism that determines how we reward different categories of workers and work in our culture. Other mechanisms for determining value are communicative: we socially construct, via decision-making, how some organizational members are symbolically and materially valued over others. These decisions, says Deetz, are political decisions, not simply market decisions. When he uses the term "political," he is not referring to a political party (e.g., Republican, Democrat, Libertarian, or Green), but instead to how decision-making privileges the interests of some members of the organization over those of others. The politics of how we distribute corporate resources are evident when we look at how CEOs are rewarded relative to other categories of workers. Table 11.1 demonstrates how organizational decision-making values top members of an organization at exponentially greater rates than most rank-and-file employees.

Deetz is not arguing that CEOs should not be well compensated. Rather, he believes the needs of everyone who contributes to and is affected by organizations should be represented in critical decisions. He is proposing that we change the way we conceive of organizational communication. Specifically, he recommends using organizational communication as a means to negotiate values rather than assuming that values are already fixed and that organizational decision-making processes merely express and manifest values. This is critical for us, he claims. As he argues, "The problem is not that values enter into decisions; that much is inevitable and can be positive. The problem is that all important values do not enter in equally."[30] The challenge is to think of organizational decision-making as an appropriate political site to address these fundamental value questions. His multiple stakeholder model outlines just such a theory. His theory serves as a model for how communication can be used to make organizations more responsive to all stakeholders' needs and to recover the democratic potential of organizing.

Table 11.1 CEO Compensation Compared to Minimum Wage and Median Wage Workers

CEO/Company	Annual/Hourly Compensation (Salary, Bonuses, Stock Options, and other Remuneration)	Annual/Hourly Compensation for Minimum Wage Worker	Annual/Hourly Compensation for Median Wage Worker	Number of Years Minimum/Median Wage Worker Would Work to Earn one year of CEO Salary
Ray R. Irani/ Occidental Petroleum Corp	$76,107,010/ $36,589.91	$15,080/ $7.25	$33,190/ $15.96	5046 years (Completion Date 7057 A.D.)/2293 years (Completion Date 4304 A.D.)
Randall L. Stephenson/ AT&T Inc	$27,341,628/ $13,145.01	$15,080/ $7.25	$33,190/ $15.96	(1813 years Completion Date 3824 A.D.)/823 years (Completion Date 2834 A.D.)
Wayne T. Smith/ Community Health Systems	$20,960,569/ 10,077.20	$15,080/ $7.25	$33,190/ $15.96	1389 years (Completion Date 3400 A.D.) /631 years (Completion Date 2642 A.D.)

ASSUMPTIONS OF THE MULTIPLE STAKEHOLDER MODEL

In *Transforming Communication, Transforming Business: Building Responsive and Responsible Workplaces,* Deetz lays out five assumptions of his multiple stakeholder model of organizational communication that can recover and invigorate the democratic potential of our ways of living and being in contemporary culture:[31]

Assumption 1: We need widespread participation because diverse group participation in corporate decision-making will lead to better decisions than are currently being made. The spate of questionable, even unethical corporate decisions at organizations such as Enron, WorldCom, Bernard L. Madoff Investment Securities, Rupert Murdoch's News of the World, and a host of others suggests that there are systemic problems with current decision-making models.

Assumption 2: People can make good collaborative decisions if given the chance and forum. Although many of us have had to sit through ineffective, time-wasting meetings, there is empirical evidence that decision quality, effectiveness, and efficiency are improved by participatory—instead of top-down—decision-making.

Assumption 3: If people are to make the high-quality collaborative decisions necessary in complex situations, they will need better information and training. Too often, organizational members are not given access to the information that provides a context and fuller understanding of decision situations, nor are they trained in effective decision-making processes. These problems are relatively easy to correct.

Assumption 4: The understanding of communication that underlies most models of collaboration and joint decision- making is misleading and leads to shortcomings. Too often, communication is considered an act of simply "expressing" what is already in one's head. Deetz suggests that we have to engage in communication to understand what's in our heads, how it got there, and how it might be changed to better represent our interests.

Assumption 5: Fundamental change is possible. Change requires new ways of thinking about what it means to be an organizational member, what it means to talk with others, and what it means to do business.

KEY CONCEPTS IN THE MULTIPLE STAKEHOLDER MODEL

Although the concepts in Deetz's multiple stakeholder model are simple, the transformation he calls forth through his use of those concepts is complex. One central concept is a stakeholder (a riff, perhaps, on the term *stockholder,* a person who has a monetary investment in an organization). A **stakeholder** is simply a person or group who has a "stake" or an interest in an organization's decision-making. A stakeholder invests in and is affected by decisions made by corporations. Stakeholders include consumers, workers, investors, suppliers, host communities, and society at large.

Investors are typically seen as having a stake in an organization. What about the community in which an organization is located? What stake does the general society have in an organization's decisions? It is in a society's interest to have a stable economy, a high quality of life, a civil and secure public sphere, and fair treatment of members. Those goals can be realized through participatory decision-making.

A second concept in the multiple stakeholder model is **coordination**. As may be clear from the preceding list, creating organizational spaces and practices to satisfy the needs of all the various stakeholders is a tall order. Management's role in democratic organizations is to coordinate competing needs and interests through negotiated and participatory decision-making.

A final concept in the multiple stakeholder model is **outcomes**. Through participatory decision-making, organizations can become sites where diverse stakeholders negotiate meaningful and satisfying outcomes around the following issues such as goods and services, income redistribution, use of resources, environmental effects, economic stability, labor force development, life styles, profit, personal identities, and childrearing practices. (Note how profit is only one of many meaningful outcomes.)

When stakeholders have the opportunity to negotiate critical issues like their lifestyles, their ability to care for their children, and their use of natural resources, organizations may be able to fulfill their democratic potential for the betterment of all those stakeholders, not just a limited set.

CLAIMS OF THE MULTIPLE STAKEHOLDER MODEL

To recover the democratic potential of organizations, we need to allow for conflict over meanings that can no longer be assumed as fixed, consensual, or pre-determined by managers but that must be created through communication as part of our everyday lives. In other words, the multiple stakeholder model prescribes conflict of a particular sort. Deetz and his colleagues urge us to use productive conflict to create new meanings that have not been used in organizations before.[32]

He suggests that the most central conflicts that can be negotiated through participatory decision-making center on our identities, the social order, knowledge, and policy. Negotiating identities refers to the process of deciding who we are and who we might become as individuals and groups through the organizing process. The social order has to do with how we relate to one another in organizations. The traditional models of hierarchical authority are less compelling to many employees today. Finding new ways to work together—as teams, for example—is an outcome of negotiating a new social order. Knowledge negotiation refers to considering a broader set of data and experience to "count" in organizational decision-making. Although the "bottom line" remains a critical metric, the experience of employees, host communities, and other relevant stakeholders should also be considered. Finally, we create new policies and practices that better address stakeholder interests.

Deetz doesn't believe that every decision should be participatory or involve all stakeholders. If only a small portion of organizational decisions were made using stakeholder principles, we might see fairly dramatic changes. He offers four specific strategies to move organizations toward a multiple stakeholder model:

1. Creating a workplace in which every member thinks and acts like an owner.
2. Integrating the management of work with the doing of work.

3. Widely distributing quality information for decision-making.
4. Growing social structures from the bottom up rather than enforcing them from the top down.

These changes are relatively simple. The greater challenge requires that we change our conceptions of organizational life to reflect a commitment to stakeholder participation and to taking up these conflicts in ethical, open, and representative ways. We have the communication theory and tools—better listening, story telling, ideology critique, group decision-making, advocacy—to do so. The point of the multiple stakeholder model, says Deetz, "is not a revolution in business, that's too easy. The point is making each day better in living a good life." [33]

▲　▲　▲

Theory into Practice
What organizations do you belong to? What decisions do those organizations make that impact you, your life, your community, your future? How do your interests and needs get represented in the decisions made by those organizations? What kinds of decisions would you like to be able to participate in? What communication mechanisms might best enable your participation in those decisions? Now that you have considered important decision-making opportunities in your organization, take this opportunity to create a participatory action plan. First, provide a clear statement to the organization's leader about why you believe this decision is important. Second, articulate the benefits of having multiple stakeholders involved in the decision making. Third, generate a plan—an agenda, location, and mechanism (e.g., formal vote or brainstorming session)—for making a decision with multiple stakeholders.

▲　▲　▲

FOR FURTHER DISCUSSION

1. Sense making theory assumes that humans organize to make complex environments meaningful. In what ways do you organize your own life to make complex environments meaningful for you?
2. Think about an organization that you belong to. How, if at all, are the cultures in that organization (such as employees, customers, etc.) fragmented?
3. When have you made better decisions as part of a group than you would as an individual?

KEY TERMS

Artifacts
Coordination
Environment
Equivocality
Outcomes
Retention
Selection
Stakeholder
Values
Variation

12

THEORIES OF GROUP AND FAMILY COMMUNICATION

HOW CAN I MAKE GROUP WORK A POSITIVE EXPERIENCE?

MAI AND LOGAN were excited to be taking political science to-gether. That is, until the first day of class, when Dr. Cox announced that one of their major assignments for the semester would involve participating in a group project to develop a new foreign policy plan for the United States in its dealings with China.

Logan sighed. "Not another group project! I am so tired of having to carry someone else's weight. Why can't we just write individual papers?"

"I know what you mean," said Mai. "In my family communication class last semester, I had two group members who rarely showed up, and everyone else waited on me to do all the work. You and I should be in the same group." As Mai tried to encourage Logan, however, Dr. Cox announced that he would be randomly assigning students to their groups—and as fate would have it, Logan and Mai ended up in different groups.

Over the next several weeks, Logan got to know her group members and found that her group really enjoyed working together as a team. Different group members contributed to their meetings by helping to analyze the issues involved, identifying criteria for judging the policies, brainstorming relevant and realistic alternatives, and comparing each option to their criteria to find the best plan for their presentation. At the same time, Logan noticed that some of her group members would occasionally share personal stories or anecdotes to help lighten the mood. Her group was focused on completing the task and earning an 'A' on the project, and yet, they developed a sense of team spirit as they caught up on each other's lives and got to know each other on a more personal level.

Mai's group experience did not go quite as well. Most of her group members were apathetic about the class and the assignment. Despite her efforts, Mai's group rarely met. And when they did meet, the conversation was stilted. The others resisted Mai's attempts to help them brainstorm policy plans and most of them showed little interest in anything other than doing the bare minimum to complete the assignment. Not surprisingly, when Mai and Logan's groups gave their policy plan presentations at the end of the semester, Mai's group earned a C+ on its presentation while Logan's group earned an A.

For many students like Mai and Logan, working in groups to complete course assignments is challenging at best. From the difficulty of coordinating schedules to the frustration of dealing with lazy and apathetic members, group projects often generate a sense of annoyance and dread. When groups come together and develop a common identity and a sense of team spirit, however, they can often accomplish more than any one individual can alone, producing very rewarding experiences.

What led to such different experiences for Mai and Logan? How does communication enhance or inhibit the successful completion of group goals? What types of communication behaviors help build team chemistry and a sense of group identity? And to what extent are these behaviors first learned in our families of origin—our original "group" experiences?[1] These are but a few of the questions that scholars have addressed as they develop theoretical explanations of how groups and families communicate.

In this chapter, we will explore three theories that help us understand how individuals develop a common group identity, analyze problems, develop effective solutions, and accomplish group goals through communication. First, we discuss symbolic convergence theory, which explains how group members develop a shared group identity and culture through the process of sharing group fantasies. Then, we turn our attention to functional theory, which examines how communication enables (or constrains) group members as they seek to accomplish the various tasks necessary for developing effective solutions to problems. Finally, we discuss family communication patterns theory, which guides our understanding of how families develop a shared social reality through conversation and conformity orientations to family interaction. By learning how the communication process works in group and family contexts, you will develop a better understanding of why some groups are more successful than others.

SYMBOLIC CONVERGENCE THEORY

Have you ever noticed that some people are really good storytellers? Or that some people know just the right thing to say at the right moment to help lighten the mood and bring humor to an otherwise serious situation? When asked to identify the skills that are most important for having a great group experience, many of us would likely identify problem-solving skills, time management skills, and organizational skills. We may be less likely to identify the rhetorical skills with which group members tell stories and share personal anecdotes to help release the tension of task activities. As we will soon learn, however, such sharing among group members is equally important in determining the success of the group. Scholars have developed symbolic convergence theory (SCT) to help us understand how the sharing of dramatizing messages and group fantasies creates common symbolic ground, which in turn builds group cohesiveness, a shared group identity, and enhanced group creativity and decision-making.

INTELLECTUAL TRADITION OF SYMBOLIC CONVERGENCE THEORY

Ernest G. Bormann was the communication scholar primarily responsible for advancing symbolic convergence theory (SCT). In the 1960s, Bormann and his students at the University of Minnesota were investigating the decision-making processes of **zero-history groups**— leaderless groups brought together for the first time to accomplish a task.[2] In what he called the Minnesota Studies, Bormann and his students studied the transcripts (and audio- or videotapes) of group meetings in a manner similar to that of a critic who analyzes public messages. They used content analyses and qualitative case studies of group meetings over time to provide an interpretive understanding of group interaction.[3] Their approach stood in stark contrast to the laboratory approach of studying small groups that was so popular in their time, wherein groups were artificially created to perform a task in the lab. As they studied the natural language of decision-making groups, Bormann and his colleagues noticed moments in group deliberations when group members would dramatize by telling a joke, sharing a personal experience, or discussing some other anecdote that seemed to be unrelated to the task at hand.

Bormann's observations were revolutionized in 1970 when Robert Freed Bales published *Personality and Interpersonal Behavior.*[4] Bales was a social psychologist at Harvard who had previously published *Interaction Process Analysis* (IPA) in 1950.[5] The IPA included a coding scheme of 12 categories that enabled group scholars to observe and code group interaction. One of the categories was "shows tension release," which Bales later renamed "dramatizes."[6] Inspired by Bales's research, Bormann and his students focused on dramatizing messages that occurred when the communication of group members would leave the "here and now" and members would tell stories that had happened, or could happen, and talked about the past or future.[7] They began to analyze the dramatic themes (what they would later call "fantasy themes") that chained out in small group discussions (that is, themes that sparked further discussions and increased participation among group members). They discovered that although some fantasy themes failed to catch on and chain out, others "caused a greater or lesser symbolic explosion in the form of a chain reaction."[8] For Bormann, small groups developed their own group history, traditions, cohesion, and identity by sharing dramatizing messages and participating in these chain reactions.

SCT represents a marriage of social science and humanism that was particularly important in the late 1970s, when a number of communication departments were rife with conflict between humanistic (or rhetorical) and social scientific (usually post-positivist) scholars.[9] Unlike most other theories in the communication discipline, Bormann argued that SCT is a *general theory* of communication, one that spans contexts and cultures. In other words, Bormann believed that the tendency of people to share group fantasies so as to release tension in group contexts and help meet rhetorical or psychological needs was relatively universal. He developed SCT in an effort to help us understand how the sharing of group fantasies helps build a shared social reality for the group, which in turn guides and directs the meanings, motives, and communication behaviors of individual group members. With this general assumption in mind, let's briefly review some of the remaining assumptions behind SCT before examining its key concepts.

ASSUMPTIONS OF SYMBOLIC CONVERGENCE THEORY

Symbolic convergence refers to the communication process that emerges as group members create a climate and culture that allows them to achieve a "meeting of the minds." It is *symbolic* because it involves the human tendency to interpret and assign meaning to signs, signals, experiences, and human actions. *Convergence* refers to the process of two or more individuals inclining their private symbolic worlds toward each other as they come more closely together. In other words, convergence occurs when two or more individuals begin to make sense of and understand things in similar ways. Bormann assumed that as group members develop portions of their private symbolic worlds that overlap as a result of symbolic convergence, they begin to share a common group consciousness.[10] For instance, Logan's expression of "Not another group project!" likely triggered a set of emotions and meanings in Mai based on her own experiences with frustrating groups. Had they been assigned to the same group, Logan and Mai's convergence on what it means to participate in a group project may have led them to share some of their previously frustrating group experiences with other group members (i.e., dramatizing messages). If the other group members had experienced similar circumstances in the past, then the sharing of their experiences could create a chain reaction and a sense of empathy that bonds the new group together. In essence, their symbolic convergence around what it means to have a frustrating group experience might, in fact, help them build a level of group cohesion necessary for making their current group project a more successful and enjoyable experience.

As a general theory of group communication, SCT is argued to be *transhistorical* and *transcultural*. Bormann argued that SCT is transhistorical in that it explains what took place in groups in the past, what takes place in groups in the present, and what will take place in future group discussions. For instance, SCT assumes that the sharing of dramatizing messages and the creation of a common group identity took place (to greater or lesser degrees) when President John F. Kennedy met with his cabinet to deliberate the Cuban missile crisis; it is taking place right now as members of Congress meet with their sub-committees to develop public policies for the U.S.; and it will take place in future semesters as the authors of your textbook meet with their faculty committees to deliberate departmental policies.

Bormann believed that SCT is also transcultural, meaning the process of symbolic convergence applies to events in cultures as diverse as those of ancient China and modern-day Germany, as well as future Brazil. In fact, Bormann believed that SCT operates in much the same way as the law of gravity, insofar as both apply equally across different time periods, cultures, and/or historical contexts. He also compared the dynamic of people sharing group fantasies with Darwin's process of natural selection, in that both processes are believed to be transcultural.[11] In short, SCT assumes that humans are storytelling creatures and that the narrative material in a dramatizing message helps provide the social glue necessary for bonding group members to each other as they seek to accomplish a common goal. With these assumptions about focus and scope in mind, let's examine the key concepts of SCT and discuss how they fit together to describe the symbolic convergence process.

KEY CONCEPTS IN SYMBOLIC CONVERGENCE THEORY

SCT begins by focusing on the relationships among a dramatizing message, a fantasy chain among group members, and the shared group fantasy that emerges out of the convergence process. According to Bormann, a **dramatizing message** is a message that contains any form of imaginative language, including figures of speech, metaphors, puns, and analogies, as well as anecdotes, allegories, and personal narratives.[12] The most important element of dramatizing messages is that they are always set in a time and place other than the "here-and-now" communication of the group. For example, group members may become involved in a disagreement that is dramatic and filled with tension, but because their disagreement is occurring in the immediate experience of the group, it would not qualify as the sharing of a group fantasy. If group members began talking about disagreements they have had in the past, or if they envisioned how they might respond to future disagreements or to potential conflicts with external parties, then such comments would qualify as dramatizing messages.

The expression of a dramatizing message often sparks the sharing of group fantasies. In SCT, the term "fantasy" does not refer to something imaginary. Rather, **fantasy** is a technical term that refers to the creative and imaginative interpretation of events that fulfills a psychological or rhetorical need (e.g., telling a story to change the subject and avoid a conflict, or to help the group make sense of new information). Some fantasies include fictitious and fanciful stories, whereas others have actually happened to members of the group, in various media outlets, or in the history of the group.[13]

As they analyzed the transcripts of both informal social groups and task-oriented groups, Bormann and his colleagues noticed moments when the discussion dropped off and members were at a stalemate. Group members often seemed tense and unsure of what to say next. Then, someone would dramatize by cracking a joke, sharing a personal experience, or telling a story that portrayed some character at some place and time other than the here-and-now meeting of the group. Some dramatizing messages had little effect on the stilted atmosphere of the group, as members paid very little attention to what was being shared. However, other dramatizing messages caused a symbolic explosion in the form of a chain reaction, as various group members became more and more interested in what was being shared and began to participate in the telling of the story. One person might respond with a laugh while another person adds to the story, and soon the entire group comes alive as everyone begins to talk and become more emotional. The end result of sharing dramatizing messages is a **group fantasy**. And then suddenly, a member may abruptly break off the episode by changing the subject, often by pulling the group back to the task at hand.

According to SCT, communication episodes in which group members are pulled into participating in the sharing of a group fantasy are referred to as **fantasy chains**, and the content of the dramatizing message that sparked the fantasy chain is a **fantasy theme.** Bormann suggested that the fantasy theme is an observable record, or social artifact, that provides evidence of the group's shared imagination and common culture. When members of a small group share a fantasy, they have jointly experienced the same emotions and interpreted some aspect of their common experience in the same way. In short, they have *achieved symbolic convergence* about that part of their common experiences. Thus, fantasy themes represent the fundamental unit of analysis in SCT research.

To conduct a fantasy theme analysis, we first seek evidence that symbolic convergence has taken place. To do so, we look for one of two forms of evidence. First, we can look for the repetition of similar dramatizing messages. When similar dramatizing material (e.g., wordplays, narratives, figures of speech) comes up repeatedly in different group contexts, that repetition suggests that symbolic convergence has occurred. Second, we can look for symbolic cues. According to SCT, a **symbolic cue** is a cryptic reference to common symbolic ground. When group members have shared a fantasy theme, they have shared a set of meanings and emotions that can be activated by a commonly agreed-upon symbolic cue that only they know. For instance, an "inside joke" is an example of a symbolic cue: only those individuals who have shared the fantasy theme and are on the "inside" will respond in an appropriate fashion to the joke.

Symbolic cues can arouse a range of emotional responses, including tears, anger, hatred, and love, or perhaps illicit laughter and humor. For example, one of us (P.S.) teaches interpersonal communication each semester. When discussing obsessive and controlling relationships, he shares the same story about one of his ex-girlfriends ("Stacy")[14] who gradually became more obsessive and controlling during their nine-month dating relationship. Although the story is filled with instances of humor, it also includes some of the shocking behaviors Stacy used to exercise greater levels of control over the relationship (e.g., hitting Paul on the head with a pool stick in the middle of the student union), until Paul finally decided to end the relationship. Of course, he embellishes certain parts of the story to illicit laughter, but he also uses it to illustrate some of the behaviors that students should watch for when determining whether a partner is becoming obsessive and controlling. The story is so memorable that when students take a second or third course from him, all he has to do is reference the "Stacy" situation and they begin to laugh and request that he re-tell the story for the benefit of first-time students. In other words, the name "Stacy" becomes a symbolic cue for students who have taken his interpersonal communication class. At every mention of the name "Stacy," a common set of meanings and emotions from the fantasy theme is cued, and this provides evidence that symbolic convergence has taken place.

In addition to symbolic cues and fantasy chains, SCT helps us understand what happens over time as group members share a number of fantasy themes with similar scenarios. According to the theory, symbolic cues make possible the development of a **fantasy type**, a stock scenario repeated again and again by the same or similar characters that covers several of the more specific fantasy themes. For instance, in their analyses of zero-history student groups in the classroom, Bormann and his colleagues found that group members would share personal experiences about parties they had recently attended.[15] These stories would often fall into a stock scenario of what the students would do at such gatherings, including those behaviors that they celebrated as enjoyable. Rather than dramatizing a fantasy theme with specific characters in a specific setting, students would present only the general plot line. One member might come to a group meeting in a Friday morning class and simply refer to the fantasy type by saying "Did I have a crazy night last night! We went on a pub crawl and didn't come home until 4 a.m. I've got a massive head-ache, but it was totally worth it!" Another member might respond with a laugh and say "Let's all keep the noise down for Scott's sake." A third member might use an inside cue referring to a previously shared group fantasy with something like "Did you end up 'calling for Earl' last night?" (a cue that refers to throwing up), and the other group members might then break out in laughter. To an outsider, the cryptic remark about "calling for Earl" might be confusing. But to the members of the group, this symbolic cue touched a common set of meanings that they had all shared when discussing the fantasy type called "pub crawl."

Finally, the culmination of dramatizing messages, fantasy themes, and fantasy types is the emergence of a **rhetorical vision**, a unified collection of the various themes and types that gives group members a broader view of things.[16] According to Bormann, rhetorical visions provide a coherent view of the group's shared social reality. Although SCT was developed to help us understand how rhetorical visions emerge in groups that share group fantasies over time, the concept can be applied to larger communities of people as well. For example, during the Boston Marathon on April 15, 2013, Chechen brothers Dzhokhar and Tamerlan Tsarnaev detonated two pressure cooker bombs that killed three people and injured another 264. In the days that followed this attack, the citizens of Boston and surrounding communities shared their personal accounts and stories as they coped with the loss of life and made sense of this act of terror. In time, the phrase "Boston Strong" emerged as a symbolic cue that referenced the larger rhetorical vision of a community of people who bonded together to overcome adversity and support each other through charity and commemoration.

"Boston Strong" is one example of a symbolic cue that alludes to a common set of meanings and emotions that a group of people (i.e., Bostonians) share based on previously shared group fantasies. Such cues need not be slogans or catch phrases, however. Check out "Baseball, God Bless America, and the Rhetorical Vision of a Nation" for further illustration of how the symbolic convergence process can extend beyond small groups.

▲ ▲ ▲

Baseball, God Bless America, and the Rhetorical Vision of a Nation
In the seventh-inning stretch of most Major League Baseball (MLB) games, "God Bless America" is either sung or performed by a musical artist. What some may not realize, however, is that the practice of singing this song during the seventh-inning stretch did not begin until after the tragic events of September 11, 2001. In the weeks that followed 9/11, MLB teams across the country instituted the singing of "God Bless America" to commemorate those lost, to honor those who protect our nation, and to communicate the courageous and determined spirit of the American people. Just as "Never Forget" and "United We Stand" represent similar kinds of symbolic cues, the singing of "God Bless America" during one of America's most beloved sports represents a cue that taps into the rhetorical vision of America as the "land of the free and the home of the brave."

▲ ▲ ▲

As you can see, SCT provides an array of key concepts that illustrate how the sharing of group fantasies helps bond group members together, creating a unified and coherent sense of group identity. That being said, why do some groups share fantasies while others do not? And how does the sharing of group fantasies and the development of a group identity aid in motivating group members, enhancing group creativity, and facilitating group decision-making? For answers to these questions, we turn our attention to the claims advanced by SCT.

CLAIMS OF SYMBOLIC CONVERGENCE THEORY

One central claim of SCT is that *the sharing of group fantasies and the process of symbolic convergence helps create a common group identity by identifying who is "in" and "out" of the group.*[17] Think back to the example of the inside joke, one type of symbolic cue that references previously shared experiences and emotions among a group of people. An implicit function of inside jokes is that they re-affirm who is considered to be a part of the group and who is not. If you have ever been on the outside of an inside joke, you may have asked your friends what they are talking about. If your request is met with a response of "Oh, don't worry about it, it's just an inside joke," you may feel left out. In one sense, inside jokes celebrate a common group identity that has previously emerged as a function of symbolic convergence. According to Bormann, such convergence helps create a sense of community among a group of people. Once the sharing of fantasies distinguishes between the insiders and the outsiders of a group, the members have a much clearer idea of the communication boundaries that serve as guidelines for initiating new members into the group and/or forcing existing members out.[18]

A second set of claims advanced by SCT pertains to the issue of *why some group members are predisposed to share some types of fantasies, respond nonchalantly to other types, or actively reject some fantasy types altogether.* Here, Bormann offered three explanations for why people share dramatizing messages and are inclined (or not) to participate in the sharing of group fantasies. First, group members may already be predisposed to share certain kinds of group fantasies because they bring common experiences or personal problems to the group context. Take, for example, the student who is experiencing a lot of pressure from her parents to earn high grades in college. If she dramatized briefly about something her parents had said about doing well or losing their financial support, the other students in her group may be inclined to empathize with her and start a fantasy chain with a theme of "school pressure and academic performance." Second, Bormann suggested that common group concerns can lead to the sharing of group fantasies, particularly when such concerns relate to external pressures or problems the group is facing, or internal matters related to role struggles, leadership, and task conflicts. A common concern for zero-history student groups is earning an "A" on whatever project they have been assigned. If the students have an unfavorable impression of the instructor, however, they may vilify that instructor and bond over the shared negative experiences they each have had with difficult and frustrating professors. Finally, Bormann argued that some members may participate in the sharing of a group fantasy because of the rhetorical skill with which a member tells the story. Although good storytellers may dramatize during group meetings simply because they enjoy being the center of attention, their dramatizing may nonetheless help release social tensions in the group and create a common group identity conducive to effective problem-solving.

The final set of claims advanced by SCT connects the symbolic convergence process to group motivation, creativity, and decision-making. First, Bormann suggested that *the sharing of group fantasies provides the group with shared motivations for accomplishing its tasks.* He identified three types of fantasies associated with different forms of group motivation: (1) **mastery fantasies**, which include dramatizations describing commendable people whose basic goals are to gain power and control; (2) **affiliation fantasies**, whose central characters have basic goals related to making friends and having good times; and (3) **achievement fantasies**, which portray sympathetic people motivated to do a good job.[19] Second, SCT predicts that *the sharing of group fantasies may fuel both individual and group creativity.* As Bormann noted, "People caught up in a chain of fantasies may experience moments similar to the creative experience of individuals when they daydream about a creative project or an important problem and suddenly get excited about the direction of their thinking."[20] In essence, the sharing of group fantasies may free individuals within the group to experiment with new ideas and play with new concepts. Finally, Bormann contended that *during the process of sharing group fantasies, the members of task-oriented groups will often dramatize in ways related to how the group processes information, solves problems, and makes decisions.* For example, members may portray their group as a "crime scene investigating team" that gathers the facts and weighs the evidence until the "team" reaches a "consensus." Of course, group members may also share fantasies about more specific details relating to the nature of sound evidence, the use of good reason, and the most efficient and effective ways of making good decisions.

Taken as a whole, SCT provides an array of key concepts and claims that describe and explain how the expression of dramatizing messages, the sharing of group fantasies, and the development of fantasy types and rhetorical visions helps bring individuals together as they converge around common symbolic ground. This process not only helps to create a common group culture and identity, but it also can facilitate higher levels of group motivation, creativity, and enhanced decision-making. For task-oriented groups, however, the ability to make sound decisions and develop effective policies and plans involves so much more than the sharing of group fantasies. In the next section, we look at the functional perspective on communication in problem-solving groups, which seeks to explain how the fulfillment of certain task requirements through social interaction enables task-oriented groups to select the "best" solution to their problems. Before we move on, though, let's take a moment to evaluate SCT using our criteria for evaluating theories.

▲ ▲ ▲

Test Your Understanding

SCT represents one of the more provocative and elaborate theories in our field, and yet, it is not without its fair share of criticism. Remember that Bormann advanced SCT as a general theory of communication, one that frames the sharing of group fantasies to create common symbolic ground as a universal principle that holds true for all people, in any culture, at any point in time.[21] Despite this universal principle, which is consistent with the theoretical goals of the post-positivist paradigm, Bormann's method of conducting a fantasy theme analysis to describe and explain the fantasy types and rhetorical visions shared by a community of people involves both interpretive methods of case study analysis and rhetorical criticism. In some ways, his attempt to merge social scientific theoretical claims with humanistic methods of analysis has generated concerns about the assumptions and concepts of SCT. For instance, some scholars have argued that SCT is a re-labeling of old concepts with trivial jargon that lacks precision and clarity; others have suggested that SCT's insights are researcher-based, not theory-based; and still others have argued that SCT focuses too much on the psychological needs that prompt the sharing of fantasies.[22] Bormann and his colleagues have responded to each of these criticisms and demonstrated that most of them are relatively inadequate.

Using our criteria for evaluating theories, how would *you* assess SCT in terms of its theoretical scope (i.e., is it too broad, too narrow)? To what extent does SCT generate new questions or give you new insights about group communication (i.e., does it have heuristic value)? How well does SCT fare in terms of parsimony (i.e., is it appropriately simple)? Clearly, SCT is verifiable (or testable) as evidenced by more than 1,000 original research studies that have examined and applied the theory.[23] But how useful is SCT? Practically speaking, can we strategically share dramatizing messages for the explicit purposes of sparking fantasy chains, sharing group fantasies, and building group cohesiveness? Or might symbolic convergence simply be an emergent process that unfolds over time in the natural dialogue of the group?

▲ ▲ ▲

FUNCTIONAL THEORY

Inspired by true events, *Apollo 13* tells the story of astronauts Jim Lovell, Fred Haise, and Jack Swigert who are forced to abandon their mission to land on the moon when two of their oxygen tanks rupture. In response to this emergency, the astronauts use the lunar module attached to their spacecraft as a "lifeboat," conserving energy and oxygen as they make their way back home. In one scene, the carbon dioxide filters in the lunar module begin to fail as the crew was given only enough filters to help two men survive for a day and a half—not enough for three men for what would eventually become four days of survival. To make matters worse, the square filters from the command module were never intended for use in the lunar module, whose filters were round. When Gene Kranz, Director of Mission Control, is apprised of their situation, he charges a small group of engineers with the task of inventing a way to "put a square peg in a round hole." Faced with life-threatening circumstances, limited resources, and tremendous pressure, the engineering team analyzed the problem, brainstormed possible solutions, and worked tirelessly to construct a new filtration system by piecing together only those materials that the astronauts had available to them on the lunar module. The engineers communicated with each other in ways that enabled them to fulfill their task requirements so that the immediate problem of saving the astronauts' lives could be solved.

Although you may never experience the kind of problem-solving pressures that the astronauts and engineers of NASA faced in *Apollo 13*, you might someday participate on a committee or in a problem-solving group responsible for developing a new policy plan or solution to some existing problem. Like Mai and Logan, perhaps you have already been in a small group whose purpose was to complete a problem-solving project in class. Maybe you are currently serving on a committee for a local church, community group, or non-profit organization. Perhaps you wish to participate in student government and help make decisions about how best to spend financial resources on behalf of the student body. What steps will you take to ensure that your committee or group makes the best decisions? How will you communicate effectively to analyze the problem, brainstorm possible solutions, and determine which course of action is best? To address these kinds of questions, communication scholars have developed functional theory, which explains how communication operates as the primary tool by which members of groups reach decisions and generate solutions to problems.[24]

INTELLECTUAL TRADITION OF FUNCTIONAL THEORY

The scholars primarily responsible for advancing functional theory are Randy Y. Hirokawa, Dean of the College of Arts and Sciences at the University of Hawai'i Hilo, and Dennis S. Gouran, Professor of Communication Arts and Sciences at the Pennsylvania State University. Hirokawa and Gouran developed functional theory to explain and predict how communication helps problem-solving groups fulfill certain task requirements. When satisfied, these task requirements (or **functions**) contribute to the appropriateness of the decisions groups make.[25] In other words, at the heart of functional theory is the question of why some groups make good decisions and others make bad ones.[26] For Hirokawa and Gouran, the answer lies in group interaction, as the communication of group members works either to promote or to counteract effective decision-making. According to Gouran, "Communication per se is not what distinguishes effective from ineffective groups. Rather . . . the distinction lies in the extent to which interaction gives warrant to particular choices."[27] That is, the communication process is a tool that can be used either to facilitate effective decision-making and problem-solving or to inhibit both outcomes in groups. Thus, functional theory is a social scientific theory of group communication grounded in the post-positivist paradigm.

Although functional theory emerged in the 1980s, elements of the theory can be traced back to John Dewey's work on reflective thinking in the early 1900s,[28] Robert F. Bales's *Interaction Process Analysis* (IPA) in the 1950s,[29] and Irving Janis's research on groupthink in the 1970s.[30] Dewey was among a group of influential thinkers in philosophy and psychology whose thoughts on reflective thinking found their way into college classrooms as communication scholars taught methods of group discussion. According to Dewey, reflective thinking involves five steps: (1) defining the problem to be addressed, (2) identifying criteria for assessing alternative solutions, (3) brainstorming possible solutions, (4) evaluating the solutions in relation to the criteria, and (5) selecting the "best" solution.

Like symbolic convergence theory (SCT), functional theory can also be traced back to social psychologist Robert Bales and his IPA (a method for analyzing group interaction). Bales argued that a small group should be viewed as a social system, one that has four "functional problems" that group members must overcome if the group is to successfully accomplish its goals: (1) *adaptation,* or adjusting to the social environment outside of the group, (2) *instrumental control,* which involves removing or managing existing situational barriers to goal achievement, (3) *expression,* or cultivating positive sentiments and managing intragroup tensions that may prevent task completion, and (4) *integration,* which involves the formation of group solidarity and unity. Whereas Bormann extended Bales's notion of "dramatizing" to build his own ideas of symbolic convergence (and group integration), Hirokawa and Gouran drew upon the notion of functions that groups must manage if they are to be successful in their tasks, and the idea that group interaction serves a key role in dealing with functional goals.[31]

Finally, functional theory was informed by Irving Janis's research on **groupthink**, which refers to "a mode of thinking that people engage in when they are deeply involved in a cohesive in-group, when the members' striving for unanimity overrides their motivation to realistically appraise alternative courses of action."[32] Groupthink tends to emerge when members have a strong desire to maintain group harmony and good feelings about the group. In that condition, individual members often feel reluctant to share opposing points of view. They may pressure others to agree with the group as a whole, and they may maintain a false sense of agreement that makes them feel invincible. Janis spent considerable time analyzing the dysfunctional interaction patterns that produce group-think in problem-solving and policy-making groups. His research reinforced the basic premise of functional theory that communication contributes to the fulfillment of particular task requirements. It suggested that rational approaches to group problem solving and decision-making help facilitate effective solutions and sound decisions.

Collectively, then, the work of Dewey, Bales, and Janis provided the intellectual foundation for functional theory. At its core, functional theory assumes that communication operates primarily to ensure that task requirements are adequately addressed. With this general assumption in mind, let's briefly review the remaining assumptions behind functional theory before we examine its key concepts and claims.

Assumptions of Functional Theory

Compared to SCT, functional theory is much narrower in focus and scope. The theory limits its predictions to decision-making and problem-solving groups that are attempting to work in a rational way, where group members are equipped with the necessary resources to accomplish their tasks and are motivated to make good decisions. Like other functional theories of social interaction, this theory assumes that human behavior is goal directed.[33]

With this in mind, Gouran and Hirokawa outline seven assumptions that set the limits for situations in which functional theory should accurately predict the quality of decisions made by groups:[34]

Assumption 1: The members of a decision-making or problem-solving group are motivated to make an appropriate choice.

Assumption 2: The choice confronting the group is nonobvious.

Assumption 3: The collective resources of the group in respect to the particular task exceed those of individual members.

Assumption 4: The requirements of the task are specifiable.

Assumption 5: Relevant information is available to the members or can be acquired.

Assumption 6: The task is within the intellectual capabilities of the members to perform.

Assumption 7: Communication is instrumental.

When any one of these seven conditions does not apply, functional theory predicts that groups are unlikely to make a good decision or generate an effective solution to a problem. In other words, functional theory claims that these assumptions have a systematic order to them, such that if any one of them does not hold, it matters little whether the others do. With these assumptions in mind, let's review the key concepts of functional theory before discussing its claims.

KEY CONCEPTS IN FUNCTIONAL THEORY

Unlike many other communication theories we have covered thus far (including SCT), functional theory does not contain a large number of key terms and definitions. Rather, the theory identifies two ways that communication functions to help problem-solving groups make appropriate and effective decisions.[35] First, the **promotive function** of communication is evident when group members state the problem to be solved or the issue to be addressed; when they identify criteria for evaluating solutions; and when they offer possible solutions to the problem. In other words, any time group members exchange messages to meet the requirements of the task, their communication is fulfilling a promotive function. On the other hand, the **counteractive function** of communication can be seen when group members attempt to deal with some difficulty or barrier interfering with their ability to complete the task. For instance, group members may digress from the agenda or go off on tangents unrelated to the task. Or perhaps one group member shares information that is irrelevant, incomplete, or entirely inaccurate, while another member gets involved in an interpersonal conflict over differences in personality. In each of these examples, the messages that are exchanged generally work against the group's efforts to complete the task at hand.

To further our understanding of how communication can function counteractively to undermine group performance, Gouran and Hirokawa reviewed three types of constraints that Janis identified in his research on decision-making processes in organizations.[36] **Constraints** are negative sources of influence that undermine effective group performance. First, **cognitive constraints** come into play when group members face a decision or confront a problem for which little information exists, time is severely limited, and/or complexity is too high. Second, **affiliative constraints** can emerge when the relationships among group members become a dominant concern for the group. Some relationships between members may have deteriorated because of differences in personality or interference from members whose thinking is inconsistent with the will of the group. Finally, **egocentric constraints** tend to surface when someone tries to seize control of the group.

Taken together, these concepts help us understand how communication works to either promote or inhibit effective decision-making while group members seek to overcome any potential constraints that stand in the way. With this in mind, let's examine some of the more specific claims advanced by functional theorists.

CLAIMS OF FUNCTIONAL THEORY

Functional theory is unique in that it begins with one overarching claim, namely, that *decision-making and problem-solving groups make the best (or most useful) decisions when the frequency with which group members communicate satisfies fundamental task requirements.*[37] The theory then claims that decision-making groups are most likely to make the best decisions when group members:[38]

1. Develop a thorough and accurate understanding of the issue(s) to be resolved;
2. Establish criteria for evaluating possible solutions, and achieve an understanding of what an acceptable decision will include;
3. Generate a relevant and realistic set of alternative decisions (or choices) the group could make;
4. Compare and contrast the alternatives according to their criteria for good choices; and
5. Select the alternative most likely to have the desired characteristics of an acceptable solution.

As part of function four (i.e., comparing alternative solutions), the theory further suggests that groups should evaluate the positive and negative consequences of all available alternatives. When the group's deliberations focus on fulfilling these five task requirements, the group will be likely to make an appropriate and effective decision.

In response to the three types of constraints that often undermine group performance, Gouran and Hirokawa later added two additional sets of propositions (or claims) to these five functions.[39] First, they added *preventative actions* that group members should take to watch for potential difficulties facing the group. These include (a) clearly expressing an interest in arriving at the best possible decision; (b) identifying the resources necessary for making such a decision; (c) recognizing potential obstacles that the group may have to confront; (d) specifying the procedures to be followed; and (e) establishing ground rules for group discussions. Once these measures have been taken, the group will be better prepared to fulfill the five task requirements noted above. Depending on the degree to which the group is constrained in its performance, however, the group may choose to take *corrective actions*. Such actions may include (a) finding ways to overcome the constraints that are interfering with the satisfaction of the five task requirements, (b) reviewing the process by which the group comes to a decision and, if needed, (c) reconsidering decisions that have been reached (even to the point of starting over).

Of course, with so many functions to fulfill and/or actions to take, the question arises as to whether some tasks are more important than others. For example, some might consider brainstorming to be one of the more critical functions a group must fulfill. But is brainstorming the *most important* function that groups must fulfill in order to reach the *best decision*? Take a look at the following box to see what researchers have to say about the importance of brainstorming in groups.

▲ ▲ ▲

How Important is Brainstorming to Group Decision-Making?

Although many people believe brainstorming is one of the most important tasks of decision-making and problem-solving groups, scholars Marc Orlitzky and Randy Hirokawa found evidence to the contrary.[40] They performed a meta-analysis to compare the relative importance of the communication functions in functional theory to the quality of group decisions. Meta-analysis is a method of summarizing research and integrating the findings from several studies on the same topic. After summarizing more than two decades of research on functional theory, Orlitzky and Hirokawa found that *assessing the negative consequences of alternative solutions* is the most important function to ensure a quality decision. Another important function was problem analysis, or the degree to which members assessed what was required of the decision-making group. Ironically, the least important function was the identification of alternative solutions, what many of us call brainstorming.

▲　▲　▲

In sum, functional theory helps us understand how communication contributes to sound decisions. In the case of *Apollo 13*, engineers at NASA communicated with each other and worked together to identify the best possible solution to the CO_2 problem on the lunar module. Their communication fulfilled the fundamental task requirements necessary for creating an alternative filtration system and, ultimately, saving the astronauts' lives. What would've happened, however, if the engineers had failed to fulfill all five functions? And how might groupthink and other constraints undermine group decision-making and problem-solving in an organization such as NASA, particularly when so many resources and peoples' lives are at stake? Let's take a moment to consider how these questions and others emerged nearly two decades later when a different group of NASA engineers and decision-makers failed to communicate in ways that fulfilled all five functions of group decision-making.

▲　▲　▲

The *Challenger* Disaster and the (Dis)Functional Nature of Faulty Decisions

On the morning of January 28, 1986, the space shuttle *Challenger* exploded 73 seconds into its launch and killed all seven of its crew. In the months that followed this tragedy, government officials and academic researchers devoted much effort to identifying what went wrong. A Presidential Commission charged with investigating the explosion concluded that the technical answer to this question lay in the "O-rings" (a type of rubber gasket) that had not been properly tested at environmental temperatures as low as those on the day of the launch. Upon further investigation, however, the Commission discovered that the decision to launch the *Challenger* was made despite knowledge of the potential hazard. In fact, many came to believe that the primary answer to "what went wrong" was faulty decision-making at NASA and Morton Thiokol, the contractor that designed the faulty O-rings.

Using functional theory, Hirokawa, Gouran, and Martz analyzed the group decision-making processes that led to the *Challenger* launch.[41] They identified a number of cognitive and egocentric constraints that undermined the communication effectiveness of key decision-makers within NASA's chain of command. For instance, there was substantial political pressure from high-level decision makers to dismiss or ignore any recommendations not to launch. Some decision-makers reviewed the information but drew the wrong conclusions from it, whereas others shifted their thinking from the belief that "a launch should be canceled if there is any doubt," to "a launch should proceed unless there is conclusive evidence that it is unsafe to do so." Still others were either ineffective in their attempts to persuade their superiors to abort the launch, or used ambiguous language when discussing the O-rings and other launch-related problems. Hirokawa and his colleagues concluded that the decision to launch the *Challenger* was ultimately the result of a complex interplay among a number of cognitive, psychological, and communicative forces that undermined effective decision-making.

▲ ▲ ▲

Taken together, functional theory and SCT provide two different frameworks for understanding how communication helps or hurts group decision-making and performance. Whereas Bormann provided a general theory that ties the sharing of group fantasies to group identity, creativity, motivation, and decision-making, Hirokawa and Gouran advanced a more specific theory of decision-making wherein communication is viewed as a tool that either promotes or counteracts the fulfillment of fundamental task requirements. Both theories acknowledge the importance of information-processing and decision-making skills, and both focus on the degree to which communication helps create a shared social reality among group members.

That being said, how do people learn to process information in group settings and communicate in ways that fulfill group tasks and enhance group decision-making? Where does the tendency to dramatize come from? And how is it that some group members are rhetorically skilled at dramatizing and sharing group fantasies while others are not? We believe the answers to these questions can be found, to some extent, in our families-of-origin, as the family represents the first "group" experience that most of us encounter.[42] Consequently, in the final section of this chapter, we review family communication patterns theory, which seeks to explain how families develop uniquely shared world views that ultimately shape how family members communicate with each other and with those outside of the family.

FAMILY COMMUNICATION PATTERNS THEORY

Take a moment and think about the family communication environment in which you were raised. How often did your parents ask for your opinion about something important? Did your family frequently talk about topics such as politics and religion, for which disagreement is common? Were your parents open and honest about their emotions and did they encourage you to express your own feelings?

Or were you instead raised by parents who were rather strict and discouraged open disagreements and conflicts? For instance, did your parents say things like "You should give in on arguments rather than risk making people mad" and "My ideas are right and you should not question them"? Would your parents become irritated with your views if they were different from their own? And did they expect you to obey their rules without question and to always let them have the last word?

Depending on your answers to these questions, family communication patterns (FCP) theory identifies orientations to family interaction that influence how you think and talk about various kinds of information. Although FCP theory is focused primarily on family communication, it shares a common interest with SCT in its efforts to explain how groups develop a shared social reality. It also provides some insight into the kinds of information-processing and decision-making behaviors that we learned are central to functional theory. With these similarities in mind, let's briefly review the intellectual tradition of FCP theory before turning our attention to some of its assumptions and key concepts.

INTELLECTUAL TRADITION OF FAMILY COMMUNICATION PATTERNS THEORY

FCP theory is the product of more than 40 years of research spanning two generations of scholars in mass communication and family communication.[43] It began with Jack M. McLeod and Steven R. Chaffee's program of research at the University of Wisconsin, which investigated how parents helped their children make sense of television programming and other forms of mass media messages.[44] McLeod and Chaffee believed it was difficult for us to know how much of our information comes from direct experience with our physical environment and how much comes indirectly from other people and the mass media.[45] They suggested that we tend to believe the information we obtain from others is, in fact, *real*, as if it were no less valid than if we had directly observed it in our physical environment. Our tendency to treat information that we receive indirectly as real is often reinforced by the fact that others seem to have the same information and ideas we do. Thus, we may find ourselves agreeing that everyone *ought* to see things the way we do. McLeod and Chaffee refer to this as a process of constructing a *social reality*, or your more general understanding of how people think and behave based on your interactions with family members and others. According to this theory, your social reality emerges primarily from two different orientations to communication in the family environment.

First, families vary in their *concept-orientation*, which represents the extent to which parental discussions of ideas and concepts influences how children process information and make decisions during social interaction. A family high in concept-orientation values the discussion of ideas over the preservation of harmony within parent-child relationships. In other words, they privilege open discussions on a wide variety of topics despite differing opinions among family members. Second, families also vary in their *socio-orientation*, which represents the extent to which social roles and relationships have a greater influence than the discussion of ideas on how children process information and make decisions. A family high in socio-orientation privileges harmony in parent-child relationships at the expense of openly discussing ideas and opinions on a variety of topics. That is, they tend to avoid conflict and expressing differences of opinion for the sake of family peace (and compliance).[46]

A second generation of FCP theory emerged in the 1990s as scholars in family and interpersonal communication found several inconsistent research findings within McLeod and Chaffee's mass media framework. Theorists such as David Ritchie at Portland State University, Mary Anne Fitzpatrick at the University of South Carolina, and Ascan Koerner at the University of Minnesota re-conceptualized and re-labeled the two underlying dimensions of FCP theory to capture more accurately the communication behaviors that reflect both family orientations. Since a concept-orientation emphasizes the importance of ideas, Ritchie and Fitzpatrick re-labeled this dimension the *conversation orientation* to reflect a concern with open discussion of ideas between parents and children. On the other hand, socio-orientation emphasizes compliance to parental authority and the avoidance of conflict. Thus, Ritchie and Fitzpatrick re-labeled this dimension the *conformity orientation*.[47] Using this re-conceptualization of FCP theory, Koerner and Fitzpatrick have studied how different combinations of both orientations predict meaningful differences in the information processing, decision-making, and conflict behaviors of individual family members.[48]

FCP theory is a social scientific theory from the post-positivist paradigm. It assumes that all families possess conversation and conformity orientations that ultimately help family members create their shared social reality. With this general assumption in mind, let's explore the remaining assumptions of FCP theory before discussing the four types of families it identifies.

ASSUMPTIONS OF FAMILY COMMUNICATION PATTERNS THEORY
Three principal assumptions underlie FCP theory.

Assumption 1: All families are characterized by shared world views that are unique to each family and that provide individual family members with value and belief systems, or **schemas**.[49] Recall from Chapter 5 that schemas represent organized knowledge structures (or "blueprints") that we use to make sense of different phenomena. FCP theory assumes that we develop an initial set of schemas from working models of how parents and children interact. Ultimately, these schemas shape how we perceive our social environments and how we communicate with family members and others.

Assumption 2: Family communication patterns emerge from the process of co-orientation, without which human communication would not be possible.[50] According to Koerner and Fitzpatrick, **co-orientation** "occurs when two or more persons focus on and evaluate the same object in their social or material environment and are aware of their shared focus." Koerner and Fitzpatrick do not necessarily limit their use of the term "object" to mean something that is tangible and relatively unchanging (e.g., a table), but rather anything that a person can observe and direct thought or energy toward understanding. For example, suppose you and your mother watched an episode of AMC's *Breaking Bad*. After watching the show, you both talk to each other about the episode, your beliefs about using and dealing drugs, and your more general opinions about how our society views doing whatever it takes to care for and defend one's family. As you discussed these issues with your mother, a process of co-orientation would take place as you both focused on, and evaluated, the ethical issues raised by *Breaking Bad*, and expressed either similarities or differences of opinion on the matter.

In families, co-orientation results in two distinct cognitions for each family member involved in a given interaction. The first cognition is your perception of the observed object or stimulus (e.g., the episode), and the second cognition is a representation of the other person's perception of the same object or stimulus (e.g., your take on your mother's perception of the episode). These two cognitions determine three attributes of the co-oriented dyad, family, or group: agreement, accuracy, and congruence. *Agreement* is the similarity between people's perceptions or attitudes about the object. *Accuracy* is the similarity between one person's representation of the other person's perception and the other person's actual perception. Finally, *congruence* is the similarity between one person's own attitude about the object and the same person's representation of the other person's attitude about the object. These three attributes are interdependent, such that the state of any two determines the state of the third.[51] Returning to our previous example, if you believe that methamphetamine use is a pervasive problem in the United States and you perceive that your mother agrees with you, then the combination of accuracy and congruence between your attitude and your mother's attitude about meth use produces agreement. Suppose the conversation changed to the topic of marijuana use, however, and the arguments for and against its use as a medicinal aid. If your mother perceives that you agree with her position that marijuana is like every other drug that has no place in our society (i.e., congruence), but in fact, you do not given the benefits you see in its medicinal use (i.e., inaccuracy), then the combination of congruence and inaccuracy would produce disagreement. Figure 12.1 provides further illustration of how agreement, accuracy, and congruence work together to produce the process of co-orientation.

Figure 12.1 The Process of Co-Orientation (© Paul Schrodt)

Assumption 3: A shared social reality becomes possible only when family members have agreement, accuracy, and congruence. It further assumes that all humans are driven by a psychological need for consistent cognitions (congruence) and by a pragmatic need to predict other people's behaviors correctly (accuracy). These two needs create a social situation that often motivates us to seek agreement.[52] Consequently, family members can seek agreement and attempt to achieve a shared social reality in two distinct ways. One way is for individuals to anticipate another family member's attitude about an object and to adopt the same attitude. That is, they can *conform* to other family members. The other way is for family members to *discuss* the object of co-orientation and its role in the family's social reality and co-construct a shared perception of it. These two ways of achieving a shared social reality lead to the development of relational schemas, or orientations to communication, that guide and direct how family members process information, make decisions, and coordinate their shared activities.

KEY CONCEPTS IN FAMILY COMMUNICATION PATTERNS THEORY

FCP theory provides two sets of key concepts. These include two orientations to family communication and four family types that emerge from different combinations of both orientations. First, FCP theory defines **conversation orientation** as "the degree to which families create a climate where all family members are encouraged to participate in unrestrained interaction about a wide array of topics."[53] Individuals in high conversation oriented families are free to interact with one another as they share ideas, express concerns, and make decisions. There are few limitations regarding time spent in family interaction and the topics that are discussed, and family members frequently share their individual activities, thoughts, and feelings with each other. By comparison, individuals in low conversation oriented families talk far less frequently with each other about thoughts, feelings, and activities. Few topics are openly discussed. Family activities are not deliberated in great detail as parents often exclude children when making family decisions.

Second, FCP theory defines **conformity orientation** as "the degree to which family communication stresses a climate of homogeneity of attitudes, values, and beliefs."[54] In other words, a conformity orientation emphasizes uniformity of beliefs and attitudes between parents and children. Families high on conformity tend to place family interests before those of individual family members. Their interactions typically focus on conflict avoidance, adherence to social rules and norms, and strict obedience to parental authority. Families with a low conformity orientation, however, tend to focus on the individuality and equality of each family member. In these families, parents value the beliefs and opinions of their children and use participatory decision making to encourage independent thinking.

Using high/low combinations of conversation and conformity orientation, FCP theory identifies four types of families that share similarities and differences in terms of family member outcomes.[55]

First, **pluralistic families** are high in conversation orientation but low in conformity orientation. Communication in pluralistic families is open, unrestrained, and involves everyone. Parents do not feel the need to control their children or to make all of their decisions for them. Rather, they encourage family discussions in which opinions are evaluated on their merit. Moreover, parents in pluralistic families are willing to let their children participate equally in family decision making, and they openly address and resolve their conflicts with one another (rather than avoid conflict). As a result, children in these families learn to value open conversations and independent thinking, which in turn enhances their communication competence[56] and their confidence in making decisions.

Families that are low in conversation orientation but high in conformity orientation are called **protective families**. In many ways, these families are the polar opposite of pluralistic families, as their communication reflects an emphasis on strict obedience to parental authority with little concern for open discussions of ideas. Parents in protective families believe they should make the decisions for their families, and they see little value in explaining their reasoning to their children or seeking their children's input. Conflict is perceived negatively and is generally avoided, as family members often lack the necessary skills to manage conflict productively. Children in protective families learn to place little value in family conversations and to question their own decision-making abilities.

Families that are high in conversation orientation and high in conformity orientation are referred to as **consensual families**. According to FCP theory, consensual families are characterized by an ongoing tension between 1) valuing open discussions and exploring ideas, and 2) feeling pressure to agree with parents and preserve the existing hierarchy within the family. Parents demonstrate a sincere interest in their children and in what they have to say, yet they believe that they (as parents) should make final decisions for the family. To resolve this tension, parents listen to their children and explain their decisions, hoping that their children will understand their reasoning and adopt their values and beliefs. Although these family members generally view conflict as negative and harmful to the family, they demonstrate a willingness to engage in conflict so that unresolved disputes do not threaten their relationships.[57] Consequently, children in consensual families typically learn to value family conversations, although they tend to adopt their parents' values and beliefs.

Finally, **laissez-faire families** are low in both conversation and conformity orientations. Their communication can best be described as infrequent, uninvolved, and limited to a small number of topics. Parents believe that all family members should be able to make their own decisions—yet, unlike in pluralistic families, they have little interest in communicating with their children and helping them learn how to make good decisions. Most members are emotionally uninvolved with one other, and most tend to avoid conflict. Children in laissez-faire families learn that there is little value in family conversation and that they have to make their own decisions. Because they receive so little support from their parents, however, they typically question their own decision-making abilities.

Considered together, conversation and conformity orientations and the four family types provide a useful vocabulary for describing and understanding meaningful differences in family communication environments. Remember, these orientations represent relational schemas that guide how family members process information and communicate with individuals both inside and outside of the family. Thus, FCP theory provides a series of claims that link both orientations and the four family types to different kinds of outcomes.

CLAIMS OF FAMILY COMMUNICATION PATTERNS THEORY

The first claim advanced by FCP theory is that *high conversation orientations produce positive outcomes in families and in individual family members.*[58] Research has shown, for instance, that conversation orientation is positively associated with children's interpersonal skills in romantic relationships,[59] parents' use of confirming messages and affectionate behaviors,[60] constructive conflict management skills,[61] and children's well-being.[62] When families, and particularly parents, create a climate in which everyone is encouraged to talk openly about a variety of topics, children are more likely to develop the kinds of information-processing and decision-making skills that enhance self-esteem, reduce stress, and enable them to cope with life's challenges.[63]

FCP theory also suggests that *high conformity orientations produce negative outcomes in families and in individual family members, although this trend is less clear and more dependent on the subtle nuances of authority that parents enact within the family.*[64] For example, conformity orientations are negatively associated with the same outcomes noted above for conversation orientations.[65] High conformity orientations are also positively associated with communication apprehension,[66] conflict avoidance,[67] and perceived stress in young adult children.[68] Researchers have speculated, however, that these trends may vary as a function of how parental authority is expressed within the family. For example, some parents may expect their children to obey, to adopt their attitudes and beliefs, and to abide by family rules and norms, but because these expectations are communicated in love, their children ultimately view their parents' behaviors as being in their own best interest (e.g., a form of "tough love"). For others, parents' expectations and authority may have been communicated in a dictatorial manner that stifled the children's sense of self-esteem and confidence, leading to more harmful outcomes. In short, subtle differences in how parental authority is expressed may alter the degree to which a conformity orientation is associated with family member outcomes.

The final set of claims advanced by FCP theory focuses on the unique and combined contributions of both orientations and the four family types to information processing, behavioral, and psychosocial (or well-being) outcomes in family members. Specifically, research generally supports the idea from FCP theory that *children from pluralistic families usually fare better on a variety of outcomes than children from the other three family types.*[69] In other words, when parents create a family communication environment that is high in conversation and relatively low in conformity, children tend to develop more competent communication and conflict-management skills that enable them to cope with stress and be more successful as young adults. Along with this claim, FCP theory also suggests that (1) *conversation orientation is a stronger predictor of well-being outcomes, on average, than conformity orientation*, and (2) *conversation orientation is more predictive of well-being outcomes than information processing and behavioral outcomes.*[70] Considered together, these claims suggest that when families encourage unrestrained conversations on a variety of topics, participatory decision making, and freedom in expressing different opinions and viewpoints, such open family environments are likely to enhance the general well-being and health of individual family members. Consequently, FCP theory ultimately teaches us an important lesson about parenting, namely, that a conversation orientation may equip children with the information-processing skills and communication behaviors necessary for developing healthy relationships with people outside of the family.

SUMMARY AND CONCLUSION

In this chapter, we discussed three theories that illustrate how communication helps groups and families process information, make decisions, and develop a shared social reality. Symbolic convergence theory highlights the importance of dramatizing messages and shared group fantasies in the development of a common group identity and group culture. Functional theory explains how group members communicate either to promote or to inhibit the fulfillment of certain task requirements necessary for making effective and appropriate decisions. Finally, family communication patterns theory provides an insightful look at how family conversation and conformity orientations combine to produce different types of family communication environments. These environments have important implications for the personal and relational well-being of family members, and they may ultimately influence how children learn to interact in other group settings once they become young adults. To conclude, let's return to the scenario from the beginning of this chapter to see if we can use what we have learned from these three theories to make sense of Mai and Logan's experience.

FOR FURTHER DISCUSSION

Looking back at our opening scenario, use the three theories that we discussed in this chapter to provide some possible reasons as to why Mai and Logan had such different group experiences.

SYMBOLIC CONVERGENCE THEORY

1. How did the sharing of personal stories and anecdotes help Logan's group have a successful experience? What might have been missing from Mai's group that prevented her

group from bonding and working more closely together on their group project?

2. How might the sharing of group fantasies have helped the members of Logan's group to be more motivated to attend group meetings? How might it have led to more creative group discussions? And how might getting to know other members of the group through the sharing of personal stories aid the group in its decision-making?

3. If you could talk to Mai and Logan prior to their first group meeting, what advice would you give them based on what you now know about symbolic convergence theory? And how has your new knowledge of this theory changed your thinking about future group projects that you may participate in?

FUNCTIONAL THEORY

1. What functions did Logan's group fulfill that may have enabled them to come up with the best possible plan for their group presentation? What functions did Mai's group fail to fulfill that may have prevented them from coming up with the best possible plan for their presentation?

2. Briefly describe the communication process that likely unfolded in the two groups. How did the communication of Logan's group help promote the fulfillment of necessary task requirements? And how did the communication of Mai's group counteract any efforts by the group to fulfill necessary task requirements?

3. Based on what you now know about functional theory, what advice would you give someone who has agreed to participate on a committee charged with developing a new policy plan?

FAMILY COMMUNICATION PATTERNS THEORY

1. How might we use FCP theory to understand how individuals in group settings process information and make decisions?

2. SCT and FCP theory both explain how groups of individuals (and/or members of families) develop a shared social reality. How might we use the assumption of co-orientation from FCP theory to understand the symbolic convergence process that occurs as individuals share group fantasies?

3. How might family conversation and conformity orientations provide relational schemas that guide and direct young adults in their social interactions with other group members? In other words, how might a conversation orientation help someone generate discussions in the group and brainstorm ideas? How might a conformity orientation create unrealistic expectations of group harmony based on the avoidance of conflict and the tendency to encourage groupthink?

KEY TERMS

Achievement fantasies
Affiliation fantasies
Affiliative constraints
Co-orientation
Cognitive constraints
Conformity orientation
Consensual families
Constraints
Conversation orientation
Counteractive function
Dramatizing message
Egocentric constraints
Fantasy
Fantasy chains
Fantasy theme
Fantasy type
Functions
Group fantasy
Groupthink
Laissez-faire families
Mastery fantasies
Pluralistic families
Promotive function
Protective families
Rhetorical vision
Schemas
Symbolic convergence
Symbolic cue
Zero-history groups

13

THEORIES OF HEALTH
COMMUNICATION

HOW DO PEOPLE USE COMMUNICATION TO MAKE
SENSE OF HEALTH ISSUES?

ADAM COULDN'T BELIEVE what he was hearing.

"How long have you had this spot on your arm?" Dr. Bateman asked.

"Oh, I don't know . . . at least a year or so. To be honest, I haven't paid much attention to it."

"Well, I'd like to take a biopsy and give it a closer look. I'll be right back."

As Dr. Bateman closed the door, Adam felt a sudden sense of panic. What began as a routine visit to his dermatologist was now becoming unsettling. Although he had never personally experienced cancer, hearing the word "biopsy" brought thoughts of cancer to mind, triggering a sense of fear and uncertainty that took him by surprise. *I hope it's not skin cancer. How can this be? I'm only 22 and I hardly ever get sick! I know I spend a lot of time in the sun, but I love the outdoors. I hope it's not malignant. I wonder if Dr. Bateman is going to recommend surgery or worse yet, radiation.* Adam was lost in his thoughts until

Dr. Bateman returned with her medical supplies and proceeded to biopsy the spot on Adam's arm. "We'll know more in a couple of days," she said. "Until then, try not to worry about it."

Despite his best efforts not to worry, Adam's uncertainty and fear grew in the days that followed. He began researching skin cancer online, and he asked several of his family members and friends what they knew about it. He learned that there are three types of skin cancer, and that each may require different forms of treatment. Although he tried not to obsess about it, he felt bombarded by online ads and TV commercials that called skin cancer the "Silent Killer" and encouraged protective measures. He found himself spending a little less time outdoors, and he began planning the courses of action he might take if his test results came back positive.

Finally, after three long days, Dr. Bateman called with the results. Adam had tested positive for basal cell carcinoma. She informed Adam that basal cell skin cancer was the slowest growing and easiest form of skin cancer to treat, and she recommended surgery to remove the cancer cells. Although the results of the biopsy were not what Adam had hoped for, he was relieved that his condition wasn't more serious. Nevertheless, he learned that he would have to make some changes in his lifestyle and leisure activities to protect himself from future occurrences of skin cancer.

Like Adam, many of us have experienced the uncertainties, fears, challenges, and opportunities associated with health and illness. From the abundance of health and fitness programs, diets, and public health campaigns to the routine check-ups and screenings that many healthcare professionals and insurance companies require, our society is obsessed with disease prevention. As communication scholar Dale Brashers concluded, "Constant surveillance of people's health, combined with improved methods for screening and monitoring, virtually guarantee finding something wrong with every person, creating a society divided into the chronically ill and the worried well (i.e., those waiting to be diagnosed)."[1]

Consequently, living in a "culture of chronic illness"[2] creates a need for understanding how communication can enhance or impede an individual's ability to make sense of health and wellness.

In this chapter, we explore three theories that help us understand how people manage the uncertainties and fears associated with illnesses, as well as how their attitudes, beliefs, and intentions influence their health behaviors. First, we examine uncertainty management theory, which explains how people make sense of health uncertainty and how they manage it through information seeking or avoiding behaviors. We then discuss the extended parallel process model (EPPM), which explains how perceived threats to people's health combine with their sense of efficacy to predict whether they accept or reject persuasive messages about health. Finally, we explore the theory of planned behavior, which combines our beliefs, attitudes, intentions, and feelings of control to predict behavior (and behavior changes). By learning how people use communication to cope with their uncertainty, to make sense of healthcare messages, and to persuade others to take preventative actions, you will gain a greater understanding of the importance of communication to your own personal health and well-being.

Uncertainty Management Theory

If there is one thing that many of us take for granted, it is our health… that is, until we experience an illness or health-related crisis of some kind. Prior to working on this chapter, for example, one of us (P.S.) attended his grandmother's 97th birthday party and celebrated with family and friends despite his grandmother's dementia and her inability to recognize anyone at the party. As he privately wondered how much time his grandmother had left, he caught up with his stepfather, who currently suffers from Parkinson's disease. During their conversation, he shared how he needed to stop by the pharmacy on the way home to pick up his son's new asthma medication.

As these events illustrate, health and illness represent two funda-mental concerns of the human experience that permeate our every-day lives and relationships in ways that often create uncertainty and fear. To help us understand how people respond to the uncertainty of illness and communicate to manage it, scholars have advanced uncertainty management theory (UMT).

INTELLECTUAL TRADITION OF UNCERTAINTY MANAGEMENT THEORY

The scholar primarily responsible for developing UMT was Dale E. Brashers, who was a professor of communication at the University of Illinois until his untimely death in 2010. Brashers and his colleagues developed UMT partly as a response to Berger's uncertainty reduc-tion theory (URT). As we learned in Chapter 8, URT was developed to explain and predict how uncertainty influences communication when people first meet. For instance, when you meet people for the first time, you may know little about who they are, where they are from, how they will act toward you, and how the conversation will go. According to URT, this lack of data generates a sense of uneasiness or anxiety that prompts you to seek information. As you ask ques-tions and make small talk, you learn about people and become able to predict how they will behave. According to URT, getting to know people reduces the anxiety associated with your uncertainty.

Contrary to URT, Brashers and his colleagues argued that *man-aging uncertainty* and *managing the emotions associated with it* are two distinct but related tasks that people perform as they adapt to the experience of uncertainty.[3] Rather than assuming that all uncertain-ty produces anxiety, Brashers believed that uncertainty was some-thing that people appraise or make sense of. In the context of health and illness, he argued that people will sometimes seek information to *increase* rather than reduce their uncertainty (e.g., getting another doctor's opinion on a diagnosis), or will avoid information to *main-tain* their uncertainty (e.g., refusing to see a doctor despite having symptoms of a disease).

To explain appraisals and how people manage uncertainty, Brashers drew from Richard Lazarus and Susan Folkman's cognitive theory of coping,[4] and from Merle H. Mishel's cognitive theory of uncertainty in illness.[5] First, Lazarus and Folkman's theory of coping suggests that people manage stressful situations by assessing (a) the seriousness of the situation and its potential for positive or negative outcomes, and (b) the skills and resources they have available for coping with the situation.[6] Second, Mishel argued that illness-related uncertainty is inherently neither bad nor good. Rather, it is something for which the value depends on context and thus, it must be appraised. According to Mishel, uncertainty can take one of four forms in the context of illness: (1) *ambiguity* concerning the state of the illness; (2) *complexity* regarding treatments and systems of care; (3) a *lack of information* about the diagnosis and seriousness of the illness; and (4) the *unpredictability* of the course of the disease and prognosis.[7] Hence, the appraisal of uncertainty determines how uncertainty is "managed," and managing the uncertainty of an illness and its treatment is essential to coping with the disease.[8]

Taken together, the works of Berger, Lazarus and Folkman, and Mishel provided the intellectual foundation for UMT. Although UMT can be applied to many contexts, Brashers developed the theory primarily to help us understand how people appraise the uncertainties of illness and communicate to manage it. UMT is a social scientific theory that, despite its post-positivist heritage, shares the interpretivist belief that meanings—such as the meaning of uncertainty—depend on context.[9] In fact, most researchers who have used UMT have relied primarily on interpretive methods of inquiry. Nevertheless, Brashers considered the theory to be post-positivist in nature.[10] With this in mind, let's review two primary assumptions of UMT before examining its key concepts and claims.

ASSUMPTIONS OF UNCERTAINTY MANAGEMENT THEORY

UMT rests on two key assumptions.

Assumption 1: Individuals appraise uncertainty for its meaning.[11] In other words, people appraise (or make sense of) their uncertainty to determine its meaning and the meaning of their emotional responses to it. Accordingly, uncertainty can represent *danger* if the inability to predict future events leads to heightened stress and anxiety, or it can represent *opportunity* if knowing the typical progression of a disease enables the individual to take preventative action. Thinking back to our opening example, consider how Adam might have appraised his uncertainty if his test results had come back positive for Stage 4 melanoma, a much more serious condition than he has. If he had been diagnosed with a more deadly form of skin cancer, he may have likely appraised his uncertainty as danger and experienced even greater levels of stress and anxiety over the life-threatening status of the disease. With the diagnosis of an early onset basal cell carcinoma, however, Adam appraised his uncertainty as an opportunity to remove the cancer cells, to adjust his leisure and outdoor activities (e.g., using suntan lotion and more protective clothing), and to improve his overall health. Consequently, when we appraise uncertainty as danger, UMT assumes that we are more likely to experience stress and anxiety. When we appraise uncertainty as an opportunity, however, we are more likely to experience hope or optimism.

Assumption 2: Communication is a primary tool for managing appraised uncertainty.[12] UMT assumes that individuals can manage their uncertainty and their emotional reactions to it by choosing to seek information or to avoid information. For example, a person might choose to *reduce* uncertainty by seeking information from a trusted doctor about a set of symptoms. Another individual might choose to *increase* uncertainty about the same set of symptoms (perhaps to increase hope) by seeking information from multiple sources, including healthcare professionals, web-based information services (e.g., WebMD), and close friends and family. Still others might avoid information altogether so as to *maintain* uncertainty, deny the existence of an illness, and/or help their loved ones not to worry about them. Thus, UMT assumes that people may seek to manipulate uncertainty by increasing it, decreasing it, or maintaining it through a variety of information-seeking and information-avoiding behaviors. They may also re-appraise their uncertainty or adapt to chronic uncertainty (e.g., in the case of AIDS) through resignation and/or relief.

Unlike URT and other uncertainty reduction models, then, UMT assumes that uncertainty is something that individuals appraise, that appraisals of uncertainty may not always produce anxiety, and that uncertainty management includes behaviors other than information-seeking behaviors. Before we turn our attention to the key concepts of UMT, let's take a moment to consider how the appraisal of uncertainty led one Hollywood celebrity to take preventative measures to protect her own health.

▲ ▲ ▲

The "Culture of Chronic Illness" and the Case of Angelina Jolie

In a May 2013 issue of the *The New York Times*, Angelina Jolie revealed her decision to undergo a preventative double mastectomy.[13] She made the decision after her doctors had informed her just three months before that she carried the "faulty gene" BRCA1 and had roughly an 87% risk of getting breast cancer. Her decision has inspired countless women who are either at risk for breast cancer themselves or are currently undergoing treatment for the disease.[14] Jolie admitted it was a difficult decision to make, but one that she is nonetheless happy with, as her risk of breast cancer has dropped to under 5%. "I chose not to keep my story private because there are many women who do not know that they might be living under the shadow of cancer. It is my hope that they too will be able to get gene tested, and that if they have a high risk they, too, will know that they have strong options."[15]

Jolie was also informed by her doctors that she has approximately a 50% risk of developing ovarian cancer. The Oscar-winning mother of six lost her own mother, Marcheline Bertrand, to ovarian cancer in 2007 at the age of 56. Consequently, Jolie has announced her plans to undergo surgery again to remove her ovaries.[16]

Although some consider Angelina's decisions to be inspirational, her actions raise interesting questions about how people manage the uncertainty of health-related information. Ultimately, Angelina appraised her uncertainty as an opportunity to take what some might call "drastic" measures to prevent the occurrence of two different forms of cancer, neither of which she had been diagnosed with. This, of course, raises interesting questions about how far someone might be willing to go *on the chance* of developing a potentially life-threatening disease. How far would you go to prevent an illness based on probability alone?

▲ ▲ ▲

KEY CONCEPTS OF UNCERTAINTY MANAGEMENT THEORY

As is evident from the intellectual tradition and core assumptions, the central concept in UMT is uncertainty. Recall that Berger defined uncertainty more generally as a lack of knowledge about what is inevitable; it is a function of the number and likelihood of alternatives that may occur in a particular context. Uncertainty is high when several outcomes are equally likely to occur, and it is low when only one outcome is likely to occur.[17] Within the context of health and illness, however, Mishel defined uncertainty as "the inability to determine the meaning of illness-related events."[18] Whereas Berger's definition of uncertainty is based upon probability estimates of certain events occurring, Mishel's definition is tied to meaning-making and to appraisals of illness-related events. In UMT, both definitions are relevant, as they inform the cognitive and behavioral processes by which people make sense of, and respond to, illness.

Once an individual experiences uncertainty, he or she then appraises it. An **appraisal** refers more generally to the act of estimating or judging the nature or value of something. In UMT, that "something" is the uncertainty associated with an illness. The concept of appraisal plays a key role in UMT, as it often motivates individuals psychologically and behaviorally to manage uncertainty.[19] According to the theory, **uncertainty management** consists of three distinct, yet related processes: information acquisition, information handling, and information use.[20] Figure 13.1 depicts these categories within the larger context of uncertainty management, with the smaller dotted circle representing the bulk of UMT research that has been conducted thus far (focusing largely on information seeking and avoidance behaviors).

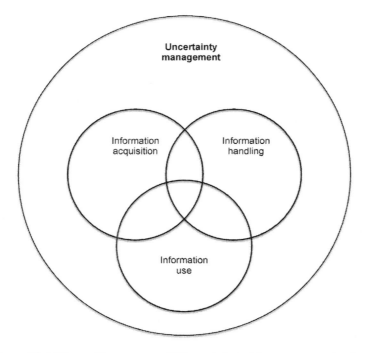

Figure 13.1 Three Processes of Uncertainty Management (redrawn and printed with permission of Timothy Hogan, on behalf of Dale Brashers, from *The theory of communication and uncertainty management*)

The first process, **information acquisition,** refers to all of the available means by which people come into contact with information in the course of their daily lives.[21] This includes our information-gathering activities that are intentional, purposeful, and goal-directed, as well as those moments when we encounter information unintentionally, inadvertently, or through happenstance. **Information seeking** represents one type of information acquisition that involves the intentional gathering of information through any number of strategies, including asking questions, observing others, and searching information systems such as libraries or online databases. Although people often make conscious decisions to seek information in response to uncertainty, they also may intentionally *avoid* information or prevent its entry into their lives so as to maintain a positive outlook and keep hope alive in an otherwise bleak situation. Consequently, **information avoidance** is a complex activity that involves more than *not seeking* information; like information seeking, it is an intentional and goal-directed behavior, one that UMT includes within the larger category of information acquisition.

The second process of **information handling** refers to how people handle the information they acquire while managing their uncertainty. For instance, they may commit the information to memory, jot down notes, or use some form of digital text, audio, or video equipment to store the information. UMT suggests that there is a wide range of activities related to the handling of personal information, including not only the storing of information (in written or digital form), but also the related tasks of labeling, filing, reviewing, weeding, and discarding information as it becomes more or less useful.

The third uncertainty management process is **information use**. This involves understanding *who* uses *what* information, *how* the information is used, for what *purpose* (or *why*), and to what *effect*. For example, Robert Taylor identified eight ways that people often use information to solve problems:

1. to contextualize and make sense of a situation
2. to understand a problem in more specific terms
3. to determine what and how to do something
4. to bring precise data to bear on the problem (i.e., fact-finding)
5. to verify other instances of information (or cross-check information)
6. to develop future-oriented estimates and probabilities
7. to promote one's own involvement (or increase motivation), and
8. to manage one's situation, standing, and relationships with others.[22]

Taken together, these concepts enable us to explore the various ways in which people respond to their appraisals of uncertainty, especially when that uncertainty emanates from a health crisis or illness of some kind. With these concepts in mind, let's briefly examine the claims advanced by UMT.

CLAIMS OF UNCERTAINTY MANAGEMENT THEORY

UMT makes several claims that help tie appraisals of uncertainty to information management behaviors. First, the theory claims that *as individuals appraise uncertainty for its potential harm or benefit, they may experience a range of emotional responses (e.g., hope, optimism, thrill, torment, insecurity, anxiety, and distress).* This claim challenges the previous assertion from URT that anxiety is the primary (or perhaps only) emotional response to the experience of uncertainty. Second, UMT contends that *appraisals and emotional responses motivate individuals psychologically and/or behaviorally to manage uncertainty.* This is where the communication process becomes a central feature of UMT. According to Brashers, communication can be inhibited or inspired by uncertainty and emotion, and it can also lead to decreases or increases in uncertainty.[23]

For instance, information seeking is important when the goal is *uncertainty reduction* (e.g., what are my treatment options?), when new information invites a re-appraisal of the uncertainty itself (e.g., when a self-examination reveals a lump), or when managing uncertainty involves locating contradictory or disconfirming evidence to escalate uncertainty (e.g., asking for second and third opinions on a potentially devastating diagnosis). Information seeking can also *increase uncertainty* by increasing the number of alternatives, by blurring the distinction between or among alternatives, or by challenging existing beliefs.

At the same time, information avoidance is important when individuals choose not to confront potentially upsetting news, or when they want to retreat from information that has become overwhelming to them. In essence, it *maintains* uncertainty by allowing individuals to ignore challenges to their current belief system.[24] As Brashers and his colleagues aptly concluded, "There likely are many other situations in which 'ignorance is bliss.'"[25]

To help us understand how UMT can be applied to information management behaviors and retrieval systems, Brashers and his colleague, Timothy Hogan, recently identified ten principles that tie together the assumptions, concepts, and claims of UMT.[26] These principles appear in Table 13.1.

Table 13.1: Ten Principles of Uncertainty Management Theory

Principle One:	Uncertainty is a perception about insufficient knowledge, which has both cognitive and affective components.
Principle Two:	There are many sources and forms of uncertainty.
Principle Three:	There are many sources and forms of information.

Principle Four:	The relationship between information and uncertainty is not straightforward.
Principle Five:	Uncertainty is appraised for its meaning.
Principle Six:	Interacting with information can reduce, maintain, or increase uncertainty.
Principle Seven:	Encountering new information fuels the re-appraisal of uncertainty.
Principle Eight:	Gathering information is often a social process, and includes collaborators in an individual's social network.
Principle Nine:	Uncertainty is not inherently good or inherently bad, but something that is managed.
Principle Ten:	Variations in information acquisition, handling, and use can be important to the effectiveness of uncertainty management.

Note. Principles are reported verbatim from Brashers, D. E., & Hogan, T. P. (2013). The appraisal and management of uncertainty: Implications for information-retrieval systems. *Information Processing and Management, 49,* 1241-1249.

Collectively, these claims provide further insight into how individuals make sense of the uncertainties associated with health conditions and chronic illnesses. They also tie together the concepts of uncertainty, appraisals, and information management in a way that allows researchers and practitioners to investigate people's varied reactions to messages about health and wellness.

Uncertainty is not the only experience people have when they receive health-related news, however. Fear is also a common emotional reaction. In the next section of this chapter, we explore a theory that helps us understand how researchers and healthcare professionals can use fear constructively to motivate changes in health behavior. Before we turn our attention to that theory, let's consider how

Brashers applied UMT to the study of people living with HIV or AIDS.

▲ ▲ ▲

UMT and The Case of People Living with AIDS

In one of his early applications of UMT to health and illness, Brashers and his colleagues conducted focus group interviews with individuals diagnosed with HIV or AIDS.[27] Like many other chronically or terminally ill patients, individuals living with HIV or AIDS must manage high levels of uncertainty about their illness. Consistent with UMT, Brashers and his colleagues found that when these individuals appraised their uncertainty as *danger*, they experienced anxiety or fear and their uncertainty management activities focused primarily on seeking information and monitoring the symptoms and progression of the disease. When they appraised their uncertainty as *opportunity*, however, they often experienced hope or optimism and managed their uncertainty by either avoiding information or seeking information to increase (rather than reduce) their uncertainty. As one focus group member noted, "I want to hear good news. I *don't* want to hear bad news."[28] To avoid information about the disease, HIV-infected individuals would often avoid situations in which they would be exposed to information, including HIV support groups. Interestingly, when these individuals appraised their uncertainty as a chronic condition, their emotional responses ranged from resignation to relief, and acceptance became very important to how they adapted to the illness and managed their uncertainty. In the end, Brashers and his colleagues concluded that the successful and adaptive management of uncertainty involves the negotiation of personal identities, relationships, levels of knowledge, and physical and psychological well-being. They demonstrated that theory matters.

▲ ▲ ▲

THE EXTENDED PARALLEL PROCESS MODEL

In 1987, the Partnership for a Drug-Free America (PDFA) launched an anti-narcotics campaign that began with the following public service announcement (PSA):[29]

> (A man holds up an egg.) "This is your brain."
> (He then picks up a frying pan.) "This is drugs."
> (He cracks open the egg and fries the contents.) "This is your brain on drugs. Any questions?"

The PSA quickly became one of the most recognizable and memorable advertisements to air on public television. In fact, *TV Guide* named the commercial one of the "100 most recognized TV advertisements," and it has since been parodied in both popular films (e.g., *Batman Forever*) and television programs (e.g., *Breaking Bad*).[30]

This PSA is an example of a fear appeal. **Fear appeals** are persuasive messages designed to scare people by describing the terrible things that will occur if they fail to do what the message recommends.[31] These include PSAs featuring disfigured people warning of the dangers of drunk driving, smoking, or texting and driving. They also include ads that encourage health-maintenance behaviors, such as exercising or getting vaccinated, by depicting the dangers of avoiding those behaviors. The use of scare tactics and other fearful messages to promote health and wellness in our society is pervasive, but what determines the success or failure of such messages? How well do fear appeals work—and why are some successful while others fail? To help answer these questions, communication scholars have developed the extended parallel process model (EPPM).

INTELLECTUAL TRADITION OF THE EXTENDED PARALLEL PROCESSING MODEL

The communication scholar primarily responsible for advancing the EPPM is Kim Witte, a professor of communication at Michigan State University. In the early 1990s, Witte noticed that theoretical explanations of fear appeals focused almost exclusively on how and why people *accepted* fear appeals, rather than why they *reject* them. For Witte, a more complete understanding of fear appeals required accounting for when and why they fail, as well as when and why they work. She believed that arousal was the key to understanding why people rejected certain kinds of fear appeals, and she set out to "put the fear back into fear appeals."[32] In fact, Witte recently lamented her decision to label her theory "the extended parallel process model" because, in many ways, a simpler name would have worked better in the real world: " . . . I took to calling the EPPM the *Fear Management Model*, because really, the EPPM focuses on how to *manage fear* to promote behavior change . . ."[33]

Witte designed the EPPM to address the limitations of previous fear appeal theories, and to expand our understanding of how perceived threats, efficacy, and fear work together to influence people's responses to persuasive healthcare messages. According to Witte, elements of the EPPM can be traced back to Irving Janis's drive model from the 1960s,[34] as well as Howard Leventhal's parallel process model (PPM)[35] and Ronald Rogers's protection motivation theory (PMT)[36] from the 1970s. First, Witte adopted Janis's argument that some fear arousal was necessary to create tension and motivate individuals to action, but that too much fear would result in negative outcomes (e.g., defensive motivation, paralysis). Second, Witte incorporated Leventhal's idea that people enact protective behaviors when they try to control a perceived danger or threat (which is a cognitive process), but not when they attempt to control the fear associated with the threat (which is an emotional process). According to the EPPM, the former is called *danger control processes* and the latter is referred to as *fear control processes*. Finally, Witte extended Rogers's PMT by critiquing his exclusive focus on danger control processes and by re-introducing fear into the appraisal process. She added a set of predictions related to fear control processes, and she provided a more complete explanation of why some fear appeals work and others do not. The result was a message design theory that helps us understand effective communication of health and risk-related information.[37]

The EPPM is a social scientific theory of health messaging grounded in the post-positivist paradigm. At its core, the theory assumes that individuals appraise their level of fear and their sense of self-efficacy as they process fear appeals and other health-related messages. With this assumption in mind, let's briefly review the remaining assumptions behind the EPPM before we examine its key concepts and claims.

ASSUMPTIONS OF THE EXTENDED PARALLEL PROCESSING MODEL

Before we discuss the assumptions of the EPPM, it is important to note that the theory explains and predict people's reactions to fear appeals only. That is, fear appeals are only one of a variety of different persuasive message techniques, and they are not always the most appropriate technique for motivating health behaviors.[38] Witte and her colleagues suggested that the EPPM is most effective when (a) audience members do not already have high levels of pre-existing fear, and when (b) messages alone can help increase perceived efficacy enough to help people overcome a perceived threat.

Assumption 1: Threat and fear are two related but distinct constructs. **Fear** is an internal emotional reaction to a threat that is perceived to be significant and personally relevant. The experience of fear is characterized by physiological arousal (e.g., increased heart rate) and subjective assessment (e.g., "I am scared").[39] A *threat* is a danger or harm (e.g., a message cue) that exists in the environment, whether a person knows about it or not.[40] Witte suggested that an actual threat is different from a *perceived* threat, as the latter involves cognitions or thoughts about the threat. If a person believes that a threat exists, then he or she perceives a threat, whether or not that threat actually exists in the real world.[41] (For instance, you may perceive a threat by believing you have contracted a serious illness, even though you actually haven't.) The distinction between fear and threat helps clarify how and why people make sense of fear appeals and other persuasive messages in different ways. As Witte and her colleagues concluded, "True threats do not always inspire fear, and people sometimes experience fear in the absence of a true threat."[42]

Assumption 2: Fear appeal messages often fail when individuals perceive little to no threat, or when high levels of threat (e.g., "Lung cancer is a severe disease that you are susceptible to because you smoke cigarettes") are combined with the belief that the threat is inevitable.[43] The EPPM considers not only those fear appeals that succeed in prompting protective behaviors, but also those appeals that fail. The failure of an appeal leads either to message rejection or to **boomerang effects**, wherein people actually increase the very behavior that the appeal is designed to reduce. With these assumptions in mind, let's identify the key concepts in the EPPM before discussing its claims.

KEY CONCEPTS IN THE EXTENDED PARALLEL PROCESSING MODEL

The three central concepts in the EPPM are fear, threat, and efficacy. As we discussed earlier, the terms *fear* and *threat* are related but distinct phenomena that influence how people interpret and respond to fear appeals. Such appeals attempt to arouse the emotion of fear by depicting a personally relevant and significant threat (e.g., "Texting while driving causes fatal accidents"). After presenting a threat, a fear appeal recommends actions to deter the threat (e.g., "Don't text and drive—it can wait"). Fear appeals are often defined in terms of their content (e.g., gruesome or gory images, vivid and personalized language) or by the reactions they evoke from the audience.[44]

According to the theory, people make sense of perceived threats in terms of the severity of the threat and their perceived susceptibility to the threat. **Perceived severity** is an individual's beliefs about the seriousness of the threat (e.g., "Elevated cholesterol leads to heart disease"), whereas **perceived susceptibility** is an individual's beliefs about his or her chances of experiencing that threat (e.g., "I'm at risk for heart disease because I eat a lot of fast food").[45] The perceived severity and susceptibility of a threat represent only half of what a person appraises when processing a health-related message, however. The individual also assesses his or her level of efficacy relative to the perceived threat. **Perceived efficacy** refers to a person's beliefs about how feasible the recommended behavior is and how effectively it can reduce the threat. The EPPM distinguishes between **response efficacy**—a person's belief about whether an action will effectively prevent the threat (e.g., "I believe that exercise and diet can reduce my cholesterol levels")—and **self efficacy**—the person's belief that he or she can perform the behavior (e.g., "I think I can eat out less and reduce my fat intake, but I doubt I can commit to exercising every day").[46]

To explain how individuals respond to fear appeals and change their health behaviors, the EPPM provides an additional set of concepts related to message acceptance and rejection. First, **danger control processes** are changes in beliefs, attitudes, intentions, and/ or behaviors that are prompted by a message's recommendations. These processes are more likely to occur when people (1) perceive a threat, (2) perceive high levels of response efficacy and self efficacy, and (3) are motivated to protect themselves by accepting the message's recommendations. **Fear control processes**, on the other hand, are coping responses that seek to diminish the fear itself, rather than deal with the threat. These processes motivate people to reject the message. Examples of fear control processes are *denial* (choosing to be inattentive to the appeal), *defensive avoidance* (minimizing or suppressing thoughts about the threat), and *reactance* (actively resisting the message).[47]

Together, the danger and fear control processes described by the EPPM provide a useful vocabulary for understanding why people either accept or reject fear appeals based on their appraisals of fear, threat, and efficacy. Now that we have a basic understanding of the key terms embedded within the EPPM, let's turn our attention to the theory's claims.

CLAIMS OF THE EXTENDED PARALLEL PROCESSING MODEL

According to the EPPM, the appraisal process begins when an individual is presented with a fear appeal.[48] The fear appeal prompts the individual to make two appraisals. First, *the person appraises the perceived threat of the hazard.* If the threat is low, then the appraisal process stops and there is no response to the fear appeal. If the threat is moderate to high, however, then fear occurs and the individual is motivated to begin the second appraisal. Second, *the person evaluates the efficacy of the recommended response and his or her ability to enact that response.*

An important claim of the EPPM is that people's appraisals of perceived threat and efficacy often depend on each other. Specifically, the theory claims that *when both perceived threat and perceived efficacy are high, danger control processes are initiated.* In other words, when people believe the treat is serious *and* that they can do something about it, they are motivated to control danger by acting to prevent or minimize the threat. In these instances, people respond to the danger, rather than to their fear.[49] As Witte noted, "As long as perceptions of efficacy are greater than perceptions of threat (e.g., 'I know that AIDS is a terrible threat, but if I use condoms correctly, I can protect myself'), danger control processes will dominate, and the message will be accepted."[50]

Conversely, *when perceived threat is high but perceived efficacy is low, fear control processes are initiated.* In other words, the fear associated with a personally relevant and meaningful threat is intensified when people believe they are unable to prevent the threat from occurring. Witte argued that when fear control processes dominate, people will respond to their fear, not to the danger.[51] In other words, individuals in this situation are motivated to cope with the fear (i.e., defensive motivation) by engaging in maladaptive responses, such as denying the threat or reacting against the communicator or the message.

To illustrate this first set of claims, let's return to our opening example and consider how Adam might have responded prior to his diagnosis to ads describing skin cancer as the "Silent Killer." As a young person who enjoyed outdoor leisure activities, Adam may have given little thought to using sun screen or other forms of skin protection. After hearing a public service announcement about the dangers of skin cancer, he may have appraised that message as having a moderate level of severity (e.g., "Skin cancer can be serious, especially when it involves melanoma."), but a low level of susceptibility (e.g., "I'm too young to get skin cancer and I tan easily, so I don't have to worry about it right now."). In this instance, the EPPM predicts that Adam would perceive no threat from the PSA, and would therefore experience no fear, causing him to reject the recommended actions.

Upon receiving his diagnosis of basal cell carcinoma, however, Adam's appraisals of the same message would probably change. Specifically, he would likely perceive greater levels of severity and susceptibility to skin cancer. He would assess the efficacy of Dr. Bateman's recommendation (i.e., surgery) and the PSA's recommendations (i.e., sun screens and protective clothing), as well as his own abilities to have the surgery and to use sun screens and protective clothing. If he perceives high levels of self- and response efficacy, then the EPPM predicts that he will be motivated to accept the messages about skin cancer and enact danger control processes. However, if he perceives either that he cannot perform the recommended course of action (e.g., "I can't afford the surgery"), or that the treatments and protection won't be effective (e.g., "I doubt that the protective clothing really works"), then fear is likely to take over and prompt him to reject Dr. Bateman's advice and the PSA, as well as to deny his susceptibility to skin cancer.

In addition to predictions about danger and fear control processes, the EPPM also claims that fear plays two different roles within the theory.[52] On one hand, the theory claims that *fear directly causes maladaptive responses*, such as defensive motivation, denial, or reactance. Thus, when people perceive high levels of threat coupled with low levels of efficacy, their emotional responses of fear will dominate and lead them to deny or reject the message. On the other hand, *fear may also indirectly cause adaptive responses* (e.g., message acceptance) depending on the level of perceived threat. That is, people's initial experience of fear from a message may prompt them to assess the severity of the threat, their susceptibility to the threat, and their perceived efficacy, which may lead them to change their health behavior in response to the message. When combined, the EPPM proposes that perceived threat determines the *degree or intensity of the reaction* to the message, whereas perceived efficacy determines the *nature of the reaction*.

Of course, people respond in different ways to fear appeals, health care messages, and other forms of persuasion. To account for this, the EPPM claims that *individual differences influence appraisals of threat and efficacy, as well as degrees of fear in response to fear appeal messages*. People with low self-esteem may perceive low self-efficacy when appraising a fear appeal or weighing a particular course of action. Likewise, those who are anxious or who lack coping skills may perceive a heightened susceptibility to a particular threat when no threat actually exists, and may cope with their fear by engaging in maladaptive behaviors. Such differences are important to the EPPM because they often foretell the **critical point**, or the moment when perceived threat exceeds perceived efficacy and fear control processes begin to dominate over danger control processes. In other words, if people believe they cannot prevent a serious threat from occurring, because they think the response ineffective or they cannot perform the recommended action, then fear control processes will begin to dominate (e.g., "AIDS is terrible and easy to get; I don't think I can do anything to prevent contracting it").

As you can see, the EPPM offers a set of claims that tie together the concepts of threat, efficacy, and fear. These claims help us predict whether an individual will accept or reject a fear appeal. Based on people's response to a fear appeal, the theory also predicts whether or not they will adapt their health behaviors. Whereas Brashers developed UMT to give insight into how individuals manage the *uncertainty* of illness and healthcare behaviors, Witte advanced the EPPM to shed light on how individuals manage the *fear* of illness and healthcare behaviors. Once we know how people communicate to manage the uncertainty and fear associated with a particular disease, however, what determines their willingness to change? How can healthcare professionals encourage their patients to change their lifestyles, habits, and health behaviors for the better? How might patients' attitudes and beliefs influence their motivation to make changes to improve their health? And, what role does their level of efficacy play in determining whether or not they follow through on their good intentions? To answer some of these questions, we turn our attention to a third theory that has been applied to health communication, the Theory of Planned Behavior. Before doing so, however, let's take a moment to evaluate the EPPM using our criteria for evaluating theories.

▲ ▲ ▲

Test Your Understanding
In a recent review and update of the EPPM, Erin Maloney, Maria Lapinski, and Kim Witte evaluated the theory using some of the same criteria that you learned about in Chapter 3.[53] For instance, after Witte's original articulation of the EPPM, scholars have continued their efforts to enhance the *parsimony* of the theory. Likewise, the EPPM has been *tested* or *verified* across a variety of contexts, although

it has been used most extensively in the context of HIV/AIDS prevention.[54] Researchers and health practitioners have also used the theory to support a wide range of different prevention health behaviors, including skin cancer,[55] teen pregnancy,[56] the HPV virus,[57] meningitis,[58] and adolescent substance abuse.[59]

Despite the strengths of the EPPM, however, some scholars have questioned its *utility*, given its limited theoretical scope. For example, Maloney and her colleagues noted that the EPPM is limited to predicting people's reactions to fear appeals only, and that fear appeals are not always the most appropriate (or the most ethical) technique for motivating health behaviors. In fact, some have argued that using fear appeals to persuade people with high levels of pre-existing fear is ill-advised and ineffective.[60]

Using our criteria for evaluating theories, how would *you* assess the EPPM in terms of its theoretical scope (i.e., is it too broad, too narrow)? To what extent does the EPPM generate new questions or give you new insights about health communication (i.e., does it have *heuristic value*)? Although Maloney and her colleagues suggested that this theory is fairly parsimonious, how would you evaluate its *elegance* and *simplicity*? Clearly, the theory is verifiable (or testable), but how *useful* is it? How might researchers expand the EPPM to contexts beyond health, such as to study fear appeals in personal relationships, families, or in organizations?

▲ ▲ ▲

THEORY OF PLANNED BEHAVIOR

Eat healthy and exercise regularly. Drink less. Learn something new. Quit smoking. Achieve better work-life balance. Volunteer. Save money. Get organized. Read more. Finish those household "to do" lists. What do all of these behaviors have in common? According to one online news website, they are the Top 10 most common New Year's resolutions.[61] For many people, New Year's resolutions represent moments when the best of intentions are met with minimal results. Why is that? How come so many people begin a new year with the hope of starting a good habit or ending a bad one, only to see their motivation dwindle and their intentions fade as the year goes on? More important, did you notice that four of the top five resolutions involve changing *health* or *stress-related* behaviors? If "learning something new" happens to include learning new health information, then we can conclude that what people most want to improve each year is their health.

Have you ever had a New Year's resolution? Did it involve some aspect of your health? What were your attitudes and beliefs about the desired change? How motivated were you? And, how well did you keep your resolution? If you have ever wondered *why* your good intentions failed to produce desired changes in your own behavior, you're not alone. More than 30 years ago, scholars developed the theory of planned behavior to help us understand what predicts people's behavior. This theory explains how beliefs, attitudes, and efficacy contribute to people's intentions, which in turn predict their behaviors.

INTELLECTUAL TRADITION OF THE THEORY OF PLANNED BEHAVIOR

Icek Ajzen is the scholar primarily responsible for advancing the theory of planned behavior (TPB). Ajzen is a social psychologist and professor emeritus at the University of Massachusetts, Amherst. His TPB modified and extended an earlier theory, the theory of reasoned action, which he developed with his colleague Martin Fishbein.[62] According to the theory of reasoned action, people's voluntary behavior is predicted by 1) their attitudes toward the behavior, and 2) how they think other people would view them if they performed it (i.e., their *subjective norms*).[63] What the theory of reasoned action failed to explain, however, were involuntary behaviors, those that people are unable to control. According to Ajzen, people's intentions can predict only their *attempt* to perform a behavior, not necessarily their *actual* performance. To provide a better explanation of human behavior that accounted for both voluntary and involuntary actions, Ajzen added *perceived behavioral control*, a concept that is nearly identical to the concept of *self-efficacy* that we discussed in the EPPM. Thus, the TPB extends the theory of reasoned action by describing how people's perceptions of their ability to perform the behavior in question (i.e., their perceived behavioral control) combine with their attitudes and subjective norms to predict their *intention* to perform the behavior.

Since its inception, the TPB has become one of the most influential and frequently cited frameworks for predicting human social behavior. Although researchers cited the theory only 22 times in 1985, that number had risen to 4,550 by 2010.[64] Given its theoretical goals of explanation and prediction, the TPB represents a social scientific theory of human behavior that is grounded in the post-positivist paradigm. Even though it represents a more general theory of human behavior, communication scholars have used the TPB to study healthcare campaigns and messages, as well as people's attempts to alter risky health behaviors.[65] With this mind, let's briefly discuss the assumptions of the TPB before we examine its concepts and claims.

Assumptions of the Theory of Planned Behavior

Three key assumptions underlie TPB.

Assumption 1: Human behavior is goal-directed. Like many of the theories we have covered thus far (e.g., Berger's Planning Theory in Chapter 5), the TPB assumes that people's behaviors result from their plans (hence, the theory of *planned behavior*). Ajzen assumes that most of us behave in a sensible manner as we weigh available information and consider (either implicitly or explicitly) the implications of our actions.[66]

Assumption 2: Actions are controlled by intentions, but not all intentions are carried out.[67] We sometimes do what we intend to do. At other times, we revise our intentions to fit changing circumstances or we abandon our intentions altogether. Thus, it matters to TPB *when* a person's intentions are observed relative to his or her actions. Intentions are expected to predict behavior only when they are observed just prior to performance of the behavior. The longer people wait to act after declaring their intention to do so, the less likely they are to follow through.

Assumption 3: Although many of our everyday behaviors are voluntary and can easily be performed when we motivated to act, motivation and ability interact to predict behavior. In other words, you may be strongly motivated to enact a particular behavior, but if your ability to perform that behavior is impaired, your possibility of failure is relevant, and your actual control over the behavior is limited, then your motivation won't matter much. For example, consider couples who want to have kids but struggle with infertility issues. Although they may be highly motivated to have children of their own, the inability of one or both partners to reproduce prevents them from accomplishing their goal. As Ajzen observed, "Every intended behavior is a *goal* whose attainment is subject to some degree of uncertainty."[68] Hence, Ajzen accounted for **perceived behavioral control**, or people's perceptions of their ability to perform a given behavior.

In summary, TPB assumes that human behavior is goal-directed and that people's intentions to perform a behavior flow from their beliefs and attitudes about the behavior. Whether or not someone's intentions produce *actual* behavior depends on that person's perceived behavioral control. Remember that assumptions represent ideas or beliefs that are taken for granted by theorists, and that not all theorists agree about a given set of assumptions. Before we turn our attention to some of the other key concepts in the TPB, then, let's take a moment to consider some alternative perspectives to the ideas of *intention* and *control*, particularly as they apply to communication in the context of health and wellness.

KEY CONCEPTS IN THE THEORY OF PLANNED BEHAVIOR

Although the TPB contains an array of key concepts, the core is composed of *beliefs, attitudes, intention,* and *behavior.* First, **beliefs** represent the information people think they have about a message, a person, an object, or a phenomenon.[69] For instance, many women believe that using birth control pills (i.e., the object or behavior) will prevent pregnancy (the attribute). The TPB identifies three types of beliefs that ultimately predict the attitudes, subjective norms, and perceived levels of behavioral control that a person has about a behavior. **Behavioral beliefs** refer to the individual's understanding of the likelihood that the behavior will produce a specific outcome (e.g., "Will using the pill prevent pregnancy?"). **Normative beliefs** refer to the expectations that people think important others (e.g., romantic partners, relatives, close friends) have of them as they consider a particular behavior (e.g., "What will my partner think if I choose not to use the pill?"). Finally, **control beliefs** are the factors that an individual believes will either facilitate or impede performance of a behavior (e.g., "Can I afford the pill? Will I be consistent in using it every day?").

According to the TPB, each of these beliefs predicts a corresponding attitude or perception that ultimately affects an individual's intention to perform a behavior.[70] Specifically, behavioral beliefs predict an individual's **attitude toward a behavior**, which the theory defines as the person's positive or negative evaluation of the behavior. If a person believes that exercise and diet are the preferred forms of treatment for high blood pressure, then he or she is likely to have a positive attitude toward walking 30 minutes a day and reducing fat intake. Likewise, the TPB uses normative beliefs to predict the **subjective norm**, which is the perceived social pressure to engage in or avoid a particular behavior. For instance, if the person seeking to reduce blood pressure has a spouse who exercises regularly and a close friend who wants to run a 5K race, then the TPB predicts that the subjective norm for exercise will enhance the individual's intention to walk 30 minutes a day. Finally, control beliefs predict people's perceived behavioral control, or their perceptions of their abilities to perform a given behavior. Someone who needs to increase daily exercise to reduce blood pressure, for example, might believe that having asthma is a barrier to walking 30 minutes a day.

Once we know people's attitudes toward a behavior, their subjective norms, and perceptions of behavioral control, we can then predict their intentions to perform the behavior. An **intention** is an indication of a person's readiness to do something. Intention is considered the immediate antecedent of **behavior**, which the TPB defines as an individual's observable response in a given situation with respect to a given target. Behavior is what the TPB is ultimately trying to predict, and according to Ajzen, it is most likely to occur when a person's intentions are compatible with his or her perceptions of behavioral control.[71]

To illustrate how these concepts fit together, let's consider how women's beliefs about birth control pills might influence their actual use. For many women, the question of whether to use birth control pills revolves around issues of physiological side effects, morality, and effectiveness.[72] Although most women believe that using the pill will lead to minor side effects, such as weight gain, they often differ in their beliefs about severe consequences. The more a woman believes that using the pill will not produce severe negative outcomes, such as blood clots and birth defects, the greater her intent to use the pill is likely to be. Likewise, women who believe birth control pills are the best available method for preventing pregnancy (a behavioral belief), who have friends who also take the pill (a normative belief), and who believe they can afford the pill and are capable of taking it consistently (control beliefs) will be more likely to hold a favorable attitude toward the pill and use it. Conversely, women who believe that their loved ones and doctors oppose the use of birth control pills (subjective norms) may form intentions not to use them.

The key concepts of the TPB help us understand how beliefs, attitudes, norms, and perceptions of control influence intentions, which, in turn, predict behavior. With the general goal of the TPB in mind, let's turn our attention to the theory's claims.

CLAIMS OF THE THEORY OF PLANNED BEHAVIOR

TPB claims that a person's intention to perform a behavior flows from both personal and social influences. Personally, *people are more likely to perform a behavior when they evaluate it positively, and less likely to perform it when they evaluate it negatively.* In other words, a person who believes that performing a given behavior will lead to mostly positive outcomes will hold a favorable attitude toward performing the behavior, whereas someone who believes that performing the behavior will lead to mostly negative outcomes will hold an unfavorable attitude.[73] Consider, for example, the use of tanning beds. Some individuals believe that using a tanning bed increases their chances of getting skin cancer and is therefore not worth the benefits of looking tan all year long. Such people hold a negative attitude about tanning bed use. For others, the use of tanning beds is convenient, efficient, and affordable, and it allows them to look the way they want. They hold a positive attitude about tanning bed use. According to the TPB, those individuals with a positive attitude about the use of tanning beds will be more inclined to use them—and will *actually* use them more—compared to people whose attitude is negative.

Socially, the TPB predicts that *individuals' intentions to perform behaviors increase when they perceive social pressure to do so; and the social pressure to perform behaviors comes from the belief that important people think they should perform them.* In other words, the more we believe that specific individuals (e.g., a partner, spouse, or close friend) or important groups (e.g., families or social networks) think that we should perform a behavior (i.e., normative beliefs), the more likely we are to perceive social pressure to do so (i.e., subjective norm). This social pressure, in turn, predicts our intentions to perform the behavior. For example, one of your authors (P.S.) enjoys diet soft drinks and holds a positive attitude toward drinking them in lieu of regular soft drinks. Many of his students, close colleagues, and family members, however, believe that the consumption of artificial sweeteners is unhealthy (i.e., normative beliefs), and they often try to persuade him to stop drinking diet soft drinks (i.e., a subjective norm). According to the TPB, his positive attitude toward drinking diet soft drinks must be weighed relative to his perceptions of the subjective norm for doing so before we can accurately predict his *intentions* to drink diet soft drinks.

In general, *the stronger an individual's intention is to engage in a behavior, the more likely that individual will be to perform the behavior.* Despite the value of knowing someone's attitudes and subjective norms, however, the TPB goes one step further to claim that a person's intentions depend on his or her *perceptions of control* over the behavior and *abilities to perform* the behavior in question. For instance, some individuals have the power to overcome bad habits but perceive that they are unable to control them (i.e., that they are helpless), whereas others may think (or perceive) that they have the same power when, in fact, they do not. According to the TPB, intentions can only turn into behaviors when people *perceive* they have control over the behavior and are *actually* able to perform the behavior. Although some behaviors are under a person's volitional control (i.e., his or her ability to perform), many are not. Many of the behaviors we enact depend in part on factors outside of our immediate control, such as time, money, skill, and the cooperation of others. Nevertheless, what matters most to the TPB is people's *perceived* behavioral control over a behavior, rather than their *actual* control.

Using these claims, researchers have applied the TPB to everything from laboratory games to decisions regarding abortion and smoking marijuana.[74] Researchers have also used the TPB to predict intentions toward genetic testing,[75] precautionary sexual behavior,[76] and the use of skin protection to help prevent occupational skin disease.[77] As a general rule, scholars have found that when behaviors pose no serious problems of control (i.e., when they are volitional), they can accurately be predicted from intentions. When situations call for behaviors that are beyond our control, however, we must take into account both intentions and perceived behavioral control. Consequently, both intentions and perceived control can be used to predict behavior, although intentions are usually more influential. For an exception to this trend, however, check out what researchers discovered when they applied the TPB to weight loss among college women.

▲ ▲ ▲

Weight Loss and the Theory of Planned Behavior

In one of the first tests of the TPB, Deborah Schifter and Icek Ajzen recruited 83 college women to participate in a study that focused on weight loss.[78] At the beginning of a six-week period, the participants were weighed and asked to complete a questionnaire measuring their attitudes, subjective norms, perceived control, and intentions with respect to weight loss. The women also reported whether or not they had made a detailed plan for losing weight. In support of the theory, the women who lost the most weight were those who (a) believed that they had control over their body weight, (b) strongly intended to lose weight, (c) developed a detailed plan of action, and (d) believed they were capable of following the plan and losing the weight. In fact, the amount of actual weight lost was more strongly associated with the women's intentions and perceived control than with their attitudes and subjective norms. More important, however, Schifter and Ajzen found that a strong intention increased weight loss only for those participants who believed they could control their body weight. These results not only provide support for the TPB but also offer further insight into a common health concern for many women and men. In other words, they demonstrate that theory matters.

▲ ▲ ▲

SUMMARY AND CONCLUSION

In this chapter, we explored three theories that help us understand how communication enables people to make sense of health and illness, to design persuasive messages for healthcare campaigns and interventions, and to understand how attitudes, beliefs, and intentions predict people's behaviors. Uncertainty management theory provides a useful lens for examining how people appraise the uncertainty associated with an illness, as well as the information management strategies they use to reduce, increase, or maintain their uncertainty. In a somewhat different vein, the extended parallel process model focuses our attention on how people manage the fear associated with fear appeal messages. By knowing how individuals appraise the threat of a fear appeal and make sense of their efficacy in responding to it, we can predict whether or not they will accept the recommendations behind the appeal. Taking the idea of efficacy one step further, the theory of planned behavior adds the idea of perceived behavioral control to our understanding of how beliefs, attitudes, and intentions predict behavior. The theories have some elements in common, such as the appraisals of uncertainty, fear, and control, and the central question of self-efficacy in determining how people respond to healthcare messages and/or change their health behavior. Nevertheless, each theory provides unique insight into the communication processes that enable us to make sense of health and illness. To conclude, let's return to the scenario from the beginning of this chapter to see if we can use what we have learned from these three theories to make sense of Adam's experience.

FOR FURTHER DISCUSSION

Looking back at our opening scenario, use the three theories that we discussed in this chapter to provide some possible explanations for Adam's behavior, as well as some plausible predictions for how he might act in the future.

UNCERTAINTY MANAGEMENT THEORY

1. How did Adam appraise his initial uncertainty about his biopsy? In what ways did he try to make sense of his visit to Dr. Bateman's office and understand the meaning behind his uncertainty?
2. While waiting for three days to receive his test results, how did he choose to manage his uncertainty? Did he seek to reduce his uncertainty about skin cancer? To increase it? To maintain it? What types of information management strategies did he use?
3. Suppose Adam learned that once he has had basal cell carcinoma, he has a 50% chance of getting it again. How might he manage the uncertainty associated with the possibility of having skin cancer again? What steps might he take to stay informed of his condition and prevent future occurrences of this disease?

THE EXTENDED PARALLEL PROCESS MODEL

1. Analyze Adam's likely response to the recommendations of the online ads and TV commercials that depicted skin cancer as the "silent killer." How great was Adam's perceived threat, both in terms of the severity of the threat and his susceptibility to it? How might he have evaluated the response efficacy and self-efficacy of using high-SPF suntan lotions and protective clothing for his outdoor activities?
2. How do you think Adam appraised his fear of getting skin cancer again? Would Adam's fear lead him to reappraise the perceived threat of a fear appeal to skin cancer and accept

the message's recommendations (i.e., a danger control process)? On the contrary, might his fear become chronic and lead him to reject the message's recommendations (i.e., a fear control process)?

3. Suppose you were tasked with developing a public service announcement about skin cancer. Based on your knowledge of the EPPM, how would you use fear appeals, perceptions of threat, and perceptions of efficacy to persuade people to protect themselves from this disease?

The Theory of Planned Behavior

1. How might Adam's beliefs about sun protection influence his attitude toward wearing sunscreen and protective clothing?
2. To what extent might his friends and family's understanding of skin cancer influence his decision to have or forego the surgery? How might this social pressure (or support) influence his motivation to have the surgery?
3. If Adam has a successful surgery, how might his attitudes toward sun protection and his feelings of control over future occurrences of skin cancer combine to predict his intentions to change how he enjoys outdoor activities?

KEY TERMS

Appraisal
Attitude toward the behavior
Behavior
Behavioral beliefs
Beliefs
Boomerang effects
Control beliefs
Danger control processes
Efficacy
Fear
Fear appeals
Fear control processes
Information acquisition
Information handling
Information seeking
Information use
Intention
Normative beliefs
Perceived behavioral control
Perceived severity
Perceived susceptibility
Response efficacy
Self-efficacy
Subjective norm
Uncertainty management

14

TECHNOLOGY AND MEDIA PROCESSING

HOW DO WE MAKE SENSE OF A MASS OF INFORMATION?

THE AMOUNT OF information available today is unparalleled in human history. Advancements in a range of technologies and the role of the media on information formation and distribution can strongly influence how each of us thinks about our social, political, organizational, cultural, and personal experiences. For example, a recurrent theme in the U.S. news media involves race-based conflicts between citizens and police. The police shooting of Michael Brown in Ferguson, Missouri, as well as the police strangulation of Eric Garner in New York City, were widely reported in the media as examples of suspected police abuse. How much do you know about these stories? In what ways has the media shaped your perceptions and judgments about the police? To what extent are race-based conflicts between police and citizens still a central headline in major national and local news outlets today? These and other questions are important for understanding the role of media and communication technology in our everyday lives. In this chapter we examine three theories that relate to information technologies and media. We will ask you to consider broad questions about the types of information you consume, the news outlets you use to understand current social and political topics, and the ways in which media facilitates the development of relationships. First, *agenda setting theory* examines the role of media in setting the news agenda and assigning the relative importance of news issues for the general public. This theory acknowledges that the media—rather than individuals—determines which events are worthy of attention. Second, *uses and gratifications theory* explores how people respond to media and the ways in which media gratifies or satisfies a variety of human needs. The central tenet of this theory is that individuals use media as a way to satisfy needs, unplug from stressful life events, gain information, and seek entertainment or information. Third, *media multiplexity theory,* which emerged from studies in computer-mediated environments, describes how media creates social networks of ties between people. Scholars using this theory examine how online communication contributes to intimacy and emotional connection, as well as how media outlets sustain group networks. Each of these theories frames the role of media in our lives in a slightly different way—but considered together, they help us understand the role of media in our everyday communication practices.

AGENDA SETTING THEORY

What are the most important issues facing our nation today? How concerned are you about the economy? About healthcare? About politics and the future leaders of our nation? And depending on how you answer these questions, where do you go to find out more? For decades, communication scholars have considered the powerful effects that the mass media have on public opinion. From politicians tracking people's reactions to their political ads and campaigns, to the television programs, news columns, and magazine stories devoted to foreign affairs, economic trends, and healthcare reform, the mass media have helped form and shape our societal viewpoints and practices in both subtle and not so subtle ways. In late 2014, for example, many students were preoccupied with issues such as the Ebola virus and the ISIS terrorist group. It just so happened that stories related to both were dominating most of the major news outlets at the time.

By the time you read this chapter, different issues will be at the top of the public's agenda. Those issues will still receive the most media coverage, however. For those interested in how public issues receive media attention and how public opinion functions in a democracy, questions of media coverage and use abound. To help us understand how the media's agenda guides and directs the public's interests, scholars have developed agenda setting theory. **Agenda setting theory** offers one explanation of how social change occurs in modern society by considering how media attention influences people's perceptions about what matters.[1]

INTELLECTUAL TRADITION OF AGENDA SETTING THEORY

The communication scholars primarily responsible for developing agenda setting theory are Maxwell E. McCombs of the University of Texas and Donald L. Shaw of the University of North Carolina. McCombs and Shaw were interested in the mass media's ability to shape political reality, and in 1972, they published an analysis of the media's role in the 1968 presidential campaign in Chapel Hill, North Carolina.[2] They believed that editors, journalists, and broadcasters provided much of the information that people used to make their voting decisions, and that readers learned not only about a given issue via the media, but also how much importance to attach to the issue based on the placement of a news story and the amount of information it provided. In essence, McCombs and Shaw believed that the media set the "agenda" of the campaign, because people learned most of they knew about each of the candidates and the issues from the media.[3]

Although McCombs and Shaw coined the term *agenda setting*, the concept itself first emerged nearly 50 years before, in Walter Lippmann's book, *Public Opinion*.[4] Lippmann argued that the mass media create images of events in people's minds and that policy makers should pay careful attention to those images. Despite his call, however, media scholars in the middle of the 20th Century focused more on explaining the direct effects of the media on individuals and societies. Driven primarily to understand the effects of World War I propaganda and the involvement of the media in Hitler's rise to power in Europe, these scholars developed a theoretical tradition known as the **magic bullet** or **hypodermic needle paradigm** of mass media.[5] Within this tradition, the media are thought to work like a magic bullet or a hypodermic needle, shooting their ideas and desires directly into the thoughts, attitudes, and behaviors of the public. According to this perspective, the mass media shape public opinion and influence individual behavior in whatever ways they choose.[6]

Although that idea may sound intuitive, researchers rarely found such strong, direct effects of media use on individual thoughts, attitudes, and behaviors. As a result, many theorists considered how the media might have less direct, but still important, effects on the public. Rather than focusing on how the media shape people's attitudes, these scholars focused instead on how the media influence people's thoughts about what issues are important. In his 1963 book on foreign policy, for example, Bernard Cohen argued that "the press may not be successful much of the time in telling people *what to think*, but it is stunningly successful in telling its readers *what to think about*" [emphases added].[7]

In other words, the media influence society not by directing people's opinions about a given topic, but instead by guiding the topics they think are important enough to have opinions about. Cohen's work, along with the earlier writings of Lippmann, provided the intellectual foundation for McCombs and Shaw's first agenda setting study.[8] Today, agenda setting theory represents one of the strongest social scientific theories within the field of mass communication, with nearly 300 articles on the topic.[9] At its core, **agenda setting** is the process by which the news media lead the public to assign relative importance to various public issues.[10] With this core concept and tradition in mind, let's review some of the assumptions of agenda setting theory before examining its key concepts and claims.

ASSUMPTIONS OF AGENDA SETTING THEORY

Agenda setting theory rests on three key assumptions.

Assumption 1: Most of what people know comes to them second- or third-hand from the mass media and/or from other people. Consider politics, for example. Most of us will never have the opportunity to meet the candidates in the next presidential election. How will we know their positions on the issues that matter to us? What kinds of information will guide our voting decisions? In other words, how will we learn what we need to know?

Agenda setting theory assumes that media provide most of our information about domestic and foreign affairs.[11] Some of us gather than information directly, such as by watching television news programs, reading newspapers or news magazines, or checking relevant web sites. Others of us receive that information indirectly by talking or texting with friends, relatives, and co-workers who follow the news. To illustrate one method of the media's indirect influence, let's consider how college students today might be receiving their news "second-hand" from an increasingly popular and unique type of news outlet.

▲ ▲ ▲

What's "The Skimm?" Agenda Setting in Email Newsletters

Two of the many news outlets from which individuals can learn about current events are online newsletters and blog posts. In 2012, two friends who met in college and later became producers for NBC News started their own e-mail newsletter and web site, known as "The Skimm." Recognizing that not everyone has the time or the interest to scour the news each day, the Skimm provides subscribers with daily e-mail newsletters that link readers to the news stories they consider to be most important. In their own words, "News is not only our career, it's our passion. Because of this, we have always been the go-to source for friends seeking the scoop on current events or breaking news."[12] Their daily newsletters promise to provide everything you need to know to start your day, by reading across subject lines and party lines to provide fresh editorial content.[13]

Websites such as www.theskimm.com are becoming increasingly popular for college students who want to stay informed and connected with current events. They also help illustrate one of the fundamental assumptions of agenda setting theory, namely, that some people gather their information indirectly from other individuals who read and watch the news themselves. Although reporters, editors, and program directors also serve as agenda setters, in that they determine what gets reported in newspapers and television news programs, the content they provide is often thought of as a primary source of information that readers (or viewers) can interpret and evaluate for themselves. For those individuals who rely only on websites and blog posts like "The Skimm," however, the news they receive has passed through a second level of agenda setting. It has been filtered by individuals who may or may not possess the journalistic credentials and news reporting experience of reporters, editors, and program directors. In many ways, "Skimms" are engaged in *meta-agenda setting* for their subscribers, as only those stories that they believe are important (rather than all of the news stories for a given day or week) receive coverage in their e-mail newsletters and blog posts. With this in mind, what other web sites do you visit to find the latest on a current event or political topic? And how might the political views and interests of the people who run those sites influence what you consider to be the most important topics of the day?

▲ ▲ ▲

Assumption 2: Mass media play a critical role in guiding and directing public attention because we cannot focus on every issue. It does so by directing our attention to certain issues and indicating the *weight* of importance that each issue deserves.[14] As McCombs noted, agenda setting theory assumes not only that attention is directed toward some issues and away from others, but also that comprehension enables readers and viewers to form opinions about the issues. By better understanding the important issues of the day, people become motivated to participate in resolving problems.[15]

Assumption 3: In any modern society, agenda setting includes the consideration of three related agendas: the media agenda, the public agenda, and policy agenda. First, the **media agenda** includes those topics addressed by media sources, such as public and cable television programs, local and national newspapers, and radio. The **public agenda** includes those topics that members of the public believe are important. Finally, the **policy agenda** represents issues that legislators and other governmental officials believe are important. Together, these three agendas are influenced by key members of a society, such as news editors, broadcasters, and popular radio personalities; by influential media (e.g., most watched television programs); and, by other indicators of the importance of an agenda issue (e.g., a global pandemic). Although some issues are likely to appear on all three agendas (as may be the case with global health crises or the war on terror), other items might be included on only one agenda.

With these assumptions in mind, let's review the key concepts of agenda setting theory before discussing its general claims. First, however, take a moment to review Figure 14.1, which provides an overview of the agenda setting process and how the three agendas relate to each other.

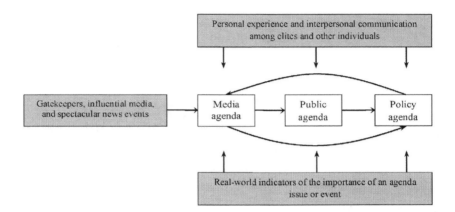

Figure 14.1 An Overview of the Agenda Setting Process (recreated from Rogers, E. M., & Dearing, J. W. (1988). Agenda-setting research: Where has it been, where is it going? In J. A. Anderson (Ed.), *Communication yearbook 11* (pp. 555-594). Newbury Park, CA: Sage.

KEY CONCEPTS IN AGENDA SETTING THEORY

Agenda setting theory provides a number of key concepts to help us understand how the media work to set the public and policy agendas of a given society. First, the theory distinguishes between first-level and second-level agenda setting. According to McCombs and Shaw, **first-level agenda setting** focuses primarily on the media and public agendas.[16] Historically, this has been the primary focus of agenda setting research, as scholars examine the topics on the media agenda and how they match the topics that the public identifies as being most important. For instance, an investigation of first-level agenda setting might find that media coverage of immigration reform has established this topic as an agenda item for the public. In recent years, however, agenda setting theorists have grown increasingly interested in **second-level agenda setting**, wherein the media not only suggest *what* the public should think about, but also influence *how* people should think. Also known as *attribute* agenda setting, this level occurs when the way in which media cover issues becomes the way people think about them.[17] In 2007, for instance, one researcher found agenda-setting effects for 12 attributes of the Japanese economy, including "The economy is stagnant with no prospect of recovery" and "Pension premiums might not pay off, especially for the young."[18] These attributes not only provided substantive information about issues on the media's agenda, but also carried a negative tone that was likely to shape how members of the public viewed the Japanese economy.

Central to the idea of second-level (or attribute) agenda setting is the concept of **framing**, a process through which the media emphasize some aspects of reality and minimize others.[19] Framing can be accomplished through: (1) the size and placement of a news item or story; (2) the narrative form and tone of language used to explain the news item; (3) the inclusion or exclusion of particular subtopics; and (4) the details included in the media coverage.[20]

Consider, for example, the issue of public health and safety that emerged September 2014, when Thomas Eric Duncan, a Liberian, became the first patient in the United States to be diagnosed with Ebola. When news broke eight days later that Duncan had died from his infection and that two nurses who had cared for him were also infected, the media had a variety of options for framing the issue of public health and safety. One news station might run a story on the government's protocols for diagnosis of the disease and quarantine of infected individuals. Another might focus on the screening of passengers at major airports and raise questions about border control and immigration. Still other media may focus on the two nurses who contracted the disease and examine nursing practices at the hospital where Duncan was treated, all while using highly sensational pictures and quotations to heighten concerns over public health. Whatever the story might be, the way in which media professionals frame the issue of public health and safety in the wake of Duncan's diagnosis and death influences not only what the public should be thinking about (i.e., the Ebola virus), but also how people should be thinking about it (i.e., that it represents a serious threat to the health and well-being of Americans).

In addition to the concept of framing, agenda setting theorists have also considered how people receive and interpret news stories. Drawing from the fields of social and cognitive psychology, for example, scholars have looked at priming as one psychological mechanism that helps to explain agenda setting effects.[21] **Priming** refers to the effects of a specific prior context on the retrieval and interpretation of information.[22] If an idea or topic is frequently on your mind, the notion of priming suggests that it will affect how you interpret ambiguous information. Someone who reads an article about the Ebola virus, for example, and then later overhears a conversational reference to a "virus" that really ruined a co-worker's day, is likely to think of "virus" as the cause of infectious disease rather than as a rogue program that crashed the co-worker's computer. Thus, priming extends one assumption of agenda setting theory: Because we have limited information-processing capabilities, we rely on primed topics to make sense of ambiguous information.

The last few concepts in this theory focus on characteristics of the audience, the issue, or the media that heighten the effects of agenda setting. One such factor is an individual's **need for orientation**, which represents a combination of high interest in an issue and high uncertainty about that issue.[23] For example, one of your authors (P.S.) is the parent of two boys and a huge sports fan. When Minnesota Vikings' running back Adrian Peterson was charged with felony injury to a child for spanking his four-year-old son with a "switch," news stories surrounding the investigation caught his attention (high interest). He knew little about the circumstances surrounding Peterson's interactions with his son and NFL policies related to domestic violence (high uncertainty). Because he had high interest and high uncertainty, agenda setting theory would suggest that his need for orientation was high, leading him to be influenced by media stories regarding Peterson's case. Other factors can also change the degree to which the media sets the agenda for an individual, such as educational level and political interest.

Besides individual characteristics, scholars have also considered how some issues facilitate the agenda setting effect more than others. Specifically, **issue obtrusiveness** refers to whether or not members of the public have had direct contact with the issue at hand.[24] The less experience the audience has had with the topic, the less obtrusive the topic is and the more susceptible the audience becomes to the media's agenda setting effect. On the other hand, people who have had direct contact with the issue are less affected by media coverage in terms of how they think. In general, domestic policy issues are considered more obtrusive than foreign policy issues because people generally have more experience with events that occur in their own country.

Together with framing and priming, an individual's need for orientation and an issue's obtrusiveness provide a useful vocabulary for understanding how the media sets the public agenda. Let's turn our attention next to the theory's claims.

CLAIMS OF AGENDA SETTING THEORY

As mentioned, the primary claim of agenda setting theory is that the media guide and direct both *what is on the public's agenda* and *how the public should think about it.* To extend this central idea, agenda setting theory offers three additional claims that help tie some of its key concepts to the agenda setting process.

First, the theory claims that *framing influences how citizens think about issues.* According to communication scholar Dietram Scheufele, it does so "not by making aspects of the issue more salient, but by invoking interpretive schemas that influence the interpretation of incoming information."[25] Consider our earlier example of Thomas Eric Duncan's Ebola diagnosis. When the *New York Times* posted headlines that read "Is the U.S. Prepared for an Ebola Outbreak?", "White House Takes Drop-Everything Approach to Respond to Public Health Crisis", and "Waste from Ebola Poses Challenge to Hospitals,"[26] the language used in each headline helped frame how the public viewed the issue. Referring to an "outbreak" that represents a "health crisis" and a "challenge to hospitals" is likely to cultivate a heightened sense of concern and anxiety that guides and directs how people think about and talk about the Duncan case and about infectious disease in general.

Second, the theory suggests that *priming influences both first-level and second-level agenda setting.*[27] When the media devote a great deal of space and time to certain issues, these issues are more likely to be on the top of people's minds. The more time people spend thinking about issues the media have primed, the more important those issues become (first-level agenda setting). Because people have limited information-processing capabilities, however, these primed topics also help them make sense of other news stories, particularly those that contain ambiguous information (second-level agenda setting). For example, students on one college campus recently reported what appeared to be a suspicious package that ultimately turned out to be an unattended backpack. Campus police, firefighters, and the bomb squad were dispatched to investigate the package before the university community had been informed, and students took to social media to vent their frustrations over what they perceived to be a nonchalant attitude toward keeping students informed of emergency situations. In the days that followed, several students referenced the need to be kept fully informed of all potential threats to their safety, given recent terrorist activity that had captured news headlines in the previous weeks and months.[28] In this instance, students had been primed to think about terrorism and other acts of violence that provided framework for making sense of the "bomb" threat and for evaluating how campus authorities distributed information about it.

The final claim advanced by agenda setting theory deals with issue obtrusiveness: *The results of agenda setting should be strongest for unobtrusive issues because audience members must rely on the media for information on these topics.*[29] For example, as a college student, issues related to campus life, university housing, and parent-provided health insurance are likely to be very relevant, or obtrusive, for you. Thus, you probably don't need the media to help you decide if these issues are important. You might rely more on the media to help you determine if issues such as trade deficits or campaign finance reform are important to you, however, because these may not affect you as directly—they are more unobtrusive, that is.

These three claims of agenda setting theory help us understand how media set the public agenda and guide how people think. Of course, the need for information isn't the only need that the media help satisfy. In the next section of this chapter, we explore a theory that helps us understand how and why people use particular forms of media and media programming to satisfy a wider variety of needs. Before we turn our attention to that theory, let's consider how communication scholars have applied agenda setting theory to breast cancer screening.

▲ ▲ ▲

Theory Matters: Agenda Setting and Breast Cancer Screening
In one application of agenda setting theory, communication scholars Karyn Ogata Jones, Bryan Denham, and Jeffrey Springtson compared the effects of mass and interpersonal communication on the breast screening practices of both college- and middle-aged women.[30] They surveyed 284 women, including 158 mothers and 126 daughters, about how often they read about breast cancer in

magazines and newspapers or heard about breast cancer on television. Participants were also asked how often they communicated with their relatives and social networks about breast cancer, as well as with personal physicians, health practitioners, and/or genetic counselors. For daughters, communication with physicians and relatives emerged as meaningful predictors of their breast cancer screening practices, such as self-examinations, mammograms, and clinical breast exams. For mothers, however, exposure to a news article about breast cancer or a television program about screening predicted how often they received a mammogram or a clinical breast exam, respectively. Jones and her colleagues concluded that middle-aged women were more likely than young women to rely on mass media messages for information about breast cancer. Nevertheless, they concluded that "differing media behaviors across individuals do not necessarily mean that those who do not gain most of their information from media are 'tuned out' to important topics of the day." Consistent with agenda setting theory, women who read a news story or watched a TV program about breast cancer were more likely to screen for breast cancer, providing further evidence that theory matters.

▲ ▲ ▲

Uses and Gratifications Theory

Are you one of the millions of Americans who loves reality shows? Reality television has exploded in popularity in the last 15 years. In 2003, one scholar noted that there were more applications to the reality show *The Real World* than to Harvard University.[31] One important question that media scholars ask is "What is the appeal?" Why are people watching so much reality TV?

Part of the answer can be found in *uses and gratifications theory* (UGT), which examines how people and groups use television, the Internet, and other media to fulfill a variety of needs and gratify their interests and desires. Uses and gratifications theory was developed in response to limitations of media effects theories (including agenda setting theory) that explored the influences of media on people's thinking and behavior. UGT shifted the attention away from the influences of powerful media and toward the motives, behaviors, and needs of individuals and groups. Communication scholar Denis McQuail noted that in UGT, we consume media because we have "an awareness of 'being lost' in something, 'involved,' 'carried away,' 'caught-up,' 'taken out of oneself,' or simply 'excited' or 'thrilled.'"[32]

INTELLECTUAL TRADITION OF USES AND GRATIFICATIONS THEORY

The central intellectual framework for UGT is based on the intersection between basic human need fulfillment (getting what we want or think we want) and the use of media for the gratification of numerous goals, motives, and needs.[33] Media scholar Denis McQuail noted that a focus on people's consumption of media is "a logical and sequential process of need-satisfaction and tension-reduction, relating the social-psychological environments to media use: a set of assumptions about the audience (notably its activity, rationality, [and] resistance to influence, capacity for reporting about itself)."[34] Thus, UGT is considered a broad framework for looking at media in social and cultural contexts from the users' point of view.

Prior to the emergence of UGT, theories of media effects tended to disregard the consumer—that is, the individual user of media. These theories (including agenda setting theory) proposed that the media strongly affect what users of media believe, conceiving of people as relatively passive receivers of media influence. In contrast, UGT suggested that people make thoughtful, deliberate choices about the media they read, watch, or listen to. In other words, UGT sought to explain *how people use media* rather than simply *how they are affected by it.*

Numerous theorists, working from multiple traditions, contributed intellectually to the development of UGT.[35] Communication scholar Thomas Ruggiero says the evolution of UGT began in the 1940s with research on the influence of films on audiences, and extends to the present-day influences of the Internet and new media.[36] Media scholar Denis McQuail explains that UGT started "as a fairly simple and straightforward attempt to learn more about the basis of appeal to popular radio programs and about the connection between the attraction of certain kinds of media content and other features of personality and social circumstances."[37] The UGT tradition developed broad questions that focused on the reception, choice, and manner of audience response rather than on the influence of messages. This focus lead to an expanded range of meanings associated with media experiences, one that views the reception and meaning of messages as diverse, complex, and ambiguous.[38]

As research explored the complex and messy processes of active audience involvement, UGT intersected with more than one theoretic tradition. For example, McQuail and Gurevitch compared three perspectives on human behavior that influenced audience gratifications perspectives: functional sociological analysis, structural cultural perspectives, and the action/motivation framework.[39] The functional perspective claimed that certain human needs explain media behavior and that an individual's psychological and social characteristics determine how well those needs are met. The structural/cultural perspective recognized that people are embedded in a modern industrial society and that that materials available to the media—along with social customs, conventions, and norms—affect media consumption. Finally, the action/motivation perspective suggests that people have the freedom not only to choose media products (such as what books to read or apps to buy) but also to evaluate the same products differently than other people do. Consider how often you disagree with others about what you're going to watch on TV or about the quality of a movie you saw over the weekend. Disagreements such as these deal with your freedoms to choose.

These three orientations to UGT were prevalent in the 1960s and 1970s. Since that time, UGT has been linked to many more perspectives, including social cognitive theory,[40] dependency theory and deprivation theory,[41] and expectancy value theory.[42] Although these traditions make a variety of assumptions about people's uses and gratifications of media, we will explore the assumptions linked most directly to UGT.

ASSUMPTIONS OF USES AND GRATIFICATIONS THEORY

Elihu Katz, Jay Blumler, and Michael Gurevitch identified five key assumptions that provide a degree of structural coherence to an otherwise diverse set of orientations to UGT.[43]

Assumption 1: Audience members are active information seekers and directed toward goal achievement. In contrast to media effects theories depicting individuals as passive, UGT assumes that we make conscious choices about media content and type; in other words, we are active and purposeful in our media choices. According to Thomas Ruggiero, our level of involvement in media can range from "high audience activity to low levels of involvement," and is potentially influenced by factors such as our income level, confinement to home, or our experiences with life stressors.[44]

Assumption 2: Audience members take the initiative in linking media choices with gratification. Unlike media effects theory, which assumed that there was a direct link between media messages and consumption behaviors, UGT focuses on empowering individuals to make their own decisions about the media they use. The argument is that *individuals use media,* rather than *media using individuals.* A classic example is the role of television in the perpetuation of violence. Researchers using the media effects model examine how violence in the media *causes* violence in real life, but UGT suggests that people gravitate toward violent programs to meet their personal and social needs.

Assumption 3: Media compete with various other sources of need fulfillment for individuals. Researchers using UGT recognize that people have a wide range of needs and that mass communication fulfills some of them. People meet some of their needs through other activities or life experiences, however. Consider how much time and energy you spend engaging media on a daily basis. Is consuming media an integral and critical part of your work, family, and or leisure activities? Do you ever take a media break?

Assumption 4: Individuals are sufficiently self-aware to be able to report their interests and motives. Being self-aware means being able to verbalize your interests and motives across a variety of media consumption circumstances. Scholars who assume self-awareness design studies to explore how people explain their interests and motives for consumption of media. This assumption highlights people's ability to *verbally explain* both the reasoning for their media choices and the gratifications they derive from those choices.

Assumption 5: As explained by researchers Katz and Blumler, "value judgments about the cultural significance of mass communication should be suspended while audience orientations are explored on their own terms"[45] After World War II, much research into media effects focused on the role of popular culture. Much of the debate centered on whether popular entertainment (such as songs, films, and stories) eroded long-held social and cultural traditions.[46] Media scholar Denis McQuail argued that the consumption of media was not merely a stage in a person's adjustment to social or cultural expectations and media messaging, but that "attention should thus be concentrated on the *making of choices* and on the meaningful encounter with cultural products" [italics added].[47] As UGT developed, scholars did not want to assume that popular culture determined viewer motives and interests. Rather, UGT scholars acknowledged that a host of individual and cultural factors influences the use of different media.

KEY CONCEPTS IN USES AND GRATIFICATIONS THEORY

To remedy the limitations of media effects models, UGT theorists identified a number of key concepts that shifted attention from persuasive messages to people's motives, interests, and gratifications when using media. The first key concept in UGT is based on the recognition that individuals use media for a variety of purposes. **Use** refers to "any engaged, purposeful media consumption that individuals select. In other words, there is an interrelationship between media and people. Using media implies that there are reasons for its use—that is, there are explanations for what people get from media use.

The second key concept is that people derive gratifications from media consumption. **Gratifications** refer to the anticipated interest, value, and/or benefit of media that satisfies social and psychological needs. UGT helps us think about the various sources of media, their use, and their value. One important way UGT scholars have explained gratification is through a related concept, **media satisfaction**, which refers to the experience of benefits from media use.[48] Media scholar Denis McQuail recognized that satisfaction with media fulfills people's needs for guidance, social exchange, identity development, orientation to new ideas, wonder, arousal, diversion, and endorsements, among others.[49] In some ways, media satisfaction can be understood by differentiating between gratifications that are sought and gratifications that are gained.[50] Gratifications sought are the anticipated gratifications we believe will occur from media use, and gratifications gained are actual gratifications we receive. There can be, and often is, a difference in the level or type of satisfaction we anticipate compared with actual satisfaction achieved after the media encounter. More importantly perhaps, satisfaction with media means that people gain specific and tangible benefits by using media.

The third key concept in UGT is that individuals constitute an **active audience**.[51] In other words, people actively seek out media to meet a variety of interests and needs. Consider the options you have when you want to purchase something, for example. If you need new shoes, you could check Amazon.com or go to the website of a particular company. In this case, your choice to buy new shoes is driven by a need (such as your old shoes being worn out), not by an advertising blitz from Nike or Ecco shoe brands. As this example illustrates, you can make choices about fulfilling your needs that are not necessarily driven by media messages or campaigns.

Media scholar Jay Blumler argued that numerous elements influence how people orient toward media.[52] Specifically, our involvement in media consumption is related to our degree of attention, our reflection on media materials, our conversations about media materials, and the relationship of media to other life activities. Blumler also observed that social roles and circumstances, personality dispositions, patterns of media consumption, and processes of media use and effects will *moderate* our responses to media.[53] For example, how might you use media differently than your professor does? How do your wants or needs differ from those of other students? Each of us seeks out media for specific reasons, and those reasons are often explained in UGT as our consumption motives, goals, and desires. What motivates you to use certain media? Is there a specific goal or desire that you hope to fulfill?

The fourth key concept is **audience need**, which consists of three interrelated ideas.[54] First, the *cognitive orientation* of the media consumer is influential—we use media that reflect our cognitive frames, further our cognitive development, and create satisfying cognitive stimulation. Second, we use media as a *diversion* from the stressors of everyday life or as an antidote to boredom. For instance, you may choose particular media sources that help you unwind at the end of a challenging day. Finally, our use of media is tied to our *personal identity*, which means we seek something important for our sense of self. In media, we may find support for our existing ideas or inspiration to think differently about social issues, relationships, or other important concerns.

The fifth key concept is **interactivity**, which means that our degree of control over media and our ability to engage in media discourse influence our use and gratification.[55] Interactivity is highly relevant today because technological innovation increase our ability to participate in media. We can chat online and use *Zoom, FaceTime, Skype,* or other technologies that allow our direct input into mediated communication environments. Greater interactivity (especially with the proliferation of smart devices) lets us find information instantaneously, rate the quality of services and products, and give immediate feedback in a host of human and organizational environments. Although high levels of interactivity offer clear benefits, they also raise some legitimate concerns, such as who has access to smart devices and what types of destructive messages are expressed online.

▲ ▲ ▲

Explore the Relevance of Uses and Gratifications

Think about at least three media sources that you use on a regular basis. Your list might include *Facebook* or other social media outlets, television shows, listservs, or magazines. For each, describe *why you use that media source* (identifying your goals, desires, and motives) and *how that source is valuable to you.* How satisfied are you with each of the media sources on your list? What are their similarities and differences? Share your thoughts with another student, and discuss the value each of these media sources has for each of you. Are there disadvantages or downsides to each of the media sources? If so, what are they? How would your life be different if you were no longer able to use these sources of media?

▲ ▲ ▲

CLAIMS OF USES AND GRATIFICATIONS THEORY

The central claim in UGT is that people seek out and use media to gratify numerous individual, community, and social needs. UGT scholars have focused on a variety of media, audiences, and variables that shed light on media uses in everyday life. When researchers collect data from people about their media use and related gratifications, the focus is on each person's activity and related social and psychological contexts, as well as his or her media dependence and ritualization, experiences of using or avoiding specific media sources and programs, learning, fulfillment of needs, and other concerns.[56] Below, we describe some of the findings across UGT contexts and approaches to give you a flavor of UGT uses and insights.

An important issue in media effects research is the role of violence in media. The effects model explores how viewing media violence influences or increases violence among individuals. Although findings are mixed, communication scholar Andrew Weaver reviewed numerous studies to see whether the intentional selection of media violence increases or decreases a person's desire to see the particular program.[57] As he explained, "violence increases selective exposure but decreases enjoyment."[58] This means that people select programs because of their violent content, but the violence actually decreases their enjoyment of those programs.

Why are people attracted to media depictions of violence in the first place? Weaver suggested that we are drawn to "forbidden fruit," intrigued by watching what society does not approve of. We may also be drawn to the suspense created by movie trailers and teasers, or we may simply enjoy being voyeurs of violence (as when we can't avoid staring at the aftermath of a car accident). Perhaps not surprisingly, men enjoy violence more than women do, and aggressive men enjoyed it more than non-aggressive men. Although men enjoy violence more than women do, Weaver's research noted that they also enjoy non-violent content more than women do, and that both sexes prefer non-violent content to depictions of violence. These and similar findings help to illustrate that we actively choose media for specific reasons, including intrigue and enjoyment.

Another compelling line of UGT research focuses on how we use media to gain information. As one example, communication scholar Nupur Tustin examined how medical patients seek information from online health sources.[59] The study assumed that patients' needs determine how—and from whom—they seek medical advice and information. Image you are a cancer patient unhappy with the relationship you have with your cancer specialists. Where would you turn for information about your condition? If you're dissatisfied with your health care providers, you might imagine looking to the Internet as a primary source of information. That's exactly what Tustin found: The less happy patients were with their specialists, the more likely they were to go online for health information. Patients therefore used the Internet to gratify their needs for information when their doctors failed to meet those needs.

Recall our observation that widespread interest in reality television programs exemplifies how people use media to satisfy various needs. A central question for UGT scholars is, "What needs do reality television programs serve?" One study by communication scholar Zhana Bagdasarov and colleagues linked the attraction of reality TV programming to both voyeurism and sensation seeking.[60] Media scholar Misha Kavka noted that, Reality TV relies on audience member interest in voyeuristic elements like "the *performance of intimate elements* in public and the *transformation of ordinary events* from unwatchable to something worth watching (italics added)."[61]

Both voyeurism—which is stimulation through visual means—and sensation seeking—a tendency to seek intense, novel experiences—were linked to the viewing of reality television, as well as situation comedies and animate satire. In this study, then, gratifications of television viewing for specific types of programming were linked to specific personality predispositions.

In mid-2014, a new late-night comedy called *Last Week Tonight with John Oliver* debuted on HBO. Oliver, a former contributor to *The Daily Show* (featuring John Stewart), continues the programming tradition of combining political information with satire, often referred to negatively as *infotainment*. Critics argue that infotainment diminishes the boundary between news and entertainment. But does it actually matter whether viewers watch these programs from a news perspective rather than an entertainment perspective? Communication scholar Lauren Feldman argued that infotainment programs "have emerged as important sources of political information."[62] In her study of *The Daily Show*, Feldman predicted that whether viewers sought information or entertainment would affect how they processed political information. As expected, people who oriented toward such shows as sources of news—*or* as a mix of news and entertainment—"activated greater mental resources" than those who watched for entertainment only.[63] UGT is central to the study because of its exploration of viewer orientation (news versus infotainment), cognitive orientation (how individuals cognitively framed the media event), and gratification (needs and gratification of *The Daily Show* as news, entertainment, or infotainment). Thus, UGT continues to serve as an important theoretical framework for understanding media consumption and the numerous types of gratifications that audience members experience in their intersection with different media.

Media scholar Denis McQail argued that we should not lose sight of the broad issues and questions connected with the UGT tradition. He asserted that:

An attention to the audience requires a sensitivity to the full range of meanings of that experience and thus to its diversity and fragility. It also means accepting that making, sending, choosing, and responding to media messages involves a set of understandings which are, up to a point, shared by "makers" and "receivers" and which are usually both complex and unspoken, Thus diversity, ambiguity and even some mystery are to be expected on the "side" of production and content as well as on the "side" of reception.[64]

What may be an interesting development in media use relates to innovation in technologies: wrist computers that display virtually any media content in any location, or virtual reality glasses that personalize media consumption in ways yet unimagined, are both developing technologies that will likely influence audience use and gratifications. Consider the different functions that media serves your everyday life and think about both its value and its possible limitations.

MEDIA MULTIPLEXITY THEORY

Take a moment to think of everyone you have talked to or interacted with over the last 24 hours. How many are close friends or family members? How many are casual friends or acquaintances from school? Co-workers or professional contacts? Now, think about the variety of media forms—telephone, text messaging, e-mail, and the like—your conversations represented.

Many of our lives have become increasingly *multimodal*. In other words, we use a variety of media to maintain our relationships with others. We may use different media in different relationships, but our choices are not random. Rather, decisions about which media to use and how often to use them convey messages about the relationship itself (just ask anyone who has ever been dumped via text message).[65] The strength of an interpersonal or professional bond is associated with the number of media people use to maintain it. To help us understand why, scholars have advanced media multiplexity theory (MMT).

INTELLECTUAL TRADITION OF MEDIA MULTIPLEXITY THEORY

The scholar primarily responsible for developing MMT is Caroline Haythornthwaite of the University of Illinois. Her research examines how the Internet and computer media support social interactions among members of online learning and work communities.[66] She developed MMT to explain how people's uses and effects of media depend on—and are predicted by—the types of relationships they have. For instance, Haythornthwaite has studied how media use by members of distance learning classes facilitates the development of community: that is, how students learn to be part of an online program, how they communicate social and emotional support across various media, and how they integrate their online social interactions into their offline lives.[67]

In the late 1970s and early 1980s, scholars studying computer-mediated communication (CMC) argued that moving social interaction from rich, face-to-face contexts to lean, text-based media would inhibit understandings and contribute to antisocial behavior.[68] More recent research has confirmed, however, that new media are vital for creating and sustaining a variety of professional and personal relationships in everyday life.[69] To support this idea, Haythornthwaite adopted a social network approach that examined how people in professional and academic communities support their ties to each other using a variety of media. Specifically, she sought to extend Mark Granovetter's classic work on social network ties by identifying how the number of media people use in their relationships can strengthen or weaken the bond between them. Granovetter was a sociologist who defined **tie strength** as a "combination of the amount of time, the emotional intensity, the intimacy (mutual confiding), and the reciprocal services which characterize the tie."[70]

He suggested that strong and weak ties provide different kinds of resources. And for Haythornthwaite, an important indicator of tie strength is the number of media used people use in their dyadic (2-person) relationships.

Rather than focus on the characteristics of any one particular medium, such as text or video, MMT focuses on how the introduction of a medium creates a social network of ties. It also explains how the addition or removal of a medium sustains or disrupts the network. MMT is a social scientific theory that emanates from the post-positivist paradigm and ties together different stands of research from information science, sociology, and communication. The first wave of studies using MMT focused on how members of work and educational groups develop and sustain their social ties. Later, a second wave of research used survey methods to examine how friends, romantic partners, and family member use various media to sustain satisfying and close relationships.[71] With both waves of research in mind, then, let's review the assumptions of MMT before examining its key concepts and claims.

Assumptions of Media Multiplexity Theory
Three basic assumptions underlie MMT.[72]

Assumption 1: The characteristics of ties hold in the mediated environment as they do in the offline environment. In other words, what characterizes your personal and professional relationships in everyday life persists regardless of whether or not you are talking to an individual in a mediated environment or face-to-face. Consequently, it is not the medium of social interaction—but rather, the messages that are exchanged—that primarily determines the nature of the tie between conversational partners. Like offline ties, online ties are expected to be stronger and closer to the extent that they demonstrate a wider variety of interactions and exchanges of emotional support. For example, let's say you wanted to express gratitude to your best friend for always supporting you in your endeavors. You could choose to do that face to face, over the phone, or via Skype. Your choice of medium may affect how the message is interpreted, but your expression of gratitude is likely to strengthen your relational tie regardless of the medium you use.

Assumption 2: Online exchanges are as real as offline exchanges in terms of their effects on relationships. That is, MMT assumes that your online interactions with close friends, family members, casual acquaintances, business associates, and the like are equally and proportionally influential as are your face-to-face interactions with each of these groups of people. For example, MTT assumes that "friends" who communicate online communicate more frequently, about a wider variety of things, and using a wider variety of media than "casual acquaintances" or "business associates." This is because individuals who consider themselves to be friends are more likely to socialize and communicate emotional support online than individuals who do not. In this example of social support, MMT assumes that support given online helps maintain an offline tie—that ties flourish not only when they receive support in offline contexts, but when they are supported by online information exchanges, social support, work interaction, and play.[73]

Assumption 3: A social tie drives the number and types of exchanges that occur between conversational partners, regardless of whether the tie is maintained online, offline, or both. Many people find it hard to separate the effects of online and offline messages in their relationships. We so often switch back and forth from between communicating online (such as by texting or e-mailing) and offline (such as by talking face to face). To understand the nature of a social tie, then, we have to consider all types of interactions within pairs or among members of a social network, not just whether those exchanges are occurring online or offline.[74] With these assumptions in mind, let's review the key concepts of MMT before turning our attention to its claims.

KEY CONCEPTS IN MEDIA MULTIPLEXITY THEORY

Building from Granovetter's work on social networks, MMT identifies three types of ties that differ in terms of strength.[75] **Strong ties** include people with whom we have established close relationships. They provide us a sense of belonging, emotional fulfillment, and greater access to both personal and professional resources. According to the theory, the value of strong ties is their willingness to help us accomplish individual, relational, and/or organizational goals by sharing their information, resources, and contacts. **Weak ties**, on the other hand, include people we know only somewhat well—not as well as we know our close friends and family members. Those include casual acquaintances, professional contacts, and perhaps our co-workers or fellow students. People who have weak ties are often dissimilar to each other and interact in different social circles.[76] Because of their varied experiences and social circles, the value of weak ties is the access they provide to a diverse range of information, resources, and contacts. For example, social networking sites such as Facebook help facilitate the formation of weak ties.[77]

In addition to strong and weak ties, Haythornthwaite defines **latent ties** as those "for which a connection is available technically but that has not yet been activated by social interaction."[78] In other words, a latent tie is a social connection that exists only in a theoretical sense until one member chooses to contact the other, at which point the tie becomes a weak tie. People who use the social networking site LinkedIn, for example, often send e-mail invitations to join networks with individuals whom they have never met, but with whom they share a professional connection. Prior to submitting an e-mail invitation to "link in," such contacts represent latent ties. Once an invitation has been sent and the latent tie accepts it, however, the individuals establish a weak tie (and perhaps, with time, a strong tie). As Haythornthwaite noted, an important characteristic of latent ties is that they are not established by individuals, but instead depend on structures governed by the system administrators (e.g., the administrators of LinkedIn), the management of an organization, or community organizers.

By focusing on tie strength and examining what distinguishes strong ties from weak ties in online environments, Haythornthwaite noticed that indicators of strong ties correspond to using more modes of communication. Specifically, MMT suggests that people in strong ties are communicate more often, and to provide social and emotional support across a variety of media, relative to people in weak ties. As Haythornthwaite put it, "Asking 'who talks to whom about what and via which media' revealed the unexpected result that more strongly tied pairs make more use of the available media."[79] She labeled this phenomenon **media multiplexity**.

The final concept in MMT references how different types of media are organized across different types of social networks. Specifically, Haythornthwaite observed that within an educational or task-oriented group, the use of media conforms to a unidimensional scale, such that "those individuals who use only one medium, use the same one medium; those who use two, tend to use the same second medium, etc."[80] In other words, people use one or two "base" media, such as e-mail or telephone, for a variety of weak ties within an organizational or educational group. They then tailor other media for use only with strong ties.

For example, you may have a weak tie with a fellow student in your communication theory class with whom you only visit when the opportunity presents itself. If you're assigned to the same group project, however, you may exchange e-mail addresses and start corresponding online as well as in class. If a friendship emerges, you transition from a weak tie to a strong tie, and you might exchange text messages and phone calls too, discussing things that go beyond your group project and classroom material.

KORY FLOYD, ET AL

As we've seen, MMT includes several concepts that help us understand social network ties, as well as how the organization and use of media contribute to them. With these concepts in mind, let's turn our attention to the claims advanced by MMT.

CLAIMS OF MEDIA MULTIPLEXITY THEORY

MMT advances four general claims about media use and tie strength.[81] First, the theory states that *media use indicates tie strength*. In her research, Haythornthwaite observed two patterns of media use that help us distinguish between weak and strong ties. The first pattern of media use, which typically describes networks of weak ties, depicts a group of individuals who are widely connected within an organization or community, but who communicate infrequently and opportunistically only when a specific need arises. This pattern emerges as individuals (a) take advantage of passive opportunities to interact (e.g., hallway encounters, class sessions), (b) use only organizationally established media (e.g., e-mail, professional listserv), and (c) communicate infrequently via one or two media. For example, students often develop networks of weak ties with others by working together on class projects. They may communicate in person during class or by e-mail outside of class. They might also interact with each other when they cross paths on campus, although their association may never grow from a weak tie to a strong tie.

The second pattern of media use depicts a network of individuals who are much more selective in who they share connections with, as they communicate more frequently through the use of face-to-face, private, and/or optional means of communicating with one another. This pattern involves both using mandated media in organizational settings (such as a person's work e-mail) and communicating in private interactions (such as through personal e-mail). Again, in some classes, students develop friendships that begin as weak ties but grow into strong ties as the students communicate more frequently, use a wider range of media, and share both public and private

— 468 —

information. According to MMT, therefore, the way media are used in different networks teaches us about the strength of the ties among network members.

The second claim advanced by MMT is that *the presence of a medium can provide a level of "latent tie connectivity" upon which weak and strong ties may grow.* **Latent tie connectivity** refers to the potential connections that individuals can create and add to their social networks by using a new medium for the first time or by joining a new social media group. In other words, adding any network-based means of communicating helps to connect formerly unconnected people to each other.[82] From online social support groups and listservs to Facebook, Twitter, and Instagram, different media help create a connection that is available technically, even if it hasn't been activated socially. According to MMT, social interaction activates latent social network ties, turning them into weak ties. Consider, for example, two people who both use Facebook but aren't connected to each other as friends. Facebook offers a latent tie by offering the *potential* for one of those people to "friend" the other. If the two become friends and start communicating, they then have a weak tie instead of a latent one.[83] If they later start communicating in other ways, such as by telephone or text message, their weak tie can become a strong one.

To further illustrate how latent ties can become weak ties (and perhaps strong ones as well), let's consider how communication scholars use MMT to study online interactions and personal relationships.

▲ ▲ ▲

Theory Matters: Xbox LIVE and the Relational Maintenance of Men's Friendships
In a recent application of MMT to personal relationships, communication researchers Andrew Ledbetter and Jeffrey Kuznekoff surveyed 180 men regarding their attitudes toward online social connection

and self-disclosure. They wanted to know how the men's communication in Xbox LIVE (XBL), as well as their offline communication, predicted how close they felt to each other.[84] Their study found that the men had closer friendships if they used *both* XBL *and* offline interactions to maintain their friendship. This result supports MMT's claim that using more media, more frequently, enhances tie strength.

▲　▲　▲

A third claim advanced by MMT is that *adding or removing a type of media alters people's weak and strong ties.* To understand this claim, it is useful to note that MMT uses a broad definition of *media.*[85] Instead of defining an individual medium only as a communication channel (such as text messaging), MMT defines a medium based on the intersection of *channel* and *social context.* For instance, think about an annual reunion with extended family and a weekly lunch with immediate family. Both occur face to face, yet their differing social goals and context would qualify each as a different medium. According to Haythornthwaite, adding or subtracting a medium affects weak and strong ties differently. For weak ties, introducing a new medium can creates new weak ties by connecting previously unconnected people to each other. Losing a medium, on the other hand, can potentially dissolve a weak tie. Students in a college course might maintain weak ties with each other through online bulletin boards, for example, but their weak ties dissolve at the end of the term unless they communicate in other ways as well.

According to MMT, adding or subtracting a communication medium has less of an effect on a strong tie. In a corporation or an extended family, for instance, a change in a group-wide medium is unlikely to weaken a strong tie because people maintain their ties through several media, not just one. People with strong ties are also more motivated to maintain their relationship, so if they lose one way of communicating, they look for others to take its place.[86]

The final claim of MMT is that *different levels (or patterns) of media use carry different kinds of information because of the various ways in which individuals use media to maintain their weak and strong ties.*[87] In other words, MMT suggests that meaningful differences exist in the kinds of information that circulate through different media based on the strength of the social network tie. In educational and organizational groups, new information is likely to be retrieved from weak ties and is likely to reach individuals through group-wide media (e.g., an e-mail chain). For instance, a new sorority member is likely to seek general information about an upcoming formal through e-mail correspondence, bulletins, or other forms of organizational media. Information from strong ties, however, is more likely to be asked for and received via more private channels. If the same sorority member wanted personal advice on what to wear to the formal or if her date was acceptable, however, she would be more likely to ask her "big" (i.e., her big sister within the sorority). In effect, Haythornthwaite identified two ongoing demands for information in working groups that are often satisfied through two different tiers of media. New information, which she argues is the strength of weak ties, is typically received via widely used and mandated public media. Information or help with task completion for those working together (i.e., the strength of strong ties), however, is typically given and received via person-to-person, optional, and private media.

As you can see, MMT helps us tie together the concepts of social networks, tie strength, and media use. It is a relatively new and exciting theory of media and technology that asks who is talking to whom via which media. It connects tie strength with media use, such that conversational partners with stronger ties are more likely to use more media to maintain their tie. It introduces the idea of a latent tie, and it identifies different patterns of media use, and different strengths, for both weak and strong ties. Finally, in group settings, MMT explains how different pairs of people exchange different kinds of information, depending on media that are either publicly mandated or privately negotiated.

FOR FURTHER DISCUSSION

AGENDA SETTING THEORY

1. What does Agenda Setting Theory tell us about media agendas? Who decides what stories or events receive priority in the news cycle? Do traditional news sources accurately and effectively reflect the *public agenda*? The *political agenda*? Why or why not?

2. Think about some of the limitations of major news outlets and their control over news agendas. What do you believe are important social and political issues that traditional media outlets downplay or ignore? Are there alternative media outlets that focus more on issues that are more important to you? If yes, what are they, and what perspectives do they offer that you do not find in traditional media outlets?

USES AND GRATIFICATIONS THEORY

1. Consider your specific media choices within the last year. Which media tend to dominate your time and energy uses? Which media do you see as obsolete? What effects does media use have on the quality of your life?

2. UGT asserts that media use results in gratifications of human needs. Identify the kinds of needs you fulfill through media use, and try and link specific media choices to specific needs. Consider also which needs media use does not fulfill in your life.

MEDIA MULTIPLEXITY THEORY

1. According to MMT, what is the relationship between strong ties and multiple media uses? To what extent does the media influence the nature of both strong and weak ties? What are the consequences to individuals who reduce their media use to maintain connections with others?
2. Explain the concept of latent ties. What does the idea of latent ties tell us about the nature of communication in online environments? What kinds of potential relationships do you think exist in your current possibilities for latent ties, and which media are more likely to increase latent tie connections?

Key Terms

Agenda setting
Audience involvement
First and second level agenda setting
Hypodermic needle paradigm
Interactivity
Issue obtrusiveness
Latent ties
Magic bullet
Media agenda
Media consumption
Media effects
Media gratifications
Media multiplexity
Media use
Need for orientation
Policy agenda
Priming
Public agenda
Strong ties
Tie strength
Weak ties

15

THEORIES OF COMMUNICATION, CULTURE, AND CRITIQUE

HOW DOES YOUR CULTURE AFFECT YOUR EVERYDAY LIFE?

THERE IS AN old joke that goes something like this: An older fish swims by two younger fish. The older fish says, "Hey, how's the water?" The young fish swim past him, look at each other quizzically, and say "What water?" The point of the joke, of course is that for fish, water is such a taken-for-granted part of their everyday experience that they simply don't notice it. And yet, it is the context that shapes every single aspect of their lives. For many communication theorists, culture is our water. Our culture—whether the culture we were raised and socialized in as children, our national culture and its expectations for polite behavior, or our mediated popular culture representations—shapes and limits our communication practices in ways that we may not be fully aware. Indeed, cultural studies scholar Stuart Hall says, "Culture is a *dimension of everything*. Every practice exists in the material world and simultaneously signifies, is the bearer of meaning and value. Everything both exists and is imagined.

And if you want to play in the area where deep feelings are involved, which people hardly understand, you have to look at culture."[1]

This chapter addresses the connections between communication and culture. We explore how power relations, taken-for-granted values and assumptions, and ideologies are embedded and (re) produced in the context of everyday interactions. Rather than assuming that culture is a neutral backdrop against which individuals engage in conversation, the theories in this chapter describe how we bring our cultures to life through our speech and how and cultures "speak us into being."

Each of the theories expresses the tension between the individual and the collective. We begin with the theory of genderlects, which explains how the gendered culture into which we are socialized creates different ways of speaking and understanding conversations for men and women. We then explore face negotiation theory, which posits that different cultures enact notions of "face" differently, making culture a significant influence one our experience and understand of conflict. Finally, we investigate the theoretical tradition of cultural studies, which unpacks how cultural messages, particularly those found in popular media, influence our day-to-day communication patterns and our identities. What unites these three theories is that each one addresses whether people produce their own unique communicative behaviors or whether their behaviors are determined by their culture?

GENDERLECTS

Perhaps you can recall a conversation you had with someone of the other sex that did not quite go according to plan. Maybe you walked away from an interaction thinking to yourself, "I was hoping she would help me figure out how to do better on my next exam, and all she did was talk about how she struggles with her own tests." Or maybe your partner has informed you that a couple of your mutual acquaintances just started dating, but when you ask for the details, he looks at you with a confused expression on his face and says, "I *just* told you." Men and women often enter conversations with both different assumptions about the purpose of the conversation and competing or contradictory goals and strategies. As a result, everyday interactions between women and men (at least, white middle-class men from Western cultures) can seem as complicated as interactions between people from different cultures. Linguist Deborah Tannen's **genderlects** is a theory that explains those gendered differences and their communicative foundations and consequences.

INTELLECTUAL TRADITION OF GENDERLECTS

Deborah Tannen is interested in how messages are interpreted and understood within the context of particular situations. She drew upon the work of interdisciplinary scholars Gregory Bateson[2] and Irving Goffman[3] to help explain how men and women emerge from the same conversation with such different and contradictory interpretations. Specifically, she built on the concept of frames or "structures of expectations" that guide interpretations. Tannen and her colleague Cynthia Wallat defined **frames** as the "definition of what is going on in interaction, without which no utterance (or movement or gesture) could be interpreted."[4] If someone asked you, "What are you looking at?" your response would be based on your frame for the interaction. Think about how having a playful frame, a confrontational frame, or a quizzical frame would greatly change the tenor of your interpretation and response.

Closely related to the concept of frames is anthropologist Gregory Bateson's articulation of metacommunication, which emerged from his research on animals' play behaviors. Bateson was interested in how monkeys could engage in behaviors and signs that look like fighting but were interpreted by other monkeys as "play" fighting. As psychologist Robert Mitchell described it, animals must "both appear to be fighting . . . and simultaneously not appear to be fighting."[5] In this case, animals need to understand the "mood signs" or the communication about communication to make sense of the behaviors as "play" and not combat.

Metacommunication is communication about communication. For Bateson, it reflected a mode of communicating that was more abstract than the actual words being spoken, wherein the "subject of discourse is the relationship between the two speakers."[6] In her theory of genderlects, Tannen explains how men and women often can hear the same content, yet understand the effect of the message in very different ways. Even a simple statement such as, "I'm sorry" may have multiple meanings at the relational level. For example, when Beverly learned of her husband Rob's difficult day at work, she said "I'm sorry." Rob's response was, "Why are you apologizing? It's not your fault." Both parties found the interaction disorienting, because although they heard the same words ("I'm sorry"), they interpreted those words differently. Beverly intended to express empathy for Rob's difficult day, but Rob interpreted her statement as admitting a sense of responsibility. These metacommunication problems are a focus of Tannen's theory.

ASSUMPTIONS OF GENDERLECTS

In her book, *You Just Don't Understand: Women and Men in Conversation*, Tannen suggests that men and women in contemporary Western culture grow up speaking different dialects, if not exactly different languages.[7] She calls these different ways of speaking *genderlects* (for "gender dialects"). As a result of genderlects, Tannen claims, men and women's communication is a form of cross-cultural interaction in which miscommunication is more common than shared meaning and experience. One reason why conversations between women and men are often challenging, she suggested, is because we fail to realize that our conversational partner is using "different words" to describe "different worlds." We assume that because we speak the same basic language, we should understand each other. But, our habitual use of genderlects often creates barriers to understanding.

We learn genderlects through socialization and cultural participation. As young boys and girls, we are socialized into different speech communities with distinctive norms. In the games that young children play, gendered rules of interaction are reinforced. The games that boys often play, such as football, cops and robbers, and king-of-the-hill, tend to competitive, organized, and rule governed. In these games, status is often achieved by performing well and standing out from the crowd. In contrast, girls grow up playing house or school, activities that usually occur in smaller groups without clear-cut rules. In these games, the goal is often to include others and facilitate further interaction.

KEY CONCEPTS IN GENDERLECTS

The key concepts in genderlects are report talk, rapport talk, powerless speech, different ways of listening, and troubles talk.

Report talk / rapport talk. It is not surprising that adult men and women's conversational styles reflect their early introductions to communication. Tannen argues that, because of differences in their socialization, men and women orient themselves to conversation differently. For men, conversation is a space to assert independence, to hold an audience's attention, to compete for the talk stage, and to garner status. For women, communication is process to create and sustain relationships, to focus on and respond sensitively to others, and to build connections. More concisely, Tannen argues that, in the context of conversations, men view and experience themselves as individuals in a hierarchial social order wherein communication can be used to negotiate one's position, to maintain the upper-hand, to resists others' attempts at put-downs, to report information and knowledge, and to preserve independence. She calls this approach to conversation **report talk.** Women, on the other hand, see themselves in conversations as individuals within a network. Thus, communication is used as a strategy to seek and give information and support, to build consensus, and to create closeness and rapport. Tannen refers to women's approach to conversation as **rapport talk**.

Polite or powerless speech. Tannen claims that what men view as *subservient* speech, women view as *sensitive* speech. Compared to men, women tend to use more tag questions (don't you think?), interrupt less often, talk for shorter periods of time in mixed-gender groups, and use responsive verbal and nonverbal indicators, such as phrases like "Tell me more," and maintaining eye contact, more often. Women also use fewer direct demands, framing their requests more ambiguously. For instance, a female boss might say to an employee, "Gosh, I have a problem. I need to get next week's schedule posted, but I don't think I am going to have time." A male boss might say, "You need to post the schedule for next week by tomorrow morning." Because women's speech is less assertive than men's, Tannen calls it **powerless speech**. Importantly, however, Tannen points out that powerless speech is not necessarily problematic. For example, women's patterns of speech can be inclusive, building rapport and inviting others to join the conversation. The problem with powerless speech is that some people interpret it as weak. When women and men both use powerless speech, for instance, only women are evaluated negatively for doing so. Thus, it is not the way of speaking itself that matters, but people's attitudes towards men and women that seem to make a difference.

Different ways of listening. If men and women speak differently, it is not surprising that they also listen differently. Even seemingly mundane and inconsequential speech and listening patterns can create gendered misunderstandings. In conversational bids for status, men tend to use terms such as "yeah," "uh huh," and "I hear you," to indicate their agreement. In conversational negotiations for connection, women use the very same words and phrases to indicate listening or to encourage continued interaction. This can lead to misunderstanding in opposite-sex conversations. Specifically, if a woman says "yeah" and "uh huh," her male companion may "hear" agreement even if she was only trying to show that she was paying attention. Alternately, the woman may believe her conversational partner is *not* listening when he fails to supply a "yeah" as she recounts a story.

Troubles talk. Tannen says that women and men approach discussing their problems—what she refers to as their **troubles talk**—in very different ways. Women often share their problems with others to gain understanding and confirmation of their feelings, whereas men share problems to get advice for solving problems. Moreover, says Tannen, "If women are often frustrated because men do not respond to their troubles by offering matching troubles, men are often frustrated because they do."[8]. A recent viral YouTube video titled "It's not about the nail" humorously portrays gendered patterns of troubles talk. In the video, a man and woman are seated on a couch talking. The camera pans in on the woman's face. She appears frustrated and uncomfortable as she describes a vague, persistent pain in her head. As the camera pans back, we see that she has a nail lodged in her forehead. Her patient partner says, "Well, you *do* have a nail stuck in your head." She responds, "It's not about the nail. You always do this. You always try to fix things when what I really need is for you to just listen." Although this vignette is clearly a caricature, it does depict the different emphases that men and women place on troubles talk. Men, says Tannen, respond to troubles talk by offering solutions and advice; women respond by matching experiences. Perhaps you have heard female friends say to each other, "Oh, that happened to me once, too!" or "I had a similar experience." These conversational strategies suggest, "We are similar, we are peers, we are connected." This makes sense because, in their 'native' genderlects, men work to maintain status and women work to maintain connection.

CLAIMS OF GENDERLECTS

One key claim of Tannen's theory is that, although gendered miscommunication is pervasive, we are ill prepared for the conflicts that inevitably result. We assume that, because we speak the same language, we "speak the same language." We expect differences when we talk to people from different nationalities or cultures, but we do not expect those differences when speaking to relatives, friends, co-workers, and partners who grew up in similar contexts. Tannen's theory provides a roadmap to navigate gendered cultural differences without blaming our partners or assuming they are not trying.

The theory of genderlects remind us that much of what is "said" in a conversation does not come from the words that are spoken, but is filled in by the person listening. That's why it can seem as though the other person isn't being *clear* in what he or she is saying. Clarity is a relational variable, which has little to do with the actual words we use.[9]

Each of us decides whether we think others are speaking to gain status or to gain connection. The likelihood that we interpret someone's words as having one or the other intention depends more on our focus, concerns, and habits than it does on the speaker's actual intention. Both status and connection are often operating in conversation, so it is easy for women and men to focus on different elements in the same interaction. Thus, women who think they are displaying a positive quality such as connection may be misjudged by men as lacking independence, which to men reflects incompetence and insecurity. Similarly, when men offer definitive statements designed to solve problems, women may interpret their speech as insensitive and lacking compassion.

Tannen is clear that neither gendered style is better or more effective than the other in every instance. Instead, men and women use the ways of speaking that help them succeed in their gendered cultures—which, in turn, reproduces those gendered cultures. In the world of work, however, women's speech style tends to be negatively evaluated, whereas men's speaking style as considered normative.[10] Moreover, the pressure to maintain connection with others—while negotiating rank and appearing skillful and knowledgeable—can become a burden for boys and men. Likewise, the pressure to achieve status while avoiding conflict and appearing no better than anyone else can become a burden for girls and women.

The trick, says Tannen, is for men and women to become well versed in both genderlects. The first step is simply recognizing these gendered patterns. Doing so provides a starting point to develop self-understanding and flexibility. The next step is learning to interpret other's messages—and to explain your own messages—in a gendered style, to increase mutual understanding. Once partners realize they have different styles, they are inclined to accept differences without blaming themselves or drawing negative conclusions about each other. Tannen's more recent book, *You're Wearing That?: Understanding Mothers and Daughters in Conversation,* suggested that similar communication patterns, problems, and possible solutions can be found among mothers and daughters.[11]

▲ ▲ ▲

Theory into Practice
Think about a recent occasion when you described a problem to someone of the opposite sex. Did you receive the response you expected? How about the response you hoped for? If not, do you think differences in genderlects contributed to the mismatch between your expectations and your reality? Given what you know, what could you do differently the next time you engage in troubles talk?

▲ ▲ ▲

CRITIQUES OF GENDERLECTS
Tannen's theory has been criticized as a providing too simplistic a framework for understanding men's and women's speech. Although

Tannen recognizes that men can seek connection and women can seek status through conversation, her work is still based largely on white, middle-class norms and research participants. Linguist Heiko Motschenbacher suggests that it may be useful to abandon the "binary genderlect concept" and replace it with an understanding of genderlects as "context-dependent, community [or local culture]-based and therefore infinite in number."[12]

FACE NEGOTIATION THEORY

Tannen's work helps to explain the "cultural" differences that underlie so many of men and women's conversational challenges. In this section, we turn to the work of intercultural communication scholar, Stella Ting Toomey, whose face negotiation theory helps to explain why members of different cultures often encounter barriers to effective communication, particularly in the context of cross-cultural conflict.

According to Ting-Toomey, "The greater the cultural distance between the two conflict parties, the more likely the assessment or judgment of the conflict negotiation process would be polarized and misconstrued."[13] Indeed, Ury suggests that intercultural communication conflicts have directly contributed to international crises and the potential for large-scale nuclear actions several times in our recent history.[14] Face negotiation theory helps us understand why intercultural communication problems persist and, importantly, how we might overcome them.

INTELLECTUAL TRADITION OF FACE NEGOTIATION THEORY

Ting-Toomey developed her theory, in part, as a response to Western theories of conflict negotiation, which focused on individualistic outcomes and framing of conflict but largely ignored Asian, collectivist approaches. In general, Westerners tend to approach conflict in an open, direct manner, expecting an immediate response from the other party. In comparison, members of Asian cultures may prefer an indirect approach to conflict that emphasizes coopera- tion or harmony. When these two different approaches come into contact, communicators may interpret the same behavior in very different ways, not unlike what happens when "report talkers" meet "rapport talkers." Westerners may interpret Easterners as evasive or tentative; Easterners may interpret Westerners as disrespectful and abrupt. Ting-Toomey's theory, then, attempts to explain how conflict and culture intersect and how we can best navigate those cultural conflicts.

The foundation for Ting-Toomey's theory comes from sociologist Erving Goffman's theorizing on the presentation of the self in ev- eryday life in general and his articulation of "face," as well as Brown and Levinson's work on intercultural understandings of politeness.[15] Goffman argued that *face*, or one's self image, is a concept that is important across all cultures. According to Ting-Toomey and her col- legues John Oetzel and Adolfo Garcia, face can be "lost, saved and protected, and social interaction begs the concern for, the protection of, the self-image."[16] Closely related to the concept of face is polite- ness theory.[17] Politeness theory proposes that all members of a cul- ture work to help one another maintain face. When encountering a threat, politeness is an important and rational strategy. However, the form that politeness takes varies depending on many factors, includ- ing the power difference and social distance between the two par- ties and the particular linguistic choices that the parties have at their disposal. Ting-Toomey's theory combines these ideas to help explain how members of different cultures negotiate face in conflict episodes.

ASSUMPTIONS OF FACE NEGOTIATION THEORY

Ting-Toomey and Oetzel outlined the four simple assumptions of face negotiation theory.[18]

Assumption 1: Maintaining face is a universal goal. Although the particular strategies they employ may vary, Oetzel and Ting-Toomey note that "people in all cultures try to maintain and negotiate face in all communication situations."[19]

Assumption 2: Face concerns are highlighted in ambiguous, vulnerable, or uncertain situations, such as those characterized by conflict, embarrassment, and potential threats. These situations call participants' identities into question and thus require **facework**, or efforts to support people's face needs.

Assumption 3: Many factors determine which face concerns are highlighted in any particular interaction. In an uncertain situation, people must decide to focus on their own face or on maintaining the face of the other. Cultural factors (such as whether a culture tends toward individualism or collectivism), individual factors (such as whether people see themselves as independent interdependent), and situational factors (such as relational closeness or status differences between parties) all influence how particular face strategies are employed.

Assumption 4: Facework concerns directly influence how interpersonal and intergroup conflicts are enacted. These four assumptions have been supported in a variety of empirical studies.[20]

KEY CONCEPTS IN FACE NEGOTIATION THEORY

As explained, the concept of *face* is central to this theory. Recall that you encountered the concept of face in Chapter 8 in our discussion of uncertainty. According to Ting-Toomey, "face refers to a claimed sense of desired social self-image in a relational or international setting."[21] Face is the self-image or national image that we want to project to others. During intercultural conflict, we often try to avoid losing face or having our self- and/or national image diminished in any way. Learning to engage in conflict while maintaining or "saving" face (both our own and other people's) can lead to more productive and satisfying solutions.

A second key concept is facework. According to Oetzel and Ting-Toomey, facework "refers to the communicative strategies one uses to enact self-face and to uphold, support, or challenge another person's face."[22] Facework strategies include 1) apologizing, 2) avoiding, 3) being aggressive, 4) compromising, 5) considering the other, 6) defending the self, 7) expressing feelings, 8) giving in, 9) involving a third party, 10) pretending, 11) remaining calm, and 12) talking about the problem.

Individualist and collectivist cultures. Depending on one's culture, different face concerns are often highlighted. One critical cultural dimension influencing face is the culture's location on the individualism-collectivism spectrum. Individualism and collectivism are "value orientations" or tendencies that are present across a wide variety of cultures. **Individualism** refers to the tendency of a culture to value individual rights over group rights. **Collectivism** refers to the tendency to privilege group interests and concerns over self interests.[23] The United States and Northern and Western European countries tend to be individualistic. Many Asian, Middle Easter, and South American countries tend to be collectivistic. Of course, these are broad categories, and there is often variation with countries. For instance, although U.S. culture is highly individualistic, specific groups within the United States, such as the Amish, tend to be strongly collectivistic.

▲ ▲ ▲

Politics in America

When you think about the important political issues in U.S. culture, do they tend to center on individual concerns or group concerns? How have you seen political issues being framed by politicians, the media, and voters? When and how do we make claims based on individual right? When and how do we make claims based on group rights? Which emphasis is more important to you?

▲ ▲ ▲

Power distance. Power distance is another cultural factor that influences intercultural interactions. According to Ting-Toomey and her colleague Atsuko Kurogi, **power distance** is the "extent to which the less powerful members of institutions accept that power is distributed unequally" within that institution.[24] Power distance can range from large to small. In large-power-distance cultures, members generally accept power differences based on hierarchy, rank, role, and even gender. In contrast, small-power-distance cultures tend to value equality based on performance and merit. These two approaches to power differences result in different orientations toward face. Specifically, say Ting-Toomey and Kurogi, "[for] small power distance cultures, defending and asserting one's personal rights is reflective of self-face esteeming behaviors. For large power distance cultures, playing one's role optimally and carrying out one's ascribed duties responsibly and asymmetrically constitute appropriate facework interaction."[25]

Self-construal. Face-negotiation theory takes cultural factors into account but also acknowledges that the individual plays an important role in intercultural interactions. At the individual level, self-construal is one of the factors that affects intercultural conflict and face. **Self-construal** "refers to the degree to which degree to which people conceive of themselves as relatively autonomous from, or connected to, others," according to Ting-Toomey and Kugori.[26] People with independent self-construal conceive of themselves as unique entities, with their own feelings, motivations, desires, and ability to navigate their own path in the world, who are able to control their own circumstances and reach their own goals. Not surprisingly, individualistic cultures tend to be populated by independents. Those with interdependent self-construal, in contrast, emphasize their connections to others. As Ting-Toomey and Kurogi noted, "People who have an interdependent self-construal want to fit in with others, act appropriately, promote others, goals and value relational collaboration. The self in relation guides the behavior of high interdependents in social situations."[27] Interdependents feature more prominently in collectivist cultures. As an aside, it is worth noting how closely these portraits of independent and inter-dependent self-construal align with Tannen's descriptions of masculine and feminine genderlects.

CLAIMS OF FACE NEGOTIATION THEORY

Propositions. Face-negotiation theory lays out 32 empirically test-able propositions to explain and predict how face negotiation plays out between members of different cultures. Propositions that focus on cultural factors include the following:

1. "Members of individualistic cultures tend to use a greater degree of direct, upfront facework strategies in a conflict situation than members of collectivistic cultures. . .
2. Members of collectivistic cultures tend to use a greater degree of indirect, smoothing facework strategies than members of individualistic cultures. . .
3. High-status members of small power distance cultures tend to use verbally direct facework strategies such as direct disapproval strategies (e.g. criticism) and autonomy-threat strategies (e.g. order) to induce compliance more than high-status members of large power distance cultures. . .
4. Low-status members of small power distance cultures tend to use self-face defensive strategies to counter face threat more than members of large power distance cultures, and that low-status members of large power distance cultures tend to use self-effacing strategies to mitigate face threat more than members of small power distance cultures. . .
5. Self-face maintenance is associated positively with a dominating/ competing conflict management style. . .
6. Other-face maintenance is associated positively with an avoiding/ obliging conflict management style".[28]

Consider the following positive intercultural conflict episode. In the early 1970s, at the behest of President Richard Nixon, the United States was transitioning from away from tying the value of world currency to gold. Instead, the government established fixed exchange rates between countries that were based on the value of foreign currencies in relation to the U.S. dollar. Major players in the global economy, including Germany, Great Britain, France, Italy, and Sweden agreed, after much negotiation, to Nixon's new plan. Japan held out, refusing to go along. To satisfy the demands of other countries, U.S. government representatives demanded that the Japanese increase the value of the Yen (the official currency in Japan) by seventeen percent. Rather than having to make concessions, the Japanese Finance Minister claimed he was ill and cancelled his meeting with the U.S. Secretary of the Treasury, John Connally. Instead, Connally met with a deputy Minister who explained that 17 percent was unacceptable by, "telling the story of the finance minister who was assassinated when he revalued the Yen by that amount in 1930."[29] Connally then conceded to a 16.9% change, which was materially inconsequential but symbolically important. The Japanese official quickly accepted Connally's concession. By offering this alternative, Connally "saved the honor" of the Japanese Finance Ministry and the Japanese people by giving them a proposal to which they could agree.[30]

Face negotiation theory would have predicted that the U.S. representatives (as members of an individualistic culture) would use direct facework and dominating conflict styles, whereas the Japanese representatives (as members of a collectivistic culture) would use indirect facework and avoidant conflict styles. Those predictions were supported. When the U.S. Treasury Secretary acknowledged the cultural differences and enabled the Japanese to save face, a successful resolution was reached.

Core competencies. Based on face negotiation theory, Ting-Toomey and Kurogi offer three core competencies that increase the likelihood of successful intercultural interactions: knowledge, mindfulness, and interaction skills.[31] First, communicators must have adequate knowledge about the culture of their conversational partner. For Ting-Toomey, *knowledge* reflects an understanding of the individualism-collectivism continuum, power distance, self and other orientations to face, as well as facework styles. **Mindfulness** refers to being aware of how our own assumptions and emotions affect ongoing interactions, while simultaneously being attentive to our partner's assumptions and emotions via our five senses. In short, being mindful requires us to "'tune-in' to our own cultural and habitual assumptions during an intercultural conflict episode. Finally, effective conflict resolution in intercultural contexts requires **interaction skills,** or abilities for effective communication, such as mindful listening, mindful observation, facework management, trust-building, and collaborative dialogue. Employing these skills requires our willingness to suspend our typical responses, to refrain from making attributions without exploring alternative explanations, and to avoid imposing our worldviews on others. Armed with these core competencies, we can manage intercultural conflicts productively.

CRITIQUES OF FACE NEGOTIATION THEORY

Many of Ting-Toomey's propositions have been supported empirically. There is ample support that face explains the influence of culture on conflict behavior."[32] In short, there is good reason to believe that face negotiation theory provides a useful foundation for intercultural knowledge. However, there is still work to be done to hone this theory and improve its utility for practitioners. Ting-Toomey suggests three areas where face negotiation theory does not help to explain conflict behavior: "facework emotions, facework situations; and facework movements"[33] Ting-Toomey recognizes the need for studies that would unpack the "developmental ebbs and flows of facework emotions and facework emotional engagement." (p. 88). We know little, for example, about how the affective components of trust, dignity, betrayal, shame, pride, and other relevant emotions unfold and impact conflict episodes. Additionally, we currently do not know what situational factors move conflict negotiators along the facework evolutionary spectrum from "self-interest to mutual-interest to universal-interest concerns" (p. 88). Moreover, the theory does not address the temporal dimensions of face negotiations because most of the studies rely of self-report data of recalled or hypothetical situations. To uncover and theorize how conflict negotiations play out over time, examining actual interactions would be an important addition to the empirical support for (or critique of) face negotiation theory. Finally, Ting-Toomey would like to see more collaborative research from scholars around the globe to assess the effect of face, facework and conflict styles across a range of situations, as there are some who suggest that politeness theory (on which face negotiation theory is based) is biased toward Western norms.[34]

CULTURAL STUDIES

Cultural studies is not a theory in the traditional sense of the term. Rather, cultural studies refers is a theoretical perspective that critiques a broad array of cultural discourses, particularly those found in popular culture (television, film, social media). Early cultural studies scholars were interested in how mass culture constitutes a social reality that structures gendered, raced, sexed, aged, and classed relations in ways that create and maintain social inequities.[35] Specifically, cultural studies theorists believe that popular culture, as it is expressed and perpetuated via the mass media, is where oppression is located. Whereas earlier (Marxist) theories located power in economic and political structures, cultural studies scholars focus on how power is structured through the communication practices of popular culture. Thus, cultural studies provides the tools to engage in "political reading of popular culture" with an eye toward transforming social reality and resisting domination and oppression.

The mass media, according to early cultural studies theory, are a manipulative and influential source of power in our culture that shape who we are as individuals and communities. Aronowitz claims that, "In addition to the *overt* ideological content of films and television—transmitting new role models, values life styles to be more or less consciously emulated by a mass audience—there is also a series of *covert* messages contained within them which appeal to the audience largely on the unconscious level . . . By creating a system of pseudo-gratifications, mass culture functions as a sort of social regulator, attempting to absorb tensions arising out of everyday life and to detect frustrations which might otherwise actualize themselves in opposition."[36] In short, the media or the "culture industry" tell us who to be and how to behave, and we typically do little to resist or critique those messages.

Cultural studies hopes to change that. Indeed, according to communication scholars David Carlone and Bryan Taylor, cultural studies began in Great Britain "as an anti-elitist, radically contextual, and multi-methodological project concerned with expanding the realms of political and economic freedom for the working class."[37] Since that time, cultural studies has maintained a focus on the power of popular culture and the media, in particular. Media representations (as well as media institutions) are often framed as both "weapons and sites of conflict in struggles over access to resources, wealth, symbolic representations, and power—and over access to the media themselves," according to communication scholar Joshua Meyrowitz.[38]

The goal of cultural studies, then, is to provide those who have historically been denied access to wealth, power, and media control the tools to wield influence by interpreting, and sometimes criticizing dominant culture in ways that more fully represent and value their place in it. Cultural studies recognizes that although popular culture texts are produced or "over-determined" to be read in ways that privilege those already in power, interpretations can be contested and challenged. "Cultural studies," claim Carlone and Taylor, "typically engage artifacts (e.g., television programs) as complex embodiments of multiple, contradictory ideologies. In this view, over-determined texts are variously interpreted by audience members using their available competencies and for situational purposes. Such readings may to confirm, adapt, or reject the dominant influences inscribed through form," whether those messages take the form of films, television shows, music videos, advertisements, tweets, or any other cultural text.[39]

INTELLECTUAL TRADITION OF CULTURAL STUDIES

Cultural studies has deep roots in the traditions of literary criticism. Cultural studies moved beyond literary criticism, which focused on the assessment of particular pieces of literature and texts, to the broader criticism of everyday life. Other significant influences were the socio-economic theories of Karl Marx[40] and the neo-Marxist traditions of social critics such as Althusser[41] and Gramsci.[42] Althusser and Gramsci extended and critiqued traditional Marxist thought and its failure to attend adequately to oppression beyond that created solely by economic structures. Instead, they wanted to explain how ideologies and power are created and recreated in social structures, including the mass media. Out of this tradition, "cultural studies [came to embrace] a set of approaches that attempt to understand and intervene into the relations of culture and power," according to communication scholar Lawrence Grossberg.[43] Foucault's (1977) interest in the critique of "normalization" and "disciplinary power," as well as the work of feminists and scholars of color, have also influenced cultural studies by causing questions of power and its relation to culture to consider gender, race, sexual, and age dynamics. Cultural studies is therefore designed to engage in a continual critique of dominant cultural assumptions. Cultural studies is thus, "a vigorous, but fragmented" field of study that has been explored across a wide variety of academic disciplines.[44] Communication scholars were among the first disciplines to take up this tradition.[45]

According to scholar Richard Johnson, the object of cultural studies is "historical forms of consciousness or subjectivity."[46] Cultural studies explores the communication processes through which we come to understand ourselves as individuals and groups. Cultural studies scholars do not assume that our identities are fixed or given, but instead assume that "subjects" or socially constructed individuals are produced through language, discourse, and social relations. Particular kinds of subjects, or individuals, are produced in and through our consumption of messages. Particular "ways of being" are created and recreated through mediated messages. If, for example, we think about what it means to be a "blue collar worker," a "corporate executive," an "unemployed dropout," a "politician," a "whistleblower," or a "college student," much of our understanding of those identity categories is produced and reproduced in mediated images.

For many young Americans who belong to social media networks, the "selfie" has become a common form of representing oneself to others. The selfie, a self-portrait taken with one's own camera and posted to one's social networking site, has become a mainstay for "freezing and sharing the thinnest slices of life," as one article put it.[47] On Instagram alone, over 23 million photographs with the hashtag *selfie* have been posted. Although many of us understand what a selfie is, the question of what this representational form *means* is hotly contested. Some argue that the selfie represents the pinnacle of self-obsession, narcissism, cries for attention, and an inward focus. Others believe that selfies are a documentary form, a democratizing way of telling one's story. Historically, self-portraits were reserved for members of dominant classes. Today, the self-portrait is as common as the smart phone. As one Instagram user says, "Instead of saying you're going to work, a photo of you in your uniform does that."[48] The selfie, then, is a form of representation that presents us to others as we want to be seen. It is a way of attempting to control how others make sense of us, although we can never control that fully. Cultural studies scholars might explore the practice of sharing selfies to understand how it both enables and constrains our way of being as individuals and as members of social networks.

Assumptions of Cultural Studies

Cultural studies shares many of the same general assumptions of critical approaches that we discussed in Chapter 2. Grossberg articulates three specific assumptions of cultural studies.[49]

Assumption 1: According to Grossberg, cultural studies assumes that "reality is continually being made through human action."[50] As a work in progress, reality can therefore be contested. Indeed, struggles over meaning are both a fact of experience and a critical practice.

Assumption 2: Cultural studies attends to "the popular" rather than the state, the official, or the "high culture." "The popular," says Grossberg, is the "terrain on which people live and political struggle must be carried out."[51]

Assumption 3: Cultural studies is committed to what Grossberg calls "radical contextualism." Rather than assuming that a culture or a text exists or can be defined in a particular way, cultural studies assumes that any cultural practice (e.g., posting "selfies," producing films, or being a woman) is, according to Grossberg, a "complex and conflictual place that cannot be separated from the context of its articulation since it has no existence outside of that context. And if this is the case, then the study of culture can be no less complex, conflictual and contextual."[52] How we make sense of our everyday cultural worlds, then, can only be understood within context.

KEY CONCEPTS IN CULTURAL STUDIES

The key concepts in cultural studies are the circuit of communication, the dominant code, negotiated codes, oppositional codes, and resisting intellectuals.

The circuit of communication. Although he was not a communication scholar, Stuart Hall, a British cultural theorist and sociologist and founding figure in the British Cultural Studies tradition, offered readers a model of communication. His model revised the linear subject-message-context-receiver model to address how power relations operate at every communicative moment, producing ideological meanings through cultural representations (such as television programs and films).[53] Hall called this process the **circuit of communication.**

For Hall, the circuit "begins" when messages are produced, circulated via the media, used by audiences to understand their place in the world, and reproduced when audiences either accept or challenge their meaning. Importantly, power is involved at each stage of the process, insofar as ideologies limit the messages that can be produced. There can never be a "raw" or totally transparent message because each message must take some sort of institutional form. For example, when television news organizations produce a news story, that process is already framed by meanings, knowledge, skills, ideologies, and assumptions about the audience. Even before it begins, production is already affected by the presumed audience reception and use of the message. The messages are pieced together and edited into a recognizable form for audience enjoyment and pleasure— and, according to Hall, the perpetuation of capitalist cultural and social relations. Similarly, world events are never presented as "raw" data; rather, they are encoded into a particular form, the recognizable news story. Thus, audiences are primed in many ways to receive a message *in the way its production was intended.* Production and consumption are not related, but they are not identical. The encoding of a message sets limits. Therefore, audiences do not simply "read whatever they like into a message." Instead, as we shall see below, messages may be coded or read differently depending on the positions from which audiences decode them.

Dominant reading. An interpretation of a media text in which audience members accept, take pleasure in, and reproduce the message intended by the producer the message without critique or question. The dominant media, argues Hall, make information available in codes (in story forms, recognizable patterns, and ways of speaking) that tend to support and reproduce the status-quo. Hall refers to these messages as preferred codes. However, audience members may or may not decode messages in the way producers intended. If audience members accept a produced message "full and straight," with all its attendant meanings, they are said to be engaged in a preferred or **dominant reading** of the text.[54]

After the post-housing-bubble financial crisis of 2007-2008 that resulted in the collapse of some of America's largest financial institutions, a sharp and extended downturn in the stock market, the bailout of banks by many governments around the globe, many mainstream news organizations reported that the U.S. government's $700 billion emergency bailout was an economic necessity. Failing to provide the bailout, they argued, would have placed the country in serious financial jeopardy. At the time, many members of the American public accepted, without question, the notion that the major financial institutions of American were in fact "too big to fail."[55] By doing so, they reproduced the preferred or dominant code. In other words, the message that financial institutions are more necessary and worthy of taxpayer support than any other institution (including education, health care, or social services) is taken for granted when audiences engage in the preferred reading. This reading then reproduces the broader power structures and social inequities that reward those who benefit most from the financial institutions, namely the rich and powerful.

Negotiated reading. A **negotiated reading** is an interpretation of a message in which audience members generally accept the dominant or preferred code, but resist or modify that code in ways that reflect their particular social position. A part-time bank teller, for example, may accept the capitalist ideology that privileges the banking sector and generally agree with the idea that the major banks in our system are, indeed, "too big to fail." At the same time, she may modify that code by articulating her belief that banking profits should be shared more equitably by all employees, rather than just the CEOs and major shareholders. Negotiated codes reveal the contradictions that are inherent in ideologies, as audience members rarely interpret or consume messages in exactly the manner the producers intended. Negotiated codes, according to Hall, "accord a privileged position to the dominant definition of events, whilst reserving the right to make a more negotiated application to 'local conditions."[56]

Oppositional reading. Finally, an **oppositional reading** is an interpretation of a message in which audience members oppose the dominant or preferred ideology. According to Hall, when an individual "detotalises the message in preferred code in order to retotalise the message within some alternative framework of reference ... He or she is operating in what we must call an oppositional code."[57] After the bank bailout, when some bankers' unethical behaviors were revealed, some commentators, bloggers, and journalists began claiming that the banks were "too big to jail."[58] Indeed, a wide spectrum of oppositional voices in the Occupy Wall Street movement argued that banks and the "rich guys in suits" had engineered a global crisis to their own benefit, but were not being held accountable.[59] By arguing that current capitalist structures benefit the few at the expense of the masses, these oppositional readings do not accept the preferred ideology. Although those oppositional voices did not directly control the major media outlets, they presented an oppositional message through "sit ins," web-based campaigns, and other strategies.

Resisting intellectuals. Because cultural studies was developed to critique dominant ideologies, one of its goals was to enable working-class individuals to raise their political awareness and engage in political struggles over meaning.[60] Since that time, however, cultural studies scholars have helped a wide variety of people to question and change the ways in which they are portrayed, rendered, and constructed in popular-culture texts. Traditional theory has identified university-based intellectuals, leaders of industry, government technocrats, and members of the ruling or upper classes as the "knowers"—the moral and intellectual leaders who maintain, protect, and often benefit from the current power relations in a culture. Cultural studies seeks to prepare lay people to serve as leaders who can recognize and challenge that status quo. Cultural studies scholar Henry Giroux and his colleagues refer to these individuals as **resisting intellectuals.**[61] Resisting intellectuals, say Giroux et al., "can emerge from and work with any number of groups which resist the suffocating knowledge and practices that constitute their social formation. Resisting intellectuals can provide the moral, political and pedagogical leadership for those groups which take as their starting point the transformative critique of the conditions of oppression."[62] The members of the Occupy Wall Street movement are examples of lay leaders who are interested in critiquing the status quo to create conditions of greater equality and enhanced democracy.

CRITIQUES OF CULTURAL STUDIES
Although the spirit of cultural studies is egalitarian and revolutionary, it is difficult to determine how cultural studies theory has affected material culture and practice. Certainly, is has influenced the field of communication studies, as well as disciplines such as geography, anthropology, and English. It has encouraged communication scholars to complicate the way they understand, study, and explain the role of popular culture in everyday life.[63] However, English professor and renowned cultural studies scholar, Michael Bérubé has

lamented the fact that cultural studies theory has lost its center, that is has become conflated with "cultural criticism" and now means "everything and nothing."[64] Perhaps, more importantly, cultural studies has not had the sort of transformative impact that many of the early theorist's hoped for, precisely because power relations are "much more complicated" than one theory can explain. Organizing civil society "to try to forge an egalitarian response" is a project that might just be too much for cultural studies theory to handle.

SUMMARY AND CONCLUSION

The theories in this chapter take up the question, how does culture influence individual communication, in everyday conversation, in intercultural interactions, and in our relationship with and to media. Tannen's theory of genderlects helps to explain how the gendered cultures into which we are socialized shape and 'frame our everyday conversations in ways that create distinct and sometimes conflictural ways of speaking across gendered lines. Genderlects offers a 'roadmap' for understanding the often unspoken frames that can create misunderstandings, particularly between men and women. Genderlects also offers the means to become more fluent interpreters and participants in gendered conversations.

Face negotiation theory how our cultural practices, particularly those that center on issues of face, individualistic or collectivist culture, power distance and self-construal, impact interactions. Ting-Toomey and her colleagues are particularly interested in conflict episodes and the impact that individualistic and collectivist cultural notions of face, or a preferred "self-image" in a social situation, has on conflict resolution or escalation.

Cultural studies represents not a theory, per se, but a general orientation toward media and popular discourse that adopts a critical stance. Cultural studies advocates argue that the media is, in many ways, an oppressive force in contemporary life because it represents or encodes the worldviews of powerful groups in society and by providing pleasures and gratifications to those who are less powerful, it tends to appropriate and redirect any real oppositional movements on the part of those less powerful groups. To counteract that oppressive influence of the media, cultural studies scholars advocate that media consumers decode media texts in alternative ways that better represent their interests. Rather than simply engaging in dominant readings, consumers of media may engage in negotiated or oppositional interpretations of popular culture texts. In so doing, consumers may be better able to critique the status quo and create more favorable conditions for society's less powerful individuals.

FOR FURTHER DISCUSSION

1. Name and describe the key concepts of Tannen's genderlects. Which concept offers you the most useful tool to understand your own experiences in conversations with gendered others? Which concept is the least useful? Why?
2. Tannen's theory rests on the assumption that men and women do not speak the same language. In what ways to you think gendered communication is an intercultural experience?
3. How might you approach a cross gender conversation differently after encountering the theory of genderlects?
4. When you think about your own facework, what face needs influence your behavior in conflict situations? How have those face needs been shaped by your cultural upbringing?
5. Which facework strategies do you tend to use most in conflict situations? Do you adjust those strategies depending on the context? Why or why not?

6. Can you think of an instance in which mass media messages have created oppressive conditions for you? What about for others like you? What about others different from you?

7. Think of your favorite recent film. Now, explain how the film could be interpreted through a dominant code or reading? How does the film mean differently if engage in a negotiated reading of the film? What about an oppositional reading?

KEY TERMS

Circuit of communication
Collectivism
Dominant reading
Facework
Frames
Genderlects
Individualism
Interaction skills
Metacommunication
Mindfulness
Negotiated reading
Oppositional reading
Power distance
Powerless speech
Rapport talk
Report talk
Resisting intellectuals
Self-construal
Troubles talk

GLOSSARY

Accommodation: In schema theory, the process of either initiating a new schema or giving up attempts to interpret information.

Accommodation: The process by which individuals vary their behaviors for the purpose of convergence and divergence.

Achievement fantasies: In symbolic convergence theory, dramatizations portraying sympathetic people motivated to do a good job.

Action: Human behavior.

Action fluidity: In planning theory, the fluency with which a plan is enacted.

Active audience: In uses and gratifications theory, the idea that people actively seek out media to meet a variety of interests and needs.

Adaptive structuration theory: An adaptation of structuration theory developed by Marshall Scott Poole and Geraldine DeSanctis.

Affiliation fantasies: In symbolic convergence theory, dramatizations whose central characters have basic goals related to making friends and having good times.

Affiliative constraints: Limitations to decision-making ability introduced by an overriding concern for relationships among group members.

Agenda setting: The process by which news media lead the public to assign relative importance to various public issues.

Agenda setting theory: A theory claiming that media attention influences people's perceptions about what matters.

Antithesis: A counter-argument or counter-claim.

Appraisal: The act of estimating or judging the nature or value of something.

Archetypes: In coordinated management of meaning, the common physical properties, neurological structures, and physiology shared by all humans.

Argument quality: A measure of how solid and strong a persuasive message is.

Argument quantity: A measure of how many arguments a message contains.

Aristotle: A student of Plato, founder of the Lyceum, and author of *Rhetoric*.

Artifacts: Tangible features of organizational experience that members can see, hear, touch, taste, smell, or otherwise encounter.

Assimilation: The process of absorbing new pieces of information into an existing schema.

Assumptions: Beliefs whose truth is taken for granted.

Attitude: An enduring way of thinking or feeling about someone or something.

Attitude toward a behavior: In the theory of planned behavior, a person's positive or negative evaluation of a behavior.

Audience need: In uses and gratifications theory, the needs of an audience for cognitive orientation, diversion, and personal identity.

Authority: A source whose education, background, or wisdom make him or her knowledgeable on a particular topic.

Autonomy versus connection: A dialectical tension between needs for closeness and needs for distance.

Axiom: A plausible assumption or untestable claim in a theory.

Becoming: In dialectical theories, a focus on the potential, dreams, or desires for who one wants to be.

Behavior: An individual's observable response in a given situation with respect to a given target.

Behavioral beliefs: A person's understanding of the likelihood that a behavior will produce a specific outcome.

Being: In dialectical theories, a focus on who one is.

Beliefs: Information people think they have about a message, a person, an object, or a phenomenon.

Boomerang effect: A failure of a fear appeal wherein people actually increase the behavior the appeal is designed to reduce.

Breadth: The range of topics about which one talks with others.

Central route processing: In the elaboration likelihood model, the tendency to carefully examine the information in a message, scrutinize the arguments and evidence, and consider other relevant details before being persuaded by the message.

Centrifugal forces: In dialectical theories, forces that separate and divide people.

Centripetal forces: In dialectical theories, forces that bring people together.

Change: The difference observed in a phenomenon over time.

Chronotope: In dialectical theories, the connection of time and space.

Circuit of communication. A model depicting how power relations operate at every communicative moment.

Claims: A theory's declarative statements about how its concepts fit together.

Co-orientation: In family communication patterns theory, the result of two or more people focusing on and evaluating the same object without recognizing their shared focus.

Cognitive complexity: The ability to think about people, relationships, and social interaction in sophisticated ways.

Cognitive constraints: Limitations to decision-making ability introduced by having too little information or too much complexity.

Cognitive dissonance: A mental state characterized by tension between competing attitudes and behaviors.

Collectivism: A cultural tendency to privilege group interests and concerns over self interests.

Comforting communication: Messages that seek to lessen the emotional distress experienced by others.

Communication accommodation theory: A theory that explores the communication strategies people use to increase or decrease their social distance from one another.

Communication channels: The means by which people exchange messages.

Communication theories: Theories that focus on how people send and receive messages to created shared meaning in societal, relational, and mediated contexts.

Comparison level for alternatives: One's assessment of how good or bad a current relationship is compared with one's other options.

Comparison level: The realistic expectation of what one wants and thinks one deserves from a relationship.

Compatibility: The link between an innovation and the experiences, needs, and values of a potential adopter.

Complexity: In diffusion of innovations theory, the difficulty in understanding and using an innovation; in planning theory, the degree to which a plan is specific and includes action contingencies.

Concepts: Abstract ideas that theories discuss.

Conceptual definition: An explanation of what a variable means.

Conceptual framework: A vocabulary of defined terms that helps people use a theory to understand some form of interaction.

Conflict: An active struggle in social practices between people or groups.

Conformity orientation: In family communication patterns theory, a communication climate in which all family members are encouraged to have the same attitudes, values, and beliefs.

Consensual families: In family communication patterns theory, families that are high in both conversation and conformity orientation.

Constant: Any concept whose values or properties do not vary.

Constraints: In functional theory, negative sources of influence that undermine effective group performance.

Construct: Attitudes and ideas that people have about their own experiences (especially as used in research).

Content analysis: A qualitative method for summarizing and drawing inferences about the substance of a message.

Content: In coordinated management of meaning, the raw sensory data that people process at any given moment.

Context: A situation, environment, or particular type of experience.

Contracts: In coordinated management of meaning, the belief that relationships have particular identifiable attributes that help explain the conditions under which they function.

Contradiction: The state that occurs when principles negate one another, so that enacting one principle makes it impossible to enact another. In dialectical theories, the dynamic interplay between unified opposites.

Control and ownership: In communication privacy management theory, the ability to exert power over private information

Control beliefs: The factors that an individual believes will either facilitate or impede performance of a behavior.

Control: The ability to influence and manage the outcomes that a theory predicts.

Convergence: In communication accommodation theory, the process of becoming more like someone else.

Conversation orientation: In family communication patterns theory, a communication climate in which all family members are encouraged to participate in unrestrained interaction.

Coordinated management of meaning: A theory that explains how individuals create, coordinate, and manage meanings during the process of communication.

Coordination: In the multiple stakeholder model, creating organizational spaces and practices to satisfy the needs of various stakeholders.

Corax: The person credited by most classical theorists and historians with inventing communication theory.

Counteractive function: In functional theory, a function of communication in which group members attempt to deal with some difficulty or barrier interfering with their ability to complete a task.

Counterargument: A claim that contradicts something one already thinks or believes.

Critical point: In the extended parallel processing model, the moment when perceived threat exceeds perceived efficacy.

Danger control processes: Changes in beliefs, attitudes, intentions, and/or behaviors that are prompted by a persuasive message's recommendations.

Data: The specific points of information that researchers want to know about.

Deductive approach: A process of doing research that involves deriving hypotheses from a theory and then testing them.

Depth: The level of intimacy in one's disclosures.

Description: A report of the conditions, experiences, events, and stories that are reflected in communication contexts.

Dialectical: Characterized by tension between two opposing but desirable outcomes.

Diffusion: The process by which members of a social community convey information about innovations.

Diffusion of innovation theory: A theory that explains how new ideas and technologies spread through societies.

Discourse: The way people talk and use texts in social interaction.

Dissonance ratio: In cognitive dissonance theory, the comparison between how many of a person's beliefs are consistent with, versus inconsistent with, his or her behaviors.

Divergence: In communication accommodation theory, the process of behaving in such a way as to differentiate oneself from others.

Dominant reading: A preferred interpretation of a message.

Domination: The extent to which people exercise control over other people, organizational rules, or institutional resources.

Dramatism: Theoretic approach to understanding human social action through an analysis of motives, stories, and language use.

Dramatizing message: A message that contains any form of imaginative language.

Duality of structure: The recursive nature of social practices.

Egocentric constraints: Limitations to decision-making ability introduced when one member tries to seize control of a group.

Elaboration: In the elaboration likelihood model, the extent to which one thinks carefully about issue-relevant information.

Elaboration likelihood: In the elaboration likelihood model, the probability that high elaboration will occur.

Elocution: The study of voice, articulation, and gesture.

Emancipation: The act of freeing people from oppression.

Empiricism: Careful observation of the physical world.

Entropy: In interactional/systems theory, the level of randomness and disorder of a system.

Environment: In sense making theory, the product of organizing.

Episode: In coordinated management of meaning, the period of time in which communicators engage in meaningful interaction.

Epistemology: The study of knowledge.

Equifinality: In interactional/systems theory, the process in which a system can reach the same final state in more than one way.

Equivocality: The condition of having more than one possible and plausible meaning.

Ethnography: A research method of describing the culture and cultural practices of a group that makes use of participant observation, note-taking, and interviewing.

Ethos: The personal character and integrity of a speaker.

Event schema: Description of the typical sequence of events in a standard social occasion.

Exchange: A transfer of something in return for something else.

Experience: Previous exposure to or involvement with an activity.

Experiment: A study in which one variable is manipulated by the researchers to determine its effect on another variable.

Explanation: The process of communicating why something occurs.

Face: The public image or identity people portray when communicating with others.

Face threats: Challenges to, or criticisms of, one's preferred public image.

Facework: Efforts to support people's face needs.

Falsifiable: Able to be proven false.

Fantasy: The creative and imaginative interpretation of events that fulfills a psychological or rhetorical need.

Fantasy chains: Communication episodes in which group members are pulled into participating in the sharing of a group fantasy.

Fantasy theme: The content of a dramatizing message that sparked a fantasy chain.

Fantasy type: A stock scenario repeated over time by the same or similar characters.

Fear: An emotional reaction to a threat that is perceived to be significant and personally relevant.

Fear appeals: Persuasive messages designed to scare people by describing the terrible things that will occur if they fail to do what the message recommends.

Fear control processes: Coping responses that seek to diminish one's fear, rather than diminishing the threat.

Findings: The results of a study.

First-level agenda setting: In agenda setting theory, the media and public agendas.

Focus: The breadth of topics that a theory covers.

Focus group: A small collection of people who are asked to discuss their beliefs, attitudes, or perceptions with one another as part of a research study.

Frames: Definitions of what is going on in an interaction.

Framing: A process in which media emphasize some aspects of reality while minimizing others.

Genderlects: A theory that explains gendered differences and their communicative foundations and consequences.

General functions: Tasks that all good theories, regardless of their subject matter, perform for the people who use them.

Generalizable: Applicable to people beyond just those who were in a study.

Generalized other: A general sense of appropriate social behavior based on group roles and norms.

Goals: In planning theory, desired end states that an individual is committed to achieving or maintaining.

Grand theories: Theories that seek to provide comprehensive, global explanations covering broad ranges of phenomena.

Gratifications: In uses and gratifications theory, the interest, value, and/or benefit of media.

Grounded theory: A formal theory that is created inductively.

Group fantasy: The end result of sharing dramatizing messages.

Groupthink: A condition in which group members' striving for unanimity overrides their motivation to consider alternative courses of action.

Guilt: A constellation of human emotional states including anxiety, disgust, and embarrassment.

Heuristic value: The ability of a theory to help researchers formulate interesting, worthwhile research questions.

Hierarchy: In interactional/systems theory, the arrangement of power and authority from top to bottom in a system.

Hierarchy principle: In planning theory, the idea that changing plans at specific levels is easier than changing plans at abstract levels.

Holarchies: In interactional/systems theory, the nesting of parts within wholes.

Homeostasis: The ability of a system to regulate its function and maintain a "steady state."

Human agency: How individuals act in social circumstances over time.

Hypodermic needle paradigm: The idea that mass media work like a hypodermic needle, shooting their ideas and desires directly into the thoughts, attitudes, and behaviors of the public. See also *magic bullet.*

Hypotheses: Specific predictions for a study to test.

Identification: In dramatism, the process by which people attempt to share symbols, perspectives, and life.

Individualism: A cultural tendency to value individual rights over group rights.

Information: Usable knowledge.

Inductive approach: A process of doing research that involves collecting data and then generating theories of broader claims on the basis of those data.

Information acquisition: In uncertainty management theory, all available means by which people come into contact with information.

Information avoidance: In uncertainty management theory, the practice of intentionally failing to seek information.

Information handling: In uncertainty management theory, the process by which people handle the information they acquire while managing their uncertainty.

Information seeking: In uncertainty management theory, the practice of intentionally gathering information.

Information use: In uncertainty management theory, the practice of applying information toward some purpose.

Innovation: An idea, practice, or object perceived to be new.

Inoculation message: In inoculation theory, the presentation of a weak counterargument and then a refutation of that argument.

Inoculations: Defenses that introduce a weak strain of whatever they are designed to prevent. Also called *vaccinations* and *immunizations*.

Insight: An understanding of the subjective experiences of others.

Integration: The reciprocity of actions and practices among individuals

Intellectual tradition: A general way of thinking about some aspect of the communication process.

Intention: An indication of a person's readiness to do something.

Interaction skills: Abilities for effective communication.

Interactivity: In uses and gratifications theory, the idea that one's degree of control over media and ability to engage in media discourse influence one's uses and gratifications.

Interdisciplinary: Recognizing and valuing the contribution of more than one academic field.

Intuition: A form of understanding that does not rely on logic or conscious reasoning.

Issue obtrusiveness: In agenda setting theory, the extent to which members of the public have had direct contact with an issue.

Knowledge: A person's understanding of the information, facts, or skills related to a topic.

Knowledge elaboration: A general function in which theories organize, anticipate, summarize, and extend knowledge about principles, practices, and experiences.

Laissez-faire families: In family communication patterns theory, families that are low in both conversation and conformity orientation.

Latent ties: Relationships that are available but not yet activated.

Legitimacy: The perception that something is beneficial.

Life scripts: In coordinated management of meaning, the narrative of the self, or the overarching self-concept of an individual. Also called *identity constructs.*

Logology: A way of thinking about how humans acquire knowledge of non-symbolic experiences.

Logos: The logical content of a message or argument.

Magic bullet: See *hypodermic needle paradigm.*

Maintenance: The process of continuing to use one's original communication style, regardless of the communication behaviors of others.

Mastery fantasies: In symbolic convergence theory, dramatizations describing commendable people whose basic goals are to gain power and control.

Meaning: The message that a symbol conveys.

Media agenda: The topics addressed by media sources.

Media multiplexity: The phenomenon in which more strongly tied pairs make more use of available media.

Media satisfaction: The experience of benefits from media use.

Message source: The entity that produces a message.

Metacommunication: Communication about communication.

Middle-range theories: Theories that provide explanations of specific categories of phenomena.

Mind: The collection of cognitive faculties that allows for consciousness, judgment, and perception.

Mindfulness: Awareness of how assumptions and emotions affect ongoing interations.

Model: A formal description of a process.

Narrow theories: Theories that explain specific aspects of a phenomenon, such as one or two recurring patterns of behavior.

Need for cognition: A persons' inclination toward effortful thought.

Need for orientation: In agenda setting theory, a combination of high interest in an issue and high uncertainty about that issue.

Negotiated reading: An interpretation of a message in which audience members generally accept the dominant reading but resist or modify that reading in ways that reflect their social position.

Non-accommodation: A strategy of making no attempt to converge or diverge from others in particular interactions.

Norm of reciprocity: The idea that self-disclosures should be reciprocated.

Normative beliefs: The expectations that people think important others have of them.

Observability: In diffusion of innovations theory, the extent to which the outcomes of an innovation are visible to others.

Ontology: The study of existence and reality.

Openness versus closedness: A dialectical tension between being disclosive and being non-disclosive.

Operational definition: A determination of how a variable will be observed or measured.

Oppositional reading: An interpretation of a message in which audience members oppose the dominant reading.

Organization: A general function in which theories help researchers classify data, understand concepts and relationships, and arrange human experiences.

Outcomes: In the multiple stakeholder model, the results of participatory decision-making.

Over-accommodation: The process by which people appear to condescend to others because they are trying too hard to increase social connection.

Over-benefited: A state in which one receives more from a relationship than one contributes to it.

Paradigm: A set of general assumptions, ideas, and procedures for viewing and studying a phenomenon.

Parsimony: A theory's simplicity.

Participant observation: A research method in which researchers learn about a social group or cultural phenomenon by becoming involved in it themselves.

Partner uncertainty: Questions or doubts people have about their partner's participation in a relationship.

Pathos: An audience's emotions.

Pentad: In dramatism, a set of five interrelated concepts: the act, the scene, the agent, agency, and the purpose.

Perceived behavioral control: People's perceptions of their ability to perform a given behavior. See also *self efficacy*.

Perceived efficacy: An individual's belief about how feasible a recommended behavior is and how effectively it can reduce a threat.

Perceived importance: In cognitive dissonance theory, the significance attributed to an issue.

Perceived severity: An individual's belief about the seriousness of a threat.

Perceived susceptibility: An individual's belief about his or her likelihood of experiencing a threat.

Perceptual set: A predisposition to perceive only what we want or expect to perceive.

Peripheral route processing: In the elaboration likelihood model, the tendency not to scrutinize an argument or evidence, but instead to pay attention to less-relevant factors.

Person schemas: Understandings of the psychology of typical or specific individuals.

Person-centered messages: Messages that recognize and adapt to the emotional, subjective, and relational characteristics of a situation.

Personal constructs: Groupings of events based on similarities and differences, such as intelligent vs. unintelligent or kind vs. unkind.

Planning: The process people go through to produce a plan.

Plans: In planning theory, cognitive representations of action sequences that enable people to achieve their goals.

Plato: A student of Socrates, founder of the Academus, and author of *The Republic*.

Pluralistic families: In family communication patterns theory, families that are high in conversation orientation but low in conformity orientation.

Policy agenda: The topics that legislators and other governmental officials believe are important.

Power: The relationship between autonomy and dependence.

Power distance: The extent to which less powerful members of an institution accept the idea that power is distributed unequally.

Powerless speech: Unassertive communication.

Praxis: The process by which one is enable or constrained by previous communication actions.

Praxis and problem-solving: Using theoretical ideas and research practices to solve real-world problems.

Prediction: The practice of anticipating future events.

Priming: The effects of a specific prior contexts on the retrieval and interpretation of information.

Principle of distributive justice: The idea that whomever contributes the most to a relationship should receive the most benefits.

Principles of integration: In structuration theory, an idea reflecting the interdependence of actions.

Privacy: The belief in ownership and control over secret information.

Privacy boundaries: Characteristics that help people make decisions about disclosing private information.

Private information: Data that individuals prefer to keep secret.

Process: Something that unfolds over time.

Promotive function: In functional theory, a function of communication in which group members state a problem, identify criteria for evaluation solutions, and offer possible solutions.

Prosaics: In dialectical theories, a form of thinking that presumes the importance of everyday, ordinary experience.

Protective families: In family communication patterns theory, families that are low in conversation orientation but high in conformity orientation.

Public agenda: The topics that members of the public believe are important.

Qualitative: Expressed as descriptions of a quality or characteristic.

Quantitative: Expressed in numbers.

Rapport talk: Communication used to give information and support, build consensus, and create closeness and rapport.

Rationalisation of action: In structuration theory, the practice of giving reasons for actions in the context of daily life.

Rationalize: In cognitive dissonance theory, the tendency to make excuses for dissonance.

Redemption: Deliverance from guilt or negative action; making amends for sins.

Reflexive monitoring of action: In structuration theory, the practice of reflecting on actions and monitoring the environmental conditions that influence action.

Refutational preemption: In inoculation theory, the presentation of counterarguments and refutations at the same time.

Relational outcomes: The result of subtracting the costs of a relationship from its rewards.

Relationship uncertainty: Questions or doubts people have about their relationships, above and beyond their self- and partner-concerns.

Relative advantage: The degree to which an innovation is perceived as superior to alternatives.

Report talk: Communication used to negotiate one's position in a hierarchical social order.

Requisite variety: In interactional/systems theory, a system's need for diversity.

Research: The systematic process of generating knowledge.

Research question: A question that guides a study.

Research stimulation: A general function in which theories encourage people to study the ways to change and improve behavior, including communication behavior.

Resisting intellectuals: People who can recognize and challenge the status quo.

Response efficacy: A person's belief about whether an action will effectively reduce a threat.

Retention: In sense making theory, the process of preserving a chosen meaning in an interpretive database or repertoire.

Reward: Anything that a person values or perceives as beneficial.

Rhetoric: (As used in ancient Greece), the study of communication.

Rhetorical vision: In symbolic convergence theory, a unified collection of the various fantasy themes and types that broadens the view of group members.

Rhetoricians: (As used in ancient Greece), those who taught communication.

Role schemas: Understandings of the appropriate norms and behaviors for social categories (based on race, sex, age, occupation, and so forth).

Role: A perception of a person's behaviors, rights, and obligations.

Rule-based management system: In communication privacy management theory, a system for understanding and managing private information.

Rules: Formal or informal processes that guide human interaction.

Schemas: Value and belief systems shared by members of a group, such as a family.

Schools of thought: Groups of people who share assumptions about the nature of reality, truth, and language, and who jointly create ideas and practices.

Scientific method: A method of research in which a problem is identified, relevant data are gathered, and hypotheses are formed and empirically tested.

Scope: The applicability of a theory's coverage.

Scrutiny: A careful examination of a claim to look for mistakes.

Second-level agenda setting: In agenda setting theory, the process wherein media influence how people think.

Selection: In sense making theory, the process of choosing a potential meaning for something.

Selective attention: Paying attention only to information that supports one's viewpoints.

Selective exposure: Intentionally avoiding information that contradicts a person's behaviors or beliefs.

Selective interpretation: Making sense of ambiguous information in a way that supports one's behaviors or beliefs.

Selective retention: The tendency to remember only those details that support one's point of view.

Self: The recognition that an individual has both subjective and objective dimensions of human experience.

Self efficacy: A person's belief that he or she can perform a recommended behavior.

Self schemas: Understandings of ourselves.

Self uncertainty: Questions or doubts people have about their own participation in a relationship.

Self-concept: The stable ideas about who a person is.

Self-construal: The degree to which people conceive of themselves as independent from, or connected to, others.

Self-disclosure: The act of intentionally giving others information about oneself that one believes they do not already possess.

Self-report data: Data about participants that are reported by the participants themselves.

Semantics: The study of meaning; a subfield of semiotics.

Semiotics: The study of signs.

Sensitizing concepts: Theoretical tools that help orient researchers to a particular research problem.

Sign: A representation of an object.

Social exchanges: Voluntary transfers of resources that rely on trust and goodwill.

Social integration: A form of integration indexing reciprocity and interaction between people.

Social scripts: Guides to appropriate social interaction.

Social system: The interrelated units (such as individuals, groups, and organizations) that engage in joint problem solving.

Society: A collection of individuals, groups, and organizations.

Sophists: Traveling teachers in ancient Greece who practiced and refined the theories taught by Corax.

Source credibility: An audience's perception of a speaker or writer's competence, character, and goodwill.

Specific purposes: Tasks that researchers perform with theories.

Speech acts: The communication behaviors an individual enacts to achieve his or her goals.

Stability versus change: A dialectical tension between sameness and difference.

Stakeholder: A person or group who has an interest in an organization's decision-making.

Stereotypes: Expectations about people that are based on their membership in a particular group.

Story: A description of a particular experience unfolding over time.

Stratification model of action: In structuration theory, a representation of three interrelated modes of action.

Strong ties: Close, well established personal relationships.

Structuration theory: A theory that explains who practical and discursive practices help people produce and reproduce organizational structures and systems over time.

Structure: The rules and resources used in the social reproduction of a system over time.

Subjective norm: The perceived social pressure to engage in or avoid a particular behavior.

Survey: A method of colleting data by asking people for the data directly.

Symbolic convergence: The communication process that emerges as group members create a climate and culture that allows them to achieve a "meeting of the minds."

Symbolic cue: In symbolic convergence theory, a cryptic reference to common symbolic ground.

Symbolic interactionism: A theory that explores the centrality of human symbolic processes and the deep interconnections among the mind, the self, and society.

Symbols: Representations of ideas.

Synthesis: An integration of two arguments or claims.

System: The interdependence of action and patterns of relations between and among actors.

System evolution: In interactional/systems theory, the capacity of a system to move to more complex forms of differentiation and integration.

System integration: A form of integration indexing reciprocity and interaction between groups and organizations.

Terministic screens: Filters through which individuals make sense of everyday interaction.

The Lyceum: School founded by Aristotle in 335 B.C.

Theory: An organized set of statements that explains some phenomenon.

Thesis: An argument or claim.

Threat: In inoculation theory, the perception that an existing attitude or belief is vulnerable to change.

Tie strength: The time, emotional intensity, intimacy, and reciprocity that characterize a relationship.

Tisias: A student of Corax who introduced Corax's theories of legal and public communication to Athens and mainland Greece.

Totality: The inseparability of phenomena.

Transferable: Relatable to contexts beyond the ones observed in a study.

Trialability: The degree to which an innovation can be experimented with.

Troubles talk: Discussion of problems.

Unacknowledged conditions of action: In structuration theory, the idea that people cannot know how their unconscious drives and desires influence their actions.

Uncertainty management: In uncertainty management theory, the combination of information acquisition, information handling, and information use.

Uncertainty: A level of doubt or lack of knowledge about what is inevitable.

Under-accommodation: The process by which people believe that others do not engage in appropriate accommodation to their needs, goals, and desires.

Under-benefited: A state in which one receives less from a relationship than one contributes to it.

Unfinalizable: In dialectical theories, a state in which issues and tensions that relational partners encounter are never fully resolved.

Unintended consequence of action: In structuration theory, the idea that people do not necessarily control the direction of system reproduction.

Use: In uses and gratifications theory, the purpose of media consumption that individuals select.

Values: Ideas about what ought to happen.

Variable: Any concept whose values or properties can vary.

Variation: Changes in otherwise stable aspects of the environment.

Verifiable: Able to be proven true.

Weak ties: Casual personal relationships.

Wholeness and interdependence: In interactional/systems theory, the total system and the connection between its parts.

Zero-history groups: Leaderless groups brought together for the first time to accomplish a task.

ENDNOTES

Chapter One

1. The material on the history of the communication discipline is taken from two sources: Harper, N. (1979). *Human communication theory: The history of a paradigm.* Rochelle Park, NJ: Hayden; and Pearce, W. B., & Foss, K. A. (1990). The historical context of communication as a science. In G. L. Dahnke & G. W. Clatterbuck (Eds.), *Human communication: Theory and research* (pp. 1-19). Belmont, CA: Wadsworth.

2. Berger, P. L., & Luckmann, T. (1967). *The social construction of reality: A treatise in the sociology of knowledge* (p. 23). New York, NY: Doubleday.

3. According to Harper (1979), there is historical evidence supporting ancient interests in communication prior to fifth century B.C., such as the *Old Testament*, the Egyptian *Precepts of Kagemni and Ptah-Hotep*, and Homer's *Iliad*. However, we have no records of any systematic study of the communication process prior to that time period.

4. Pearce & Foss (1990).

5. Harper (1979).

6. Marrou, H. I. (1956). *A history of education in antiquity* (pp. 267-268). New York, NY: New American Library.

7. Pearce & Foss (1990).

8. Aristotle (1991). *On rhetoric: A theory of civic discourse* (G. A. Kennedy, Trans.). New York, NY: Oxford University Press.

9. Harper (1979), p. 29.

10. There were other classical writers and those during the Renaissance and modern periods who contributed to our contemporary understandings of communication theory, including Isocrates, Cicero, Augustine, Bacon, Descartes, Locke, Campbell, De Quincey, and Dewey, to name a few. For further information on the historical development of the field from ancient Greece until the late 19th century, see Harper (1979); Thonssen, L., Baird, A. C., & Braden, W. W. (1970). *Speech criticism* (2nd ed.). Malabar, FL: Robert E. Krieger Publishing.

11. The material on communication in contemporary times is taken from two sources: Delia, J. G. (1987). Communication research: A history. In C. R. Berger & S. H. Chaffee (Eds.), *Handbook of communication science* (pp. 20-98). Beverly Hills, CA: Sage; Bormann, E. G. (1989). *Communication theory* (pp. 3-55). Salem, WI: Sheffield.

12. Bormann (1989).

13. Craig, R. T. (2008). Communication as a field and discipline. In W. Donsbach (Ed.), *The international encyclopedia of communication* (pp. 675-688). Hoboken, NJ: Blackwell.

14. Lievrouw, L. A. (2009). New media, mediation, and communication study. *Information, Communication, and Society, 12,* 303-325; Merrin, W. (2009). Media studies 2.0: Upgrading and open-sourcing the discipline. *Interactions: Studies in Communication and Culture, 1,* 17-34.

15. Floyd, K. (2011). *Communication matters.* New York, NY: McGraw-Hill.

16. Siegert, J. R., & Stamp, G. H. (1994). "Our first big fight" as a milestone in the development of close relationships, *Communication Monographs, 61,* 345-360.

17. Bertelsen, D. A., & Goodboy, A. K. (2009). Curriculum planning: Trends in communication studies, workplace competencies, and current programs at 4-year colleges and universities. *Communication Education, 58,* 262-275.

18. Craig (2008); Wood, J. T. (2008). *Communication mosaics.* Belmont, CA: Thomson Wadsworth.

19. National Communication Association (www.natcom.org/Defaul.aspx?id=631&libID=652)

20. International Communication Association (www.icahdq.org/aboutica/missionstatement.asp)

21. Association for Education in Journalism and Mass Communication (www.aejmc.org)

22. Friedman, T. L. (2008). *Hot, flat, crowded.* New York, NY: Farrar, Straus and Giroux.

23. Chesebro, J. W., Kim, J. K., & Lee, D. (2007). Strategic transformations in power and the nature of international communication theory. *China Media Research, 3,* 1-13; Chung, C. J., Lee, S., Barnett, G. A., & Kim, J., H. (2009). A comparative analysis of the Korean Society of Journalism and Communication Studies (KSJCS) and the International Communication Association

(ICA) in the era of hybridization. *Asian Journal of Communication, 19*, 170-191.

24. Gordon, R. D. (2007). The Asian communication scholar for the 21st century. *China Media Research, 3*, 50-59.

25. Flyvberg, B. (2001). *Making social science matter: Why social inquiry fails and how it can succeed again* (Trans. S. Sampson). Cambridge, England: Cambridge University Press; Tracy, S. J. (2007). Taking the plunge: A contextual approach to problem-based research. Communication Monographs, 74, 106-111.

26. See Wang, Z., & Ramirez, A. (2008). When online meets offline: An expectancy violations perspective on modality switching. *Journal of Communication, 58*, 20-39.

27. Stephens, K. K., Houser, M. L., & Cowan, R. L. (2009). R U able to meat me: The impact of students' overly casual email messages to instructors. *Communication Education, 58*, 303-326.

28. Beatty, M. J., McCroskey, J. C., & Floyd, K. (Eds.). (2009). *Biological dimensions of communication: Perspectives, methods, and research.* Cresskill, NJ: Hampton Press.

29. See, e.g., Floyd, K., & Riforgiate, S. (2008). Affectionate communication received from spouses predicts stress hormone levels in healthy adults. Communication Monographs, 75, 351-368.

30. E.g., Dopp, J. M., Miller, G. E., Myers, H. F., & Fahey, J. L. (2000). Increased natural killer-cell mobilization and cytotoxicity during marital conflict. *Brain, Behavior, and Immunity, 14*, 10-26.

31. Halverson, J., Goodall, H. L., & Corman, S. R. (2011). *Master narratives of Islamist extremism.* New York, NY: Palgrave Macmillan.

32. Perera, D. (2010, March 17). JFCOM forecasts internet-fueled "battle of narratives." Retrieved March 5, 2011, from: http://www.fiercegovernmentit.com/story/jfcom-forecasts-internet-fueled-battle-narratives/2010-03-17

33. Kerkhof, P., Finkenauer, C., & Muusses, L. D. (2011). Relational consequences of compulsive Internet use: A longitudinal study among newlyweds. *Human Communication Research, 37,* 147-293.

34. Hmielowski, J. D., Holbert, R. L., & Lee, J. (2011). Predicting the consumption of political TV satire: Affinity for political humor, *The Daily Show,* and *The Colbert Report. Communication Monographs, 78,* 96-114.

35. Miller, J. D., Kotowski, M. R., Comis, R. L., Smith, S. W., Silk, K. J., Coliazzi, D. D., & Kimmel, L. G. (2011). Measuring cancer clinical trial understanding. *Health Communication, 26,* 82-92.

Chapter Two

1. The material on what constitutes a theory and the different parts of a theory is taken primarily from two sources: Bormann, E. G. (1989). *Communication theory* (pp. 3-55). Salem, WI: Sheffield; Klein, D. M., & White, J. M. (1996). *Family theories: An introduction* (pp. 1-30). Thousand Oaks, CA: Sage.

2. Braithwaite, D. O., & Baxter, L. A. (2008). Introduction: Metatheory and theory in interpersonal communication research. In L. A. Baxter & D. O. Braithwaite (Eds.), *Engaging theories in*

interpersonal communication: Multiple perspectives (pp. 1-18). Los Angeles, CA: Sage.

3.   Braithwaite & Baxter (2008).

4.   Klein & White (1996).

5.   Bormann (1989).

6.   Shannon, C. E., & Weaver, W. (1949). *The mathematical theory of communication.* Urbana: University of Illinois Press.

7.   Schramm, W. (1954). *The process and effects of mass communication.* Urbana: University of Illinois Press.

8.   Berlo, D. K. (1960). *The process of communication: An introduction to theory and practice.* New York, NY: Holt, Rinehart & Winston.

9.   Applbaum, R. L., Anatol, K. W. E., Hays, E. R., Jenson, O. O., Porter, R. E., & Mandel, J. E. (1973). *Fundamental concepts in human communication.* San Francisco, CA: Canfield Press.

10. Klein & White (1996).

11. Spitzberg, B. H. (2006). Preliminary development of a model and measure of computer-mediated (CMC) competence. *Journal of Computer-Mediated Communication, 11,* 629-666.

12. Afifi, T. D., Schrodt, P., & McManus, T. (2009). The divorce disclosure model (DDM): Why parents disclose negative information about the divorce to their children and its effects. In T. D. Afifi & W. A. Afifi (Eds.), *Uncertainty, information management, and disclosure decisions: Theories and applications* (pp. 403-425). New York, NY: Routledge.

13. Klein & White (1996).

14. Klein & White (1996).

15. Donnelley, P. (2010). *Fade to black: A book of movie obituaries* (3rd ed.). London, England: Omnibus Press.

16. Klein & White (1996), p. 12.

17. http://inventors.about.com/library/inventors/bllego.htm

18. Schrodt, P., & Ledbetter, A. M. (2011). Parental confirmation as a mitigator of feeling caught and family satisfaction. *Personal Relationships, 19,* 146-161.

19. Scott, C. W., & Trethewey, A. (2008). Organizational discourse and the appraisal of occupational hazards: Interpretive repertoires, heedful interrelating, and identity at work. *Journal of Applied Communication Research, 36,* 298-317.

20. Berger, P. L., & Luckmann, T. (1967). *The social construction of reality.* New York, NY: Anchor Books.

21. Meisenbach, R., J., Remke, R. V., Buzzanell, P. M., & Liu, M. (2008). "They allowed": Pentadic mapping of women's maternity leave discourse as organizational rhetoric. *Communication Monographs, 75,* 1-24.

22. Burrell, G., & Morgan, G. (1979). *Social paradigms and organizational analysis.* Portsmouth, NH: Heinemann Books.

23. Miller, K. (2002). *Communication theories: Perspectives, processes and contexts.* Boston, MA: McGraw-Hill.

24. Weick, K. (1979). *The social psychology of organizing.* New York, NY: McGraw-Hill

25. Infante, D. A., Rancer, A. S., & Avtgis, T. A. (2009). *Contemporary communication theory.* Dubuque, IA: Kendall/Hunt. (Note: *Knowledge elaboration* is our term. Infante and colleague used the more narrow term *knowledge extension.*)

26. Littlejohn, S. W. (1992). *Theories of human communication.* (4th ed.). Belmont, CA: Wadsworth.

27. Gottman, J. (1994). *What predicts divorce?* Hillsdale, NJ: Lawrence Erlbaum Associates.

28. Infante et al. (2009).

29. Giddens, A. (1979). *Central problems in social theory.* London, England: Hutchinson.

30. See Poole, M. S., & McPhee, R. D. (2005). Structuration theory. In S. May & D. K. Mumby (Eds.), *Engaging organizational communication theory and research* (pp. 171-195). Thousand Oaks, CA: Sage; Poole, M. S., & DeSanctis, G. (1992). Microlevel structuration in computer-supported group decision-making. *Human Communication Research, 19,* 5-49.

31. Krone, K. J., Schrodt, P., & Kirby, E. L. (2006). Structuration theory: Promising directions for family communication research. In D. O. Braithwaite & L. A. Baxter. (Eds.), *Engaging theories in family communication* (pp. 293-308). Thousand Oaks, CA: Sage.

32. Infante et al. (2009).

33. Manusov, V. L. (2006). Attribution theories: Assessing causal and responsibility judgments in families. In D. O. Braithwaite, & L. A. Baxter. (Eds.). *Engaging theories in family communication* (pp. 181-196). Thousand Oaks, CA: Sage. (Quote is from p. 182.)

34. Floyd, K., & Haynes, M. T. (2006). The theory of natural selection: An evolutionary approach to family communication. In D. O. Braithwaite & L. A. Baxter. (Eds.), *Engaging theories in family communication* (pp. 325-340). Thousand Oaks, CA: Sage. (Quote is from p. 333.)

35. Maslow, A. H. (1968). *Toward a psychology of being* (2nd ed.). Princeton, NJ: D. Van Nostrand Co., Inc.

36. Spangle, M. L., & Isenhart, M. W (2003). *Negotiation.* Thousand Oaks, CA: Sage.

37. Infante et al. (2009).

38. Baskin, O., & Aronoff, C. (1988). *Public relations.* Dubuque, IA: Wm. C. Brown Publishers.

39. Littlejohn (1992), p. 29.

40. Baxter, L. A. (2006). Relational dialectics theory: Multivocal dialogues of family communication. In D. O. Braithwaite & L. A. Baxter. (Eds.), *Engaging theories in family communication* (pp. 130-145). Thousand Oaks, CA: Sage.

41. Kincheloe J. L., & McLaren, P. (2000). Rethinking critical theory and qualitative research. In N. K. Denzin & Y. S. Lincoln (Eds.), *Handbook of qualitative research* (2nd ed., pp. 279-313). Thousand Oaks, CA: Sage.

42.   Deetz, S. (2005). Critical theory. In S. May & D. K. Mumby (Eds.), *Engaging organizational communication theory and research* (pp. 85-111). Thousand Oaks, CA: Sage.

Chapter Three

1.   Committee on Ways and Means Democrats. (2004). *Steep decline in teen birth rate significantly responsible for reducing child poverty and single-parent families.* In *Committee Issue Brief, April 23, 2004.* Washington, D.C.: Author.

2.   Shuger, L. (2012). *Teen pregnancy and high school dropout: What communities are doing to address these issues.* Washington, D.C.: The National Campaign to Prevent Teen and Unplanned Pregnancy and America's Promise Alliance.

3.   Wilson, H., & Huntington, A. (2006). Deviant (m)others: The construction of teenage motherhood in contemporary discourse. *Journal of Social Policy, 35,* 59-76.

4.   Maynard, R. A. (Ed.). (1996). *Kids having kids: A Robin Hood Foundation special report on the costs of adolescent childbearing.* New York, NY: Robin Hood Foundation.

5.   The National Campaign to Prevent Teen and Unplanned Pregnancy. (2013). Counting it up: The public costs of teen childbearing. Retrieved October 21, 2013, from http://www.thenationalcampaign.org/costs/

6.   This example comes from Singh, S. (2004). *Big bang: The origin of the universe.* New York, NY: HarperCollins.

7. The first hypothesis is also false; women and men are equally talkative. See Mehl, M. R., Vazire, S., Ramírez-Esparza, N., Slatcher, R. B., & Pennebaker, J. W. (2007). Are women really more talkative than men? *Science, 317,* 5834.

8. Lasswell, H. D. (1948). *Power and personality.* New York, NY: Transaction.

9. Krippendorff, K. H. (2012). *Content analysis: An introduction to its methodology* (3rd ed.). Thousand Oaks, CA: Sage.

10. Tracy, S. J., Lutgen-Sandvik, P., & Alberts, J. K. (2006). Nightmares, demons and slaves: Exploring the painful metaphors of workplace bullying. *Management Communication Quarterly, 20*(2), 148-185.

11. Ibid. (Quotes are from p. 156.)

12. Geertz, C. (1973). *The interpretation of cultures.* New York, NY: Basic Books.

Chapter Four

1. Leeds-Hurwitz, W. (2009). Semiotics and semiology. In S. Littlejohn, & K. Foss (Eds.), *Encyclopedia of communication theory* (pp. 875-877). Thousand Oaks, CA: Sage

2. http://en.wikipedia.org/wiki/Semantics

3. Bach, K., & Harnish, R. M. (1979). *Linguistic communication and speech acts.* Cambridge, MA: MIT Press.

4. See introduction to *Mind, Self and Society* (1934) for fuller discussion of Mead's mentors and contemporaries.

5. Mead, G. H. (1934). *Mind, self and society.* Chicago, IL: University of Chicago Press. (Quote is from p. 5.)

6. Mead (1934, p. 7)

7. Mead (1934, p. 55)

8. Mead (1934, p.   )

9. Mead (1934, p. 229)

10. Blumer, H. (1969). *Symbolic Interactionism.* Englewood Cliffs, NJ: Prentice-Hall. (Quote is from p. 2.)

11. Blumer (1969, p. 3)

12. Blumer (1969, p. 2).

13. See Dictionary.com

14. http://en.wikipedia.org/wiki/Meaning

15. Blumer (1969, pp. 2-5).

16. Blumer (1969, p. 5)

17. A brief summary of the influences on Mead's perspective can be found in the introduction of *Mind, Self, and Society* (1934).

18. Mead (1934, p. 154).

19. Mead (1934, p. 155).

20. Mead (1934, p. 229).

21. Mead (1934, pp. 253-260).

22. Mead (1934, p. 253)

23. Burke, K. (1985). Dramatism and logology. *Communication Quarterly, 33,* 89-93.

24. Littlejohn, S. W. (1992). *Theories of human communication* (4th ed.). Belmont, CA: Wadsworth.

25. Burke, K (1984). *Permanence and change* (3rd ed.). Los Angeles: University of California Press. (Quote is from p. 295.)

26. Burke (1984, p. 295).

27. Burke (1985).

28. Burke (1985).

29. Fox, C. (2002). Beyond the 'tyranny of the real': Revisiting Burke's pentad as research method for professional communication. *Technical Communication Quarterly, 11,* 365-388. (Quote is from p. 366.).

30. Burke (1984, p. 35).

31. Blakesley, D. (2002). *The elements of dramatism.* New York, NY: Longman Publishers.

32. Burke, K. (1990). From a grammar of motives. In P. Bizzell, & B. Herzberg (Eds.) *The rhetorical tradition* (pp. 992-1018). Boston, MA: Bedford St. Martin's Press.

33. Blakesley, D (2002).

34. Burke, K. (1950). A rhetoric of motives. Berkely & Los Angeles: University of California Press.

35. Rueckert, W. (1969). *Critical responses to Kenneth Burke.* Minneapolis, MN: University of Minnesota Press.

36. Burke (1984, p. 177).

37. Appel (1993, p. 53).

38. Appel, E. (1987). The perfected drama of Reverend Jerry Falwell. *Communication Quarterly, 35,* 26-38. (Quote is from p. 28.)

39. Appel (1987, p. 36).

40. Hopper, R. (1993). Conversational dramatism: A symposium. *Text and Performance Quarterly, 13,* 181-183.

41. Hopper (1993, p. 181).

42. Fox (2002).

43. Fox (2002, p. 373).

44. Pearce, V. W., & Cronen, V. E. (1980). *Communication, action, and meaning.* New York, NY: Praeger. (Quote is from p. 1.)

45. Pearce & Cronen (1980, p. 31).

46. Pearce & Cronen (1980, pp. 61-89).

47. Pearce & Cronen (1980, p. 31)

48. Pearce & Cronen (1980, p. 139).

49. Pearce & Cronen (1980, p. 119).

50. Pearce, W. B., & Pearce, K. A. (2000). Extending the theory of the coordinated management of meaning (CMM) through a community dialogue process. *Communication Theory, 10,* 405-423. See also, Cronen, V. E., Pearce, W. B., & Harris, L. M. (1979). The logic of coordinated management of meaning: A rules-based approach to the first course in interpersonal communication. *Communication Education, 28,* 22-38.

51. Pearce & Cronen (1980, p. 132).

52. Pearce & Cronen (1980, p. 137).

53. Pearce & Cronen (1980, p. 139)

54. Pearce & Pearce (2000).

55. Orbe, M. A., & Camara, S. K. (2010). Defining discrimination across cultural groups: Exploring the [un-]coordinated management of meaning. *International Journal of Intercultural Relations, 34,* 283-293.

56. Bruss, M. B., Morris, J. R., Dannison, L. L., Orbe, M. A., Quitugua, J. A., & Palacios, R. T. (2005). Food, culture, and

family: Exploring the coordinated management of meaning regarding childhood obesity. *Health Communication, 18,* 155-175.

57.   Bruss et al. (2005, p. 156).

58.   Montgomery, E. (2004). Tortured families: A coordinated management of meaning analysis. *Family Process, 43,* 349-371.

Chapter Five

1.   Fiske, S. T., & Taylor, S. E. (1991). *Social cognition.* New York, NY: McGraw-Hill.

2.   Schank, R. C. (1982). *Dynamic memory.* Cambridge, England: Cambridge University Press; Schank, R. C. (1999). *Dynamic memory revisited* (2nd ed.). Cambridge, England: Cambridge University Press.

3.   Kellermann, K., Broetzmann, S., Lim, T.-S., & Kitao, K. (1989). The conversation MOP: Scenes in the stream of discourse. *Discourse Processes, 12,* 27-61.

4.   Honeycutt, J. M., Cantrill, J. G., & Greene, R. W. (1989). Memory structures for relational escalation: A cognitive test of the sequencing of relational actions and stages. *Human Communication Research, 16,* 62-90; Honeycutt, J. M., Zagacki, K. S., & Edwards, R. (1990). Imagined interaction and interpersonal communication. *Communication Reports, 3,* 1-8.

5.   Wicks, R. H. (1992). Schema theory and measurement in mass communication research: Theoretical and methodological issues in news information processing. *Communication Yearbook, 15,* 115-145.

6. Urberg, K. A., Değirmencioğlu, S. M., & Tolson, J. M. (1998). Adolescent friendship selection and termination: The role of similarity. *Journal of Social and Personal Relationships, 15,* 703-710.

7. Schyns, P. G., & Oliva, A. (1999). Dr. Angry and Mr. Smile: When categorization flexibly modifies the perception of faces in rapid visual representations. *Cognition, 69,* 243-265.

8. Floyd, K. (2000). Affectionate same-sex touch: Understanding the influence of homophobia on observers' perceptions. *Journal of Social Psychology, 140,* 774-788.

9. Lepore, L., & Brown, R. (1997). Category and stereotype activation: Is prejudice inevitable? *Journal of Personality and Social Psychology, 72,* 275-287.

10. Lee, Y.-T., Jussim, L. J., & McCauley, C. R. (1996). *Stereotype accuracy: Toward appreciating group differences.* Washington, DC: American Psychological Association.

11. Most of our discussion of the key claims advanced by schema theory comes from Wicks (1992).

12. Weber, R., & Crocker, J. (1983). Cognitive processing in the revision of stereotypic beliefs. *Journal of Personality and Social Psychology, 45,* 961-977.

13. Burleson, B. R., & Rack, J. J. (2008). Constructivism theory: Explaining individual differences in communication skill. In L. A. Baxter & D. O. Braithwaite (Eds.), *Explaining theories in interpersonal communication: Multiple perspectives* (pp. 51-63). Thousand Oaks, CA: Sage.

14. Burleson, B. R. (2010). Explaining recipient responses to supportive messages: Development and tests of a dual-process theory. In S. W. Smith & S. R. Wilson (Eds.), *New directions in interpersonal communication research* (pp. 159-179). Thousand Oaks, CA: Sage.

15. Kelly, G. A. (1955). *The psychology of personal constructs* (2 vols.). New York, NY: Norton.

16. Burleson, B. R. (2007). Constructivism: A general theory of communication skill. In B. B. Whaley & W. Samter (Eds.), *Explaining communication: Contemporary theories and exemplars* (pp. 105-128). Mahwah, NJ: Lawrence Erlbaum Associates.

17. Tetlock, P. E. (1983). Accountability and the perseverance of first impressions. *Social Psychology Quarterly, 46,* 285-292.

18. Burleson, B. R., & Waltman, M. S. (1988). Cognitive complexity: Using the Role Category Questionnaire measure. In C. H. Tardy (Ed.), *A handbook for the study of human communication: Methods and instruments for observing, measuring, and assessing communication processes* (pp. 1-35). Norwood, NJ: Ablex.

19. Burleson, B. R. (2008). What counts as effective emotional support? Explorations of individual and situation differences. In M. T. Motley (Ed.), *Studies in applied interpersonal communication* (pp. 207-227). Thousand Oaks, CA: Sage.

20. Berger, C. R. (1997). *Planning strategic interaction: Attaining goals through communicative action.* Mahwah, NJ: Lawrence Erlbaum Associates.

21. Berger, C. R. (2008). Planning theory of communication: Goal attainment through communicative action. In L. A. Baxter & D.

O. Braithwaite (Eds.), *Engaging theories in interpersonal communication: Multiple perspectives* (pp. 89-101). Thousand Oaks, CA: Sage.

22. Most of our discussion of the assumptions, key concepts, and claims of planning theory come from Berger (1997, 2008).

23. Lewicki, P. (1986). *Nonconcious social information processing.* Orlando, FL: Academic Press.

24. Our discussion of the key concepts in planning theory comes from Berger (1997, 2008).

25. Waldron, V. R. (1997). Toward a theory of interactive conversational planning. In J. O. Greene (Ed.), *Message production: Advances in theory and research* (pp. 195-220). Mahwah, NJ: Lawrence Erlbaum Associates.

26. Berger (2008).

27. Our summary of the claims advanced by planning theory is based primarily on Berger (1997).

28. Berger (2008).

29. Gottman, J. M. (1993). A theory of marital dissolution and stability. *Journal of Family Psychology, 7,* 57-75.

Chapter Six

1. Heider, F. (1958). *The psychology of interpersonal relations.* Hillsdale, NJ: Lawrence Erlbaum Associates.

2. Ibid., p. 20.

3. Ibid., p. 22.

4. Heider (1958, p. 23).

5. Hewstone, M (1983). Attribution theory and common-sense explanations: An introductory overview. In M. Hewstone (Ed.). *Attribution theory: Social and functional extensions* (pp. 1-26). Oxford, England: Basil Blackwell Publisher. (Quote is from p. 4)

6. Jones, E. E. (1990) *Interpersonal perception.* New York, NY: W. H. Freeman and Company; Kelley, H. A. (1972). Attribution in social interaction. In E. E. Jones et al., (Eds.), *Attribution* (pp. 1-26). Morristown, NJ: General Learning Press (see also Kelley, H. A., Causal schemata and the attribution process, pp. 151-174 same volume); Hewstone, M (1983). Attribution theory and common-sense explanations: An introductory overview. In M. Hewstone (Ed.). *Attribution theory: Social and functional extensions* (pp. 1-26). Oxford, England: Basil Blackwell; Weiner, B. (1980). *Human motivation.* New York, NY: Holt, Rinehart, and Winston.

7. Heider, F. (1958, p. 1).

8. See Giddens (1979), and Berger & Luckman (1959).

9. Heider (1958, p. 2).

10. Hewstone (1983, p. 4)

11. Ibid., p. 7.

12. Lalljee, M., & Abelson, R. P. (1983). The organization of explanations. In M. Hewstone (Ed.). *Attribution theory: Social and functional extensions* (pp. 65-80). Oxford, England: Basil Blackwell.

13. Weiten, W. (2004). *Psychology: Themes and variations.* Belmont, CA: Wadsworth/Thompson Learning. (p. 652).

14. Ibid., p. 652.

15. Heider (1958, p. 80).

16. Saks, M. J., & Krupat, E. (1988). *Social psychology and its applications.* New York, NY: Harper & Row.

17. Kelley (1972, p. 3).

18. Kelley (1972, p. 8).

19. Saks & Krupat (1988, p. 51).

20. See Saks & Krupat (1988).

21. See Jones (1990).

22. Ibid., p. 78.

23. Ibid., p. 50-51.

24. Ibid., p. 52.

25. Hewstone (1983).

26. Jones (1990, p. 224).

27. Ibid., p. 224-230.

28. Ibid., p. 225.

29. See Jones (1990_ for fuller explanation of hedonic relevance.

30. Ibid., p. 227.

31. Ibid., p. 228.

32. See Saks & Krupat (1988) for explanation.

33. Ibid (p. 147).

34. Weiner, B., Frieze, I., Kukla, A., Reed, L., Rest, S., & Rosenbaum, R. M. (1972). Perceiving the causes and success and failure. In E. E. Jones et al., (Eds.). *Attribution* (pp. 95-120). Morristown, NJ: General Learning Press.

35. Lalljee, M. Watson, M., & White, P. (1983). Some aspects of the explanations of young children. In J. Jaspers, F. D. Fincham, & M. Hewstone (Eds.). *Attribution theory and research: Conceptual, developmental and social dimensions* (pp. 165-192). New York, NY: Academic Press.

36. Ibid., p. 181-182.

37. Young, S. L. (2004). What the _ _ _ _ is your problem?: Attribution theory and perceived reasons for profanity usage during conflict. *Communication Research Reports, 21,* 338-347.

38. Hullett, C. R. (2001). Attributional support: Targeting attribu-
     tions underlying recipient emotions. *Communication Research
     Reports, 18,* 285-294.

39. Polk, D. M. (2005). Communication and family caregiving for
     Alzheimer's dementia: Linking attributions and problematic
     integration. *Health Communication, 18,* 257-273.

40. Manusov, V., Floyd, K., &Kerssen-Griep, J. (1997). Yours, mine,
     and ours: Mutual attributions for nonverbal behaviors in cou-
     ples' interaction. *Communication Research, 24,* 234-254.

41. Munton, A. G., Silvester, J., Stratton, P., & Hanks, H. (1999).
     *Attributions in action: A practical approach to coding qualitative
     data.* New York, NY: John Wiley & Sons.

42. Burgoon, J. K. (1978). A communication model of person-
     al space violations: Explication and an initial test. *Human
     Communication Research, 4,* 129-142; Burgoon, J. K., & Hale, J.
     L. (1988). Nonverbal expectancy violations: Model elabora-
     tion and application to immediacy behaviors. *Communication
     Monographs, 55,* 58-79; Burgoon, J. K., & Jones, S. B. (1976).
     Toward a theory of personal space expectations and their vio-
     lations. *Human Communication Research, 2,* 131-146.

43. Burgoon, J. K. (1993). Interpersonal expectations, expectancy
     violations, and emotional communication. *Journal of Language
     and Social Psychology, 12,* 30-48.

44. Ibid (p. 31).

45. Goffman, I. (1974). *Frame analysis.* New York, NY: Harper &
     Row.

46. Burgoon (1993, p. 32).

47. Ibid.

48. See Goffman, I. (1959). *The presentation of self in everyday life.* New York, NY: Doubleday Anchor.

49. Burgoon & Hale (1988).

50. Ibid., p. 59.

51. Kelly, G. A. (1955). *The psychology of personal constructs.* New York, NY: Norton.

52. Burgoon & Hale (1988, p. 61).

53. Ibid., p. 58.

54. Burgoon (1993, p. 32).

55. Ibid., p. 62.

56. Burgoon (1993, see p. 38 for listing of studies).

57. Burgoon & Hale (1988, p. 67).

58. Floyd, K., Mikkelson, A. C., & Hesse, C. (2007). *The biology of human communication* (2nd ed.). Florence, KY: Cengage Learning; Le Poire, B. A., & Burgoon, J. K. (1996). Usefulness of differentiating arousal responses within communication theories: Orienting response or defensive arousal within nonverbal theories of expectancy violation. *Communication Monographs, 63,* 208-230.

59. Burgoon & Hale (1988, p. 67).

60. Ibid., p. 67.

61. McLaughlin, C., & Vitak, J. (2012). Norm evolution and violation on Facebook. *New Media Society, 14,* 299-315.

62. Burgoon & Hale (1988, p. 67).

63. Ibid.

64. Johnson, D. I., & Lewis, N. (2010). Perceptions of swearing in the work setting: An expectancy violations theory perspective. *Communication Reports, 23,* 106-118.

65. See Burgoon & Hale (1998) for summary of studies.

66. Guerrero, L. K., & Bachman, G. F. (2010). Forgiveness and forgiving communication in dating relationships: An expectancy-investment model. *Journal of Social and Personal Relationships, 27,* 801-823.

67. Aune, R. K., Ching, P. U., & Levine, T. R. (1996). Attributions of deception as a function of reward value: A test of two explanations. *Communication Quarterly, 44,* 478-486.

68. Bachman, G. F., & Guerrero, L. K. (2006). Relational quality and communicative responses following hurtful events in dating relationships: An expectancy violations analysis. *Journal of Social and Personal Relationships, 23,* 943-963.

69. Houser, M. L. (2006). Expectancy violations of instructor communication as predictors of motivation and learning:

A comparison of traditional and nontraditional students. *Communication Quarterly, 54*, 331-349.

Chapter Seven

1. Grant, D., Hardy, C., Oswick., C., & Putnam. L. L. (2004). Introduction: Organizational discourse: Exploring the field. In D. Grant, C. Hardy, C. Oswick & L. L. Putnam (Eds.). *The sage handbook of organizational discourse* (pp. 1-36). Thousand Oaks, CA: Sage Publications, Inc.

2. See Contractor, N. S., & Seibold, D. R. (1993). Theoretical frameworks for the study of structuring processes in group decision support systems. *Human Communication Research, 19,* 528-563.

3. Giddens, A. (1979). *Central problems in social theory.* Berkeley and Los Angeles: University of California Press. (Quote is from p. 55.)

4. Giddens, A. (1981). *A contemporary critique of historical materialism.* Berkeley and Los Angeles: University of California Press. (Quote is from p. 27.)

5. Ibid. (Quote is from p. 5.)

6. Ibid. (Quote is from p. 5.)

7. Ibid.

8. Ibid. (Quote is from p. 57.)

9. Ibid. (Quote is from p. 57.)

10.   Ibid. (Quote is from p. 7.)

11.   Ibid. (Quote is from p. 4.)

12.   Ibid. (Quote is from p. 19.)

13.   Ibid. (Quote is from p. 26.)

14.   Giddens (1979).

15.   Ibid. (Quote is from pp. 69-70.)

16.   Giddens (1979). (Quote is from p. 56.)

17.   Ibid. (Quote is from p. 57.)

18.   See Giddens, A. (1984). *The constitution of society: Outline of the theory of structuration.* Berkeley: University of California Press.

19.   Giddens (1979). (Quote is from p. 58.)

20.   Ibid. (Quote is from p. 76.)

21.   Ibid.

22.   Ibid. (Quote is from p. 6.)

23.   Ibid. (Quote is from p. 29.)

24.   Altman, I. (1993). Dialectics, physical environments, and personal relationships. *Communication Monographs, 60,* 26-41.

25.   Giddens (1981). (Quote is from p. 131.)

26. See further discussion in Poole, M. S., Seibold, D. R., & McPhee, R. D. (1996). The structuration of group decisions. In R. Y. Hirokawa & M. S. Poole (Eds.), *Communication and group decision making* (2nd ed., pp. 114-146). Thousand Oaks, CA: Sage.

27. Fay, M. J., & Kline, S. L. (2011). Coworker relationships and informal communication in high-intensity commuting. *Journal of Applied Communication Research, 39,* 144-163.

28. Golden, A. G. (2013). The structuration of information and communication technologies and work-life interrelationships: Shared organizational and family rules and resources and implications for work in a high-technology organization. *Communication Monographs, 80,* 101-123.

29. Norton, T. (2007). The structuration of public participation: Organizing environmental control. *Environmental Communication, 1,* 146-170.

30. Schrodt, P., Baxter, L. A., McBride, M. C., Braithwaite, D. O., & Fine, M. A. (2006). The divorce decree, communication, and the structuration of coparenting relationships in stepfamilies. *Journal of Social and Personal Relationships, 23,* 741-759.

31. Poole, M. S., & McPhee, R. D. (2005). Structuration theory. In S. May & D. K. Mumby (Eds.), *Engaging organizational communication theory & research* (pp. 171-195). Thousand Oaks, CA: Sage.

32. Ibid.

33. Poole, Seibold, & McPhee (1985).

34.   See Poole & McPhee (2005) for summary.

35.   Ibid. (Quote is from p. 183.)

36.   Ibid.

37.   Ibid. (Quote is from p. 183.)

38.   Giddens (1979). (Quote is from p. 85.)

39.   Rogers, E. M. (1995). *Diffusion of innovations* (4th ed.). New York, NY: The Free Press. (Quote is from p. 11.)

40.   Ibid.

41.   Ibid. (Quote is from p. 40.)

42.   Ibid. (Quote is from p. 41.)

43.   See Ibid. pp. 42-43, for extended explanation and elaboration of research within these ten traditions.

44.   See Ibid. pp. 31-35 for case study analysis of "Hybrid Corn in Iowa."

45.   Srivastava, J., & Moreland, J. J. (2013). Diffusion of innovations: Communication evolution and influences. *The Communication Review, 15,* 294-312.

46.   Papa, M. J., Singhal, A., & Papa, W. H. (2006). *Organizing for social change: A dialectic journey of theory and praxis.* Thousand Oaks, CA: Sage.

47.   Rogers (1995). (Quote is from p. 10.)

48.   Friedman, T. (2008). *Hot, flat, and, crowded*. New York, NY: Farrar, Straus & Giroux.

49.   Rogers (1995). (Quote is from pp. 5-6.)

50.   Ibid. (Quote is from p. 6.)

51.   Ibid. (Quote is from p. 11.)

52.   Heri, S., & Mosler, H. J. (2008). Factors affecting the diffusion of solar water disinfection: A field study in Bolivia. *Health Education & Behavior, 35,* 541-560.

53.   See http://www.wavesforwater.org/

54.   Rogers (1995). (Quote is from p. 12.)

55.   Ibid. (Quote is from p. 15.)

56.   Ibid.

57.   Rogers (1995).

58.   Ibid. (Quote is from p. 16.)

59.   Ibid.

60.   Ibid. (Quote is from p. 20.)

61.   http://marketingland.com/pew-61-percent-in-us-now-have-smartphones-46966

62. Rogers (1995).

63. Ibid.

64. Ibid., see pp. 28-30 for discussion.

65. Ibid., see pp. 263-266 for discussion.

66. Giles, H., & Smith, P. (1979). Accommodation theory: Optimal levels of convergence. In H. Giles & R. N. St. Clair (Eds.), *Language and social psychology* (pp. 45-65). Baltimore, MD: University Park Press. (Quote is from p. 46.)

67. Giles, H., Coupland, N., & Coupland, J. (1991). Accommodation theory: Communication, context, and consequence. In H. Giles, J. Coupland & N. Coupland (Eds.), *Contexts of accommodation* (pp. 1-68). New York, NY: Cambridge University Press. (Quote is from p. 7.)

68. Ibid. (Quote is from p. 8.)

69. Giles et al. (1991).

70. Giles & Smith (1979). (Quote is from p. 46.)

71. See Byrne, D. (1971). *The attraction paradigm.* New York, NY: Academic Free Press.

72. Giles & Smith (1979).

73. Ibid. (Quote is from p. 51.)

74. Ibid. (Quote is from p. 52.)

75. Giles, H. (2008). Accommodating translational research. *Journal of Applied Communication Research, 36,* 121-127.

76. Coupland, N., & Giles, H. (1988). Introduction: The communicative contexts of accommodation. *Language & Communication, 8,* 175-182.

77. Ibid., chapter 2.

78. Coupland, N., Coupland, J., & Giles, H. (1991). *Language, society, & the elderly.* Cambridge, MA: Basil Blackwell.

79. Giles, H., Fortman, J., Dailey, R. M., Barker, V., Hajek, C., Anderson, M. C., & Rule, N. O. (2007). Communication accommodation: Law enforcement and the public. In R. M. Dailey & B. A. Le Poire (Eds.), *Interpersonal communication matters: Family, health, and community relations* (pp. 241-270). New York, NY: Peter Lang.

80. Ibid. (Quote is from p. 247.)

81. Coupland et al. (1991).

82. Bourhis (1979), as cited in Giles et al. (2007).

83. Giles, H., Linz, D., Bonilla, D., & Gomez, M. L. (2012). Police stops and interactions with latino and white (non-latino) drivers: Extensive policing and communication accommodation. *Communication Monographs, 79,* 407-427.

84. See Giles (2008) for extended discussion.

85. Ibid.

86. Ibid. (Quote is from p. 123.)

87. Ibid.

88. Ibid. (Quote is from p. 124.)

89. Coupland & Giles (1988). (Quote is from p. 179.)

90. Coupland et al. (1991).

91. See Giles et al. (1991); Giles et al. (2012); Myers, P., Giles, H., Reid, S. A., & Nabi, R. L. (2008). Law enforcement encounters: The effects of officer accommodativeness and crime severity on interpersonal attributions are mediated by intergroup sensitivity. *Communication Studies, 59*, 291-305; Soliz, J., Ribarsky, E., Harrigan, M. M., & Tye-Williams, S. (2010). Perceptions of communication with gay and lesbian family members: Predictors of relational satisfaction and implications for outgroup attitudes. *Communication Quarterly, 58*, 77-95.

92. Huffaker, D. A., Swaab, R., & Diermeier, D. (2010). The language of coalition formation in online multiparty negotiations. *Journal of Language and Social Psychology, 30*, 66-81.

93. Giles et al. (1991). (Quote is from p. 37.)

Chapter Eight

1. Knobloch, L. K. (2008). Uncertainty reduction theory: Communicating under conditions of ambiguity. In L. A. Baxter & D. O. Braithwaite (Eds.), *Engaging theories in interpersonal communication: Multiple perspectives* (pp. 133-144). Thousand Oaks, CA: Sage.

2. Berger, C. R., & Calabrese, R. J. (1975). Some explorations in initial interaction and beyond: Toward a developmental theory of interpersonal communication. *Human Communication Research, 1,* 99-112.

3. See Gudykunst, W. B. (1995). Anxiety/uncertainty management (AUM) theory: Current status. In R. L. Wiseman (Ed.), *Intercultural communication theory* (pp. 8-58). Thousand Oaks, CA: Sage.

4. See Knobloch, L. K., & Satterlee, K. L. (2009). Relational uncertainty: Theory and application. In T. D. Afifi & W. A. Afifi (Eds.), *Uncertainty, information management, and disclosure decisions: Theories and applications* (pp. 106-127). New York, NY: Routledge.

5. p. 100, Berger & Calabrese (1975)

6. Berger, C. R. (1979). Beyond initial interaction: Uncertainty, understanding, and the development of interpersonal relationships. In H. Giles & R. St. Clair (Eds.), *Language and social psychology* (pp. 122-144). Oxford, England: Basil Blackwell.

7. Parks, M. R., & Adelman, M. B. (1983). Communication networks and the development of romantic relationships: An expansion of uncertainty reduction theory. *Human Communication Research, 10,* 55-79.

8. This example was adapted from Knobloch (2008).

9. By logically connecting all eight axioms to each other, 28 theorems can be derived (see Berger & Calabrese, 1975).

10. Berger, C. R., & Bradac, J. J. (1982). *Language and social knowledge: Uncertainty in interpersonal relationships*. London, England: Edward Arnold.

11. p. 134, Knobloch (2008)

12. Knobloch (2008)

13. Berger, C. R., Karol, S. H., & Jordan, J. M. (1989). When a lot of knowledge is a dangerous thing: The debilitating effects of plan complexity on verbal fluency. *Human Communication Research, 16,* 91-119.

14. Berger, C. R., & Kellermann, K. A. (1983). To ask or not to ask: Is that a question? In R. Bostrom (Ed.), *Communication yearbook 7* (pp. 342-368). Newbury Park, CA: Sage.

15. Berger, C. R. (1997a). *Planning strategic interaction: Attaining goals through communicative action*. Mahwah, NJ: Lawrence Erlbaum Associates.

16. Berger, C. R. (1997b). Producing messages under uncertainty. In J. O. Greene (Ed.), *Message production: Advances in communication theory* (pp. 221-244). Mahwah, NJ: Lawrence Erlbaum Associates.

17. Baxter, L. A., & Braithwaite, D. O. (2009). Reclaiming uncertainty: The formation of new meanings. In T. D. Afifi & W. A. Afifi (Eds.), *Uncertainty, information management, and disclosure decisions: Theories and applications* (pp. 26-44).

18. pp. 12-13, Berger & Bradac (1982)

19. Knobloch, L. K., & Solomon, D. H. (1999). Measuring the sources and content of relational uncertainty. *Communication Studies, 50,* 261-278.

20. Knobloch, L. K., & Solomon, D. H. (2002a). Information seeking beyond initial interaction: Negotiating relational uncertainty within close relationships. *Human Communication Research, 28,* 243-257.

21. Knobloch & Solomon (1999, 2002).

22. Knobloch, L. K. (2007). The dark side of relational uncertainty: Obstacle or opportunity? In B. H. Spitzberg & W. R. Cupach (Eds.), *The dark side of interpersonal communication* (2nd ed.) (pp. 31-59). Mahwah, NJ: Erlbaum.

23. For a detailed review, see Knobloch (2007, p. 39).

24. For a detailed discussion of the claims related to relational uncertainty, see Knobloch and Satterlee (2009).

25. Brown, P., & Levinson, S. (1987). *Politeness: Some universals in language use.* New York, NY: Cambridge University Press.

26. Knobloch, L. K., & Solomon, D. H. (2002b). Intimacy and the magnitude and experience of episodic relational uncertainty within romantic relationships. *Personal Relationships, 9,* 457-478.

27. McCurry, A. L., Schrodt, P., & Ledbetter, A. M. (in press). Relational uncertainty and communication efficacy as predictors of religious conversations in romantic relationships. *Journal of Social and Personal Relationships.*

28. Knobloch, L. K. (2006). Relational uncertainty and message production within courtship: Features and appraisals of date request messages. *Human Communication Research, 32,* 244-273.

29. Theiss, J. A., & Solomon, D. H. (2006a). A relational turbulence model of communication about irritations in romantic relationships. *Communication Research 33,* 391-418.

30. Theiss, J. A., & Solomon, D. H. (2006b). Coupling longitudinal data and multilevel modeling to examine the antecedents and consequences of jealousy experiences in romantic relationships: A test of the relational turbulence model. *Human Communication Research, 32,* 469-503.

31. Knobloch & Satterlee (2009).

32. Solomon, D. H., & Knobloch, L. K. (2004). A model of relational turbulence: The role of intimacy, relational uncertainty, and interference from partners in appraisals of irritations. *Journal of Social and Personal Relationships, 21,* 795-816.

33. Knobloch & Solomon (2002b).

34. McCurry et al. (in press).

35. The questions for each source of relational uncertainty can be found in Knobloch (2007).

36. Warner, A., Williams, J. H., Katzenberg, J. (Producers), Adamson, A., & Jenson, V. (Directors). (2001). *Shrek* [Motion picture]. United States: DreamWorks SKG.

37. Miller, G. R., & Steinburg, M. (1975). *Between people: An analysis of interpersonal communication*. Chicago, IL: Science Research Associates.

38. Mongeau, P. A., & Henningsen, M. L. M. (2008). Stage theories of relational development: Charting the course of interpersonal communication. In L. A. Baxter & D. O. Braithwaite (Eds.), *Engaging theories in interpersonal communication: Multiple perspectives* (pp. 363-375). Thousand Oaks, CA: Sage.

39. Altman, I., & Taylor, D. A. (1973). *Social penetration: The development of interpersonal relationships*. New York, NY: Rinehart & Winston.

40. p. 51 in Knapp, M. L. (1978). *Social intercourse: From greeting to goodbye*. Boston, MA: Allyn & Bacon.

41. Altman & Taylor (1973).

42. Altman, I., Vinsel, A., & Brown, B. B. (1981). Dialectic conceptions in social psychology: An application to social penetration and privacy regulation. In L. Berkowitz (Ed.), *Advances in experimental social psychology* (Vol. 14; pp. 107-160). New York, NY: Academic Press.

43. Wheeless, L. R., & Grotz, J. (1976). Conceptualization and measurement of reported self-disclosure. *Human Communication Research, 2,* 338-346.

44. The norm of reciprocity is a more general, social expectation that Altman and Taylor apply to self-disclosure in SPT – see Gouldner, A. W. (1960). The norm of reciprocity: A preliminary statement. *American Sociological Review, 25,* 161-178.

45. Miller, L. C., & Kenny, D. A. (1986). Reciprocity of self-disclosure at the individual and dyadic levels: A social relations analysis. *Journal of Personality and Social Psychology, 50,* 713-719.

46. Dindia, K. (1994). The intrapersonal-interpersonal dialectical process of self-disclosure. In S. Duck (Ed.), *Dynamics of relationships* (pp. 27-57). Thousand Oaks, CA: Sage.

47. Altman & Taylor (1973).

48. Thibaut, J. W., & Kelley, H. H. (1959). *The social psychology of groups.* New York, NY: John Wiley. See also Kelley, H. H., & Thibaut, J. W. (1978). *Interpersonal relations: A theory of interdependence.* New York, NY: John Wiley.

49. Homans, G. (1961). *Social behavior: Its elementary forms.* New York, NY: Harcourt Brace.

50. Walster, E., Berscheid, E., & Walster, G. W. (1973). New directions in equity research. *Journal of Personality and Social Psychology, 25,* 151-176.

51. Roloff, M. E. (1981). *Interpersonal communication: The social exchange approach.* Beverly Hills, CA: Sage.

52. Stafford, L. (2008). Social exchange theories: Calculating the rewards and costs of personal relationships. In L. A. Baxter & D. O. Braithwaite (Eds.), *Engaging theories in interpersonal communication: Multiple perspectives* (pp. 377-389). Thousand Oaks, CA: Sage.

53. See Canary, D. J., & Stafford, L. (1992). Relational maintenance strategies and equity in marriage. *Communication Monographs,*

59, 243-267; also Stafford, L., & Canary, D. J. (2006). Equity and interdependence as predictors of relational maintenance strategies. *Journal of Family Communication, 6*, 227-254.

54. Schrodt, P., Miller, A. E., & Braithwaite, D. O. (2011). Ex-spouses' relational satisfaction as a function of coparental communication in stepfamilies. *Communication Studies, 62*, 272-290.

55. Walster et al. (1973).

56. Klein & White (1996).

Chapter Nine

57. Baxter, L. A., & Montgomery, B. M. (1996). *Relating, dialogues and dialectics.* New York, NY: Guilford.

58. Altman, I., Vinsel, A., & Brown, B. B. (1981). Dialectic conceptions in social psychology: An application to social penetration and privacy regulation. In L. Berkowitz (Ed.). *Advances in experimental social psychology: Volume 14* (pp. 107-160). New York, NY: Academic Press.

59. Erbert, L. A. (2000). Conflict and dialectics: Perceptions of dialectical contradictions in marital conflict. *Journal of Social and Personal Relationships, 17*, 638-659.

60. Baxter & Montgomery (1996).

61. Baxter & Montgomery (1996). (Quote is from pp. 19-20.)

62. Rawlins, W. K. (1983). *Friendship matters: Communication, dialectics and the life course.* New York, NY: Aldine De Gruyter.

63. See Baxter & Montgomery (1996) for overview.

64. Conville, R. L. (1991). *Relational transitions: The evolution of personal relationships.* New York, NY: Praeger.

65. Altman, I., Vinsel, A., & Brown, B. B (1981). Dialectic conceptions in social psychology: An application to social penetration and privacy regulation. In L. Berkowitz (Ed.), *Advances in experimental social psychology: Volume 14* (pp. 107-160). New York, NY: Academic Press.

66. Bakhtin, M. M. (1981). *The dialogic imagination: Four essays by M. M. Bakhtin* (M. Holquist, Ed.; C. Emerson & M. Holquist, Trans.). Austin: University of Texas Press.

67. Baxter & Montgomery (1996); Morson, G. S., & Emerson, C. (1990). *Mikhail Bakhtin: The creation of a prosaics.* Stanford, CA: Stanford University Press.

68. Morson & Emerson (1990). (Quote is from p. 6.)

69. Baxter & Montgomery (1996). (Quote is from p. 26.)

70. Baxter & Montgomery (1996). (Quote is from p. 5.)

71. Baxter & Montgomery (1996).

72. Baxter & Montgomery (1996, p. 15).

73. Baxter & Montgomery (1996).

74. Baxter, L. A. (1990). Dialectical contradictions in relationship development. *Journal of Social and Personal Relationships,*

7, 69-88; Baxter, L. A., & Bullis, C. (1986). Turning points in developing romantic relationships. *Human Communication Research, 12,* 469-493; Baxter, L. A., & Erbert, L. A. (1999). Perceptions of dialectical contradictions in turning points of development in heterosexual romantic relationships. *Journal of Social and Personal Relationships, 16,* 547-569; Erbert, L. A. (2000). Conflict and dialectics: Perceptions of dialectical contradictions in marital conflict. *Journal of Social and Personal Relationships, 17,* 638-659; Erbert, L. A., & Duck, S. W. (1997). "Rethinking" satisfaction in personal relationships from a dialectical perspective. In R. J. Sternberg & M. Hojjat (Eds.), *Satisfaction in close relationships* (pp. 190-216). New York, NY: Guilford Press.

75. Baxter & Montogmery (1996).

76. Petronio, S. (2002). *Boundaries of privacy: Dialectics of disclosure.* New York: State University of New York.

77. Altman, I., & Taylor, D. (1973). *Social penetration: The development of interpersonal relationships.* New York, NY: Holt, Rinehart, and Winston

78. Petronio (2002). (Quote is from p. 1.)

79. Petronio (2002).

80. Petronio (2002).

81. Petronio (2002). (Quote is from p. 39.)

82. Petronio (2002).

83. Petronio (2002). (Quote is from p. 5.)

84. Petronio (2002).

85. Petronio (2002). (Quote is from p. 25.)

86. Petronio (2002).

87. Petronio (2002). (Quote is from p. 30.)

88. Petronio (2002). (Quote is from p. 31.)

89. Petronio (2002). (Quote is from p. 33.)

90. Derlega, V. J., Winstead, B. A., & Folk-Barron (2000). Reasons for and against disclosing HIV-seropositive test results to an intimate partner: A functional perspective. In S. Petronio (Ed.). *Balancing the secrets of private disclosures* (pp. 53-70). Mahwah, NJ: Lawrence Erlbaum Associates.

90. Roloff & Cloven (1990), as cited in Roloff & Ifert (2000).

91. Thorson, A. R. (2009). Adult children's experiences with their parent's infidelity: Communication protection and access rules in the absence of divorce. *Communication Studies, 60,* 32-48.

92. Hollenbaugh, E. E., & Egbert, N. (2009). A test of communication privacy management theory in cross-sex friendships. *Ohio Communication Journal, 47,* 113-136.

93. Child, J. T., Pearson, J. C., & Petronio, S. (2009). Blogging, communication, and privacy management: Development of the

blogging privacy management measure. *Journal for the American Society for Information Science and Technology, 60,* 2079-2094.

94. Roloff, M. E., & Ifert, D. E (2000). Conflict management through avoidance: Withholding complaints, suppressing arguments, and declaring topics taboo. In S. Petronio (Ed.), *Balancing the secrets of private disclosures* (pp. 151-164). Mahwah, NJ: Lawrence Erlbaum Associates.

95. Roloff & Cloven (1990), as cited in Roloff & Ifert (2000).

96. See Wilder, C. (1979). The Palo Alto group: Difficulties and direction of the interactional view for human communication research. *Human Communication Research, 5,* 171-186.

97. Almaney, A. (1974). Communication and the systems theory of organization. *The Journal of Business Communication, 12,* 35-43.

98. Von Bertalanffy (1968). *General systems theory: Foundations, development, applications.* New York, NY: Braziller.

99. Morgan, G. (1997). *Images of organization* (2nd ed.). Thousand Oaks, CA: Sage. (Quote is from p. 387.)

100. Eisenberg, E. M., Goodall, H. L., & Trethewey, A. (2010). *Organizational communication: Balancing creativity and constraint.* New York, NY: Bedford/St. Martin's. (Quote is from p. 62.)

101. Wilbur, K. (1998). *The marriage of sense and soul: Integrating science and religion.* New York, NY: Random House.

102. Wilbur, K. (1998). (Quote is from p. 67.)

103. Greene, B. (1999). *The elegant universe.* New York, NY: Random House.

104. von Bertalanffy (1979), as cited in Wilder (1979, p. 173).

105. Morgan (1997). (Quote is from p. 12.)

106. Morgan (1997). (Quote is from p. 113.)

107. Morgan (1997). (Quote is from p. 41.)

108. Senge, P., Smith, B., Kruschwitz, N., Laur, J., & Schley, S. (2008). *The necessary revolution: How individuals and organizations are working together to create a sustainable world.* New York, NY: Doubleday.

109. Heinberg, R., & Lerch, D. (Eds.). (2010). *The post carbon reader: Managing the 21ˢᵗ century sustainability crisis.* Healdsburg, CA: Watershed Media.

110. Giddens, A. (1981). *A contemporary critique of historical materialism.* Berkeley and Los Angeles: University of California Press; Poole, M. S., & McPhee, R. D. (2005). Structuration theory. In S. May & D. K. Mumby (Eds.), *Engaging organizational communication theory and research* (pp. 171-196). Thousand Oaks, CA: Sage.

Chapter Ten

1. Lau, R. L., Sigelman, L., Heldman, C., & Babbit, P. (1999). The effects of negative political advertisements: A meta-analytic assessment. *American Political Science Review, 93,* 851-875.

2.   Festinger, L., Riecken, H. W., & Schachter, S. (1956). *When prophecy fails: A social and psychological study of a modern group that predicted the destruction of the world.* Minneapolis: University of Minnesota Press.

3.   Festinger, L. (1957). *A theory of cognitive dissonance.* Stanford, CA: Stanford University Press.

4.   See Cooper, J. (2007). *Cognitive dissonance: Fifty years of a classic theory.* London, England: Sage.

5.   Tumminia, D. (1998). How prophecy never fails: Interpretive reason in a flying-saucer group. *Sociology of Religion, 59,* 157-170.

6.   Bader, C. (1999). When prophecy passes unnoticed: New perspectives on failed prophecy. *Journal for the Scientific Study of Religion, 38,* 119-131.

7.   This claim is actually false. A 2007 Harvard University study showed that countries with more gun control had *more* intentional shootings, not *fewer.* See Kates, D. B., & Mauser, G. (2007). Would banning firearms reduce murder and suicide? A review of international and some domestic evidence. *Harvard Journal of Law & Public Policy, 30*(2), 649-694.

8.   Mukherjee, D. (2009). *Impact of celebrity endorsements on brand image.* Social Science Research Network Electronic Paper Collection. Accessed January 4, 2014, from http://ssm.com/abstract=1444814

9.   Petty, R. E., & Cacioppo, J. T. (1986). The elaboration likelihood model of persuasion. In L. Berkowitz (Ed.), *Advances*

in experimental social psychology (pp. 123-205). New York, NY: Academic Press.

10. See, e.g., Mohs, A., & Hübner, G. (2013). Organ donation: The role of gender in the attitude-behavior relationship. *Journal of Applied Social Psychology, 43* (Suppl. S1), E64-E70.

11. Festinger, L. (1954). A theory of social comparison processes. *Human Relations, 7,* 117-140.

12. Petty, R. E., & Cacioppo, J. T. (1981). *Attitudes and persuasion: Classic and contemporary approaches.* Dubuque, IA: William C. Brown.

13. Petty, R. E., & Cacioppo, J. T. (1979). Issue involvement can increase or decrease persuasion by enhancing message-relevant cognitive processes. *Journal of Personality and Social Psychology, 37,* 1915-1926.

14. Petty, R. E., & Cacioppo, J. T. (1986). *Communication and persuasion: Central and peripheral routs to attitude change.* New York: Springer-Verlag. (Quote is from p. 7.)

15. Hass, R. G. (1981). Effects of course characteristics on cognitive responses and persuasion. In R. E. Petty, T. M. Ostrom, & T. C. Brock (Eds.), *Cognitive responses in persuasion* (pp. 44-72). Hillsdale, NJ: Lawrence Erlbaum Associates.

16. Benoit, W. L. (1991). A cognitive response analysis of source credibility. In B. Dervin & M. J. Voigt (Eds.), *Progress in communication sciences* (vol. X., pp. 1-19). Norwood, NJ: Ablex.

17. O'Keefe, D. J. (1987). The persuasive effects of delaying iden-tification of high- and low-credibility communicators: A meta-analytic review. *Central States Speech Journal, 38,* 63-72.

18. Benoit, W. L., & Kennedy, K. A. (1999). On reluctant testimo-ny. *Communication Quarterly, 49,* 376-387.

19. Shavitt, S., Swan, S., Lowrey, T. M., & Wanke, M. (1994). The interaction of endorser attractiveness and involvement in per-suasion depends on the goal that guides message processing. *Journal of Consumer Psychology, 3,* 137-162.

20. Mills, J., & Harvey, J. (1972). Opinion change as a function of when information about the communicator is received and whether he is attractive or expert. *Journal of Personality and Social Psychology, 21,* 52-55.

21. Benoit, W. L. (1987). Argument and credibility appeals in per-suasion. *Southern Speech Communication Journal, 52,* 181-197.

22. Petty, R. E., & Cacioppo, J. T. (1984). The effects of involve-ment on responses to argument quantity and quality: Central and peripheral routes to persuasion. *Journal of Personality and Social Psychology, 46,* 69-81.

23. Andrews, J. C., & Shimp, T. A. (1990). Effects of involvement, argument strength, and source characteristics on central and peripheral processing in advertising. *Psychology & Marketing, 7,* 195-214.

24. E.g., Petty & Cacioppo, 1984.

25. Petty, R. E., & Cacioppo, J. T. (1986). The elaboration likelihood model of persuasion. In L. Berkowitz (Ed.), *Advances in experimental social psychology* (vol. 19, pp. 123-205). San Diego, CA: Academic Press.

26. O'Keefe, D. J. (2008). Elaboration likelihood model. In W. Donsbach (Ed.), *International encyclopedia of communication* (vol. 4, pp. 1475-1480). Oxford, England: Wiley-Blackwell.

27. Leding, J. K. (2013). Need for cognition is related to the rejection (but not the acceptance) of false memories. *The American Journal of Psychology, 126,* 1-10.

28. Cacioppo, J. T., & Petty, R. E. (1983). Central and peripheral routes to persuasion: Application to advertising. In L. Percy & A. Woodside (Eds.), *Advertising and consumer psychology* (pp. 3-23). Lexington, MA: D. C. Heath.

29. U.S. Federal Trade Commission. (2011). *Federal Trade Commission cigarette report for 2007 and 2008.* Washington, DC: Author.

30. U.S. Food and Drug Administration. (2009). Tobacco control act. Retrieved January 27, 2014, from: http://www.fda.gov/TobaccoProducts/GuidanceComplianceRegulatory Information/ucm298595.htm

31. U.S. Department of Health and Human Services. (2012). *Preventing tobacco use among youth and young adults: A report of the Surgeon General.* Atlanta, GA: Centers for Disease Control and Prevention, Office on Smoking and Health.

32. McGuire, W. (1961). Resistance to persuasion conferred by active and passive prior refutation of the same and alternative counterarguments. *Journal of Abnormal and Social Psychology, 63,* 326-332; McGuire, W. (1964). Inducing resistance to persuasion. In L. Berkowitz (Ed.), *Advances in experimental social psychology* (Vol. 1, pp. 192-229). New York, NY: Academic Press.

33. Matusitz, J., & Breek, G.-M. (2005). Prevention of sexual harassment in the medical setting: Applying inoculation theory. *Journal of Health and Scoial Policy, 21,* 53-71.

34. Compton, J., & Pfau, M. (2005). Inoculation theory of resistance to influence at maturity: Recent progress in theory development and application and suggestions for future research. In P. J. Kalbfleisch (Ed.), *Communication yearbook* (Vol. 29, pp. 97-145). Mahwah, NJ: Lawrence Erlbaum Associates.

35. Pfau, M., Van Bockern, S., & Kang, J. G. (1992). Use of inoculation to promote resistance to smoking initiation among adolescents. *Communication Monographs, 59,* 213-230.

36. Pfau et al., 1992. (Quotes are from p. 219.)

37. Pfau, M., & Van Bockern, S. (1994). The persistence of inoculation in conferring resistance to smoking initiation among adolescents: The second year. *Human Communication Research, 20,* 413-430.

38. Pfau, M., Kenski, H. C., Nitz, M., & Sorenson, J. (1990). Efficacy of inoculation messages in promoting resistance to political attack messages: Application to direct mail. *Communication Monographs, 57,* 1-12.

39. Nabi, R. L. (2003). "Feeling" resistance: Exploring the role of emotionally evocative visuals in inducing inoculation. *Media Psychology, 5,* 199-223.

40. Compton, J., & Pfau, M. (2004). Use of inoculation to foster resistance to credit card marketing targeting college students. *Journal of Applied Communication Research, 32,* 343-364.

41. Pfau, M., Semmler, S. M., Deatrick, L., Mason, A., Nisbett, G., Lane, L., et al. (2009). Nuances about the role and impact of affect in inoculation. *Communication Monographs, 76,* 73-98.

42. Pfau, M., Haigh, M. M., Shannon, T., Tones, T., Mercurio, D., Williams, R., et al. (2008). The influence of television news depictions on the images of war on viewers. *Journal of Broadcasting and Electronic Media, 52,* 303-322.

43. Godbold, L. C., & Pfau, M. (2000). Conferring resistance to peer pressure among adolescents: Using inoculation theory to discourage alcohol use. *Communication Research, 27,* 411-437.

44. Parker, K. A., Ivanov, B., & Compton, J. (2012). Inoculation's efficacy with young adults' risky behaviors: Can inoculation confer cross-protection over related but untreated issues? *Health Communication, 27,* 223-233.

45. Pfau, M. (1992). The potential of inoculation in promoting resistance to the effectiveness of comparative advertising messages. *Communication Quarterly, 40,* 26-44.

46. An, C., & Pfau, M. (2004). The efficacy of inoculation in televised political debates. *Journal of Communication, 54,* 421-436.

47. Compton, J., & Pfau, M. (2005). Inoculation theory of resistance to influence at maturity: Recent progress in theory development and application and suggestions for future research. In P. J. Kalbfleisch (Ed.), *Communication yearbook* (Vol. 29, pp. 97-145). Mahwah, NJ: Lawrence Erlbaum Associates.

48. McGuire, W. J. (1964). Inducing resistance to persuasion: Some contemporary approaches. In L. Berkowitz (Ed.), *Advances in experimental social psychology* (Vol. 1, pp. 192-229). New York, NY: Academic Press.

49. United States Senate. (1956). Committee on Government Operations, Permanent Subcommittee on Investigations (84th Congress, 2nd Sesssion). *Communist interrogation, indoctrination and exploitation of American military and political prisoners.* Washington, DC: U.S. Government Printing Office.

50. McGuire, W. J., & Papageorgis, D. (1961). The relative efficacy of various types of prior belief-defense in producing immunity against persuasion. *Journal of Abnormal and Social Psychology, 62,* 327-337.

51. Ivanov, B., Pfau, B., & Parker, K. A. (2009). The attitude base as a moderator of the effectiveness of inoculation strategy. *Communication Monographs, 76,* 47-72.

52. Pfau, M., Tusing, K. J., Koerner, A. F., Lee, W., Godbold, L. C. Penaloza, L. J., et al. (1997). Enriching the inoculation construct: The role of critical components in the process of resistance. *Human Communication Research, 24,* 187-215; but see Banas, J. A., & Rains, S. A. (2010). A meta-analysis of research on inoculation theory. *Communication Monographs, 77,* 281-311.

53. For examples, see http://www.catholic.com/documents/crack-ing-the-da-vinci-code and http://www.catholic.org/national/national_story.php?id=19200

Chapter Eleven

1. Kirby, E., & Krone, K. (2002). "The policy exists but you can't really use it": Communication and the structuration of work-family policies. *Journal of Applied Communication Research, 30,* 50-77.

2. Bantz, C., & Smith, D. (1977). A critique and experimental test of Weick's model of organizing. *Communication Monographs, 44,* 171–184.

3. Baran, B., & Scott, C. W. (2010). Organizing ambiguity: A grounded theory of leadership and sensemaking within dangerous contexts. *Military Psychology, 22,* 42-69; Tracy, S. J., Myers, K. K., & Scott, C. W. (2006). Crafting jokes and crafting selves: Sensemaking and identity management among human service workers. *Communication Monographs, 73,* 283-308.

4. Weick, K. (1969). *The social psychology of organizing.* Reading, MA: Addison-Wesley. Quote is from p. 90.

5. Weick, 1969. Quote is from p. 6.

6. Weick, 1969. Quote is from p. 136.

7. Weick, 1969. Quote is from p. 126.

8. Weick, K., & Roberts, K. H. (1993). Collective mind in organizations: Heedful interrelating on flight decks. *Administrative Science Quarterly, 38,* 357-381. Quote is from p. 366.

9. Baran & Scott, 2010

10. Baran & Scott, 2010. Quote is from p. 56.

11. Eisenberg, E. (2006). Karl Weick and the aesthetics of contingency. *Organization Studies, 27*(11), 1693-1707. Quote is from p. 1703.

12. Pacanowsky, M. E., & O'Donnell-Trujillo, N. (1982). Communication and organizational culture. *Western Journal of Speech Communication, 46*, 115-130.

13. Keyton, J. (2005). *Communication & organizational culture: A key to understanding work experiences.* Thousand Oaks, CA: Sage.

14. Peters, T. J., & Waterman, R. J. (1982). *In search of excellence.* New York, NY: Harper & Row.

15. Keyton, 2005

16. Van Maanen, J. (1988). *Tales of the field: On writing ethnography.* Chicago, IL: University of Chicago Press.

17. Keyton, 2005. Quote is from p. 28.

18. Miller, K. (2009). *Organizational communication: Approaches and processes.* Boston, MA: Wadsworth Cengage Learning.

19. Schein, E. H. (1992). *Organizational culture and leadership* (2nd ed.). San Francisco, CA: Jossey Bass. Quote is from p. 9.

20. Schein, 1992.

21. Allen, R. S., White, S. W., Takeda, M. B., & Helms, M. M. (2004). Performance in Japan and the United States: A comparison. *Compensation and Benefits Review, 36,* 7-14.

22. Goo, S. K. (2006, October 21). Building a 'Googley' workforce. Retrieved June 18, 2011, from http://www.washingtonpost.com/wp-dyn/content/article/2006/10/20/AR2006102001461.html

23. Kunda, G. (1992). *Engineering culture.* Philadelphia, PA: Temple University Press.

24. Peters, T. J., & Waterman, R. J. (1982). *In search of excellence.* New York, NY: Harper & Row.

25. Martin, J. (1985). Can organizational culture be managed? In P. Frost, L. Moore, M. Louis, C. Lundberg, & J. Martin (Eds.), *Organizational culture* (pp. 95-98). Beverly Hills, CA: Sage. Quote is from p. 95.

26. Goodall, H. L., Jr. (1994). *Casing a promised land: The autobiography of an organizational detective as cultural ethnographer.* Carbondale: Southern Illinois University Press; Goodall, H. L., Jr. (2004). *A need to know: The clandestine history of a CIA family.* Walnut Creek, CA: Left Coast Press.

27. Dixon, M. A., & Dougherty, D. S. (2010). Managing the multiple meanings of organizational culture in interdisciplinary and collaboration and consulting. *Journal of Business Communication, 47,* 3-19.

28. Deetz, S. (1992). *Democracy in an age of corporate colonization: Developments in communication and the politics of everyday life.*

Albany: State University of New York Press; Deetz, S. (1995). *Transforming communication, transforming business: Building responsive and responsible workplaces.* Cresskill, NJ: Hampton Press; Deetz, S. (2008). Engagement as co-generative theorizing. *Journal of Applied Communication Research, 36,* 289-297.

29. Deetz, S., & Putnam, L. L. (2001). Thinking about the future of communication studies. In W. B. Gudykunst (Ed.) *Communication Yearbook, 24,* pp. 1-17. Thousand Oaks, CA: Sage. p. 5

30. Deetz, 1995, p. 7

31. Deetz, 1995.

32. Newton, T., Deetz, S., & Reed, M. (2011). Responses to social constructionism and social realism in organization studies. *Organization Studies, 32,* 7-26.

33. Deetz, 1995, p. 184

Chapter Twelve

1.   Socha, T. J. (1999). Communication in family units. In L. R. Frey, D. S. Gouran, & M. S. Poole (Eds.), *The handbook of group communication theory and research* (pp. 475-492). Thousand Oaks, CA: Sage.

2.   Bormann, E. G. (1996). Symbolic convergence theory and communication in group decision-making. In R. Y. Hirokawa & M. S. Poole (Eds.), *Communication and group decision-making* (2nd ed.) (pp. 81-113). Thousand Oaks, CA: Sage.

3.   Braithwaite, D. O., Schrodt, P., & Koenig Kellas, J. (2006). Symbolic convergence theory: Communication, dramatizing messages, and rhetorical visions in families. In D. O. Braithwaite & L. A. Baxter (Eds.), *Engaging theories in family communication: Multiple perspectives* (pp. 146-161). Thousand Oaks, CA: Sage.

4.   Bales, R. F. (1970). *Personality and interpersonal behavior.* New York, NY: Holt, Rinehart, & Winston.

5.   Bales, R. F. (1950) *Interaction process analysis: A method for the study of small groups.* Cambridge, MA: Addison-Wesley.

6.   Bormann (1996).

7.   Braithwaite et al. (2006).

8.   p. 5, from Bormann, E. G. (1985). *The force of fantasy: Restoring the American dream.* Carbondale, IL: Southern Illinois University.

9.   Bormann, E. G. (1989). *Communication theory.* Salem, WI: Sheffield.

10.   Bormann (1996).

11.   pp. 86-88 in Bormann (1996).

12.   Our review of SCT's key concepts comes primarily from Bormann (1985, 1996).

13.   Bormann, E. G., Cragan, J. F., & Shields, D. C. (1994). In defense of symbolic convergence theory: A look at the theory and its criticisms after two decades. *Communication Theory, 4,* 259-294.

14. The name of the ex-girlfriend has been changed to protect her identity.

15. This example of a fantasy type is adapted from Bormann (1996, pp. 96-97).

16. Bormann et al. (1994).

17. The claims of SCT were summarized from Bormann (1985, 1996).

18. Bormann (1996).

19. p. 107 in Bormann (1996).

20. p. 109 in Bormann (1996).

21. Bormann (1989).

22. For a complete review of these criticisms, see Bormann et al. (1994).

23. Cragan, J., & Shields, D., "Obituary #10694," archived in the *Communication Research and Theory Network,* January 6, 2009, http://www.natcom.org/CRTNET, accessed June 21, 2013

24. Gouran, D. S., & Hirokawa, R. Y. (1996). Functional theory and communication in decision-making and problem-solving groups: An expanded view. In M. S. Poole & R. Y. Hirokawa (Eds.), *Communication and group decision-making* (pp. 55-80). Thousand Oaks, CA: Sage.

25. Gouran, D. S., Hirokawa, R. Y., Julian, K. M., & Leatham, G. B. (1993). The evolution and current status of the functional perspective on communication in decision-making and problem-solving groups. In S. A. Deetz (Ed.), *Communication yearbook 16* (pp. 573-600). Newbury Park, CA: Sage.

26. Miller, K. (2005). *Communication theories: Perspectives, processes, and contexts.* Boston, MA: McGraw-Hill.

27. p. 579, Gouran et al. (1993).

28. Dewey, J. (1910). *How we think.* Boston, MA: Heath.

29. Bales (1950).

30. Janis, I. L. (1972). *Victims of groupthink.* Boston, MA: Houghton Mifflin.

31. Gouran et al. (1993).

32. p. 9, Janis, I. L. (1982). *Groupthink* (2nd ed.). Boston, MA: Houghton Mifflin.

33. Gouran et al. (1993).

34. Adapted from Gouran et al. (1993).

35. From p. 580 in Gouran et al. (1993).

36. Gouran and Hirokawa's (1996) summary of group constraints comes from: Janis, I. L. (1989). *Crucial decisions:*

Leadership in policy making and crisis management. New York, NY: Free Press.

37. Adapted from Propp, K. M., & Nelson, D. (1996). Problem-solving performance in naturalistic groups: A test of the ecological validity of the functional perspective. *Communication Studies, 47,* 35-45.

38. Gouran et al. (1993).

39. pp. 76-77 from Gouran & Hirokawa (1996).

40. Orlitzky, M., & Hirokawa, R. Y. (2001). To err is human, to correct for it divine: A meta-analysis of research testing the functional theory of group decision-making effectiveness. *Small Group Research, 32,* 313-341.

41. Hirokawa, R. Y., Gouran, D. S., & Martz, A. E. (1988). Understanding the sources of faulty group decision making: A lesson from the *Challenger* disaster. *Small Group Behavior, 19,* 411-433.

42. Socha (1999).

43. Schrodt, P., Witt, P. L., & Messersmith, A. S. (2008). A meta-analytical review of family communication patterns and their associations with information processing, behavioral, and psychosocial outcomes. *Communication Monographs, 75,* 248-269.

44. McLeod, J. M., Atkin, C. K., & Chaffee, S. R. (1972). Adolescents, parents, and television use: Self-report and other-report measures from the Wisconsin sample. In G. A. Comstock & E. A. Rubinstein (Eds.), *Television and social behavior, reports and*

papers: Vol. 3. Television and adolescent aggressiveness (pp. 239-313). Rockville, MD: National Institute of Mental Health.

45. McLeod, J. M., & Chaffee, S. R. (1972). The social construction of reality. In J. Tedeschi (Ed.), *The social influence processes* (pp. 50-99). Chicago, IL: Aldine-Atherton.

46. McLeod et al. (1972); Schrodt et al. (2008)

47. Ritchie, L. D., & Fitzpatrick, M. A. (1990). Family communication patterns: Measuring intrapersonal perceptions of interpersonal relationships. *Communication Research, 17,* 523-544.

48. Koerner, A. F., & Fitzpatrick, M. A. (2002). Understanding family communication patterns and family functioning: The roles of conversation orientation and conformity orientation. *Communication Yearbook, 26,* 36-68.

49. Fitzpatrick, M. A., & Ritchie, L. D. (1994). Communication schemata within the family: Multiple perspectives on family interaction. *Human Communication Research, 20,* 275-301.

50. Koerner, A. F., & Fitzpatrick, M. A. (2013). Communication in intact families. In A. L. Vangelisti (Ed.), *The Routledge handbook of family communication* (2nd ed.) (pp. 129-144). New York, NY: Routledge.

51. p. 137, Koerner & Fitzpatrick (2013).

52. Koerner, A. F., & Fitzpatrick, M. A. (2004). Communication in intact families. In A. L. Vangelisti (Ed.), *Handbook of family communication* (pp. 177-195). Mahwah, NJ: Erlbaum.

53. p. 138, Koerner & Fitzpatrick (2013).

54. p. 139, Koerner & Fitzpatrick (2013).

55. Our summary of the four family types is paraphrased from Koerner and Fitzpatrick (2013).

56. See Schrodt, P., Ledbetter, A. M., Jernberg, K. A., Larson, L., Elledge, N., & Glonek, K. (2009). Family communication patterns as mediators of communication competence in the parent-child relationship. *Journal of Social and Personal Relationships, 26,* 853-874.

57. Koerner, A. F., & Fitzpatrick, M. A. (1997). Family type and conflict: The impact of conversation orientation and conformity orientation on conflict in the family. *Communication Studies, 48,* 59-75.

58. Schrodt et al. (2008).

59. Koesten, J. (2004). Family communication patterns, sex of subject, and communication competence. *Communication Monographs, 71,* 226-244.

60. Schrodt, P., Ledbetter, A. M., & Ohrt, J. K. (2007). Parental confirmation and affection as mediators of family communication patterns and children's mental well-being. *Journal of Family Communication, 7,* 23-46.

61. Koerner & Fitzpatrick (1997).

62. Schrodt, P., & Ledbetter, A. M. (2007). Communication processes that mediate family communication patterns and

mental well-being: A mean and covariance structures analysis of young adults from divorced and non-divorced families. *Human Communication Research, 33,* 330-356.

63. Schrodt et al. (2007).

64. Schrodt et al. (2008).

65. Schrodt et al. (2008).

66. Elwood & Schrader (1998). Family communication patterns and communication apprehension. *Journal of Social Behavior and Personality, 13,* 493-502.

67. Koerner & Fitzpatrick (1997).

68. Schrodt et al. (2007).

69. The differences between pluralistic and consensual families are not always present, nor are they always consistent with what FCP theory would predict. This may be due, in part, to subtle nuances in how parental authority is communicated in consensual families (Schrodt et al., 2008).

70. Schrodt et al. (2008).

Chapter Thirteen

1. Brashers, D. E. (2001). Communication and uncertainty management. *Journal of Communication, 51,* 477-497. (Quote is from p. 477.)

2. Brashers (2001).

3. Brashers, D. E., Neidig, J. L., Haas, S. M., Dobbs, L. K., Cardillo, L. W., & Russell, J. A. (2000). Communication in the management of uncertainty: The case of persons living with HIV or AIDS. *Communication Monographs, 67,* 63-84.

4. Lazarus, R. S., & Folkman, S. (1984). *Stress, appraisal, and coping.* New York, NY: Springer.

5. Mishel, M. (1988). Uncertainty in illness. *Image: Journal of Nursing Scholarship, 20,* 225-232.

6. Lazarus & Folkman (1984).

7. Mishel, M. (1990). Reconceptualization of the uncertainty in illness theory. *Image: Journal of Nursing Scholarship, 22,* 256-262.

8. Mishel (1988, 1990).

9. Babrow, A. S., & Striley, C. M. (in press). Problematic integration theory and uncertainty management theory. To appear in D. O. Braithwaite & P. Schrodt (Eds.), *Engaging theories in interpersonal communication: Multiple perspectives* (2nd ed.). Thousand Oaks, CA: Sage.

10. Babrow & Striley (in press).

11. Brashers (2001).

12. Brashers (2001).

13. Finn, N. (2013, May). Angelina Jolie reveals having double mastectomy to prevent breast cancer. *E! Online News.* Retrieved from

http://www.eonline.com/news/418466/angelina-jolie-reveals-having-double-mastectomy-to-prevent-breast-cancer

14. Toomey, A. (2013, August). Angelina Jolie's double mastectomy: Surgeon says actress "waited to find the perfect timing." *E! Online News.* Retrieved from http://www.eonline.com/news/449797/angelina-jolie-s-double-mastectomy-surgeon-says-actress-waited-to-find-the-perfect-timing

15. Finn (2013).

16. Macatee, R. (2013, May). Angelina Jolie planning to remove her ovaries following preventive double mastectomy. *E! Online News.* Retrieved from http://www.eonline.com/news/419113/angelina-jolie-planning-to-remove-her-ovaries-following-preventive-double-mastectomy

17. Berger, C. R., & Bradac, J. J. (1982). *Language and social knowledge: Uncertainty in interpersonal relationships.* London, England: Edward Arnold.

18. Mishel (1988). (Quote is from p. 225.)

19. Brashers et al. (2000).

20. Our discussion of uncertainty management processes comes from Hogan, T. P., & Brashers, D. E. (2009). The theory of communication and uncertainty management: Implications from the wider realm of information behavior. In T. D. Afifi & W. A. Afifi (Eds.), *Uncertainty, information management, and disclosure decisions: Theories and applications* (pp. 45-66). New York, NY: Routledge.

21. Definitions for the three broad categories of information behavior are based on Hogan and Brashers (2009), pp. 49-58.

22. Taylor, R. S. (1991). Information use environments. *Progress in Communication Sciences, 10,* 217-255. Also cited in Hogan and Brashers (2009).

23. Brashers et al. (2000).

24. Brashers, D. E., & Babrow, A. S. (1996). Theorizing communication and health. *Communication Studies, 47,* 243-251.

25. Brashers et al. (2000). (Quote is from p. 81.)

26. Brashers, D. E., & Hogan, T. P. (2013). The appraisal and management of uncertainty: Implications for information-retrieval systems. *Information Processing and Management, 49,* 1241-1249.

27. Brashers et al. (2000).

28. Brashers et al. (2000). (Quote is from p. 72.)

29. Twohey, M. (2000, November 4). From the frying pan into the fire. *National Journal,* p. 3491. Retrieved from http://www.psa-research.com/casD201.html

30. http://en.wikipedia.org/wiki/This_Is_Your_Brain_on_Drugs

31. Witte, K. (1992). Putting the fear back into fear appeals: The extended parallel process model. *Communication Monographs, 59,* 329-349.

32. Witte (1992).

33. Witte, K. (2013). Introduction: Pathways. *Health Communication, 28*, 3-4.

34. Janis, I. L. (1967). Effects of fear arousal on attitude change: Recent developments in theory and experimental research. In L. Berkowitz (Ed.), *Advances in experimental social psychology* (Vol. 3, pp. 166-225). New York, NY: Academic Press.

35. Leventhal, H. (1970). Findings and theory in the study of fear communications. In L. Berkowitz (Ed.), *Advances in experimental social psychology* (Vol. 5, pp. 119-186). New York, NY: Academic Press.

36. Rogers, R. W. (1975). A protection motivation theory of fear appeals and attitude change. *Journal of Psychology, 91*, 93-114.

37. Maloney, E. K., Lapinski, M. K., & Witte, K. (2011). Fear appeals and persuasion: A review and update of the extended parallel process model. *Social and Personality Psychology Compass, 5*(4), 206-219.

38. Maloney et al. (2011).

39. Witte (1992). (Quote is from p. 331.)

40. Witte, K. (1994). Fear control and danger control: A test of the extended parallel process model (EPPM). *Communication Monographs, 61*, 113-134.

41. Witte (1994).

42. Maloney et al. (2011).

43. This example was adapted from Witte (1992).

44. Witte (1992, 1994).

45. Witte (1992). (Quote is from p. 332.)

46. Witte (1992). (Quote is from p. 332.)

47. Witte, K., Cameron, K. A., McKeon, J., & Berkowitz, J. (1996). Predicting risk behaviors: Development and validation of a diagnostic scale. *Journal of Health Communication, 1,* 317-341.

48. Our discussion of the EPPM's claims are based primarily upon pp. 337 – 345 in Witte (1992).

49. Witte (1992). (Quote is from p. 338.)

50. Witte (1994). (Quote is from p. 115.)

51. Witte (1992).

52. Witte (1992). (Quote is from p. 338.)

53. Maloney et al. (2011).

54. See Witte (1992, 1994); also Murray-Johnson, L., Witte, K., Liu, W., & Hubbel, A. P. (2001). Addressing cultural orientations in fear appeals: Promoting AIDS-protective behaviors among Mexican immigrant and African American adolescents and

American and Taiwanese college students. *Journal of Health Communication, 6,* 335-358.

55. Stephenson, M., & Witte, K. (1998). Fear, threat, and perceptions of efficacy from frightening skin cancer messages. *Public Health Review, 26,* 147-174.

56. Witte, K. (1997). Preventing teen pregnancy through persuasive communications: Realities, myths, and the hard-fact truths. *Journal of Community Health, 22,* 137-154.

57. Carcioppolo, N., Jensen, J. D., Wilson, S. R., Collins, W. B., Carrion, M., & Linnemeier, G. (2013). Examining HPV threat-to-efficacy ratios in the extended parallel process model. *Health Communication, 28,* 20-28.

58. Gore, T. D., & Bracken, C. (2005). Testing the theoretical design of a health risk message: Reexamining the major tenets of the extended parallel process model. *Health Education & Behavior, 32,* 27-41.

59. Choi, H. J., Krieger, J. L., & Hecht, M. L. (2013). Reconceptualizing efficacy in substance use prevention research: Refusal response efficacy and drug resistance self-efficacy in adolescent substance use. *Health Communication, 28,* 40-52.

60. Muthusamy, N., Levine, T. R., & Weber, R. (2009). Scaring the already scared: Some problems with HIV/AIDS fear appeals in Nambia. *Journal of Communication, 59,* 317-344.

61. Costello, K. (2013, January). New Years 2013: The 10 most common New Year's resolutions. Retrieved September

11, 2013 from http://www.policymic.com/articles/21328/new-years-2013-the-10-most-common-new-year-s-resolutions

62. Fishbein, M., & Ajzen, I. (1975). *Belief, attitude, intention, and behavior: An introduction to theory and research.* Reading, MA: Addison-Wesley.

63. Ajzen, I. (1985). From intentions to actions: A theory of planned behavior. In J. Kuhl & J. Beckmann (Eds.), *Action control: From cognition to behavior* (pp. 11-39). New York, NY: Springer-Verlag.

64. Ajzen, I. (2011). The theory of planned behaviour: Reactions and reflections. *Psychology and Health, 26,* 1113-1127.

65. A September 11, 2013 search of the Communication & Mass Media Complete database revealed more than 75 citations to the TPB.

66. Ajzen, I. (1991). The theory of planned behavior. *Organizational Behavior and Human Decision Processes, 50,* 179-211.

67. Ajzen (1985).

68. Ajzen (1985). (Quote is from p. 24.)

69. Fishbein & Ajzen (1975).

70. The key concepts of the TPB can be found in Ajzen (1985, 1991).

71. Ajzen (1991).

72. This example and the findings associated with it were adapted from Ajzen, I., & Fishbein, M. (1980). *Understanding attitudes and predicting social behavior.* Englewood-Cliffs, NJ: Prentice Hall.

73. These and the other claims found in this section are paraphrased from Ajzen (1985, 1991).

74. Ajzen (1991); see also McEachan, R. R. C., Conner, M., Taylor, N., & Lawton, R. J. (2011). Prospective prediction of health-related behaviors with the theory of planned behavior: A meta-analysis. *Health Psychology Review, 5,* 97-144.

75. Wolff, K., Nordin, K., Brun, W., Berglund, G., & Kvale, G. (2011). Affective and cognitive attitudes, uncertainty avoidance and intention to obtain genetic testing: An extension of the theory of planned behaviour. *Psychology and Health, 26,* 1143-1155.

76. Richard, R., de Vries, N. K., & van der Pligt, J. (1998). Anticipated regret and precautionary sexual behavior. *Journal of Applied Social Psychology, 28,* 1411-1428.

77. Matterne, U., Diepgen, T. L., & Weisshar, E. (2011). A longitudinal application of three behaviour models in the context of skin protection behaviour in individuals with occupational skin disease. *Psychology and Health, 26,* 1188-1207.

78. Schifter, D. E., & Ajzen, I. (1985). Intention, perceived control, and weight loss: An application of the theory of planned behavior. *Journal of Personality and Social Psychology, 49,* 843-851.

Chapter Fourteen

1. Rogers, E. M., & Dearing, J. W. (1993). The anatomy of agenda-setting research. *Journal of Communication, 43,* 68-84.

2. McCombs, M. E., & Shaw, D. L. (1972). The agenda-setting function of mass media. *Public Opinion Quarterly, 36,* 176-185.

3. McCombs & Shaw (1972).

4. Lippmann, W. (1922). *Public opinion.* New York, NY: Harcourt Brace.

5. DeFleur, M. L., & Ball-Rokeach, S. (1982). *Theories of mass communication.* New York, NY: Longman.

6. Miller, K. (2005). *Communication theories: Perspectives, processes, and contexts* (2nd ed.). Boston, MA: McGraw-Hill.

7. p. 13 from Cohen, B. C. (1963). *The press and foreign policy.* Princeton, NJ: Princeton University Press.

8. Tankard, J. W., Jr. (1990). Maxwell McCombs, Donald Shaw and agenda-setting. In W. D. Sloan (Ed.), *Makers of the media mind: Journalism educators and their ideas* (pp. 278-286). Hillsdale, NJ: Lawrence Erlbaum Associates.

9. According to an October 14, 2014 search in the academic database Communication & Mass Media Complete.

10. Zhu, J. H., & Blood, D. (1997). Media agenda-setting theory: Telling the public what to think about. In G. Kovacic (Ed.),

Emerging theories of human communication (pp. 88-114). Albany: SUNY Press.

11. Yang, J., & Stone, G. (2003). The powerful role of interpersonal communication in agenda setting. *Mass Communication and Society, 6,* 57-74.

12. http://www.theskimm.com/about

13. http://blog.theskimm.com/

14. Moon, S. J. (2013). Attention, attitude, and behavior: Second-level agenda-setting effects as a mediator of media use and political participation. *Communication Research, 40,* 698-719.

15. McCombs, M. E. (2004). *Setting the agenda: The mass media and public opinion.* Cambridge, England: Blackwell.

16. McCombs, M., Shaw, D. L., & Weaver, D. (Eds.). (1997). *Communication and democracy: Exploring the intellectual frontiers of agenda-setting theory.* Mahwah, NJ: Lawrence Erlbaum Associates.

17. Muddiman, A., Stroud, N. J., & McCombs, M. (2014). Media fragmentation, attribute agenda setting, and political opinions about Iraq. *Journal of Broadcasting & Electronic Media, 58,* 215-233.

18. Takeshita, T. (2007). Agenda-setting and framing: Two dimensions of attribute agenda-setting. *Mita Journal of Sociology, 12,* 4-18.

19. Takeshita (2007).

20. Miller (2005).

21. Wilnat, L. (1997). Agenda setting and priming: Conceptual links and differences. In M. McCombs, D. L. Shaw, & D. Weaver (Eds.), *Communication and democracy: Exploring the intellectual frontiers in agenda-setting theory* (pp. 51-66). Mahwah, NJ: Lawrence Erlbaum Associates.

22. Fiske, S., & Taylor, S. (1991). *Social cognition.* New York, NY: McGraw-Hill.

23. Weaver, D. H. (1977). Political issues and voter need for orientation. In D. L. Shaw & M. E. McCombs (Eds.), *The emergence of American political issues: The agenda-setting function of the press* (pp. 107-119). St. Paul, MN: West.

24. Zucker, H. G. (1978). The variable nature of news media influence. In B. Ruben (Ed.), *Communication yearbook 2* (pp. 225-246). New Brunswick, NJ: Transaction Books.

25. p. 309 in Scheufele, D. A. (2000). Agenda-setting, priming, and framing revisited: Another look at cognitive effects of political communication. *Mass Communication & Society, 3,* 297-316.

26. Sample headlines retrieved on October 17, 2014 from http://topics.nytimes.com/top/reference/timestopics/subjects/e/ebola/index.html

27. Wilnat (1997).

28. Retrieved on February 16, 2015 from http://dallas.culturemap.com/news/city-life/10-02-14-tcu-alert-campus-bomb-threat-suspicious-package-student-tweets/

29. Zhu & Blood (1997).

30. Jones, K. O., Denham, B. E., & Springston, J. K. (2006). Effects of mass and interpersonal communication on breast cancer screening: Advancing agenda-setting theory in health contexts. *Journal of Applied Communication Research, 34,* 94-113.

31. Andrejevic, M. (2003). *Reality TV: The work of being watched.* Lanham, MD: Rowman & Littlefield.

32. McQuail, D. (1984). With the benefit of hindsight: Reflections on uses and gratifications research. *Critical Studies in Mass Communication, 1,* 177-193. (Quote is from p. 187.)

33. Rosengren, K. E. (1974). Uses and gratifications: A paradigm outlined. In J. G. Blumler & E. Katz (Eds.), *The uses of mass communications* (pp. 269-286). Beverly Hills, CA: Sage.

34. McQuail, D. (1984, p. 185)

35. Ruggiero, T. E. (2000). Uses and gratifications theory in the 21st century. *Mass Communication & Society, 3,* 3-37. (Quote is from p. 8.)

36. Ruggiero (2000).

37. McQuail (1984, p. 177).

38. McQuail (1984).

39. McQuail, D., & Gurevitch, M. (1974). Explaining audience behavior: Three approaches considered. In J. G. Blumler &

E. Katz (Eds.), *The uses of mass communications* (pp. 287-301). Beverly Hills, CA: Sage.

40. Larose, R., Mastro, D., & Eastin, M. S. (2001). Understanding internet usage: A social-cognitive approach to uses and gratifications. *Social Science Computer Review, 19,* 95-413.

41. See Ruggiero (2000) for brief summaries.

42. See Littlejohn, S. W., & Foss K. A. (2011). *Theories of human communication* (10th ed.). Long Grove, IL: Waveland Pres.

43. Katz, E., Blumler, J. G., & Gurevitch, M. (1974). Utilization of mass communication by the individual. In J. G. Blumler & E. Katz (Eds.). *The uses of mass communications* (pp. 19-32). Beverly Hills, CA: Sage.

44. Ruggiero, T. E. (2000. P. 8).

45. Katz & Blumler (1974, p. 22).

46. Carey, J. W., & Kreiling, A. L. (1974). Popular culture and uses and gratifications: Notes toward an accommodation. In J. G. Blumler & E. Katz (Eds.), *The uses of mass communications* (pp. 225-248). Beverly Hills, CA: Sage.

47. McQuail (1984, p. 186).

48. See Blumler (1979) and Katz, Blumler, & Gurevitch, (1974).

49. McQuail (1984). See also Blumler (1979).

50. Ruggiero (2000).

51. Blumler, J. G. (1979). The role of theory in uses and gratifications studies. *Communication Research, 6,* 9-36.

52. Blumler (1979).

53. Blumler (1979).

54. Blumler (1979).

55. See Ruggiero (2000) for discussion.

56. Ruggerio (2000).

57. Weaver, A. J. (2011). A meta-analytic review of selective exposure to and the enjoyment of media violence. *Journal of Broadcasting & Electronic Media, 55,* 232-250.

58. Weaver (2011, p. 244).

59. Tustin, R. (2010). The role of patient satisfaction in online health information seeking. *Journal of Health Communication, 15,* 3-17.

60. Bagdasarov, Z., Greene, K., Banerjee, S. M., Krcmar, M., Yanovitzhy, I., & Ruginye, D. (2010). I am what I watch: Voyerism, sensation seeking, and television viewing programs. *Journal of Broadcasting & Electronic Media, June,* 299-315.

61. Kavka, M. (2004). The queering of reality TV. *Feminist Media Studies, 4,* 220-223 (quote cited in Bagdasarov et al., 2010, p. 301).

62. Feldman, L., (2013). Learning about politics from *The Daily Show*: The role of viewer orientation and processing motivations. *Mass Communication and Society, 16,* 586-607.

63. Feldman (2013, p. 602).

64. McQuail (1984, p. 183).

65. Ledbetter, A. M. (2015). Media multiplexity theory: Technology use and interpersonal tie strength. In D. O. Braithwaite & P. Schrodt (Eds.), *Engaging theories in interpersonal communication: Multiple perspectives* (2nd ed.) (pp. 363-375). Thousand Oaks, CA: Sage.

66. Haythornthwaite, C. (2005). Social networks and internet connectivity effects. *Information, Communication & Society, 8*(2), 125-147.

67. Haythornthwaite, C. (2002). Strong, weak, and latent ties and the impact of new media. *The Information Society, 18,* 385-401.

68. Haythornthwaite (2005); see also Short, J., Williams, E., & Christie, B. (1976). *The social psychology of telecommunications.* London, England: Wiley.

69. Ledbetter, A. M., & Kuznekoff, J. H. (2012). More than a game: Friendship relational maintenance and attitudes toward Xbox LIVE communication. *Communication Research, 39,* 269-290. See also Ledbetter, A. M., & Mazer, J. P. (2013). Do online communication attitudes mitigate the association between Facebook use and relational interdependence? An extension of media multiplexity theory. *New Media & Society.* Advance

publication online retrieved from sagepub.com on January 29, 2014. doi:10.1177/1461444813495159

70. p. 1361 in Granovetter, M. S. (1973). The strength of weak ties. *American Journal of Sociology, 78,* 1360-1380.

71. Ledbetter (2015); Ledbetter & Kuznekoff (2012).

72. The assumptions of MMT are summarized from Haythornthwaite (2002).

73. Haythornthwaite, C. (2001). Exploring multiplexity: Social network structures in a computer-supported distance learning class. *The Information Society, 17,* 211-226.

74. Haythornthwaite (2002, 2005).

75. To Granovetter's (1973) discussion of strong and weak ties, Haythornthwaite (2005) added latent ties.

76. Haythornthwaite (2005).

77. Ledbetter (2015); see also Ellison, N. B., Steinfield, C., & Lampe, C. (2007). The benefits of Facebook "friends:" Social capital and college students' use of online social network sites. *Journal of Computer-Mediated Communication, 12,* 1143-1168.

78. p. 389 in Haythornthwaite (2002).

79. p. 130 in Haythornthwaite (2005).

80. p. 130 in Haythornthwaite (2005).

81. Summarized primarily from Haythornthwaite (2002, 2005).

82. Haythornthwaite (2005).

83. Ledbetter (2015).

84. Ledbetter & Kuznekoff (2012).

85. Ledbetter (2015).

86. Haythornthwaite (2005).

87. Haythornthwaite (2005).

Chapter Fifteen

1. Hall, S. (2007). Living with difference. *Soundings, 37,* 148-160. (Quote is from p. 153.)

2. Bateson, G. (1972). *Steps to an ecology of mind.* New York, NY: Ballantine Books.

3. Goffman, E. (1974). *Frame analysis.* New York, NY: Harper & Row; Goffman, E. (1981). *Forms of talk.* Philadelphia: University of Pennsylvania Press.

4. Tannen, D., & Wallat, C. (1987). Interactive frames and knowledge schema in interaction: Examples from a medical examination/interview. *Social Psychology Quarterly, 50,* 205-216. (Quote is from p. 206.)

5.   Mitchell, R. W. (1991). Bateson's concept of "metacommunica-tion" in play. *New Ideas in Psychology, 9,* 79-87. (Quote is from p. 75.)

6.   Bateson, 1972, p. 178

7.   Tannen, D. (1990). *You just don't understand: Women and men in conversation.* New York, NY: Ballentine Books.

8.   Tannen, 1990, p. 51

9.   Eisenberg, E. (2006). *Strategic ambiguities: Essays on communica-tion, organization, and identity.* Thousand Oaks, CA: Sage.

10.   Tannen, D. (2001). *Talking from 9 to 5: Women and men at work.* New York, NY: William Morrow.

11.   Tannen, D. (2006). *You're wearing that?: Understanding mothers and daughters in conversation.* New York, NY: Ballentine Books.

12.   Motschenbacher, H. (2007). Can the term 'genderlect' be saved? A postmodernist re-definition. *Gender & Language, 1,* 255-278. (Quote is from p. 225.)

13.   Ting-Toomey, S. (2007). Intercultural conflict training: Theory-practice approaches and research challenges. *Journal of Intercultural Communication Research, 36,* 255-271. (Quote is from p. 256.)

14.   Ury, W., (1999). *Getting to Peace: Transforming Conflict at Home, at Work, and in the World.* New York: Viking.

15. Goffman, E. (1959). *The presentation of self in everyday life.* New York, NY: Anchor Books.

16. Oetzel, J.G., Garcia, A. J., & Ting-Toomey, S. (2000). An analysis of the relationships among face concerns and facework behaviors in perceived conflict situations: A four-culture investigation. *International Journal of Conflict Management, 19,* 382-403. (Quote is from p. 384.)

17. Brown, P., & Levison, S. C. (1987). *Politeness: Some universals in language usage.* Cambridge, England: Cambridge University Press.

18. Oetzel, J. G., & Ting-Toomey, S. (2003). Face concerns in interpersonal conflict: A cross-cultural empirical test of the face negotiation theory. *Communication Research, 30,* 599-624.

19. Oetzel & Ting-Toomey, 2003, p. 600

20. Oetzel, J. G., Ting-Toomey, S., Masumoto, T., Yokochi, Y., Pan, X., Takai, J. et al. (2001). Face and facework in conflict: A cross-cultural comparison of China, Germany, Japan, and the United States. *Communication Monographs, 68,* 235-258; Oetzel, J. G., Ting-Toomey, S., Yokochi, Y., Masumoto, T., & Takai, J. (2000). A typology of facework behaviors in conflicts with best friends and relative strangers. *Communication Quarterly, 48,* 397-419.

21. Ting-Toomey, 2007, p. 256

22. Oetzel & Ting-Toomey, 2003, p. 620

23. Ting-Toomey, S., & Kurogi, A. (1998). Facework competence in intercultural conflict: An updated face-negotiation theory.

International Journal of Intercultural Relations, 22, 187-225. (Quote is from p. 189.)

24. *Ting-Toomey & Kurogi, 1998, p. 194*

25. Ibid., p. 194

26. Ibid., p. 196

27. Ibid., p. 197

28. Ibid., pp. 199-200

29. Irwin, D. A. (2013). The Nixon shock after forty years: The import surcharge revisited. *World Trade Review, 12,* 29-56.

30. Cohen, R. (1991). *Negotiating across cultures: Communication obstacles in international diplomacy.* Washington, D.C.: United States Institute of Peace Press.

31. *Ting-Toomey & Kurogi, 1998*

32. Ting-Toomey, 2007

33. Ting-Toomey, S. (2005). The matrix of face: An updated face negotiation theory. In W. B. Gudykunst (Ed.), *Theorizing about intercultural communication* (pp. 71-93). Thousand Oaks, CA: Sage.

34. *Kisselburgh, L. G., & Dutta, M. J. (2009). The construction of civility in multicultural organizations. In P. Lutgen-Sandvik & B. D. Sypher (Eds.), Destructive organizational communication: Process, consequences, and constructive ways of organizing (pp. 121-142). New York, NY: Routledge.*

35. Aronowitz, S. (1973). *False promises.* New York, NY: McGraw-Hill.

36. Ibid., p. 111

37. Carlone, D., & Taylor, B. (1998). Organizational communication and cultural studies: A review essay. *Communication Theory, 8,* 337-367. (Quote is from p. 340.)

38. Meyrowitz, J. (2008). Power, pleasure, patterns: Intersecting narratives of media influence. *Journal of Communication, 58,* 641-663. (Quote is from p. 646.)

39. Carlone & Taylor, 1998, pp. 340-341

40. Marx, K. (1961). *Das Kapital: A critique of political economy.* F. Engels (Ed.). Washington, D.C.: Gateway Editions.

41. Althusser, L. (1971). Ideology and ideological state apparatuses. Printed in L. Althusser, *Lenin and philosophy and other essays* (1971, pp. 121-176). B. Brewster (trans). New York: Monthly Review Press.

42. Gramsci, A. (1971). *Selections from the prison notebooks of Antonio Gramsci.* Q. Hoare & G. Nowell Smith (trans). London, England: International Publishers.

43. Grossberg, L. (1993). Can cultural studies find true happiness in communication? *Journal of Communication, 43,* 89-97. (Quote is from p. 89.)

44. Johnson, R. (1986/1987). What is cultural studies anyway? *Social Text, 16,* 38-80.

45. Grossberg, 1993

46. Johnson, 1986/1987, p. 43

47. USA Today. What did Narcissus say to Instagram? Selfie time! Retrieved September 9, 2013, from: http://www.usatoday.com/ story/tech/2013/06/25/what-did-narcissus-say-to-instagram-selfie-time/2456261/

48. BBC News Magazine. Self-portraits and social media: The rise of the 'selfie." Retrieved September 9, 2013, from: http://www. bbc.co.uk/news/magazine-22511650

49. Grossberg, 1993

50. Ibid., p. 89

51. Ibid., p. 89

52. Ibid., p. 89

53. Hall, S. (1973). The television discourse – encoding and decoding. *Education and Culture, 25,* 8-14.

54. Ibid.

55. Barofsky, N. M. (2011, March 29). Where the bailout went wrong. *The New York Times Online.* Retrieved September 9, 2013, from: http://www.nytimes.com/2011/03/30/opinion/30barofsky.html?_r=1&

56. Hall, 1973, p. 14

57. Ibid., p. 14

58. Taibbi, M. (2013, February 14). Gangster bankers: Too big to jail. *Rolling Stone*. Retrieved September 9, 2013, from: http://www. rollingstone.com/politics/news/gangster-bankers-too-big-to-jail-20130214

59. Scherer, M. (2011, November 18). Occupy Wall Street's day off message. *Time*. Retrieved September 9, 2013, from: http:// swampland.time.com/2011/11/18/occupy-wall-streets-day-off-message/

60. Gramsci, 1971

61. Giroux, H., Shumway, D., Smith, P., & Sosnoski, J. (1984). The need for cultural studies: Resisting intellectuals and oppositional public spheres. Retrieved September 9, 2013, from: http://theory.eserver.org/need.html

62. Ibid., paragraph 27

63. Grossberg, 1993

64. Bérubé, M. (2009, September 14). What's the matter with cultural studies? The popular discipline has lost its bearings. *The Chronicle of Higher Education*. Retrieved September 9, 2013, from: http://chronicle.com/article/Whats-the-Matter-With/48334/

Made in the USA
Charleston, SC
04 January 2017